# STORIES
# FROM SIERRA LEONE

Farid R. Anthony

Farid and Joan Anthony

The author at Stonehenge

# STORIES
# FROM SIERRA LEONE

## by

## Farid Raymond Anthony

MERESBOROUGH BOOKS

STORIES FROM SIERRA LEONE
BY
FARID R. ANTHONY

Published for the author by
Meresborough Books
17 Station Road, Rainham, Kent. ME8 7RS.

ISBN 0948193905

Further copies may be ordered from the publisher at £9.99 plus
postage (Inland £1.00 per copy, five or more copies post free.
Overseas post at cost) or from www.rainhambookshop.co.uk.

Copies of the author's previous book 'Sawpit Boy' are also available
at £7.99 (plus 80p post. Combined orders over £50 post free inland)
from Meresborough Books or the Rainham Bookshop.

Printed by Lanes Printers, Broadstairs, Kent.

DEDICATED

TO

MY WIFE JOAN,

MY CHILDREN

AND GRANDCHILDREN

OTHER BOOKS BY THE SAME AUTHOR

Sawpit Boy  -  Historical (about Sierra Leone) and Autobiographical

Questions and Answers on Immigration to Britain - Legal textbook

# Stories from Sierra Leone

# List of Contents

# Acknowledgements

My most sincere thanks go to my wife Joan, who all along has helped me in my researches and who remembered and recounted some of the stories in this book.  She did all the typing and all the corrections and alterations, and carried a notebook and pen at all times to be ready when she or I thought of something worthy of inclusion.  Without her help this book may not have been written.

My sincere thanks go to the following friends and relatives who in one way or another made contributions to this book:-  Drs Kitty and Ahmadu Fadlu-Deen and their children, the late Dr Arthur Stuart, Mrs Tungie Stuart, Dr Peter Tucker, Sir Phillip Bridges, Shakib N.K. Basma,  Father Martin Nott,  Professor Cyril P. Foray, Dr Michel Aboud, Professor Arthur Abraham, Dr Rolv Holst-Roness, Dr Farouk Blell, Michael Blell, George Farrah, John Farrah, Caroline Munklinde, the late Mrs Salma Courban, Samir and Nancy Courban, Choukri Courban, Tunde and Lovetta Savage, Osman Cole, Melik Sabrah, Paddy Warren, Albert Metzger, Suru Davies, Arnold Gordon, Rose Howes, Farid Hassib, Fuad Hassib, Frank Isaac, Maureen Marke.

I must make special mention of my children, who have contributed to this book in so many various ways.

# Preamble

I was born and grew up in Sierra Leone, West Africa, and spent most of my life there, so it is hardly surprising that most of the stories in this book are about Sierra Leone while just a few are about our travels abroad. According to the Concise Oxford Dictionary, the word 'story' is defined as 'Facts or experiences that deserve narration'. I hope that the reader will find the following stories come into that category.

It is a very difficult process to keep events in chronological order and the reader will find we do not keep strictly to it. No doubt the reader will not know everything we have put in this book (anyway I hope not). I am not writing a straightforward history of Sierra Leone, and the reader will find that he or she is asked to jump from story to story as I remember them. Some are humorous incidents I want to share with you, and others are interesting and important events in the chronicles of Sierra Leone.

Sierra Leone got its name from a Portuguese explorer who "discovered" it in 1462, and called it Serra Lyoa. Pedro de Sintra, so called because he came from a Portuguese town known as Sintra, named the country Serra Lyoa (mountain of lions) because the high mountains that can be seen from the sea look like lions. Other people believe that the Portuguese heard the thunder echoing among the mountains and thought that it sounded like the roaring of lions (even though there were no lions in Sierra Leone), hence the name.

It has a tropical climate and consists of two seasons, the rainy season and the dry season. The rainy season starts in April, when the rain comes in occasional light showers, usually at night. The showers increase in length and density until by July it may rain all day and night without stopping. I was born in July so perhaps that is why I always enjoyed the rains. By mid October the rains stop completely. Harmattan, an Arabic word, is part of the dry season. It is a dry, dusty, wind that blows from the Sahara Desert to the West Coast of Africa and can be felt in December and January. The dust gets everywhere, any food set out on the table has to be covered if it is not going to be eaten immediately. The view from the hills gives the impression of mist as the air is so full of dust. The wind is very dry, your lips become chapped, and people reach for the moisturising cream. It is all the more noticeable in that the water in Sierra Leone is very soft and kind to the skin and for most of the year skin lotions are not really needed. Furniture also is affected, and it is not uncommon to have a table-top crack from end to end, and if covered with Formica, the glue used dries out and the Formica lifts up and sometimes cracks. It is the reverse of the rainy season, when the air, even inside your home, is so damp that leather shoes, belts and bags turn white with mildew. The temperature around Freetown ranges from 25 to 30 degrees Centigrade.

Some people believe that Hanno the Carthaginian visited Sierra Leone in 500 BC to get fresh water for his ships. Carthage was a colony near Tunis in North Africa founded by the Phoenicians, who came from Tyre in Lebanon in the early ninth century BC. Amongst seafarers of various countries that visited Freetown, it is known that the Dutch Admiral M. de Ruyter visited Sierra Leone in 1664, where he attacked an English fort at Tasso Island, the Dutch being at war with England at the time. De Ruyter stopped at King Jimmy in Freetown for water, and carved his name on a rock. This stone was buried for many years but was discovered in 1923 and a copy made which can be seen in the Sierra Leone Museum. The original stone was reburied to preserve it. In 1667 a Dutch fleet led by Admiral de Ruyter sailed to England and up the River Medway to Chatham, where they bombarded Chatham Docks, set fire to several ships and took possession of the 'Royal Charles', the pride of the English Fleet.

Before De Ruyter, an Englishman, John Hawkins, made several visits to the bays of Freetown to buy slaves in about the 1560s. His tall young cousin, Sir Francis Drake, who was born near Plymouth in Devon, moved with his family to Rochester in Kent when still a boy and grew up around the ships and sailors on the River Medway and in Chatham Dockyard. He got his early experience of long sea voyages by serving in one of Hawkins' ships as third officer. Drake called at Freetown for water around 1580 as captain of his own ship on his voyage to become the first Englishman to circumnavigate the globe. He is famous for being one of the English captains who defeated the Spanish Armada sent to attack England by Phillip II of Spain in 1588. John Hawkins also helped command the English ships in that battle and was knighted for his services to his country during the battle. Hawkins is reputed to have founded a hospice in Chatham for sailors maimed or disabled in the navy.

I have often been surprised when delving into Sierra Leone history to find a link, however tenuous, between early visitors to Sierra Leone and the Medway Towns in Kent where I now live (see also John Newton, Chapter 6).

Street and place names in Freetown, being a British colony from 1787 up to 1961, were often named after British people and places. Waterloo, Gloucester, Bathurst, Regent, Charlotte and Wellington, amongst others, are both street and place names. Kent, Lumley, Russell, York, Leicester, Aberdeen and Hastings are villages in the Western Area. The park in Freetown was named after Queen Victoria, and Albert Academy was possibly named after her Consort. The deep-water quay at Cline Town, opened in 1954, was named after Queen Elizabeth II. Connaught Hospital was named after the Duke of Connaught, and the Prince of Wales Secondary School was named after Edward, Prince of Wales, son of King George V, when he visited Sierra Leone in 1925 and performed the official opening ceremony. Many streets in Freetown were named after past Governors such as Rowe, Mereweather, Blackhall, Kortright, Cardew, King-Harman, and many others.

I was born at 8 Little East Street in Freetown, Sierra Leone. When I was a few months old I was christened in the Protestant St George's Cathedral. My parents sent me to a Catholic school, and later I was baptised as a Roman Catholic on 11 December 1943 at the Sacred Heart Cathedral in Freetown by Reverend Father W. Hagan, C.S.Sp. (This stands for Communioni Spiritus Sancto, or Community of Holy Fathers.)

I lived with my parents at 8 Little East Street until I was sixteen years old, when we moved to Sackville Street. By this time (1949) my mother Rahme (nee Khoury) had died, and I was living with my father John Anthony, my sister Victoria, who was the oldest, my younger brother John, who was always known as Anthony, and my sister Mary who was the youngest. My father and mother, who met and married in Freetown in 1922, were Lebanese. They both came from large families, so I had twenty-eight first cousins on my mother's side alone, and numerous other relatives. I also had some first cousins and other relatives on my father's side as well, but as they did not come to Sierra Leone I did not meet them until I visited Lebanon. Sadly I am now the only surviving child of my parents, although I have nephews and nieces in Gambia, Senegal and France.

I married for the first time in 1955 and had three children, a girl and two boys. My daughter, Rahme, was named after my mother, but is now generally known as Margaret. Rahme is a Lebanese name and difficult for the English tongue to pronounce. My eldest son is Jamal Edward, followed by Michael Kamal.

After my studies in England I returned to Freetown as a fully-fledged barrister with my new wife Joan and my daughter Mary, less than one year old. Some time later my son John was born, in Sawpit just two houses away from where I was born. We then moved to a larger flat in East Street (now Ecowas Street), whilst I was building a house in Lumley. In 1967 I finished the house and we moved out of Freetown. I soon brought the rest of my family to live with us in Lumley. In 1968 Margaret was ready for secondary school, and I sent her to school in England, as most of my friends did with their own daughters. When she finished her schooling Margaret studied nursing. On 30th December 1975 I received a card from her telling me that she had qualified as a State Enrolled Nurse. This was a very pleasant ending for the year. Margaret spent some time working in a hospital in Iran, before returning to England. She has two children, Christopher and Catherine. Christopher is the first of my thirteen grandchildren!

In 1968 my youngest child, Linda, was born. Joan had wanted to have the baby at home in Freetown, in the house we had just finished building, as she said it would be a blessing on the house to have a child born there. She also said that as we had not been back to England since we left in January 1964, she did not want to go on holiday heavily pregnant and not be able to travel around and visit her family and friends. She preferred to wait a year or so before travelling. For some reason, which I still do not understand and still baffles me, I insisted that we went to England that year, and ignored all her protests. It turned out to be a good thing, because as the time for the birth approached complications were found that were not apparent earlier. Linda was born in the same hospital in London where her elder sister Mary was born about five years before. My family was now complete with three girls and three boys.

My three sons all attended St Edwards Secondary School. The eldest, Jamal, went on to Fourah Bay College and did an Honours degree in Geography. His results came out in July 1978, and he achieved a Second Class in the First Division. He was awarded a scholarship to study in France, and went to Strasbourg in September 1978. He got his doctorate, and then became the youngest professor in France. He is at present Vice-Principal of a University in Dunkirk, and specialises in coastal geomorphology. He sometimes travels abroad to advise on the conservation of mangrove swamps. He is married to Iman, whom he met in Sierra Leone, and they have three daughters, Miriam, Hannah and Sarah.

My second son, Michael, also went to Fourah Bay College where he studied mechanical engineering. After working in Sierra Leone for a while designing and building various machines, he and his wife Afaf, who is sister to Jamal's wife Iman, went to America to live with their two sons. They also have two daughters, both born in America, and Michael has his own engineering business in Florida. He holds many patents for his inventions, one of which is the 'chill can', a system which will make the contents of a can or bottle cold upon opening, thus avoiding the need for ice or a refrigerator to make drinks cold.

My third son, John, came to England. Among other things, he is an experienced diver and also an expedition leader, having travelled to Malaysia and Peru, among other places. He has one son, Alexander.

My two youngest daughters both attended St Joseph's Secondary School. Mary came to England and did an Honours degree in Biochemical Analysis. She later went to America, where she is married to Steve and has three sons.

Linda also came to England to study. She worked for some years in a bank, rising to first cashier, then branched out into a new career to become a driving instructor. She is married to Kevin and has two stepsons.

Following my return to Sierra Leone as a barrister and registering at the Sierra Leone Bar, I became a member of the Sierra Leone Bar Association in

February 1964. Two pictures of me appeared in the Sierra Leone Daily Mail, one announcing my return to Freetown as a qualified barrister, and the other showing me at the Students Union Annual Dance in London together with Mr A.R. Virani, President of the Union, and Sir Frederick Pritchard, Director of the Council of Legal Education.

The Historical Society of Sierra Leone was formed on 16 April 1975 and was revived in 1980, at which time I became a member. In 1981 I was Vice-President of the Society. Dr J.S. Lenga-Kromah was President. In 1987 the Conservation Society of Sierra Leone was formed and I was a Founder Member. My wife was also a member. The aims of the Society were to attempt to preserve the rain forest and the flora and fauna of the country. One instance of this was in trying to introduce methods of cooking that would use less wood and so avoid the cutting down of so many trees for firewood.

The Heritage Society of Sierra Leone was formed in 1990 and I was also a Founder Member of this organisation which included, amongst others, Professors Eldred Jones and C.P. Foray and Dr W.F. Conton. Its aims were a little different to those of the Historical Society in that it was principally concerned in locating and then preserving various historical buildings, sites and artefacts of cultural and heritable importance to the country.

It is the fervent hope of myself and my wife that the aims and ideals of these societies will not be forgotten and that those that have been discontinued will be revived in the near future.

My first book is called 'Sawpit Boy' and was printed in 1980. It is partly historical and partly autobiographical, but wholly factual, about Sierra Leone and my life there.

I have also written a book called 'Questions and Answers on Immigration to Britain'. Those who wish to buy these books may write to me at 89 Saxton Street, Gillingham, Kent, ME7 5EG, United Kingdom. Both books were reviewed in the publication "West Africa" shortly after they appeared in the shops.

If I were to follow the dictates of my heart, this book would go on and on, as I remember stories or events that I want to record. However, I have to stop somewhere, so I hope you will find pleasure and interest in the twenty chapters I have produced.

# Chapter 1

# In Days Gone By

Little East Street, Freetown, is now called Malamah Thomas Street after a well-known businessman who lived at the top end of the street before I was born, and who was eight times Mayor of Freetown. The lower end of Little East Street where I lived with my family is known as Sawpit. It is named after the saw pit that was sited there at the wharf in days gone by when boats used to be built there. Across the street from our home were just the railings to prevent people from falling over the edge and down the steep slope that led to the water. There was an iron gate and steps that led down to the wharf where the launches would tie up. On the wharf itself were two sheds for goods, and a crane that was sometimes used to load or unload the boats and lighters. The lighters would be loaded with palm kernels, coffee or cocoa to be taken out to the ships at anchor half a mile or so away in the harbour. Freetown Harbour is said to be the second largest natural harbour in the world.

At midnight on New Year's Eve the first hooter heralding the New Year would come from Mabella (the wharf from which the ships were supplied with coal by lighters, nearly a sea mile from Sawpit Wharf), then all the ships anchored in the huge harbour joined in the refrain. During the Second World War the Freetown harbour would be full of ships of all kinds, British Royal Navy and merchant navy, and troop ships, and it was not unusual to count up to three hundred or more ships at anchor. It was a treat to listen to all the ships welcoming in the New Year.

I sometimes borrowed a small boat to scull around the wharf or to cross to Mabella, just for the fun of it. One day I went out in the boat with three friends. We were only halfway out towards Mabella when two of my friends decided they wanted to turn back and they both dived overboard and swam back to Sawpit Wharf. The third, a Lebanese boy who had just come from the Provinces, remained on board with me, but several times he made diving motions as if he too wanted to swim to shore. I asked him if he wanted to go ashore with the others, and he said yes. I got fed up with him pretending to dive, and the next time he did so, I gave him a little help and pushed him overboard. But lo and behold and unknown to me, my new friend could not swim very well! I left the scull and reached over the side to grab his hand and help him back into the boat. I turned back to Sawpit Wharf to return my friend to dry land, tied up the boat and went home. Looking at Mabella from my house, it occurred to me that the

1

distance to a point at sea always looks shorter when viewed from land than it looks when you are actually swimming towards it!

Kite-flying was another activity my friends and I would do at Sawpit Wharf. I made my own kites out of coloured paper, bamboo sticks and string, with a long thin strip of cotton material for the tail. If the tail is too short, the kite will 'turn foofoo', that is it will turn round and round and not fly properly. One form of amusement would be to send a 'message' or 'telegram' up to the kite by placing a small piece of paper on the string of the kite and letting the breeze carry it all the way up to the kite. We would compete to see who could fly their kite the highest, and send up the most 'messages'. Nowadays ready-made kites, usually made from plastic and with bright pictures such as birds and butterflies, are easily obtainable. The most popular time for flying kites was at Easter, when the weather was often breezy.

Oh, one of the things I must tell you about is our device for catching pigeons. We would find a large empty basket, and prop it half upright on a stick, with a long strong thread tied to the stick. I would place a little dried corn or rice under the basket, with just a few grains leading up to the basket. I then went as far away as the thread would allow and waited patiently for a pigeon to come and eat the food under the basket. When the bird came I waited until it was right underneath the basket and then tugged the thread sharply to pull away the stick thus letting the basket drop over the bird. I then headed home with the bird. After plucking a few of the wing feathers so that it couldn't fly away, I would keep the bird in a cage as a pet.

As a boy I used to attend the Empire Cinema at Water Street. The cinema was the only one in Freetown at that time and had opened just a few years before in 1939. Most of the entertainment for my friends and me was of our own making, so a trip to watch a film was a high treat. We would watch whatever film was being screened, we were not choosy, but if the film was not up to the expectations of us small boys we would leave. If the film was exciting we would really feel a part of it, and would shout encouragement or a warning during the chase scenes, as if the actors could hear us.

Many years later I sent my sons on holiday to my sister and her family in the Gambia, where they went to an outdoor cinema near to Barra Point. They told me that if the film did not meet with the approval of the small boys in the audience, they would throw stones at the screen! This no longer happens these days in Barra, or, I believe, anywhere else.

Another incident I must tell you about concerned a Lebanese friend of mine, who would usually go on his own when going to the cinema. He would buy a bag of toffees to eat during the show. On this occasion he thought that his toffees were disappearing rather quickly, but he put it down to the excitement of the film. He found he was wrong when he put

2

out his hand to take a sweet and found another hand in the bag before him! The stranger sitting next to him was helping himself to my friend's sweets under cover of the darkness. My friend decided that his pocket was the safest place for the few toffees that were left to him.

➼ My education, both Elementary and Secondary, was obtained from start to finish at St Edward's School, whose motto was and is 'Dirige Nos In Veritate', meaning 'Guide us in Truth'. The school was divided into four houses – Wilson, O'Gorman, Blanchet and Brown, and I belonged to Wilson House. Lately Mulcahy House has been added.

During the start of my days in secondary school in 1947, I became friendly with Ahmadu Fadlu-Deen who belonged to O'Gorman House. Ahmadu used to visit me in Sawpit, and I introduced him to Charles Benjamin, whom I had known for a long time as we lived in the same street. One day in the mid-term break that year the three of us, all of us boy scouts, decided to go to a fishing village outside Freetown called Goderich and to explore some of the beautiful beaches. In pursuit of our intentions we boarded a bus to the Peninsula road and alighted just outside Goderich. We turned right and walked down the road towards the village, hoping to find a cassava plantation where we might be able to uproot some tubers, and maybe pick some mangoes for our lunch. We came across a farmer carring a bottle containing a very clear liquid which we thought was water. We asked him for a drink, and he forthwith obliged us. Charles took the first swig, then spluttered and coughed and almost choked on the 'water'. We discovered to our amazement that the liquid was a locally distilled substance called 'omole', and after what had happened to Charles, Ahmadu and I decided that we would not touch it. Then curiosity got the better of us, so Ahmadu got the farmer to pour a few drops into his palm, and when he tasted it, it was like fire burning his tongue. I, too, tried a few drops just to see what it was like, and discovered the same thing. While this tasting was going on, the farmer was drinking freely from the bottle. By the time we were ready to leave, the farmer was so drunk he was in a stupor. We three boy scouts did our good deed for the day and carried the drunken farmer back to his village. When the villagers saw three young boys carrying him they knew he had been up to his usual habits – drinking to oblivion. We left the farmer with the villagers and continued on our way to the beach.

Ahmadu and I have stayed friends throughout the years up to the present day, but sad to say, Charles died some years ago. I have watched with interest as Ahmadu became very prominent in the community. He is a doctor and did his medical studies in Ireland, where he met his wife Kitty, who comes from Singapore and has a Doctorate in music. They have four children, the eldest a boy named Yazid, then their daughter Yasmin, followed by their son Tejan, and finally a girl named Zarin.

Ahmadu is Chairman of the flour mill in Freetown, Seaboard West Africa

Ltd, and Chairman of Medical and General Insurance Company Ltd., (M.A.G.I.C.), owned and managed by Sierra Leoneans. He is also Chairman of the Campaign Against Violent Events (C.A.V.E.), a Non-Governmental Organisation. Being a staunch Muslim, Ahmadu is an Alhaji. He has a strong interest in education and is Chairman of the Board of Directors of the Sierra Leone Muslim Congress Boys Secondary School. Further to that, he has been chosen as Alghadi (Chief) of the Foulah Town Jamat or Community and endeavours to settle disputes of all kinds among the community.

For some time Ahmadu was Chairman of the voluntary organisation campaigning to Keep the City Clean (it's slogan), set up by the Government during the time that Desmond Luke was Minister of Health under the All Peoples Congress (APC) government. Many a time I saw the refuse collection lorries lined up outside the Ministry of Health building in Gloucester Street, where I had my chambers in those days before I moved to Circular Road. Ahmadu served with the United Nations Fund for Population Activities (UNFPA) in Ghana and subsequently in Somalia. He retired from the United Nations in 1992 and returned home to Sierra Leone.

Ahmadu was Electoral Commissioner, Western Region, of the Interim National Electoral Commission (I.N.E.C.), with Dr James Jonah as Chairman. With other Commissioners, Professor Bob Kandeh, Mr Ibrahim Sesay and Mr Alimamy Cylla, Ahmadu conducted the Parliamentary and Presidential Elections in 1996 that ushered in Democratic Rule in Sierra Leone. International observers were present at these elections, and it was said that they were the fairest elections ever held in Sierra Leone.

More recently Ahmadu became Chairman of the Ports Authority in Freetown.

Alhaji Dr Ahmadu Tejan Fadlu-Deen, born 27 June 1931, has sporting interests as well. In our school days Ahmadu represented St Edwards Secondary School, to which we both belonged, in the high jump, and he played rugby during his medical studies in Ireland. More lately he has turned to golf, and has been President of the famous Freetown Golf Club for three consecutive years, from 1981 to 1983, and is now a Life-Member of the club. (Previous Life-Members included Ade Hyde, Johnnie Smythe, Q.C., Peter Miller and Mr Robertson). Ahmadu was Vice-Captain of the Achimota Golf Club in 1990 when he was in Ghana.

The Freetown Golf Club can now boast of many professionals, most of whom started their careers as caddies, including well-known James Lebbie who went on to win the Nigerian Open Tournament and has played all over the world. Other professionals who now give lessons at the club include, to name a few, Bureh Kargo, Jerry Dumbuya, Mohmodu Kargbo, Ibrahima Conteh and others. I learnt recently that the first time golf was played in West Africa was in Sierra Leone on the Banana Islands in 1770.

With Ahmadu having so many interests it is not surprising that he knows a great many people. It is difficult to walk through the streets of Freetown with him, because he is stopped every few paces by someone he knows. One day we were walking together towards PZ (Paterson Zochonis) Store to buy our imported weekly English papers. I spoke to the person I thought was him, then turned to look at him only to find it was a strange woman walking next to me. Ahmadu was way behind me, talking to someone else!

Ahmadu and Kitty's beautiful house, from which you could see Lumley Beach, was completely burned down by the Revolutionary United Front, (R.U.F.) in February 1998. It was the only house I knew of in Sierra Leone that had solar panels on the roof to supply the house with electricity. This occurred as the Ecomog forces (the military wing of ECOWAS, the Economic Community of West African States) were entering Freetown to re-take the city on behalf of the Sierra Leone Government, forcing the R.U.F. to withdraw. As I write these stories Ahmadu and Kitty are rebuilding their home in Lumley.

➡ 'Long road noh kill nobody'. Roughly translated this means going the long way round does not do anybody any harm. This arose out of an experience a Sierra Leonean friend and I had when we were young. It was a public holiday, and as usual most of Freetown headed for Lumley Beach, which was about three miles long, where they played football or picnicked according to their whims. We had walked from Freetown and got as far as Wilkinson Road at the point where you can look down and see Lumley Beach. We knew that to stay on the road would take us another forty five minutes walking, so my friend and I decided that we would take a short cut from Wilkinson Road straight down to the beach, although, as we thought, it meant going through uncleared bush. We had hardly gone two or three hundred yards when we were slowed down considerably by swamps. We were sometimes knee-deep in mud and so it took us two hours to wade through the swamps to get to Lumley. Our clothes and ourselves were covered from head to toe in mud. When at last we reached the beach we both walked straight into the water with our clothes on, and washed ourselves thoroughly. We vowed that whenever we came to the beach again we would take the long road and not attempt to take a short cut. As my friend said, "Long road noh kill nobody!"

We spent the rest of the day on the beach, until evening. The setting sun was so beautiful that we stayed a few more minutes gazing at the sky and the reflections of the bright colours in the sea. We could see the fishermen in their small canoes far out at sea. Afterwards we decided to take the 'boneshaker' home (a covered lorry with seats added so it could be run as a bus). On the way home we sang a song popular at the time, which ran thus:-

"We boarded a bus to Lumley,
Five shillings he charged us
For the sake of our education.
Everywhere I go titi, palm-wine de wait for me."

Palm-wine (poyo) is a drink obtained by tapping palm trees. A cut is made at the top of the trunk just below where the leaves emerge, and a gourd is placed to gather the sap as it drops. The juice ferments as it is collected, and is a refreshing, pleasantly sour, whitish drink which can be drunk straight away. Sometimes it is distilled, to produce a far stronger form of alcohol. Palm-wine became known as 'From God to Man', in reference to the ease with which it is obtained. Palm-wine sellers wore a yoke across their shoulders with a bully of palm-wine hanging from each side, much as the milkmaids would carry the pails of milk in England in days gone by.

➥ St Edward's Secondary School was in my day situated at Brookfields where St Joseph's Secondary School for Girls now stands. The school buildings were Nissen huts left over from World War II. There were several mango trees in the compound and one day during the lunch break a schoolmate of mine decided to pick some mangoes. He glanced around and saw no-one in authority so he picked up a stone. He took his stance, with one hand pointing upwards at the mango and the other drawn back ready to let fly. Suddenly a stern voice at his elbow said, "What do you think you are doing?" The boy turned around to see one of the Priests standing right behind him. The boy, stone still in his right hand and left arm raised, said innocently, "Nothing, Father!" The Priest told him to report to his office after school. The boy was glad to have more time to try and think of a convincing reason for him to throw a stone into a tree full of ripe mangoes. When the boy reported after school, the priest said to him, "I saw you in Freetown a few days ago when you were supposed to be in school. I suppose you are now going to tell me that it wasn't you I saw." The boy replied, "Yes, Sir!" The priest let him off with a caution.

➥ Rev. Father P. Holly, C.S.Sp., who was the Principal of the school at that time, taught us Latin in 1951. Towards the end of one lesson, he suddenly stopped and ushered us all outside and told us to look up at Tower Hill where a twenty-one gun salute was being fired for some reason or the other which I cannot now remember. He wanted to use the salute to demonstrate the principle that light travels faster than sound, and that we would see the flash from the guns before we heard the sound of the cannon. We all stood and waited and watched the Hill - but nothing happened. We all began to look at each other and smile surreptitiously. Unknown to the priest, the last of the twenty-one gun salute had been fired just as he got the idea for an impromptu physics lesson. In disgust he uttered his favourite saying, "Glory be to God", and walked away.

Just then the bell rang for the lunch break and a group of us made a dash for the gamesroom to play 'roundtable'. This was a form of table tennis which started off with five or six players on each side of the table but only one bat on each side. The first player would hit the ball over the net then put down the bat and run to join the boys at the other end of the table. Each player would hit the ball only once and run to the other side, unless he played a fault in which case he was out of the game. It would continue like this until only two players remained, and these two would then play a game of normal table tennis but up to eleven points. This version of the game meant that a lot of boys could take part on one table, while a more traditional game took place on the second table with only two or four players.

➺ One day Cyril Foray, Somerset Williams and I, all from the same form in St Edwards Secondary School, were dressed in our Boy Scout uniforms and heading for the Prince of Wales Secondary School in King Tom (an area in Freetown), to take part in a Scouting Jamboree. We were strolling along in no particular hurry, but as we entered the grounds of the school we were met by a Scoutmaster who swept back his sleeve to look at his watch and snapped, "What is your idea of time?" We all gave the three-finger Scouts salute and Cyril quickly replied without hesitation, "The same as yours, Sir!" Obviously this did not please the Scouter, but we three speeded up and left him standing there, lost for words.

Signalling and bridge-building were the forte of the 8th Freetown Troop belonging to St Edwards Secondary School. A few days before the whole troop had gone by foot to Leicester Peak to cut down trees to use to build an imitation bridge in the grounds of the Prince of Wales School where the Jamboree would be held. The trees were trimmed and carried back down to Freetown on the shoulders of the boy scouts. Assembling the bridge was also a test of our knotting skills, as no nails were used, only rope. The bridge was then used as a platform from which to send a signal by Morse code, using a flag. The Governor, Sir George Beresford-Stooke, wrote out a message and gave it to Cyril and myself for us to signal to two other 8th Freetown scouts on the other side of the field, Somerset Williams and Abu Bangura. We both sent the calling-up signal of 'VE, VE, VE', each using a single flag. We received back the go-ahead signal of 'K', and then signalled the Governor's message. These two scouts in turn passed on the message in the same way to a further two scouts, who wrote down the message and ran to the Governor with it. The Governor read it out and confirmed that it was the true and correct message which he had given to us. The Governor praised the speed and accuracy by which the scouts had relayed the message, and the 8th Freetown felt very proud of themselves.

It is interesting to note that the Morse code was invented by Samuel Morse, an American artist born in 1791. Morse got the idea that it might be possible to send messages by means of electrical current while on a ship returning home after a visit to Europe in 1832. He invented the electric telegraph machine, and then devised the Morse Code, a system whereby letters and numbers were represented by dots and dashes, which could be sent by way of electrical contacts, sounds, flashes or even flags. After years of experiment, it was on 24 January 1838 that Samuel Morse gave the first demonstration of his electrical machine, but at this time the American Government was not interested. It was not until May 1844 that the first telegraph line was put into operation and messages were transmitted in a matter of seconds over long distances.

➤➤ "Worok Worok," came the shout from the wharf as a trader looked for somebody to carry his goods through the town. 'Worok' is a Krio term meaning "Who wants work?" I was strolling with a lawyer colleague of mine, Shakib Basma, when he heard this cry, and was reminded of a trick he once played as a schoolboy when being asked by his father to mind his shop for a short while. Shakib filled a sack with stones and tied it loosely, then stepped outside into the street and shouted "Worok, Worok". A tall, strong man came forward and asked what was the load to be carried. Shakib showed the man the sack, told him it was heavy, and gave him an address some distance away. It was usually wise for the employer to walk close beside the labourer who was carrying the goods if the Worok wasn't known to him, lest the labourer and the goods disappear before the destination was reached. At this point Shakib's father returned, so Shakib was able to go out. The Worok had got some distance ahead. Shakib stayed out of sight, but kept an eye on the Worok to see what he would do. As he suspected, the man, thinking that Shakib had been left way behind, soon slipped down a side road and lowered the sack to the ground. The man's expression when he found that all he had got away with was a sack of rocks was a sight to see. Shakib then appeared on the scene whilst the Worok was searching the bag, and accused him of replacing the goods he had been given to carry with stones. The man protested his innocence, and Shakib made a show of being magnanimous and told the man he would forgive him this time, but it must never happen again!

In most cases the "Worok" (labourer) was an honest man looking for casual work, and sometimes the employer knew him and would trust him to carry the goods unaccompanied to another trader. Usually the labourer would know the person he was delivering the goods to, as he had probably done casual work for him as well. It was more than likely that the "Worok" tricked by Shakib was not a Worok at all but was actually a thief who thought he was taking advantage of a young boy.

I say 'in most cases' the Worok was an honest man but there was one occasion when a friend of mine who ran a store in Westmoreland Street (now Siaka Stevens Street) had sold some bulky items to a woman. She wanted a Worok to carry her load and asked the shop assistant to call one for her. When the labourer came into the shop my friend recognised him as a petty thief and wanted to warn the woman, so he said to her, "Mama, dis nar t-i-f-f-m-a-n", spelling out the last two words. Before the woman could say anything, the Worok looked at my friend, the shop owner, and said, "Mama, nar l-i-e-!" My friend was speechless.

This incident reminded me of another story of a thief who was being chased down Sawpit. The people chasing him were shouting, "Stop, thief!" as they ran. The thief decided to draw attention away from himself by also shouting, "Stop, thief!" and pointing ahead as if he was chasing someone else. This worked very well as no one tried to stop him, as they looked for the imaginary thief who ran in front of the actual thief! The thief got away in the ensuing confusion.

➤ One day when I was a teenager I was strolling along Garrison Street, with my hands behind my back, deep in thought. I did not notice the sudden confusion around me, with everyone running in the opposite direction to where I was going. A sudden clatter on the road close to me made me look up in time to see a huge bull with large horns and a rope hanging from its neck, running past within arm's length of me. Due to my absent-mindedness I had not noticed the bull running down the street towards me so I made no move to escape like the others in his path. Apparently the bull had escaped from a Foulah who was leading him through the town. Everybody said I was very brave in not running away, but what I did not say was that had I seen the escaped bull, I would have run faster than anyone!

➤ In those days we would quite often spend our evenings playing 'Masari', meaning 'money' in Arabic. A few friends and I would go along to a billiards hall about fifteen minutes walk from my home in Sawpit. The Sierra Leonean proprietor had only one table, so instead of billiards, which can only be played by two people, we would play masari. The fifteen red balls were all numbered one to fifteen and we used one white cue ball. We would each put up our stake, usually sixpence each, then to start the game we would each draw a numbered disc from a bag and keep the number secret from all the other players. The object was to pot the ball that had your own number on it, and the first to do this won the stake, after taking out the 'table' money, ie the amount paid to the owner of the table.

If your number was a large one you could make it up by potting two or more balls to make the correct amount, for instance potting the number two and number five balls if your own number was seven, or three, five, six and one to total fifteen. Potted balls do not go back on the table. If by mistake you pot a number higher than your own you 'burn' and are out of the game. Similarly, if your number is small and somebody else has potted it and you cannot make it up with different numbers, again you are out of the game. Sometimes a player would try to give a false impression as to the number he has by pretending the near-miss of a ball with a different number if the ball with his own number is not accessible. The player who wins shouts "Masari", then shows the disc with his number on it.

9

The room we played in was narrow with just enough space to move along the sides of the table, and if you had to play a shot from the side you ask for a 'short' cue, about three feet long, so that you could play without hitting the wall behind you. I was quite good at this game and so would encourage my friends to play so that I could earn enough money to go to the cinema on the following night!

➻ A businessman who had a shop somewhere up country came down to Freetown to buy some goods. His business had been doing very badly in recent months and he was very worried about the money he had lost. He began to feel seriously unwell and was coughing constantly, so he decided to visit a doctor. The doctor examined him thoroughly and then told his patient, "I am afraid you have tuberculosis." The businessman was amazed. He said in Krio, words to the effect of: "Doctor, I do not know how you did it, being so far away from where I do business. You examine my chest, and from that you can tell I have tobacco losses? How did you know I had lost all my money trading in tobacco?"

➻ As a schoolboy I spent a short holiday with the Akar family at Rotifunk. Edward Akar was slightly younger than I was, and little did we think in those days that one day we would both be lawyers. A few years later, in 1954, John Akar, the eldest brother, took the part of the black narrator in a dramatised version of Alan Paton's famous book, "Cry, the Beloved Country" in the United Kingdom. It is a story of racial conflict as well as racial understanding set in South Africa, and the play was performed for three weeks in St Martins in the Fields at Trafalgar Square in London. Another Sierra Leonean who took part was Evelyn Dove. A Nigerian actor, Orlando Martins, played the leading role of the Rev. Stephen Kumale.

John worked with the SLBS, after studying commercial radio and television in America, Britain and other places. Professor Cyril Foray, in his book 'Historical Dictionary of Sierra Leone' published by Scarecrow Press in 1977, tells us that John became head of programmes for SLBS in 1957. In 1960 he was appointed 'the first **indigenous** Director of Broadcasting', quoting from 'Sierra Leonean Heroes, Fifty Great Men and Women who Helped to Build Our Nation'. In 1961 Sierra Leone gained its independence, and the music for the new National Anthem was written by John Akar. The words were written by Mr C. Nelson-Fyle, a tutor at the Methodist Boys High School. His composition was chosen out of 171 entries from all over the world. (See Appendix B)

John was also a playwright, having written "Valley Without Echo" in 1959 and "Cry Tamba" in 1963, which were performed by the Sierra Leone Players.

Another thing that John Akar did was to found the National Dance Troupe and to take it around the world - to the New York World's Fair in 1964, where it won first prize, to the Commonwealth Arts Festival in London in 1965 and the Festival of Negro Arts in Dakar in 1966.

Everywhere it went it was a great success. The Dance Troupe was a permanent group of dancers, who could frequently be seen performing for tourists at the Bintumani Hotel at Aberdeen when they were not on tour.

Freetown had had a dance troupe once before, in the 1930's, organised by Mr Alex D. Yaskey, a Sierra Leonean, "who used to make arrangements for native dancers from all over 'the far off Protectorate' to give performances for the tourists who were provided with the opportunity of seeing 'boneless' babies, mamakparas (stilt dancers), shegureh singers, snake charmers, fire-eaters and other performances at the Victoria Park" (quoted from my book 'Sawpit Boy' page 83).

John Akar is remembered for taking a case against the Attorney General of Sierra Leone claiming that he was a citizen of Sierra Leone (see The African Law Reports, Sierra Leone Series, 1967-1968. The same edition reported a case in which I appeared). John Akar was born in Sierra Leone, but not of Negro African descent. He wanted to stand for election to parliament in 1967, but was refused as not being eligible. Sierra Leone became independent of Great Britain on 27 April 1961. The terms of the constitution were agreed by the people of Sierra Leone and the British Government, and under this constitution John Akar was a citizen by birth, being one of the qualifications for election to the House of Representatives. An Act was passed retrospectively, however, in 1962 which disentitled persons **not** of Negro African descent from being citizens of Sierra Leone by birth. Such persons could register to be citizens, but would not be eligible for election until they had completed twenty five years residence after such registration. Akar won his case in the Supreme Court (which was then as the High Court is now). The Attorney General appealed against the decision and the appeal was granted, so John Akar lost his case.

Despite this setback, he was still able to serve his country and joined the diplomatic service. He was Ambassador for Sierra Leone to the United States, 1969-1971. He came several times to our house at Lumley when he was in Freetown, for a Saturday lunch of 'foofoo' and palmoil stew. Foofoo is made of cassava, ground up, mixed with a little water and pushed through a sieve, then cooked over a slow fire into a very thick paste that is rolled into balls. It is eaten with palm oil stew as an alternative to rice.

John Akar died in Jamaica on 23 June 1975 aged 48. His body was brought back to Sierra Leone, and was laid out for a few hours in the school which he had attended in Freetown, the Albert Academy, for people to pay their last respects, and was then taken to Rotifunk in the Southern Province of Sierra Leone for burial.

I, and many, many others attended his funeral. I travelled to Rotifunk in my car with a friend, and took the long way round instead of crossing on the ferry. We went straight to the Akar family home, where we met John Akar's wife, Connie, and other members of the family, and we joined them for lunch of cassava leaf and rice. After lunch we went to the United

Mission School where John Akar's body was laid out. The casket was of beautiful polished wood, and John was dressed in embroidered native costume with a Cross on his chest. His native hat was laid beside him in the coffin. The local school girls choir sang hymns. The coffin was then closed and we all walked behind it in procession to the Martyrs Memorial United Methodist Church. The church was packed full, and there were judges, magistrates and practising lawyers who, like me, had driven from Freetown and elsewhere. The coffin was draped with the flag of Albert Academy School, and there were many representatives from this school in attendance. There were some people of mixed race who gave a wreath with a card marked from "The Coloured Brotherhood", no doubt in memory of the case he had fought for citizenship. I heard that the President of Sierra Leone wrote a personal letter of condolence to the family. John Akar held the M.B.E., B.A. and Ph.D.

I have not been to Rotifunk since the day of the funeral, but I have learnt that the whole town has been destroyed recently due to the civil strife in Sierra Leone. This is not the first time that Rotifunk has met with destruction. During the 1898 uprising, otherwise known as the Hut Tax War, the whole of Rotifunk was burnt to the ground. The Martyrs Memorial United Methodist Church is so named in memory of those members of the clergy and their families and others who were killed at that time, and memorial plaques could be seen inside the church. One of the plaques read: "In memory of the Martyrs of 1898, United Brethren of Christ. W.M.A. 1902". It would appear that Rotifunk is completely destroyed every one hundred years! Let us hope 2098 will bring better fortune to this town.

Sadly, my friend and colleague Edward Akar, younger brother of John, died early in 2002.

➤ My late brother Anthony started smoking in his late teens, and whilst he was helping his auntie in her shop in the provinces he would also help himself to her cigarettes when she was not looking. My aunt became aware of this and took to keeping her cigarettes up on a high shelf out of sight. She also placed a mousetrap, already set, on the next shelf, ready to catch Anthony when he started searching for the cigarettes. Unknown to my aunt, my brother saw her positioning the mousetrap and realised what it was for. As soon as he had the opportunity he helped himself to a cigarette and then exchanged the positions of the packet and the mousetrap. My aunt, suspecting nothing, reached up to get herself a cigarette only to have the trap close on her fingers. Anthony, who had gone outside for a moment, came back in at the sound of her cries of agony and asked her in seeming innocence why she had a mousetrap hanging on her fingers. My aunt was in too much pain to think of a suitable answer.

➤ A man walked into a police station somewhere in the provinces. He saw on the wall a poster showing four different views of a wanted man who had escaped from custody in Freetown. He went up to the policeman on duty and told him, "I have seen all four of these men here in town." The policeman, shaking his head, sent him away.

➤ A young relative of mine, I shall call him Joe, was sent by his father to buy himself a new pair of shoes for school. Joe went to the Bata shoe shop and found a suitable pair of shoes in his size for £2.10s. On looking around he saw a similar pair in a larger adult size for the same price. Thinking that they were trying to fool him about the price – because the adult size was the same price as the smaller size – he bought the larger! Joe rushed home to his father with a pair of shoes so big that his two feet could go into one shoe, and he boasted how clever he had been in buying the bigger pair at the same price as the smaller one. His father smacked him for being so stupid, and made Joe go back to the shop and choose the pair of shoes that were his correct size.

➤ The Sierra Leone Railway (first proposed in 1872 by Dr Edward Wilmot Blyden, a West Indian-born Liberian) ran from the station at Water Street via Kissy Street in Freetown on its way to Pendembu in the Eastern Province, a distance of about 227 miles. Construction began in 1896 by Crown Agents, and the first section to be completed was Freetown to Songo. Construction continued and by 1908 the railway station at Pendembu, the end of the main line, was opened. At Bauya the line branched off and ran for about 74 miles to Makeni in the Northern Province, which station was opened around 1915.

At Kissy Street the railway line passed over a bridge which was about thirty feet above the small stream called Nicol's Brook which ran underneath. This bridge, which was popularly known as 'Overbridge', was not meant for pedestrians, having only a couple of small semi-circular platforms where the workmen could stand in safety if a train came along. However, a few brave (or foolhardy?) people would use the bridge as a way to Kissy Road. I used to use it myself on my way to the home of teacher Arthur Williams in Hagan Street, for private lessons after school about twice a week. Mr Williams taught us history at St Edwards Secondary, and did his B.A. in history in England.

One day a man was crossing the bridge when he heard a train approaching. Instead of hurrying to one of the platforms he jumped from the bridge to the waters below and broke one of his legs. For a long time after this incident no one would take the risk of crossing that railway bridge on foot. In the 1970's the Government decided that the railway was not economical and discontinued it in phases.

Many years later Kissy Street was renamed Sani Abacha Street by President Tejan Kabba. Incidentally, I have recently heard that the steam engines from the Sierra Leone railway are still in use somewhere in Wales in the United Kingdom, and S.L.R. (Sierra Leone Railway) can still be seen on the side. I shall be grateful if anyone can tell me about this.

➤ In my teens I began to take an interest in the opposite sex and would go out with my friends to the nightclubs. I remember one particular evening with a certain embarrassment. I had taken an English girl to a popular club in Freetown. The club was dimly lit and we sat at a secluded table. A friend of mine called Frank came in and saw us, and I asked him to join our table. After a while I stretched out my hand under the table, and found another hand reaching towards my own. I squeezed, and the hand squeezed mine in return. I smiled to myself, and thought I was doing very well. For quite a while I sat enjoying holding hands in secret, as I thought, with a pretty young lady. After a while the young lady said she needed to visit the ladies room and got to her feet. I realised with a shock that I could see both of her hands, while I was still holding *someone's* hand under the table! Frank and I looked at each other in dismay as we realised that for the last ten minutes we had been holding each other's hand instead of the girl's!

➤ In 1999 I was reading a book called "Diamonds are Trumps" written by Michael Boorman and published by The Book Guild Ltd in 1996. It is about his life and work as an English policeman in Africa, part of which was spent in Sierra Leone, from 1954 to 1965. He wrote about another English policeman called Michael Everitt and how he was killed during a riot in Freetown in February 1955. I have vivid memories of this riot. I clearly remember going out with a friend, Frank Isaac, whose mother rented a small house from my father in the same compound where we lived. When we came home, we met the iron gate to the compound closed and locked, due to the riot. The army had been called out and shots had been fired in our street. We were wondering how to get in, when a bullet hit the iron gate where we were standing. This made up our minds and in moments we had both climbed over the gate, a feat we had not thought possible a minute before! The same night my uncle Michael Blell's house in East Street was attacked, and one door was burnt. An Austin Station Wagon which was in the street near his house was burnt out. The following day all the Lebanese who agreed to go were evacuated to the barracks at Murray Town for their safety.

My cousin Dr John Blell, son of Michael Blell, had a surgery on the ground floor of his home in Goderich Street, where he lived with his Lebanese wife, Olga (nee Aboud), and children. A lot of the local women went to him for treatment and those who could not afford to pay him he treated free of charge. It is usually said that one good turn deserves another, and these ladies found a way to repay Dr Blell's kindness to them when the rioters reached Goderich Street. The women came out of their houses and formed a barrier in front of Dr Blell's house, shouting to the rioters, "You will have to kill us first before you touch Dr Blell!" The rioters threw a few stones, but they left the women alone and moved further on down the street.

The riot was caused by the workers who were demanding more pay. There was a strike, and thousands of workers were out in the streets. The army was guarding the Electricity Company and more soldiers were patrolling in lorries, armed with machine guns, and they opened fire on the rioters killing many of them. This brought the disturbances to an end. Eventually the workers succeeded in getting an increase of one shilling a day.

A few months later I moved to Mambolo in the Kambia District in the Northern Province. Riots took place all over the north from Kambia to Moyamba, which lasted four months. I remember clearly the women marching in Mambolo in 1955 and singing a song in Temne insulting the local Paramount Chief and blaming him as being the cause of the strikes in Mambolo. The workers complained that the cost of living was very high, so were the taxes, but their wages very low, and they were banding together to attack the Chiefs and Tribal Authorities. One day I went into Kasiri by launch along the Great Scarcies River to buy goods for my own shop from a Lebanese trader, popularly known as Ramoneh. He had bags of rice stacked outside his shop, from ground level up to the veranda of his first floor house. Armed police were lying on top of the sacks to get a good view along the main street and stationed at other points throughout the town, to prevent looting. It was estimated that hundreds of people died as a result of the riots.

An official enquiry was commissioned by the Governor, His Excellency Sir Robert de Zouche Hall, KCMG, under the chairmanship of Herbert Cox, and the leaders of the disturbances were questioned as to the reasons for their dissatisfaction. Most of their grievances were found to be justified, but the report also vindicated the actions of the police and the army.

➤ When I was a young man and we drove on the left-hand side of the road (being then a British colony), I had my first car. It had running boards on both sides and the signals for turning left or right were indicators that sprang out from the side of the car just below the roof. The headlamps were perched on top of the mudguards. I cannot now remember the licence number, but it began with C followed by numbers, as did all vehicle licences in the Colony. Cars and lorries in the Protectorate had numberplates beginning with PR. One day I was driving through Westmoreland Street (now Siaka Stevens Street) and as I approached the junction with Wilberforce Street I turned the signal knob on the dashboard to indicate my intention to turn right. I was going to the "Makroo Dispensary" – a name we gave to a sweet shop run by a Lebanese.

There was the usual policeman, dressed in his uniform that included khaki shorts and shirt, knee-high socks and brown sandals, standing on a box in the middle of the road at the junction, directing traffic. He put up his hand to stop me, and I wondered what was wrong. He came down from the box and asked me where I intended going, left or right? I told him, "It is obvious that I am going right, because I have signalled to go right." "Oh no," he said, "Your signals point in both directions at the same time, so I don't know where you are going." Small wonder that the policeman was confused. When he told me I was confused as well. I looked out and saw he was right, both indicators were out at the same time! I got out of the car and flipped down the left indicator. The observant policeman glanced down and then said to me, "Blow your nose!" This was a commonly used phrase in Sierra Leone and I realised he wasn't telling me that I had a cold. This is the usual way of telling a man that his flies are undone! I put things right and got back into my car. The police got back on his box and waved me round to the right.

As I started up I crashed the gears, and heard a nearby man call out, "How much for yard?" At first I didn't understand what he meant, but when I heard another driver crash his gears and heard the same comment, I realised that the crashing of gears sounds very like the tearing of a piece of material off of the roll of cloth, which can be heard in some of the Lebanese shops even to today.

➤ One day, round about 1958, I was visiting my relatives in Freetown. At the time I was running a shop and living in the Provinces and came down to buy a few things, planning to return the next day. During the night a slight noise woke me up. I looked up and saw my trousers floating before me. At first I thought I must be dreaming. Then I realised that I was awake and that someone standing on the veranda had poked a long stick through the guard bars of the open window and hooked my trousers from where they were hanging on a hook on the door and was slowly pulling them towards the window.

Just as my trousers were about to disappear through the window I jumped out of bed and managed to grab hold of the legs. The thief on the outside told me to let go. I, in turn, told the thief to let go of my trousers and that they were the only pair I had, but the thief continued to pull. After a tug of war between him and myself, with my trousers as the rope, it occurred to me to shout "Thief, thief", which I promptly did at the top of my voice, whilst not relinquishing my hold. At this the thief let go of my trousers and ran for it, and so I was able to retrieve them.

I folded my trousers and placed them underneath the mattress for the rest of the night. I didn't sleep much and kept waking to check that my trousers and the rest of my belongings were still where I had put them. The next day I completed my shopping as quickly as possible and returned to my peaceful home in the provinces.

➤ A Lebanese businessman had just learned to drive and had taken another Lebanese for a drive, no doubt to show off! On returning to Sawpit he had to back up into his garage so that when coming out the next day he could see in front of him. He asked his friend to get out and tell him when to stop backing up as the car was only a few inches smaller than the garage itself. The passenger stood to the side and said, "Back ... back ... back ..." waving his left hand to direct him. The driver, depending on his friend's directions, went back ... back ... back ... until he hit the rear wall of his garage with a crunch. This annoyed him and he got out of the car in his anger and slapped his so-called friend, saying, "I hit the wall, and you are still saying 'back ... back ...'!"

➤ Another story I was told was about a man who bought a second-hand Volkswagen car and set out to drive to the provinces. After about an hour the car stopped of its own. The man got out and opened the bonnet to see what was wrong, and to his surprise found only an empty compartment instead of an engine. The man panicked and ran about asking people if they had seen an engine lying in the road as his had just dropped out. Luckily for him one of the passersby was a mechanic, who was able to reassure him and show him that in this model of car the engine was at the back.

➤ In those days down near Sawpit Wharf there lived some petty thieves. I was told this story of a doctor who lived nearby and who treated these people free of charge. One day the doctor's car was left parked as usual during surgery hours. Later that day the doctor returned to the car and found one of the wheels was missing. The doctor called for the headman down Sawpit Wharf and complained to him that in spite of treating him and his companions free of charge, a wheel was missing from the car and the local thieves were the prime suspects. The doctor threatened that in future bills would be issued for all treatment given. The headman begged the doctor to take no action for the moment but to give him time to sort things out. An hour later the headman returned bearing two nearly new wheels of the correct size. The doctor protested that only one wheel had been stolen and two wheels were returned. The headman said, "One is for the wheel that was stolen, and the other is spare!"

➤ A foreign businessman from Freetown was visiting London for the first time. He saw a short queue of people and decided to join in to see what it was about. When his turn came he found himself in front of a vending machine and the people before him had all been putting money in the coin slot. He did the same, pulled the handle and the machine 'paid out' a packet of cigarettes. He put in more money, pulled the handle and received another packet of cigarettes, then went through the same procedure twice more. The man behind him in the queue tapped him on the shoulder and said, "Are you going to take much longer, I am in a hurry". The businessman turned to him and said "Do you want me to stop now whilst I am winning?" The poor man had thought that it was a new style of Jackpot machine!

The same man hired a car so that he could get about easily to do his business and visit friends and relatives. When he returned to Freetown he told me about all the many roadsigns that he saw. He was amazed that there was even one warning sign that up ahead was a man struggling in strong wind with a big umbrella! It took me some time to work out that what he had seen was the roadsign for 'Men at work' and had nothing to do with the weather!

# Chapter 2

# My Early Working Life

One of my first jobs after I left school in 1951 was keeping the books for my cousin Salma and her husband, Mr and Mrs Christo Courban, at their shop in Charlotte Street. They dealt in wholesale supplies of meat, chicken, vegetables and fruit, mostly bananas, brought to Freetown from their large farm in Songo, run for them by a Sierra Leonean called Mr Pearce. The Courbans were ship's chandlers, serving the large vessels that called in to the harbour at Freetown to discharge goods and take on supplies. I worked with them for a few months.

I then tried my hand as a continuity announcer with the Sierra Leone Broadcasting Service (SLBS). My job was a short one, to announce the next broadcaster, for instance the newsreader, and occasionally to actually read the news. I did not stay long with the SLBS, and moved up to the Provinces to stay with a Lebanese friend, Pierrindo Bamin, in Kenema. The Bamin family are well-known in Sierra Leone. On my return to Freetown I met Pierrindo's sister, Bernadette, who got me a job working for her husband, Edward Haroun, one of the proprietors of the Sierra Leone Produce and Trading Company, as a storekeeper. His business partner was Mr Edmond Moukarzel.

I worked for the company at their bottling plant in (then) Oxford Street in Freetown. I was paid £25 per month, a very good salary in those days. Wine was imported in barrels from Cyprus and we bottled it under the names 'Fefegora' and 'Taiwe'. Quite often I sampled the wines myself (I called it 'Quality Control'), and went home from work happy!

After a few months I was transferred to work as storekeeper of the produce department at Cline Town. This was a large building roofed in corrugated iron sheets on the wharf and had its own jetty. It was leased by Mr Edmond Moukarzel and Mr Edward Haroun, who were, amongst other things, agents for the Sierra Leone Produce Marketing Board. We received palm kernels from the provinces both by rail and by river, which we would weigh and pay for. The palm kernels would then be spread out on the large jetty to dry in the sun before being re-bagged to a standard weight of 168 pounds ready for shipment by lighter to the cargo ships which would carry them to the Produce Marketing Board in England. At that time Sierra Leone was still a British Colony. I recall a launch named 'High Flyer' owned by one Mr Habibu, a Sierra Leonean, who supplied us with palm kernels and smaller amounts of coffee and cocoa from Port Loko area.

Some time in 1953 I went up to the provinces, with the idea of setting up business near Segbwema, where my father had had a shop years before. I was told by Mrs Matilda Isaac, the wife of my godfather Mr Joseph Isaac, who lived and did business in Segbwema, of a small house about ten miles away that was vacant, but that it was not suitable as it was miles away from anywhere. I went to see it and found it was built of wattle and daub and roofed with old corrugated iron sheets. It was completely isolated with no other building in sight, and it was less than a hundred yards from the Moa River. I discovered that the farmers would cross the river by canoe at that point, with palm kernels and coffee that they were taking to Segbwema for sale.

I rented the two-roomed house and converted the front room to a small shop, with the hope that the farmers would bring their produce to me rather than walk all the way to Segbwema. The farmers would send their wives with large pans full of palm kernels on their heads. When they put the pans down on the ground to be weighed, I saw that some had eggs and garden produce for sale, placed on top of the palm kernels. I would buy from them, and they in turn would quite likely buy goods from my shop. Two days later I sent to a Sierra Leonean friend called Abu Bangura and asked him if he was prepared to work for me in such an isolated place. Having nothing to do at the time he agreed to come and help me out. He would do the cooking and also went out to solicit custom among the farmers passing on their way to Segbwema. The venture went quite well, but I found it nerve-racking to live so far from anywhere, especially late at night when sometimes I could hear people down by the river and I did not know who they were and why they were there. This, and the mosquitoes, drove us away after a few weeks. The mosquitoes were gigantic, the largest I had ever seen, and my mosquito-net was no defence. They seemed to chew their way in, and then feast on me all night. I decided the profit I was making was not sufficient compensation for the hardships we had to endure, so we left.

In 1955 I got married for the first time and soon moved to Mambolo in the Kambia District with my wife and opened a shop with the help of my father-in-law. I had a van, and would use it to come to Freetown to buy goods. During my stay in Mambolo I had three children, my daughter Rahme, and two sons Jamal and Michael. We moved on to Rokupr, also in the Kambia District, and later to Kailahun where my cousin Howard Lokat and his family had a shop.

After about eighteen months I moved on with my family to Koindu where the borders of Guinea, Sierra Leone and Liberia meet and there was an international market at weekends. I opened a shop where I worked throughout the week, and on Sundays I would sell at the market. After a few months my wife returned to her family in Mambolo with the children, and I moved to Freetown.

I tried several different ways of making a living, including buying a second hand car and hiring a driver to run it as a taxi service. I also worked as overseer in a laterite quarry, owned by my cousin, Elfrida and her husband Albert Gilbey, supplying ball stones to the building trade. I found this job unsuitable. I had become friendly with Sydney Warne, then a barrister and now a Judge of the Supreme Court in Sierra Leone. He knew that I had passed my Junior and Senior Cambridge exams and encouraged me to go to England and do law. I also spoke to Berthan Macauley (Senior), then Attorney General, and to James Mahoney, another leading barrister, and they all agreed that I was wasting my time in Freetown and that law was a proper outlet for my intelligence. I made up my mind to go to England to study law.

In March 1960 I left Freetown for England, with the help of my father. I travelled first to Gambia, by Ghana Airways – my first flight - to visit my sister Victoria and her family. I had to cross the River Gambia by ferry from Bathurst (now Banjul) to Barra Point, and then took a taxi to a town called Jawara where my sister lived. One afternoon while I was staying there, the place suddenly became dark. I saw locusts for the first time, as swarms of big reddish insects blocked out the sun. They ate every leaf on the trees and left them bare before they moved on.

From there I went by road into Senegal to take a ship. As I had a week or two to spare before the ship left, I spent some time with my brother-in-law's family in Rufisque. I had my first experience with the black market, when I was told that if I went to the bank I would get only 650 French Francs for my pound, whilst on the black market I would get 750 French Francs. As my resources were limited, I changed at FF750 and bought my ticket to London on the General Leclerc for FF21,000.

On our way we stopped at Funchal in Madeira, a Portuguese island famous for its wine. I went ashore with a French-Belgian author called Pierre Verger and a Nigerian whose name I cannot remember now. We went all around the beautiful town and visited the wine cellars and tasted various wines. They were all so good that we were half drunk by the time we got back to the ship. We left at 7.15pm and arrived at Bordeaux four days later. I took a train to Paris and then to Dunkirk. There I boarded the Shepperton Ferry to Dover in England, and took train again to Victoria, where I was met by my cousin George Farrah. Together we went to 46 Herne Hill where George had booked a short stay for me with a kind, elderly lady, Miss Morris. It was March, and very chilly for a young man from a hot country.

I then found another bedsitter at 60 Elmwood Road just a few minutes away. The first thing I noticed was a sign on the door of my new bedroom saying, "Please bang the door softly!" My new landlord, who I believe was Polish, was very kind and helpful to me, so I was always careful to comply with his direction and made sure that every 'bang' of the door was a soft one.   After a few months, during which time I was working and saving money to pay my fees, my landlord accompanied me to the Inns of Court in London, where he stood as guarantor for me when I enrolled as a student at the Inner Temple on 16 November 1960.   Two days later I had my first dinner in the hall as a law student.

My law studies soon began in earnest, and I found that the advice I had received from my lawyer friends in Sierra Leone was good.   From the beginning I enjoyed studying law and never looked back.   The law became my career for the rest of my working life and I found it satisfying and rewarding.

# Chapter 3

# In the Sixties

On 27 April 1961 Sierra Leone achieved Independence from Great Britain. There were celebrations all over the country, including a lantern parade and durbar in the Bombali District, a durbar in Makeni. Ali Ganda, a famous Sierra Leonean calypso singer and composer, wrote a calypso called 'Freedom, Sierra Leone' to mark the occasion which was performed by the Ali Ganda Carnival Star Orchestra.

The first Prime Minister was pipe-smoking Dr Sir Milton Strieby Margai. He was born in Gbangbatok in the Southern Province of Sierra Leone in 1895. He was educated at the Albert Academy and Fourah Bay College, then went on to study medicine in England. He was the first Sierra Leonean from the then Protectorate to become a doctor, and his half-brother Sir Albert Margai was the first from the then Protectorate to become a barrister. Quite a family, to produce a doctor and a lawyer in those days, both of whom became Prime Ministers of Sierra Leone! Although a prominent and successful doctor, Sir Milton also took a strong interest in politics and founded the Sierra Leone Peoples Party (SLPP) in 1950, and became Chief Minister in 1954. The name of the Legislative Council was changed to the House of Representatives two years later, and the Protectorate became known as the Northern, Eastern and Southern Provinces.

Sir Albert Margai was also a politician and member of the SLPP, and after the election in 1957 was elected by a majority of the parliamentarians as leader of the party. However, he was persuaded to stand down in favour of Dr Milton Margai, his elder brother, a typical Sierra Leonean sign of respect for the elder sibling. In 1959 Dr Margai was knighted by the Queen to become Sir Milton Margai.

At the Independence celebrations in Freetown Queen Elizabeth II was represented by her cousin, Edward, Duke of Kent. His Royal Highness handed over to the Prime Minister, Sir Milton Margai, the Constitutional Instruments making Sierra Leone an independent state during the State Opening of Parliament on 27 April 1961. On that auspicious day Sir Milton, known as "the Father of the Nation", said, among other things that, "Independence in fact, while it represents the fulfilment of all our political aspirations, constitutes but a greater challenge to our determination to improve the material, spiritual and cultural well-being of all our peoples".

The Duke of Kent arrived in Freetown on 24 April and stayed at

Government House as guest of the Governor and his wife, Sir Maurice and Lady Dorman. He left on Monday, 1 May.

The British Government was represented by Mr Duncan Sandys, Secretary of State for Commonwealth Relations. He presented the people of Sierra Leone with gifts of table silver on behalf of the Government of the United Kingdom. Present at the celebrations were the President of the Republic of Liberia, Dr W V S Tubman, and the Prime Minister of Nigeria, Alhaji Sir Abubakar Tafawa Balewa. On 28 April, at a special Congregation held at Fourah Bay College, the degree of Doctor of Civil Law (Honoris Causa) was conferred upon the Duke of Kent. Some years later, in 1987, the Duke and Duchess of Kent once again visited Sierra Leone, this time privately, to celebrate the bicentenary of Freetown. On this occasion the Duchess of Kent was invited to Fourah Bay College where she was conferred with the Degree of Doctor of Civil Laws (Honoris Causa) by the University of Sierra Leone.

As Sierra Leone was celebrating achieving independence, Sierra Leoneans in other parts of the world were joining in the spirit of the occasion with celebrations of their own. In London I attended a dance held at the Guildhall in the City of London. There was also a thanksgiving service held at St Paul's Cathedral. Friends of mine who were studying in Dublin told me of parties and dances held to celebrate the event.

Sierra Leone now had a new flag, horizontal bands of green (for agriculture), white (for peace) and blue (for the ocean). The country took"Unity, Freedom and Justice" as its motto.

A special set of thirteen postage stamps was issued to commemorate Independence, ranging from one halfpenny to one pound. The designs of these stamps showed a Bundu mask, Bishop Crowther and old Fourah Bay College, Palm fruit gathering, a Forces bugler, Sir Milton Margai, Lumley Beach, and a diamond miner. The difference between thirteen stamps and only seven pictures is because most of the pictures were repeated on stamps of different values.

On 29 September 1961 Sierra Leone became the 100th member of the United Nations.

Soon after Independence, Freetown was visited by Her Majesty Queen Elizabeth II and her husband the Duke of Edinburgh. They arrived on HMS Britannia for a State Visit of a few days on 25th November 1961. Thousands of Sierra Leoneans were there to welcome the Queen and the Duke, and the visit, which was the first by the reigning monarch of Britain and Head of the Commonwealth to Sierra Leone, was a great success. Several members of my family were among the guests invited to see the Queen when she went to Victoria Park in Freetown. Unfortunately I was studying in England at this time and missed all the pomp and splendour of this occasion, but a class-mate of mine, Hans Pawa Sesay, was fortunate enough to be one of those to shake hands with Her Majesty when she visited Fourah Bay College.

➼ When I first came to England in 1960 to study law, I looked for a job to help me with the financial side of my first year of studies. The first thing I saw was an advertisement by London Transport for a bus conductor, so I applied for it and naturally succeeded in my application. The training took about a month, if I remember rightly, and after that I was allocated bus number 172 in Camberwell Garage which ran between West Norwood and Highgate. My identity number was 72259. One advantage of this job was that when I was off duty I could travel free on all buses in London. One of the disadvantages was that sometimes I was allocated as conductor on the first bus out of the garage at 4.00 am, which meant I had to walk from Herne Hill to Camberwell. This could be very cold in winter, but I clearly remember doing this walk and looking back and seeing only my own footprints in the snow stretching behind me in the distance. We had two sets of uniforms, including raincoats, thick and warm for winter, and lightweight for summer.

I was issued with a free pass, as were all London Transport employees, but to save us all from the bother of getting out the pass to prove that we belonged to London Transport a password was used instead. This meant that when getting on a bus I could just say "Sticky" to the conductor and he would let me pass without asking for my fare.

The female of the species was generally known as a "clippy", probably because she would clip the ticket before issuing it to show the destination. Tickets used to come in different colours according to their value, and a hole was punched in the relevant square on the ticket to indicate where that person's journey should end. Joan has told me that during the Second World War a lot of young women took on jobs they would not have thought of doing before, because the young men had gone off to the war. One of those jobs was that of bus conducting, and that was probably when they got the nickname. Somehow men doing that work were always just known as conductors.

By the time that I had my short career as a conductor, however, the ticket system had changed. I was issued with a machine that I hung around my neck that actually printed the tickets as required with the value and fare stage, on a role of white paper.

My wife had joined me in England, but the marriage was not going well and after a few months we separated permanently and she returned to her family in Sierra Leone. By this time I was dividing my time between bus conducting and studying law.

One day a lad got on my bus and went to sit at the front upstairs. By the time I got to him to collect his fare the bus had already gone several stops. He asked me for a destination in the opposite direction. I told him he was going the wrong way, and to get off and get a bus on the other side of the road going the other way. Unfortunately for him the bus moved off very slowly due to heavy traffic, and I noticed that the lad had not crossed the road but was waiting for another bus at the same stop. I thought maybe he hadn't understood me, and then forgot about him until he got on my bus again. Once more he sat in the front seat upstairs, and again asked for a stop which was in the opposite direction. Again I told him that he was going the wrong way and should go in the other direction.

On the third occasion a few days later, when he tried it again, I told him "You can get off and go in the other direction, but first you will pay for the stops you have travelled." I knew by now what he was doing and that he thought he had found a way to get to his destination by bus free of charge. He never tried that again with me. This system would not work nowadays with the one-man buses where you have to pay the driver as you get on the bus.

After living for over a year in Herne Hill, a room became vacant in the large house at 35 Rowfant Road, Balham, where my cousin George was living. A few weeks after I moved in, a further room became empty when the young medical student staying there married and moved to a larger flat. A friend from Sierra Leone, Abdul Labi, took the vacant room and from that time on I had more companionship. I was also able to eat more African food as Abdul was a very good cook! We each had our own bedsitting room, but shared the kitchen and living room on the ground floor.

The house was quite well kept, but the garden, both in front of the house and at the back, was neglected. Other houses had flowers in their front gardens, but ours had nothing. Then one day I came home and found brightly-coloured flowers in the garden in front of the house. The landlord was outside busily watering them to keep them looking fresh. But then I took a closer look at the flowers and discovered they were all plastic! I asked the landlord why he was bothering to water them, as they were not going to die anyway. The landlord told me not to speak so loud, and said, "If the neighbours see me watering the flowers, they will not guess they are plastic!"

As a bus conductor you meet with all sorts of people. One story that is worth telling was of a man who never sat upstairs in the bus, even though there were seats there and standing room only downstairs. When I told him he could go upstairs and sit down, his reply, which I have never forgotten, was "He that is down needs fear no fall!" When I went home I checked where the quotation came from, and after consulting various books I found that it was by Bunyan and the next line reads, "He that is low no pride." Another interesting passenger was a very tall man who sat on the seat near the open doorway. I would stand there when not collecting fares, and this particular man started a conversation with me. He told me he was a professional wrestler and he was known as 'Sky High Lee'. We chatted for a while, and before he got off he gave me a signed picture of himself in his wrestling outfit, which I have to this day.

One evening I had just finished work and took a bus home. Behind me sat two African women chatting in Krio. One was telling a funny story that had happened to her, and hearing it made me laugh. The second woman said in Krio to her friend, and I translate, "What is that white man laughing at, as if he understands what we are saying." I laughed again but said nothing, until I got up to leave. I turned to the women and said, "Oona kusheh Oh". The women looked at each other and one said, "Lord a mercy, e sabi Krio en understand all watin we tok." She then turned to me and said, "Oosai you commot, way you sabi Krio so?" meaning "Where do you come from that you speak Krio so well?" I told her, "I was born in Freetown just like you!" I said a brief goodbye in Krio and left.

I have just said that as a bus conductor you meet all sorts of people. On 31 October 1961 I met a young lady called Joan as a passenger on my bus. You might wonder why I recall the date so well – it is because she became my wife and is still with me! One day I invited Joan to lunch with me at the Inner Temple, to impress her and show that I was only a bus conductor for the time being and had bigger intentions. Joan and I met up in Fleet Street and walked through to the Inner Temple, where we were joined by another student, a good friend of mine called Titus, a Nigerian. The three of us sat together in the dining hall. When we had finished our lunch, Titus gave me his contribution, and I went up to the cash desk to pay for all three meals. The cashier asked me who the lady with me was as he did not recognise her as a student of the Inns of Court. I replied, "I don't know, I have only just met her!" I told Joan some time later that only members of the Inn were allowed to eat in hall!

When studying for the English bar, as I was, it was essential for each of us to attend the dinners at the Hall at the Inner Temple at least three times per term for three years. This was taken very seriously. Take my case for instance. I was admitted to the Inner Temple on 16 November 1960, for which privilege I paid the sum of £56.17.6, and sat my first examination, Roman Law, on 5 December 1960. I ate my first dinner on Friday, 18 November 1960, but although I had finished all my exams in two and a half years, I was not called to the Bar until November 1963 when I had eaten all my dinners! In the meantime I studied International Law at the City of London College under Professor Clive Shmitoff, who was the senior Lecturer in Law, and obtained a First Class Certificate with Distinction and Merit.

Mr Pink, who ushered us into the dining hall, distributed plain gowns to the students to wear whilst dining. Benchers (senior members of the Inns who form the managing body) would sometimes sit among the students, instead of at the High Table.

Wine was served during dinner and port afterwards, included in the price of the meal, thanks to Lord Goddard who supplied the port. The students would be divided into messes of four people and a bottle of wine would be placed on the long tables to be shared amongst each four, followed by a bottle of port. Some friends and I would each sit with a group of girls who did not drink. At the end of the meal we would join up again and thus have a few full bottles of wine and port to polish off amongst us before going home, quite happy. This was one of the reasons we enjoyed dining in hall!

At about this time I went with a relative of mine to the airport to meet a friend who was arriving in London from Sierra Leone. We were a little early so we went to the information desk to ask when our friend's plane would be arriving. My relative saw on the desk a most attractive ashtray with a small model plane on the side. He made a collection of such items, so when the young lady working on the desk turned around to check the times on the board behind her, my relative pulled open the pocket of his overcoat with one hand, and with the other swept the ashtray off the desk so that it disappeared into the depths of the large pocket. The lady turned back to us and gave us the details and we thanked her and walked away. Suddenly, my relative was pulled back with a jerk, and he looked down to see a fine chain leading from his pocket to where it was attached to the desk behind him. Apparently the airport had lost a lot of ashtrays and was taking defensive measures. My kinsman, embarrassed by this experience, stepped back to the desk and carefully replaced the ashtray in its place, trying not to catch the eye of the laughing information lady!

One of the things I found hard to adjust to was the weather in England. I had never believed I could feel so cold as on winter days in London. Another thing was the fog, or London 'smog', which was occasionally so bad that you could barely see your hand in front of your face and all traffic was reduced to a walking pace. One evening dining in hall a fellow student told me of the experience of a friend of his. The friend had been driving home the evening before in thick fog, and as he could hardly tell where he was he decided to follow closely the rear lights of the car in front. After driving for some time the car in front suddenly stopped and the friend drove into the back of it. Both drivers got out and the friend complained to the other driver about him stopping so suddenly, especially in the thick fog. The driver in front got angry at this and shouted, "I am at home on my own drive, so why shouldn't I stop!"

I have a note in my diary for around that time, 'Dinner with the Home Secretary'. A few of us had been invited to have dinner at the home of Lord Henry Brookes, whose son, also named Henry, now a judge, was studying with us. The conversation was interesting and varied. Another guest asked me whether we had a Home Secretary in Sierra Leone. I told him that we did, but that he was called the Minister of the Interior.

The Inner Temple had a debating society for the students and I particularly remember taking part in one of the debates – 'Better Dead then Red'. 'Red', in those days, was a reference to Communism, and in England it was frowned upon. Of the many topics that were debated at the meetings in Niblett Hall, 'This House Considers that Marriage is Outdated' caused a very lively debate, while 'This House thinks that the age of Criminal Responsibility should have remained at Eight' provoked a serious discussion. The subject 'This House would abolish Capital Punishment' found far more students in favour than against, which was reflected a few years later, in December 1969, when the Death Sentence was abolished in the United Kingdom.

Niblett Hall was the Students' Common Room in the days when I studied at the Inn, and sometimes there would be a dance held there to celebrate the end of term. On one occasion I was appointed to the Dance Committee and it was my responsibility to arrange the music. We hired a small band, which had their own instruments except for a piano which they expected to find at the Hall. I tried to hire one for the occasion, but none seemed to be available at the time. I scoured the notice boards of all the corner shops, and finally found a piano for sale near where I was living at that time in Southfields, south-west London. The piano was purchased for the magnificent sum of £3.00 (yes, only three pounds; it cost more than that to have it transported to Niblett Hall!). The dance was a success. As I couldn't afford to transport the piano back to Southfields, and had nowhere to put it in our small rented flat, I left it at the Inner Temple in Niblett Hall. Quite some years later I visited the Inner Temple when on holiday from Freetown. I met Miss Morris, secretary to Commander Flynn who was the Sub-Treasurer for the Inn, and the first words she said to me were, "Your piano is still in Niblett Hall!"

Among the many books on different aspects of the law that I read during my studies was a small book called 'The Seven Lamps of Advocacy'. It taught me that Honesty, Courage, Industry, Wit, Eloquence, Judgement and Fellowship, were all attributes to be acquired to be a success as an advocate. "Do as adversaries do in law, Strive mightily, but eat and drink as friends," seemed like very good advice to me.

As a student in England, things were difficult financially for some of us from overseas, especially if the allowance from home was late in arriving. Another student was also studying in London. It was usual for us to find work from time to time to help our finances, and this student, let us call him Santigie, took a temporary job with the Post Office helping with the extra work at Christmas. Santigie found the work both tiring and boring, and after a couple of days trudging the streets in cold, windy and rainy weather, decided to save himself time and trouble, and "delivered" all the mail he had been given by the sorting office, to the nearest Post Box. He then went home, and spent the day studying. Unfortunately for him, when the over-flowing post-box was emptied, the postman noticed that a lot of the mail had already been franked by the Post Office. It didn't take them long to find out who had been given those particular letters and cards to deliver, and so Santigie found himself out of a job once more.

Another friend of mine told me this story of when he was studying in Dublin. He was a Catholic, and another student recommend him to see a certain priest when he wanted to go to confession, and to be sure to go into the right hand side of the confessional. My friend did as was suggested, and found a long queue on the right hand, and only one or two people on the left of the confessional. He decided he would follow the advice and joined the longer queue. When it came to his turn, he began his confession with the usual preliminary of "Father, forgive me for I have sinned ....." but before he could complete his confession he heard the Father granting him absolution and giving him a small penance to do. Then my friend realised that the Priest was deaf on that side and had given him absolution without hearing a word of his confession! Small wonder that his right ear was more popular than his left!

To come back to me, as a change from my old job, I took up a temporary job of a few hours per week with Professor Jack Berry, of the School of Oriental and African Studies if I recall correctly. Professor Berry was compiling a dictionary of Krio and I was asked to help with the intonations of spoken Krio, for which I was paid by the hour. Professor Berry was assisted by an English Reverend whose job it was to translate my spoken Krio words to music to interpret the highs and lows of the language. A friend of mine, Abdul Labi, had been working with Professor Berry before me, but as he was preparing to return to Sierra Leone, I took his place. This dictionary was later published, but I regret I do not have a copy of it. I left England to return to Freetown when my studies were completed, and to my surprise in 1964 I had a visit at my home from Professor Berry, who was once again visiting Sierra Leone.

➤ I little imagined when I was a boy in Sawpit that I would one day return to reside there for a year or so as a newly qualified lawyer with a new wife and a new baby. Our daughter Mary was born in England and was less than one year old when we arrived in Sawpit. We travelled out from England in the new Elder Dempster Lines boat M.V. Apapa. My wife and daughter Mary stayed in Barra in the Gambia with my elder sister Victoria and her family for one month, while I went on to Freetown in the Apapa to find a place for us to live.

It was my wife's first visit to Africa, in fact the first time she had left England, and she had some stories to tell me when she joined me in Freetown. On one occasion my sister and her family were going to stay for a few days with a relative who lived in a village called Jawara, some miles from Barra Point. Victoria and her children travelled by car, and her husband, also called Farid, and Joan and baby Mary travelled by poda-poda (a minibus). My wife and baby and brother-in-law sat in front with the driver. Gambia is a very flat country, and the hills they came to were very low. However, the driver started to blow his horn on the way up and continued blowing it until the poda-poda had gone down the other side of the hill and was on level ground again. When they arrived at the village the driver switched off the engine and the mini-bus slowly rolled to a halt. It was only then that my brother-in-law explained to my wife that the bus had no brakes!

Joan enjoyed her first taste of life in Africa and found Gambia a paradise for birds, with a great variety of different birds of all colours and sizes that she had never seen before. In later years when Gambia was building up a tourist industry, people would come from around the world to study the abundant bird-life of the Gambia.

I rented a flat from my uncle, Ibrahim Lokat, just two houses away from where I was born in Sawpit. The next thing I did when I arrived back in Freetown was to pay a visit to my father, who was now living in Kailahun with my sister Mary and brother Anthony. I found that my father had purchased some furniture for me from Forest Industries in Kenema, including a large wardrobe, dressing table, six sitting room chairs with padded seats and back and wooden arms, four three-legged whisky stools, and a dining table and six dining chairs. I had to hire a lorry for the return journey to Freetown!

My wife Joan took a while to get used to life in Freetown and had a lot to learn. She told me of one day when she had given the houseboy some money to go to the market to buy meat for her. He asked her, "You wan mek ah buy yabbas sef?" (Do you want me to buy yabbas as well?) Joan thought this must be some strange, exotic fruit or vegetable that she had never seen before, so she asked the houseboy to buy some and waited eagerly for his return. Joan said she was so disappointed to find that the fellow brought back the meat and some onions! She had had her first lesson in Krio, she now knew that when she wanted onions she had to ask for yabbas!

Joan had her first introduction that day to cooking on a kerosine stove. It had two burners, so she was able to cook the rice and stew side by side, and felt very pleased with herself when the meal was ready. I was not really aware of how much effort this first meal had cost a young woman used to supermarkets and gas cookers. It was Saturday morning and I had gone to the office for just a few hours. My old class-mate Cyril Foray came to see me there and invited me to his home to eat foofoo and crane-crane. Cyril and I went back to the flat to tell Joan that I was going to eat lunch with Cyril. Joan accepted this without much comment, and it was only years later that I learned how upset she was that her first struggles with the kerosine cooker were not appreciated.

At first Joan did not attempt to cook palaver sauce (palmoil stew), feeling that the strange ingredients and different method of cooking were beyond her. When she met the young Lebanese wife of my cousin, who had been brought up in Lebanon, and was cooking all the African dishes as if she had been born to them, it changed Joan's attitude. She started to ask the wives of my African friends for help and advice, and soon my friends were coming to my home to eat foofoo and crane-crane or some other African food prepared by my wife.

After my wife had shown me she could cook foofoo the way it should be done, I said to her, "So it didn't turn to starch?" When she asked me what I meant, I sang her this song:

"Ah cook foofoo e turn to starch
Ah cook agidi e turn to pap
E monah me e monah me oh.
E monah me e monah me."

I made starch myself from small balls of cassava starch bought from the market when I got someone to put up some posters in various parts of Freetown advertising my first book "Sawpit Boy".

➨ A few months after Joan and Mary joined me in Freetown our son John was born, just two houses away from where I was born thirty years or so before. Mary was now running around and getting up to all sorts of mischief. We had brought with us from England, amongst other things, a set of six small wine glasses in a stand. One day Joan walked into the sitting room to find Mary carefully building a tower out of the glasses, putting one on top of the other. Mary had just got to the fifth glass, but jumped when she saw Joan standing there. The tower collapsed in ruins and we were left with one intact glass from the six.

Another time Mary was playing a game and running across the carpet in the sitting room when she tripped. As she fell her open mouth hit the arm of one of the chairs with such force that she left a perfect impression of her upper teeth on the edge. That chair stayed with us, and when later I set up my chambers and took some chairs from the house for my waiting room, Joan would not let me have that particular one, and it remained in our home until we had to leave it behind when we came to England twenty seven years later.

After a few months back in Freetown I had saved enough money to buy a second hand car. My first cousin Nabiha's husband, Nohmi Anthony (not a blood relation), had an estate car for sale, an AutoUnion with registration number C2510 (C was for Colony and PR for Protectorate). It was light brown and had a lot of space in the boot, and seemed suitable for us. It was quite economical on petrol, but it did use a lot of water. I used to carry a gallon container of water in the boot in case it needed topping up throughout the day. It must have been quite easy to open inspite of me locking it whenever I parked it, because in the rainy season I was always losing my umbrella out of the car.

After eighteen months in that flat in Sawpit, we moved a short distance away to a larger flat in East Street (now called Ecowas Street), which had previously been rented by Nohmi Anthony. The railway passed in front of the building, and Mary would rush to watch the steam train through the window. This train had a narrow guage of two feet six inches and ran along East Street from the station which was just a short distance away, belching thick black smoke which covered everything in soot. Sometimes the train could not climb the slight gradient at East Street and had to reverse all the way back to put on more speed (and more smoke!).

One day Mary was in such a hurry to see the train that she knocked over one of the three-legged whisky stools, and broke some more glasses. Another day Joan was in the kitchen preparing lunch when the telephone rang. It was a call from a Lebanese friend who lived opposite our flat. He said to my wife, "Do you know your daughter has climbed up the guard bars on one of your parlour windows?" Joan rushed to the parlour in time to rescue Mary, who had reached to the top of the window and didn't know quite what to do next. Joan waved across to our friend who was anxiously watching from his veranda, to thank him for his concern.

Soon after Mary was again in trouble. The bedroom doors in the flat had round brass door knobs, and for some reason which she was never able to explain to us she had opened her mouth as wide as it would go and closed it again over one of the door knobs. Then she got stuck and couldn't get her mouth off the door knob again. Joan tried to help her but couldn't, so I sent for a carpenter to try and take the door knob off the door to see if that would help. As soon as our daughter saw the screwdriver in the carpenter's hand it must have given her added impetus to make a greater effort, because she removed her mouth from the door knob without further ado.

➡ When I first returned to Freetown as a fully qualified lawyer I joined the practice of the late Cyrus Rogers Wright, a well-known criminal lawyer in those days. He taught me to look up the applicable law myself from the reference books and legislations rather than asking another lawyer when I was stuck. This was good advice which I followed throughout my career. I practised in Cyrus's chambers for nearly eighteen months, before setting up practice on my own.

One of the interesting cases I did in 1964 was to defend four of the accused in a 'Borfima' case. I was appointed by the government, along with George Gelaga-King, to act for the defence, and Constance S. Davies of the Attorney General's Office was prosecuting. L.A.M Brewah, M.P., was privately instructed to act in defence of Village Chief, the only woman accused. The judge was Acting Puisne Judge Mr Justice Ronald Beoku-Betts, and a special session was held in Kenema, not far from the village where the incident occurred. The accused had been reported missing. After a search the body of the deceased was discovered by the police and eighteen people were charged with murder.

Borfima is a 'medicine' made from the blood and certain parts of the human body, and is used by members of the Hengor Society. Ritual killing was the only form of 'cannibalism' known in Sierra Leone. The person killed was normally a stranger in the area, and it was believed that the eating of certain parts of the human body gave extra powers to the eater. In the case I was concerned with, a hunter was murdered and the heart, liver and some of the fat were removed, as well as the blood. The human fat was taken by one of the accused to Liberia and sold to members of the society there.

The other lawyers and I went to Kenema, a drive of several hours, to appear in this case, which lasted about two weeks. Accommodation was provided for us, and a police guard was provided to protect us, because local feeling ran high against the accused persons and this was extended to those assigned to defend them, even though the law insists that every man (or woman) has a right to a defence. During the trial the court was moved for one day to the scene of the crime, which happened to be six miles into the bush and so we all had to walk, including the judge. Whilst I was in the bush I received a message from Freetown that my wife was in labour. I got leave to return to Freetown for the weekend, only to find that the labour was a false alarm and the child had not yet been born. I returned to Kenema to continue the case, which lasted for a further week. The decision of the Judge was that the woman chief and nine others were to hang for murder, while the others were acquitted and discharged. The accused had the right of appeal, which they exercised. The appeals failed in the case of the nine men and they were all hanged. The only woman accused was freed, on the grounds that she had not been concerned in the murder itself. Borfima, or Ritual Murder, is still practised occasionally even today.

My wife had never seen me appear in Court and asked that she might attend the Appeal hearing in Freetown. I agreed, and on the day she arrived at the Law Courts, found an Usher and asked him to direct her to the public seats for the Appeal hearing. The Usher was very polite and helpful and led Joan through the building and opened a door for her, directing her to an empty bench. She went in and sat down and I soon caught sight of her. I was shaking my head at her, trying to indicate that she should move from where she was sitting, but she did not understand and luckily no one else took any notice of her. She did not know it but the kindly Usher had put her to sit in the Jury Box (empty on this occasion as appeal cases are heard before three Judges and with no jury)! Some years later the Appeal Court was moved from the Law Courts building.

A long time afterwards I attended a party in England at the home of some English friends who had spent several years in Sierra Leone. One young Englishman came up to me and said that he understood I was a lawyer, and asked what my most interesting case had been. I replied that amongst the most interesting cases that I had done was a cannibal case when I had defended some ritual murderers. After a while the young man moved off and I saw him talking to my host. Later my host told me that the young man had complained to him that I had told him a load of rubbish about cannibals, perhaps because I was drunk. He was most surprised when he was informed that everything I had said was the truth!

➤ Sierra Leone had always been known for its attractive and colourful stamps, but it was the first country in the world to produce free-form self adhesive stamps. The first set of these stamps was issued in 1964 in the shape of the map of Sierra Leone. Some had a Lion Emblem in the middle while others had a globe, and had printed near the bottom " 1964-65 New York World's Fair". They were priced in shillings and pence, ranging from one penny to eleven shillings, as Sierra Leone, although it had become independent from Britain in 1961, was still using British West Africa currency at that time. Twelve pence equalled one shilling and twenty shillings equalled one pound.

Three months later a further set of stamps was issued, still in the shape of the map of Sierra Leone but honouring the late President Kennedy of the United States of America, who had died in 1963. These stamps were of two kinds, Airmail and ordinary postage.

In August of 1964 Sierra Leone introduced decimal currency, Leones and cents, linked to Sterling for exchange purposes. Two Leones equalled one pound, and each Leone was worth one hundred cents. The stamps already in use were now sold overprinted with values in Leones and cents.

The next issue of self-adhesive stamps was in November 1965 and these stamps, as well as being free form and shaped like kola nuts, were embossed on silver foil. Another set was on cream paper and showed the Arms of Sierra Leone in full colour and was shaped like a shield. Another set was diamond shaped, printed on black and showed a diamond necklace with the words "Harry Winston" at the bottom. In November 1966 circular stamps were issued printed on gold foil to commemorate Sierra Leone's issue of gold coinage, and in 1967 a striking set of airmail stamps were issued in the shape of an eagle.

Several more sets of self adhesive stamps were issued, all on backing paper containing advertisements, but within a few years they were discontinued and by, I believe, 1972, Sierra Leone had reverted to ordinary perforated stamps that had to be licked. The stamps continue to be very colourful and often depict the birds, butterflies, animals and flowers of the country.

➤ In 1965 Gerald Durrell, the English animal collector who had a zoo in Jersey, came to Sierra Leone in the hope of collecting some specimens of the Red-and-black and Black-and-white Colobus monkeys (which have no thumbs), as well as other animals. He came with a camera crew from BBC television to make a film to be shown on television in England. It is very unfortunate that monkey drives were necessary in Sierra Leone, because the monkeys destroyed the cocoa plantations that were a very important part of the economy of Sierra Leone. The government paid a bounty for each monkey killed. Mr Durrell managed to get the local people to organise a special monkey drive for him, but without harming any of the monkeys. He was successful in obtaining several specimens of the Colobus monkeys he came for, with the intention of taking them back to his zoo in Jersey to set up a breeding colony. However, he was forced to release back into the wild all the specimens of the Red and Black Colobus monkey as he could not get them to eat properly in captivity and would not risk them dying on his hands. He took back to Jersey some Black-and-white Colobus monkeys, a pair of young leopards, as well as some squirrels and many other animals.

When Gerald Durrell had completed his expedition to the provinces he returned to Freetown, where Joan and I were lucky to see him give a talk about his trip at the British Council hall. He illustrated his talk with lightning charcoal sketches of the animals he had seen and collected, and spoke with the same humour and warmth that is evident in his many books about animals. In 1972 William Collins Sons & Co Ltd published Gerald Durrell's book of his experiences in Sierra Leone called "Catch Me a Colobus". In the book Durrell wrote of his success in breeding the Colobus monkeys and increasing the size of the colony in his zoo.

Durrell also mentioned meeting in Freetown Sandhurst-trained Major Ambrose Genda of the Sierra Leone Army, who was also known as "Uncle Ambrose" from his appearances in shows for children on local television, which usually included an animal of some kind. I remember seeing some of these programmes myself.

I later discovered that David Attenborough, the naturalist, had also visited Sierra Leone with a camera crew to make a film about the ants of Sierra Leone in October 1954. I am sure he found plenty of material to work on, as the ants are numerous and of quite a few different species with very varying habits.

One variety is locally called 'injaloh'. They are soldier ants and march in columns several ants wide with a line of ants on each side guarding the others. The guards are usually the larger ants, which have large heads and strong pincers which once they have taken hold of you are very hard to remove. My wife and I have seen columns in our garden that are two to three hundred feet long, but we have not worked out the reason for the marches. The ants will mind their own business unless they are disturbed, such as someone stepping by mistake on their marching column, in which case they will attack to defend themselves and you will see the unwary person hopping around on one leg while he or she tries to pull the ants off the other leg.

Late one night our watchman called us to say the 'injaloh' were marching up the back wall and onto the small veranda. We went to the back door to look and found that they were already inside and the four walls of the kitchen were black with ants. We did not know what to do about them, but the watchman said to leave them alone and they will go. We did so, but keeping a wary eye on the ants to see that they went no further then the kitchen because our children were all asleep in their bedrooms. The ants all left in due course, and in daylight when we checked the kitchen we found it stripped of every spider and cockroach and every living thing. We were grateful to the ants, but asked our friends what to do if they should come again. They told us to spread freshly picked cassava leaves in their path and across doorways and windows. A few months later the ants came again. We called the watchman and asked him to pick some cassava leaves from the garden for us and told him why. The leaves worked beautifully and the ants all turned back, and they never came again.

➦ In 1966 I went to the Gambia to represent an insurance company in a court case. Whilst there I heard about the mysterious stone circles in Wassau. The circles consisted of a number of upright stones – about twenty in each circle – but I did not get to see them. The stones are cut out of laterite, which is common in the region. Some of the stones are said to shine at night. I have heard that a museum has been opened at Wassau, in May 2000, with the aim of discovering why the stone circles were built. From reference books I discovered that the stone circles were associated with early iron work and have been radiocarbon-dated to about A.D. 750. I have read that human remains have been found buried near the stones, suggesting that they might have been a kind of cemetery. There are stone circles in many parts of the world, for instance one in Japan which is said to be 12,000 years old. There will be something else on stone circles later in this book.

Although I did not see the stone circles, I consoled myself by buying a few coins in Banjul. These coins were unusual because they were four-shilling pieces. They were about one and three-tenths inches across. On one side was the head of Queen Elizabeth II with the words "The Gambia 1966", and on the reverse was a picture of a crocodile with some Arabic writing and the amount of four shillings in English. Gambia became independent of Great Britain on 18 February 1965 and planned to change the British West African currency to a decimal system of Dalasis and Bututs. One Dalasi was to be equal to four British shillings, so the new four-shilling coin was introduced to give the population time to get used to thinking in terms of Dalasis. When the new currency was introduced in 1971, the one Dalasi coin bore the same picture of a crocodile, but the head of the Queen of England was replaced with the head of Sir Dauda Jawara, then President of The Gambia. Gambia had become a Republic on 24 April 1970.

The last of the Gambian coins to be issued under the old currency was in 1970 and was most unusual. It bore the head of Queen Elizabeth, with a hippopotamus on the reverse, and was for a value of eight shillings. I believe that this coin is a unique denomination in world coinage.

➦ Before I built my own badminton court, I used to play badminton regularly at the Young Sportsmen's Club. It was a membership club owned by the Lebanese of Freetown and run by a committee elected from among the members, to promote various sports like basketball, lawn tennis and badminton amongst others. The club was founded in 1952 by a group of young Lebanese, namely Darwish Karanouh, Sammy Kudsy, Delore Yazbeck, Abess Bahsoon and Hassan Yanni, the last named being my cousin once removed. The first president was Abess Bahsoon of the 7Up factory in Freetown. The club used to play basketball and football against Sierra Leone Military Forces teams, and international matches against teams from Guinea and Liberia.

One evening I was playing a badminton match against an Englishman, who was tall and thin with a bald head. A friend of mine, who wanted to encourage the Englishman to be a regular member of the club, asked me his name. I knew his name, but as I was in a mischievous mood I said to my Lebanese friend, "He is called Mr Bald." The game continued and whenever the Englishman played a good shot my friend would shout, "Well done, Mr Bald" or "Good shot, Mr Bald". This annoyed the Englishman and put him off his game, so he lost, which annoyed him even more. At the end he walked up to my friend and said to him, "My name isn't Mr Bald, it is Mr ..........," and walked out of the club. My friend was not very pleased with me and came looking for me, but I slipped out quietly after "Mr Bald" had left.

➡ During the late 1960's a very special Englishman visited Sierra Leone, Group Captain Leonard Cheshire, V.C., D.S.O. and 2 bars, D.F.C. He was a daring and skilful pilot in World War II, and succeeded Guy Gibson in command of the famous Dam Busters Squadron 617. Later in the war he flew as an observer in the aircraft that dropped an atom bomb on Nagasaki in Japan. He had been an efficient and accurate bomber pilot throughout the war, but the terrible devastation caused by that atom bomb in 1945 changed Leonard Cheshire's life forever. He decided to devote his life to helping others, and in 1948 took a terminally ill friend with nowhere else to go into his own home and nursed him until he died. Other patients were taken in and the first Cheshire Home came into being. Over the years the Cheshire Foundation spread out and homes for the sick and disabled were opened in fifty one countries throughout Africa, the Far East, Europe, the USA and Canada, South America, India and the Caribbean. The first Cheshire Home in Sierra Leone was opened in Freetown, in Cline Town opposite the Racecourse Cemetary. The Rotary Club of Freetown became involved and built a classroom for the disabled children who were cared for at the Home. The late Dr Arthur Stuart, a Rotarian, who was chairman of the Freetown Cheshire Home, and Dr Roxy Harris, approached their friends and patients, many of them Lebanese, and got them to donate funds so that a second home could be built in Bo in the Provinces.

Group Captain Leonard Cheshire came to Sierra Leone so that he could visit the two Homes for disabled children and see for himself the good work that was being done. Dr Stuart and his wife Mrs Tungie Stuart gave a dinner party for the Group Captain, who was particularly impressed with the work Mrs Stuart, a qualified physiotherapist, was doing at the two Homes. The Diamond Corporation in Sierra Leone gave a lot of support to the Homes, including having one of their secretaries act as Secretary to the Cheshire Homes. The Corporation had its own plane, necessary for travel between Freetown and the areas where mining was carried out, and would give a lift to Mrs Stuart so that she could give treatment to the children in Bo, about 156 miles from Freetown. The disabled children were mainly polio victims, and the physiotherapy was very important in improving their mobility.

Mrs Maureen Marke, who was a secretary at the Diamond Corporation and the Cheshire Homes for several years, has told my wife and me of the challenge it was each year to help in the organising of the Red Feather Ball. The ball was one of the biggest social events in the Freetown calendar and the main Cheshire Homes annual fund raising event. The evening would include a dinner of several courses and a raffle. Attendance at the ball was an excuse for the ladies to have new dresses and the gentlemen to get out their dinner suits. The ladies were all given programme cards with a small pencil attached so that their partners could mark their names against particular dances. Gentlemen were encouraged to obtain a corsage for their ladies, in return for a donation.

In 1955 Leonard Cheshire met a lady called Sue Ryder. They had not previously heard of each other but each was committed to a life of service to humanity, Sue Ryder being the Founder of the Sue Ryder Care Centres. In 1957 Sue Ryder visited India, where she joined Leonard Cheshire in touring the country by bus and train choosing suitable sites for establishing care homes. They were married in the Catholic Cathedral in Bombay, India, on 5th April 1959, Leonard Cheshire having become a Roman Catholic in 1948.

Cheshire accepted a Peerage in 1991, having refused it previously on several occasions, and died at home on 31 July 1992. His wife Lady Sue Ryder, whose full title was Baroness Ryder of Warsaw, C.M.G., O.B.E., died in 2000, and the work to which they both dedicated their lives is still being continued in their names, including the Cheshire Homes in Freetown and Bo in Sierra Leone.

➥ On 12 February 1969, in a ceremony held in the forecourt of Parliament Buildings at Tower Hill in Freetown, the three colleges in Sierra Leone, namely Fourah Bay College, Njala Agricultural College and Milton Margai Teacher Training College, were joined to form the University of Sierra Leone.

Sir Samuel Bankole-Jones, Kt., M.A., D.C.L., a Sierra Leonean and former Chief Justice of Sierra Leone and President of the Court of Appeal, was installed as Chancellor of the new University. He was called to the English

Bar in January 1938, and two months later enrolled at the Sierra Leone Bar. Much later the College of Medicine and the Law College were added to the University of Sierra Leone. (I have read that the first university was instituted in China between 200 BC and 1 BC, many hundreds of years before universities were introduced in medieval Europe.)

➤➤ I was not a rugby player at all, but had an interest in the Freetown Rugby Club and several of the players were my friends. One day in May 1969 I attended a meeting of the F.R.C. and was elected as Honorary Vice President of the club and agreed to be the Club's legal adviser. Soon after that training began, but I became so absorbed in my work as a lawyer that I could not attend the training sessions or the meetings and so I left the F.R.C., but I agreed to advise them free of charge if they consulted me on any legal matters. Fortunately they didn't have any legal problems.

➤➤ On 20th July 1969 the Americans landed a manned spacecraft, Apollo 11, on the moon for the first time. At about the same time a lot of people in Sierra Leone began to suffer with eye problems, a very contagious form of conjuctivitis. Many people had been spending a lot of time staring up at the sky trying to catch a glimpse of the spacecraft and decided that their sore eyes were a result of this, so the eye disease became known as 'Apollo'!

➤➤ A close friend of mine, the late Dr Arthur Stuart, had a lot of good stories to tell of his days in medical practice in Sierra Leone. One such story went as follows:- He was working at the Connaught Hospital in Freetown, and from time to time had need to visit the hospital mortuary. He would usually go along with one of the hospital orderlies, who would always knock on the door and wait a while before going into the mortuary. One day Dr Stuart asked him why he knocked as there were only lifeless bodies in the mortuary. The orderly said " Sir, the dead people might get up and move around when there is no-one there to see. I am just giving them time to get back to their places." Dr Stuart told me that of course he did not give any credence to stories of that kind. Then he added, with a twinkle in his eyes, "But after that, whenever I had to go to the mortuary on my own, I always knocked ..... just in case!"

A young friend of ours from Sweden, Caroline Munklinde, told us a similar story of 'just in case'. She said that if they have cause in her home country to throw hot water outside the house they would always shout out a warning first, just in case some unseen spirit might be in the way. It was considered wise to treat the spirits well, as they would protect your farm for you if you were good to them.

➤➤ Another story was told to us by Mrs Tungie Stuart, wife of Dr Stuart. She said they had had an English woman living near them for a while. This lady had some groundnuts that she wanted chopped up into small pieces. She called her cook and told him, "Go and chop the groundnuts." The cook went away with the groundnuts. After a while the English woman called to the cook, saying "Have you chopped the groundnuts yet?" The cook answered, "Yes Ma." The lady said, "Then bring them here." The cook replied, "You told me to chop them, and I did!" 'Chop' in Krio means 'eat', and the cook had enjoyed his snack of groundnuts, much to the bewilderment of the English lady.

➤➤ A close friend told us this story that she heard when her husband was working at Delco Mines at Marampa. The wife of one of the managers was an English woman with a rather severe manner. All the domestic workers were scared of her. One day the head gardener was working clearing the bush in the compound, when he saw a big snake. He shouted, "Snake, snake!" The second gardener shouted, "Kill am, kill am!" "No," said the first gardener, "Go call Missis. Everybody de fraid am, sometem the snake sef go fraid am!" (Everybody is afraid of the Missus, maybe the snake will be as well.)

# Chapter 4

# In the Seventies

➠ On 1st March 1971 Sierra Leone changed from left-hand to right-hand traffic. The two countries that shared a border with Sierra Leone, Guinea and Liberia, already drove on the right hand side, and it would have been difficult, nay, dangerous, to drive on the left in view of the increased traffic between the three countries. It had been well publicised in advance, and drivers had been asked to stay off the roads until 6.00 am on the day of the change. There were many volunteers assisting the police to direct traffic for the first few days, and drivers were requested to keep to a very low speed limit, I think it was 20 mph, to reduce the risk of accidents. Many people found various ways to remind them to drive on the right, such as tying a piece of bright ribbon on the right side of the steering wheel that would be seen as soon as the driver sat in the car. For my own part I had a card with "Drive on the Right" in big letters stuck on the dashboard in front of me. The whole exercise went through very smoothly without a single accident, so much praise is due to those responsible for all the detailed planning and publicity that went on before the big day.

A special calypso had been written and recorded and was played on the radio several times a day to tell people about the changeover. In fact, the only accident that I heard of in connection with the change to driving on the right happened some days before March 1. A lorry driving on the wrong side of the road in the provinces had a minor collision with an oncoming car. When asked why he was driving on the wrong (right!) side of the road, he said "Every day I hear the song on the radio that we should drive on the right hand side, so that is what I am doing!" He took no notice of the date when driving on the right hand side should start!

➠ On 19 April 1971 at 1.13 pm Sierra Leone became a Republic, after a Republican Constitution had been approved by Parliament. The former Acting Governor-General, Mr Justice C.O.E. Cole, became the first Ceremonial President, and Dr Siaka Stevens was Prime Minister. The British flag flying over State House was lowered, and the flag of Sierra Leone was raised in its place.

On 21 April 1971, Parliament passed the necessary constitutional instruments and Dr Siaka Stevens became the first Executive President of Sierra Leone, sworn in by former President Mr Justice C.O.E. Cole who had held the post of Ceremonial President for only three days. As is said in Sierra Leone, "Wan day king nar king", meaning that even if you have only been king for one day you have still been a king. One legal change was that cases decided in Sierra Leone no longer went to Privy Council in the United Kingdom as the final Court of Appeal. Instead, the Courts were rearranged and all appeals were heard in Sierra Leone. The first Chief Justice and Head of the Judiciary of the new Republic was the Honourable Mr Justice C.O.E. Cole.

Three days later, Mr Sorie Ibrahim Koroma was appointed as the first ever Vice President and Prime Minister. In July 1975 further changes were made to the constitution to separate these offices, and Mr S.I. Koroma became the Vice President and Mr C.A. Kamara-Taylor became Prime Minister. Mr S.I. Koroma was appointed in addition Minister of Finance, a post formerly held by Mr Kamara-Taylor. Mr Kamara-Taylor received the portfolio of the Ministry of the Interior in addition to being Prime Minister. A few years later Mr S.I. Koroma became First Vice President and Mr C.A. Kamara-Taylor was appointed Second Vice President.

I had followed all the political changes quite closely and made notes up to that point, but the changes became too frequent and so I gave up recording them and hoped that there would not be any more changes for a long while.

➟ One discovery that is worth a mention is that of the "Star of Sierra Leone", found early in 1972. This was the third largest diamond in the world at that time, and it weighed 968.9 carats. It was widely reported around the world. A copy was made and put on show in Freetown, and the stone itself was sent to London for sale, and bought by Harry Winston of New York. It was later cut into eleven smaller gems, ranging from 143.2 carats down to 1.85. The largest stone was then re-cut and reduced to 32.52 carats, but producing six more stones, making a total of seventeen polished diamonds.

A few years later another large diamond weighing 145 carats was found and named the Treasure of Sierra Leone. The diamond, said to be flawless, again found its way to America. Sierra Leone is famous for its high quality gem diamonds which attract diamond buyers from various countries.

In 1970 the Government of Sierra Leone had acquired 51% of the Sierra Leone Selection Trust, a foreign company which mined diamonds under lease in certain areas of the Provinces. The new company thus formed was called National Diamond Mining Company of Sierra Leone, Diminco for short.

➟ In 1972 an Act was passed in Parliament called the National Honours and Awards Act No. 3 of 1972. Soon after it was announced that President Siaka Stevens, as Head of State and Fountain of Honour, had created the following Honours: the highest order is the Order of the Republic of Sierra Leone, and the next most important is the Order of the Rokel. Both Orders have four divisions, the highest being Grand Commander, the second - Commander, third - Officer and the fourth - Member. There were other less important Honours, and also a Certificate of Honour. Grand Commander and Commander of the Order of the Republic were only given to the President and Vice Presidents. The Order of the Mosquito (OM) was also created. Presumably this Order was created because it was the disease-carrying mosquitoes that prevented the white man from settling in Sierra Leone, unlike the more southern parts of Africa. This Order was soon discontinued. It was said that people did not want to accept this award. There were jokes in the bars around Freetown, as to who would get the Order of the Cockroach or the Order of the Spider, and perhaps this made the grantees reluctant to accept an order that was being made fun of.

All the national awards were designed by a well-known Sierra Leonean artist, Mr Hassan Bangura.

➻ On 5th April 1972 I went to Lebanon for the first time, at 39 years of age. I stayed at the New Melcart Hotel in Beirut. I travelled with the late Raschid Jojo, a friend and client of mine who had grown up in Lebanon but then lived in Manchester in England. He took me around to see various places of interest, such as the grotto at Jeita and the ruins at the famous Baalbek (sometimes spelt Baalbeck). He also took me to the south of Lebanon where his family lived. In the south Lebanon shares a border with Israel, one of the six or so countries to do so. For the first time in my life I went to the village in the north where my father and mother were both born, Rahbe Akar, and met many members of my family I had not known before. This visit was interesting to me as I learnt at first-hand about the country and culture of my parents. Since my return, I have often asked myself, "If Sierra Leone and Lebanon were at war, which side would I fight for?" I decided I would have to be neutral, but this is an academic question and it is most unlikely I would ever have to choose. Both countries are small and resemble each other in many ways, having mountains and beaches and a great variety of fruits and vegetables. I was lucky to have Raschid with me as I do not speak Arabic fluently, and some people would not believe that I was born of Lebanese parents until Raschid confirmed it. As I said in another book, "Sawpit Boy", there are more Lebanese living in countries around the world than there are in Lebanon, so it is not really surprising that there are many people like myself who are Lebanese in origin, but have assumed the cultures and languages of the countries in which they were born. Like some of the Lebanese born abroad, I understand spoken Arabic very well but when it comes to speaking it, I find I have to think of what I want to say.

Lebanon is a very small country, only 10,400 square kilometres, whilst Sierra Leone is seven times bigger at 72,325 square kilometres. By way of comparison, the United Kingdom is 244,755 square kilometres.

I visited Lebanon for the second time in 2001 with my wife and daughter Mary, but that is another story!

➤ A Minister of State was making a visit to England. He was asked what minerals could be found in Sierra Leone. The Minister answered with enthusiasm, "We are fortunate in having plenty of minerals, such as Fanta, 7Up, Coca Cola, Lemonade, Sprite, etc." Stories such as this one, making fun of government ministers, have been common since I was a schoolboy in Freetown.

➤ Another story along similar lines came into circulation soon after the Cape Sierra Hotel opened. It went like this:

Customer to Waiter: "Is this a four star hotel?"

Waiter to Customer: "Yes sir," and went away.

He reappeared shortly after bearing a tray with four bottles of cold Star Beer. Star Beer and Heineken were both brewed in Freetown at the Brewery in Wellington.

➤ I was in a restaurant in Freetown and had ordered Jollof Rice for my lunch. The gentleman at the next table was eating a concoction that looked something like Shepherds Pie, and he did not seem to be enjoying it very much. I was very hungry, and the serving of rice was not very big, so I called to the waiter who had served me before and, pointing to my plate, said to him "Encore". The waiter smiled, and came back in a few minutes with another plate full of Jollof Rice. The man at the next table heard my order of "Encore" and eyed my plate hungrily when it arrived. He called to the waiter and told him, "Encore". The waiter brought him a repeat order of what he had had before, Shepherds Pie. At that the man became angry and said, "When that man over there ordered "Encore" he got a plate of Jollof Rice, why is my "Encore" different from his?" The waiter had to explain to him the meaning of "Encore".

➤ Some years ago the government decided there were too many Foulahs in Sierra Leone taking jobs from the local people and planned to deport them all back to Guinea. The Foulahs were small shopkeepers, tailors (particularly skilled in machine and hand embroidery), watchmen, bakers and so on, all hardworking people. They frequently wore native gowns instead of trousers and shirts. Their small shops were to be found all over the country, but particularly in the capital, Freetown. The shops were generally very small, only a few feet square, and usually the living quarters would be at the back of the shop. They would be open from early morning to late at night, and stocked nearly everything in small quantities, from bread to tinned milk, from needles to torch batteries. Foulahs were also noted for tending cattle. They were musicians as well, and it was not uncommon to see a group of them with their instruments entertaining a small gathering. They would usually wear brightly coloured cotton trousers, ballooning between the legs but gathered tightly at the ankle, and some of the performers would turn somersaults whilst the others played.

Within a few days of the government's decision to send the Foulahs away, it became hard to get a loaf of bread, most of the small shops by the roadside were closed, and it was difficult to get a suit or a dress made up in Freetown. So many of these jobs were held by Foulahs that an outcry by the populace made the government backtrack and remove the ban. Everything came quickly back to normal, to the relief of the local inhabitants.

➤ Around this time I bought a new car. This time it was not just 'new' for me but a brand new car, something I had not been able to afford to do before. I bought it from a Lebanese friend, Salim Sabrah, who had imported three new Mazda Estate cars for sale. I got a special number for it, WR 8888, and called it 'Four fat ladies'. I found it very useful as it had a large boot with a window, and when my nieces came to stay with us from the Gambia we were able to pack extra children in the back, sitting on the floor side by side, on outings to the beach or to Aqua Club.

When I had just finished running-in the engine I had a case to do in the Provinces. I took over from my driver, Mahmoud, and put my foot down on a long straight road to test the speed of my new car. I did over 100 mph for a short while along the Vianini Road, and my driver was cowering in the seat beside me. I soon slowed down again, as even on empty roads it is not safe to drive at such high speed, but I was greatly satisfied with myself and the car. It was not the same, however, for Mahmoud, who took a little time to recover from the fright I had given him and take the wheel of the car once more. I never did tell my wife of the time I 'did a ton' in 'Four fat ladies' on the road to Bo as I was sure she would not approve, and she only found out about it when typing out this manuscript!

➤ On 13th June 1974, I read a heading in one of the local papers, "Sensation as First Sierra Leonean Cremated in Freetown". The Indian community had built a crematorium in Freetown, but up to this point it had only been made use of by the Indian families who believed in cremation. On this unique occasion the person to be cremated was a Sierra Leonean, a Mr Elba, the first time the facilities had been used by a Sierra Leonean family.

➤ Flipping through my diary for July 1974, during a period when the facilities in Freetown had not been working well, I found these entries on consecutive days:

17th: No light (electricity) in office.

18th: Light in office but no telephone (phone not working).

19th: Hooray! Light and telephone in office!

➤ In July 1974 Joan and I were invited to a reception at the Young Sportsmen's Club given by the Egyptian Embassy to mark the twenty-second anniversary of their Revolution. We were enjoying the party and chatting with friends as usual at a party of this sort, when the music seemed to be turned up a bit louder than it hitherto had been. The music changed, and everyone stood to attention in silence, thinking it was the Egyptian National Anthem that was being played. Someone then recognised the music and mentioned that it was simply a march played by a military band. Everyone relaxed and laughed at the mistake.

➤ We had quite a busy social life with invitations to cocktail parties and dinners at the homes of friends, weddings and so on. One particular evening Joan was getting dressed as we were going out to dinner. She had taken a lot of trouble with her hair, setting it on heated rollers and so forth. When she was all ready to go she suddenly remembered that she had not sprayed her hair with lacquer to keep it in place, as was the fashion in those days. She reached up on top of the wardrobe where she kept the can and sprayed lavishly. Only then did she realise that the scent was all wrong, and when she looked at the tin she found that she had sprayed her head with Shelltox! She did not appreciate my joke that at least she would not get any cockroaches in her hair that night! There was no time for her to wash her hair and start again as we were already a little late, so she added a spurt of Chanel No. 5 to the scent already on her head and hoped it would prove to be stronger than the smell of Shelltox!

➤ On 30 July 1974 we were woken up at about 3.30 am by what sounded like explosions coming from not too far away. At first I thought they came from the sea, but when I called my watchman and asked him about the explosions, he said they were coming from Wilberforce, where the army barracks are. We jokingly said to each other, "Perhaps it is another attempted coup!" and went back to bed.

I was travelling in the morning to Nigeria to meet with other lawyers acting for Mr John Christlieb. I left the house at 9.00 am to go to my office in Freetown, and took the route by way of Spur Road as usual. When I got to the ministerial quarters I saw a lot of armed policemen guarding the outside and searching the grounds. I asked a by-stander what had happened, and was told that there had been an attempted coup in the night, and the residence of the Acting Prime Minister had been bombed. What we had said in jest the night before turned out to be true! Little damage had been done, and no one was hurt. I was due to catch a flight to Nigeria within a few hours, so I was concerned as to the safety of my family in my absence. That concern stayed with me until I returned to Freetown, and I tried several times to telephone home from Nigeria, but it vain. It was not unusual to have difficulty in making international calls to and from Freetown, especially at a time like that, but it did nothing to allay my anxiety. I caught the British Caledonian flight, which made one stop in Accra before landing at Ikeja Airport in Nigeria at 6.00 pm, one hour ahead of Freetown time.

I was met at the airport by my client's chauffeur and driven to Apapa in his personal car, air conditioned and fully automatic. I was taken to the guesthouse belonging to the company owned by my host John Christlieb, whom I had met in Freetown when he visited there in his yacht. After a quick shower I was taken to the pent-house home of my host, where I walked into a champagne party in honour of his birthday which had been the day before. The block of flats was eleven storeys high and was called 'Guinea Flats', owned by Guinea Properties Ltd, a company owned by John Christlieb. I met two Ghanaians at the party – Mr Kojo Newman, a lawyer, and Mr Amartey - who were sharing the guesthouse with me.

The next morning, Thursday, I was served tea in bed, and then had breakfast before going to a meeting with the others. Afterwards we were all taken on a tour of the factories owned by John, which manufactured goods ranging from lipsticks to peppermints, face powder to plastic containers, and were given samples of each. That evening John took us in his speedboat, 'Slip Stream', to the Lagos Yacht Club, a club entirely for sailing boats with over 150 boats. A race was taking place when we arrived, and John pointed out a yacht that he had built himself, 'nail by nail and plank by plank'. I discovered that Lagos itself is an island, connected to the mainland, Apapa, by two bridges, the Eko and Carter Bridges. Later we went to a barbecue party at John's flat where I met John's daughter Debbie, a qualified pilot for non-commercial planes.

On Friday morning, after another business meeting, we all went into Apapa to do some shopping. The next event was a trip to the Aero Club of Nigeria at KiriKiri Airfield, owned by John Christlieb, where he personally had five aeroplanes belonging to him. He took us up in one of them, a Cessna 310, and gave us a 35-minute fantastic view of Lagos from the air. In the late afternoon John gave a cocktail party at the jetty where his 48-foot yacht 'Quantraille' was moored. The yacht was decorated with bunting ready for the trip that John was starting the next day for South America. One of the guests at the party, a business associate of John's, invited a few of us out to dinner that evening to Ciro's in Apapa owned, I believe, by a Lebanese called Mr Hussein Jamal, where, to me, the food seemed very expensive.

I left Apapa at 7.00 the next morning, Saturday, on my way back to Freetown. On the return journey the plane stopped at Accra, Abidjan, Monrovia and then Freetown, where I met a Sierra Leonean, Mr Musa Suma – the Assistant Director of the Sierra Leone Produce Marketing Board - who gave me a lift home from the airport. I met my family all quite well and heaved a sigh of relief from my pent up anxiety. Later that evening we went to the Atlantic Club for dinner, and I told my wife it was for the further relief of my anxiety at being away!

A few months later I had a further trip abroad. On Saturday 7 December 1974 I left Freetown by British Caledonian Airlines VC10. The Freetown to Gatwick flight was a joint venture by the Sierra Leone Government and British Caledonian. On the flight I met a colleague of mine, George Gelaga-King, who was on his way to France to take up his appointment as Sierra Leone Ambassador in that country. We arrived at Gatwick at 7.30 am. Once again I was met at the airport by a chauffeur-driven Rolls Royce and driven to a flat in Putney owned by John Christlieb's company. James, the chauffeur, then took the car back to the company offices, and I was left with two days free before doing any work. On Saturday I did some Christmas shopping and had visits from two of my cousins who were in London, George Farrah and Sam Courban, and Sam's then girlfriend Nancy, later to be his wife. On Sunday I went down to Gillingham in Kent to visit a family who had been in Freetown for some years. I say Gillingham in Kent, because I learnt then that there is another Gillingham in Dorset, both spelt the same way but the one in Kent is pronounced with a soft G while the other is said with a hard G as in 'gate'.

My friend, also called John, had grown a short beard since I last saw him. He told me it was to cover a small scar he had sustained in an accident when he first arrived back from Freetown. At this time I owned a house in Gillingham and I took this opportunity to pay a quick visit to see that everything was all right. I left Gillingham at 8.00 pm and went to Charing Cross, where I met my cousin George for a drink before taking a bus back to the flat.

On Monday I had a business meeting in Fleet Street with my client's legal advisers in England. The rest of my stay in London was spent in shopping for presents for my family and visiting friends. Among the things I bought were a prayer book and a veil from the repository at Westminster Cathedral, and a pair of white shoes from Oxford Street, for my daughter Mary. I also bought a prayer book from the Catholic Truth Society shop at Victoria for my son John, as they were both to take their First Communion on Christmas Day.

I wanted to return home on Friday 13 December, but there was no place in economy class so I had to travel first class. I went home laden with gifts, boxes of chocolates and bags of nuts ready for Christmas. I met Mr Musa Suma, whom I have mentioned before, on the plane; he was travelling first class for the same reason I was. The plane had a full load, mainly school children going to Freetown to their families for the holidays. Between Dakar and Freetown the journey was a bit rough and we had to fasten our seatbelts. A lot of people were really apprehensive – it being Friday the thirteenth! However, we landed safely on time and the company I had been working for confirmed later that they considered my trip had been well worth while. It was worth while for me as well!

On Christmas morning 1974 we attended 9.30 am mass at St Anthony's Church. Mass was said by the Irish Archbishop, Dr Brosnahan, assisted by two priests. The front row was reserved for us. My son Michael served at the mass, and Mary and John received their First Holy Communion. Mary looked lovely in a white dress and veil, and John wore white shirt and trousers with a bow tie. Following the service we had a small party at our home for a few family and friends, including Mrs Nabiha Isaac who was the godmother of Mary and John at their Baptism in 1965 in the Sacred Heart Cathedral.

➼ I was told this story by a friend who had just come back from a trip abroad, and he vouched for it being a true story. The plane on which my friend was due to travel developed some trouble and all the passengers were taken to a small hotel in a Third World country for the night whilst repairs were carried out. They were told that a bus would come for them at 8.00 and take them to the airport. At 7.00 am the passengers went down to the restaurant for their breakfast. Five minutes later the airport bus arrived and the driver and conductor came into the restaurant and told them they should get on the bus as they were leaving straight away for the airport. The passengers all left their meals, which had just been served, uneaten, and hurried to get on the bus. They sat on the bus for about twenty minutes waiting for the driver and conductor, who were nowhere to be seen. A few of the passengers decided to go and look for them, and found them in the restaurant busily eating the passengers' breakfasts, and what they couldn't eat they were packing into plastic bags! My friend said he was certain of the truth of this story, as he was one of those who lost his breakfast!

➼ On All Fools Day, 1st April 1975, I phoned one of my cousins to say that some Americans had come to my office wanting to do business in Freetown and asked me to recommend someone they could contact. Would he be interested? My cousin dashed round to my office and asked to meet the Americans. "What Americans?" I asked. He looked puzzled at first, then noticed the calendar on my desk and remembered that it was April Fools Day! He took it in good part and we laughed together. I also remember getting a friend of mine the following year. I phoned him, disguising my voice, and said that I was phoning from his bank as someone had come in with a large cheque drawn on his account. Could he come in to verify his signature. He dashed round to the bank, but no-one knew what he was talking about. A few hours later I phoned him, not disguising my voice this time, and asked him what he found out about the cheque. He was not pleased, and said I had given him a walk to the bank for nothing and a lot of worry besides!

➼ At the corner of Siaka Stevens Street and Wilberforce Street was a tall building built by a Lebanese, Rashid Jojo (now deceased), with a shop on the ground floor and offices above. Perched on top of the roof was a red Volkswagen Beetle car, placed there with great endeavour by the importers of Volkswagen cars. One result of this was that some people avoided passing near to that building, just in case the car fell off! The car was in fact securely bolted down to the roof, and had no engine, it was just the shell of the car put there for advertising purposes. After the car had been up on the roof for some time without falling off, people lost their fear of it and didn't comment about it any more. I do not know if any more people bought Beetles because of seeing the car there, but it was a great talking point for a while.

➤ In the early hours of Saturday, 21 June 1975, a mighty hurricane blew. There was not much rain but the wind was gale-force. All the lights went out at about 2.00 am. When we woke up in the morning we saw the damage the hurricane had caused. One or two corrugated sheets at the corner of our roof were lifted up and damaged, but not very badly, and in our garden two trees had fallen. The Pride of Babados shrubs in front of the house were all leaning down to the ground.

I drove into Freetown with Mary, my daughter, who had a guitar lesson at school. We found Wilkinson Road was blocked by huge trees that had been uprooted, and the electric cables were lying on the ground, so I said to Mary, "It looks like we won't have lights for a long time." When I turned back to attempt to get into Freetown by way of Spur Road I found that too was blocked by fallen trees. I had to use all the back and unmade roads to bypass the obstructions. Lots of houses had their roofs damaged, and the damage seemed greater the nearer I got to Freetown. Some roofs had flown off completely and landed in the compound. I was later told of one instance where the roof of a house was blown off and landed in the street, and the roof of the neighbours' house was blown off and landed intact on top of the first house. It was a double shock for the family who looked up to see a different roof from what they had put up! In some instances cars had been damaged by roofs collapsing on them!

When we reached St Anthony's Catholic Church in Brookfields, the weathercock on the steeple had been bent over by the wind, as if in prayer. At St Joseph's Convent Secondary School where my daughter was to have had her guitar lesson, we found that the wooden building that housed the girls who boarded at the school was completely destroyed.

By the time I was ready to leave town and go home early for the day, the air was full of the sound of hammering as people started on repairs to their homes and building materials shops were selling corrugated iron sheets like hot cakes! The older people were saying they could not remember in all their lives a storm that had done such widespread damage as this one. In spite of all the damage, however, I did not hear that anyone had died, and only a few people had minor injuries; God must have been watching over Freetown that night.

As the saying goes, it is an ill wind that blows nobody any good. The carpenters and builders had more work than they could manage for weeks to come. I was told the BBC announced that the wind had reached 120 miles per hour. In the afternoon I took Joan and the children to see the havoc caused by the windstorm.

Back at home, I climbed up to my own roof with Musa, my gardener, to see what damage there was, and found that a few nails were missing and the corrugated iron sheets at the front of the house were bent upwards. After straightening the sheets that were bent, I went all over the roof hammering down whichever nails had worked loose and covering them all with a sealant called Farotex, which looked like tar.

The children spent some time in the garden collecting over five hundred 'horse-yai', a large, very hard, inedible seed that resembles the eye of a horse, which grew on a creeper, one or two to a pod, that was growing all over the mango tree which was now lying in our garden. The weather was dry the whole day with no trace of the wind that had done so much damage the night before.

I later learned that the storm had reached other parts of the country as well, causing considerable damage to property, especially roofs, but I believe Freetown to have been the hardest hit that night - a night not easily forgotten!

➤ I started writing my book "Sawpit Boy" in 1975 and usually worked on it in my office in between clients. On 27th June I was working on the first chapter about my father's arrival in Sierra Leone in 1908, when I had a surprise visitor. Neil Leighton, an American who remembered meeting me about seven years before when he was doing research at Fourah Bay College into the Lebanese community in Sierra Leone, called in to say hello. He had by this time obtained his doctorate and had plans to publish it as a book. He had a copy of his thesis with him and left it with me to read. His book is called "The Lebanese Middleman in Sierra Leone" and deals with the Lebanese traders acting as middlemen between the Sierra Leonean farmers and the produce-buying companies.

I invited Neil to join my wife and me for dinner that evening. We picked him up from Brookfields Hotel where he was staying and drove out to the Atlantic Club on Lumley Beach, where we had a good meal and interesting conversation about Sierra Leone and the position of the Lebanese in trade. We left at about midnight and I dropped Joan off at our home in Lumley before driving Neil back to his hotel. Later Neil gave me a signed microfilm copy of his thesis to keep, dated July 17th 1975, which I still have. Neil's study concentrated on the Eastern Province, and I was interested to read that at the time of his field research in 1967-68 there were only eight Lebanese shops in Kailahun, of which my father's was one.

➤ The Old Edwardians Association had a dinner each year in October on or near 13th October, the Feast Day of St Edward the Confessor after whom the school was named. At the end of the evening the School Song was sung loudly and lustily. The only problem with this was that some years before the words of the school song were changed. Those of us who attended St Edwards in earlier years sang the original words, whilst the younger old boys among us sang the new words! The tune was the same, but it was funny to hear the older and younger groups trying to drown each other out!

➤ Sierra Leone Development Company, commonly known as DELCO, closed down its operations in Sierra Leone on 17th October 1975 after more than forty years.   It went into liquidation, putting about three thousand workers out of a job.   The company had been mining for iron ore at Marampa in Lunsar

➼   One weekend late in 1975, I went with some friends to visit the National Diamond Mining Corporation at Tongo Fields for water skiing on the lake.   We were all members of the Freetown Aqua Sports Club and were invited by the staff of NDMC, to visit their club called the Geliama Club.   Accommodation had been arranged for us at Tongo Fields by the manager.   After lunch of sandwiches and drinks at the club we drove about two miles to the lake of fresh water, about a mile in diameter, which supplied water to the NDMC plants.   There was only one boat, a red Fletcher with an 85 hp engine, owned by Jack Stoll.   The evening was spent back at the club where they laid on a buffet for us of a variety of African and English dishes.   During the evening they had a "Ten cents hour", a variation of the Happy Hour in similar clubs, when all drinks were served at ten cents a shot, which in those days was the equivalent of one English shilling or five pence.   The hour lasted in fact for more like three hours, so there were some very happy people around.

After breakfast the next day I went with Paul Steiner, a Swiss engineer working with my cousins who owned a construction company in Freetown, to visit Panguma Sawmills.   We were shown around the mill, which was beautifully clean and had a lovely smell of fresh woodshavings.   The timber was mainly mahogany and was cut from the forest reserves for miles around, and a royalty was paid for each tree cut at twelve cents per opus foot, irrespective of the kind of tree.   The mills had their own power plant and one of the generators in use when I was there was over forty-five years old!   We then took a stroll around the rest of the compound.   The house belonging to Jack Stoll and his wife, Jeanine, was fantastic, built of mahogany throughout.   Even the bathtubs had mahogany surrounds.   I believe Jack Stoll, who had been at Panguma for twenty years, was one of the two owners of the mill.   It was really a beautiful house and it is not surprising that the Stolls were happy there.

The whole compound was like a huge park, and surrounded by green hills.   I never imagined that such a place existed, it was really a paradise.   Four expatriate families lived within the compound, and the Company employed over 180 workers.   At the time I was there, a swimming pool was under construction near Jack's house.

There was some more skiing on the lake in the afternoon, and then Jack took some of us out in his boat round the lake.   After a bite and a drink we took leave of our hosts at 4.00 pm.   On our way to Freetown, Paul Steiner, who was driving, inadvertently ran over and killed a 'Muskiat' (a civet cat) which had run out from the bushes at the side of the road, and as we didn't want to leave it by the roadside we took it home.   I had it skinned and cleaned, and put it in the freezer, although my wife did not like the idea as it was so much like a large cat.

The next weekend we invited Paul and a few other friends over for lunch and barbecued the 'Muskiat'. We also barbecued some chickens, and I mixed some of the chicken with the bush cat so that the children would try it without knowing which was which. They ate it without noticing the difference. The bush cat was very tender and tasted surprisingly good. My wife ate a little and agreed it was very tasty, but asked me not to make a habit of 'Muskiat hunting', to which I promptly agreed.

➡ Dr Arthur Stuart and his wife Tungie, a physiotherapist and chiropidist, have been friends of mine since I lived and had a shop in Kailahun in the Eastern Province of Sierra Leone in 1955. The friendship was renewed when I returned to Freetown as a lawyer, and when we had Linda baptised in 1969 we asked Tungie to be her Godmother. Tungie Stuart is a descendent of the May family and inherited May House, which had housed the May family and the Sierra Leone Weekly News Press from September 1884 until it closed, I believe sometime in the 1950's. The original May House, at the corner of East Street (now Ecowas Street) and Wallace-Johnson Street, was an old wooden building which was pulled down in 1976 and a new concrete building put in its place.

When the construction of the new building had reached a certain stage, the Stuarts arranged a ceremony for laying the foundation stone, and invited us to take part on 10 February 1976. I had found out what the usual custom was, and so assembled a collection of all the different denominations of Sierra Leone coins, eg fifty cents, twenty cents, ten cents, five cents, one cent and half cent. These were all placed in a large glass bottle, together with a copy of the Sierra Leone Weekly News of 1929 and an obituary notice of the late Claudius May, publisher of the above-named paper. Also enclosed was a copy of the Sunday We Yone dated 8 February 1976, and a current copy of the local Daily Mail. Tungie invited us to include a short history of the Anthony family, reproduced in full below:

### THE ANTHONY FAMILY

Mr. John Anthony was born in the Lebanon in 1894 and he emigrated to Sierra Leone in 1908 at the age of 14 years. He married Rahme Khoury in 1922 and they had four children, Victoria, Farid, John and Mary, all born in Sierra Leone. Mrs. Rahme Anthony died on 7$^{th}$ October 1949. John Anthony died 29$^{th}$ September 1974. Their daughter Victoria died on 24$^{th}$ May 1972.

Farid Anthony, born 12$^{th}$ July 1933, became acquainted with the Stuart family in 1955, when he was a small trader in Kailahun and Dr. Arthur Stuart had been posted to Kailahun as the Medical Officer in charge of the hospital there.

Farid and Arthur became friendly. At that time Farid was married and had three children: Rahme (named after his late mother) now aged 20, Jamal aged 19, and Michael aged 17½.

In 1960 Farid left and went to the United Kingdom to study law. He qualified in 1963 and came out to Sierra Leone in 1964 as a Barrister. He had divorced and he remarried Joan Howes.

Joan is a Londoner and was born on 2$^{nd}$ November 1939. Her father, Mr. Henry Howes, died in 1951. Her mother, Mrs. Hilda Howes, resides in Tooting Broadway, London.

Joan and Farid have three children: Mary aged 12½, John aged 11 years, and Linda aged 7 years.

LINDA ANTHONY IS TUNGIE STUART'S GOD-CHILD.


10$^{th}$ February, 1976.

The coins, copy of the Weekly News, and Obituary Notice of Cornelius May, Editor of the Sierra Leone Weekly News, were provided by the Anthony family (the last two items from the small archives of the Anthony family).

On this site stood the old building containing the Weekly News Press, established in 1884 by Reverend Principal J.C. May, which produced the Sierra Leone Weekly News, a copy of which is enclosed.

Tungie Stuart nee May is a descendant of the May family. This Foundation Stone is laid jointly by the Stuart family and Linda Anthony, and in accordance with local custom (seldom applied now) this container has been placed with the coins and Daily Mail Paper of today, 10$^{th}$ February, 1976, by F.R. Anthony, Esq.

We all gathered at the site at 5.30 pm, where a hole had been made in the foundations to hold the bottle. Prayers were said by the Reverend Ivan Johnson and he read from an old Bible owned by the Stuart family which was over a hundred years old at that time. The bottle was placed in the hole by Mrs Stuart, Arthur's elderly mother. The hole was already lined with cement. Mortar was mixed and three trowels-full were placed in the hole by Mrs Stuart Senior. Then Tungie, Arthur, Linda (my daughter) and others each placed three trowels-full in the hole. After this one of Tungie's friends poured a libation, a glass of water and a glass of brandy, and called upon the spirits of the departed Stuart and May families to make the paths of Arthur and Tungie smooth and pacifying all anger. Finally, bottles of champagne were opened (for our refreshment) and snacks were served to all the guests. We were happy as a family to share a ceremony that was new to us with Arthur and Tungie.

➹ One evening in March 1976 I took my family up to the Mary Kingsley Theatre at Fourah Bay College to watch a play, "The Gods Are Not to Blame", put on by the English Department Dramatic Society. The cost was one Leone for an adult ticket and fifty cents for children.  The play was based on the story of Oedipus Rex, but the characters had all been given African names and the action took place somewhere in Nigeria.  My son Jamal was a student at the college and took three parts in the play, as the Royal Bard, Royal bodyguard Akilapa, and the Towncrier.  He did very well in all three small parts, and we all enjoyed the play.

➤➤ Freetown and its environs were developing rapidly and in 1977 I took my family to see the Port War Signal Station, which stood on a slight hill at Aberdeen, before it was pulled down to make way for development of the site.  As a Boy Scout in 1951 leading the 8th Freetown Troop (St Edward's School Troop), I had signalled in the MV Aureol belonging to Elder Dempster Lines on its maiden voyage to Freetown in 1951 from that very point.

I had become very friendly with Mr Galibert, the head of the Port War Signal Station.  He used to teach the 8th Freetown Scout Troop signalling, which included Morse code and Semaphore.  I was studying for my Coast Watchman badge, and the use of the various flags that were used by the ships and signal stations was an essential part of this.   The other signallers at the Station were Mr John and Mr Tucker, who helped in teaching me signalling.  In those days a signal lamp was used to send and receive messages by Morse code to the ships coming in to the harbour to direct them to where they should anchor.  This was in the days before the Queen Elizabeth II deep-water quay was built, which enables the ships to slam alongside the jetty.  I used to watch the ships signalling each other using either Morse code, or semaphore, which involved the use of two flags, held in varying positions to spell out the message.  By chance I was at the Station when the M.V. Aureol was approaching Freetown for the first time.  To my delight, Mr Galibert and the others agreed to my request to signal in this ship.  Mr Galibert wrote down the message and stood beside me, and I used the lamp to signal in the ship.   It was not necessary in obtaining the Coast Watchman badge to actually signal in a ship, and I was the only scout in Freetown to actually do so – much to my pride, and I enjoyed boasting to my fellow scouts that I not only knew how to do it, I had actually signalled in a ship and directed it to its anchorage!

The M.Vs. Aureol, Apapa and Accra were large passenger liners that travelled between Liverpool and West Africa.  Every fortnight one of these ships left England and made its first stop at Las Palmas.  Passengers had a few hours to go ashore and view the town, while the ship took on freight of fresh fruit and vegetables that had been ordered by the supermarkets and traders in the West African ports.  Fruit such as grapes and apples, and items such as bacon, cheese and butter which needed to be transported in refrigerated containers, were eagerly awaited.  Shops that sold these goods in Freetown would open specially on Sunday afternoon after collecting their wares from the 'mail boat' (as they were popularly called, because they also brought the parcels, letters and magazines that would be too expensive to send by airmail). The ports of call on the West African coast were Bathurst in the Gambia, Freetown in Sierra Leone, Accra in Ghana and Lagos in Nigeria.

On 10 October 1974 the MV Aureol, the last of the Elder Dempster liners on the West Africa route, left Freetown on its final voyage after regular trips bringing passengers and goods to Freetown and other ports on the West Coast of Africa for twenty-three years. She was seen out of the harbour by a flotilla of small craft, all hooting and decorated with bunting and flags. This was the end of an era.

The M.V. Aureol, a 16 knots ship with twin screw diesel engines and a crew of over 140, carried 253 first class passengers and 76 cabin class. She was sold to Panama and renamed M.V. Marianna VI. She was finally laid up in Eleusis, Greece, 1989, and eventually sold as scrap in 2001, when she was towed to India to be broken up.

➼ A new hotel, costing about Le5.5 million, was built on Aberdeen Hill. It was called Bintumani, after a mountain in the interior of Sierra Leone. The management of the hotel wanted to give their staff a little practical experience before the actual opening, so they invited the members of the Freetown Rotary Club, of which I was one, to hold their lunchtime meeting of Thursday, 24th November 1977, at the hotel. We were not charged by the hotel for our lunch, but we paid what our lunch would usually cost towards the Rotary Club fundraising committee. There was no speaker arranged for that day, so at short notice I was called upon to speak, thus possibly making history as the first person to make a speech at the Bintumani Hotel!

The hotel management had also generously invited Rotarians to spend a night at the hotel, with their wives, before the official opening. About ten of the members accepted the invitation for Saturday, 3rd December 1977, and arrived with their wives dressed for dinner. The evening started with drinks outside on the terrace by the swimming pool, then we moved inside to the restaurant. This was large, and it was a little strange having so few of us in such a huge place, but it was helped by everyone knowing each other as members of the same club. The dinner was very good, with large portions, and a band played music for dancing.

At about one o'clock Joan and I retired to our bedroom, over-looking the Atlantic Ocean. We stood for a while looking at the moonlight and the waves breaking on the rocks below. We had been assigned a room with two single beds which we pushed together to make a double bed. The beds moved easily on castors. Too easily in fact! Just turning over in bed was enough to set it going. Before we could settle down to sleep we had to find a method of wedging the beds together to keep them in one place. In the morning I reached out to see if my wife was awake but found an empty space.

The beds had moved apart in the night and my wife was fast asleep in her bed in the middle of the room whilst mine was still against the wall. My first thought was, "What have I done now!" I got out of bed and woke her up and she was surprised that her bed was not against mine as it had been when she went to sleep. We laughed over the situation and my wife said that perhaps the beds were not married and that is why they moved apart!

We met up with all the others for breakfast and found that most of them had had similar experiences with their beds, so we passed our comments on to the management. We left at 10.00 am to go home having thoroughly enjoyed our stay. The members of Rotary Clubs are usually working in some way for the benefit of people who needed our help, and we all appreciated this occasion when Rotarians received the benefit, but still served the public by telling the hotel management about the 'runaway beds'!

The Bintumani Hotel was officially opened by the President, Dr Siaka Stevens, on 10th March 1978, in the presence of foreign journalists. The Hotel was run by Caledonian Hotel Management, connected with British Caledonian Airways which ran direct flights between London and Freetown three times a week at that time.

➥ Dr Kenneth Kaunda, President of Zambia, arrived in Freetown on a short visit on Thursday, 20 January 1977. President Kaunda was on a tour of West Africa with a delegation to try to raise support for the Zimbabwe Patriotic Front, which was led by Mr Robert Mugabe and Mr Joshua Nkomo. During the visit, President Kaunda and President Stevens issued a joint communique recognising the Patriotic Front. Before he left Freetown, President Kaunda was made a Freeman of the City of Freetown.

➥ On Saturday 29 January 1977 I heard of the students' demonstration at Fourah Bay College during the Convocation held for the conferment of degrees, particularly when the President of Sierra Leone, Dr Siaka Stevens, who was Chancellor of the University, stood up to make a speech. The next day I heard further that the students had called upon the President to resign. I kept a daily journal in those days, and give here my entries for the next few days:-

"Monday, 31 January. Counter demonstration by APC (All Peoples Congress) Women, Youths, etc. Clashes between students and counter-demonstrators at FBC (Fourah Bay College). It is said a lot of damage was caused to buildings. I had a telephone call to say that my son Jamal (studying Geomorphology at FBC) had been arrested and brought down to CID in Freetown, with some other students. I left my breakfast uneaten and drove into Freetown. The atmosphere was tense and electric. I went to the CID. I was allowed to see Jamal and he told me he knew nothing of the demonstration except what he had seen from the window of one of the buildings, and had taken no part in it. I returned later in the day and took food for him, which he shared with the other students, including a

Lebanese girl student arrested at the same time who was studying Marine Biology. There were about sixty students in custody. Later that evening, at 8.30 pm, Jamal and about fifty other students were released.

Tuesday, 1 February.  Did not take my children to school.  School children who did attend left school early and joined up in town, singing "No school, no college", meaning that as Fourah Bay College has been closed down they, too, are closing down in sympathy.  ISU (Internal Security Unit, later changed to Special Security Division) called out to disperse the crowd.  I went home at 1.00 pm.  Announcement by the President at 8.00 pm of a State of Emergency and Curfew from 7.00 pm to 6.00 am.  Also announcement from Minister of Education that in view of the demonstration by school children all schools are closed down for the rest of the week.  Heard over the radio of serious clashes in the East End of Freetown.

Wednesday, 2 February.  Majority of the town closed due to student unrest.  I did not go to work today and my children all stayed at home.

Thursday, 3$^{rd}$ February.  Still people are not sure what's happening.  Half the shops in town had only one door open, ready for any emergency.  Closed at 1.00 pm, went to the Aqua for a drink.  Closing time was 6.00 pm to allow the bar boys to get home.  Lumley is quiet at night.  Hear that Medical Association is to meet tomorrow regarding the present unrest.  Parliament to meet on 7$^{th}$ instead of 14$^{th}$.  Rumours all round town that the students have planned a big demonstration on the 7$^{th}$.  Collected Jamal's clothes, books, etc from Ivor Patnelli, his room-mate at Block G.111 at FBC, who escaped on Monday during the demonstration with Jamal's things as well his own.  How nice of him.  He resembles his father Patrick Patnelli, an old schoolmate but my senior in school.

I collected my Curfew Pass from the Sierra Leone Police.  It contains my photograph and permits me to go about my duties during curfew hours.

Friday, 4$^{th}$ February.  All seems calm on the surface.  Everyone is talking about the mass students' demonstration planned for Monday next.  Quiet; those businesses that opened used only one door.

Saturday, 5$^{th}$ February.  Curfew relaxed by two hours, that is from 9.00 pm to 6.00 am.  ISU seem to have had their arms withdrawn, only truncheons left.  Medical Association, Bar Association, religious bodies and Students Union had individual discussions with President at State House this morning.  Schools to remain closed for the time being.  Students Union and FBC Executive to meet at FBC on Tuesday.

The religious leaders of the United Christian Council, the Roman Catholic Church and the Muslim Community issued a Joint Memorandum calling on the Government "to have an independent inquiry into the incidents arising out of the approved peaceful demonstrations in the vicinity of Fourah Bay College and to take the necessary steps to see that in the highly sensitive situation counter demonstrations are not encouraged. ...."

Sunday, 6th February. All seems quiet. Went to Mass at Sacred Heart Cathedral in Freetown.

Monday, 7th February. Businesses open although most were still apprehensive.

Tuesday, 8th February. Students met at FBC. Jamal attended. They came down later and presented a memorandum to the President. There were a few hundred students outside State House, and I am informed that they demanded an immediate reply to their demands and would not leave State House until they have had it. News of rioting in Bo, Kenema and Kailahun. At night the SLBS announced at 11.00 pm that the President would make a speech before they closed down. Normally they closed at 11.30 pm but they were kept open with music until about 1.00 am, when the President came on. He talked of riots in Bo and Kenema by students and others, and that the full powers of the State of Emergency would now be evoked. I hear that the ISU were out again and armed, and that roadblocks were set up by demonstrators.

Wednesday, 9th February. I went to my office at 10.00 am. All seems calm. Some shops open, some closed. I saw some writings painted on the streets against the President, but I could not read them properly. Closed my office at noon due to rumours of further unrest. Curfew still 9.00 pm to 6.00 am. Late announcement of apology by students.

Thursday, 10th February. Schools reopened today. Kept my children at home. All quiet in town. Curfew still on.

Friday, 11 February. Took all my children to school. At Linda's school (St Annes) only a handful of children attended. At John's school (St Edward's) less than half turned up, and so too at Mary's school (St Joseph's). Linda's school broke up at 10.30 am as there were only three children in the class. The University Senate meets today to decide on when FBC should reopen. All quiet so took children into town at 4.00 pm to go on board MV Logos, a ship that travels round the world selling books, mainly educational and religious. We bought a few. The books were priced in 'Logos' units, each Logos being worth two cents. Left at 6.00 pm. Curfew 9.00 pm."

The schools were operating normally by Monday 14th February, although on Tuesday, 15th February Parliament ratified the State of Emergency by 84 votes in favour and none against. On Monday 21st February the curfew was shifted to 11.00 pm to 6.00 am, and on 1st March it was changed again to 12.00 midnight to 6.00 am. Throughout the second half of February I heard of rioting in various towns in the provinces such as Makeni, Bo and Kenema, and also Pujehun, Bonthe and Kailahun. On 10th March the curfew was lifted completely and I presume the State of Emergency was also lifted. On Monday 4th April Parliament was dissolved to pave the way for elections on 5th May. The result was a landslide win for the All Peoples Congress and President Siaka Stevens was returned to power.

➥ Some time in 1977 I bought a piece of land consisting of just over three and a half acres at Bungalow Road in Adonkia in the Western Area of Sierra Leone. When all the formalities had been completed, I took the family there to see our piece of land. The land was bounded by Bungalow Road along the front and by a stream on the side. Right by the first beacon on Bungalow Road was a most unusual piece of granite standing upright and known locally as "Beah-beah stone" (beah-beah in Krio means bearded in English). It stood about four feet high and three feet wide and the surface was full of scoop marks as if someone had taken pieces out with a giant spoon. The stone was very significant in the area and had a local tradition. In the olden days people travelling on foot from Hill Station or Wilberforce took that path and when they arrived at "Beah-beah stone" they would pause and give thanks for their safe journey so far.

It was at this piece of land that my wife saw a scorpion for the first time. We would often go there at weekends to check the boundaries and pick some fruit, including mangoes and malombo (I do not know the English equivalent of the name for this fruit, and I have never seen it in England). We would all wander about to explore the land, and Joan was turning over some small pieces of granite when underneath one of them was a black scorpion about two inches long. It raised up its tail with the sting ready for action, but we moved back and let it scuttle safely away without killing it. When we went home we looked up scorpion in an encyclopaedia and found that it belongs to the arachnid family. Spiders, mites and ticks also belong to this class. Joan was lucky that she was not stung, as the poison from a scorpion is potentially dangerous and painful, though not usually lethal. Scorpions eat insects and spiders, and the mothers bear live young.

➥ 15th June 1977. Today, I see from my diary, is the first time a jumbo jet has landed at Lungi Airport. The DC10 jet belonged to UTA, and to honour the inaugural flight President Siaka Stevens was on board, returning from the Commonwealth Heads of State Conference in the United Kingdom. I was listening to the commentator on SLBS (Sierra Leone Broadcasting Service) as he described the occasion. He said in an agitated voice, "Any minute now the door will open and the President will be the first to come out. Yes, the door has just opened and ... and ... and a woman has come out! She is an airhostess wearing a pale green dress, yes a pale green one. The weather has been good and clear. In fact clear enough to see the pale of her green!" I burst out laughing as I realised what the commentator had said!

➥ On a wet morning at the end of June 1977, even though I was suffering from a bout of malaria, I drove to my chambers to pay my staff and to finish writing an article about "The Lebanese in Sierra Leone" to be published in the "We Yone", a bi-weekly newspaper. I discovered that thieves had opened the window of my library and fished out from between the guard bars the oval tin box with my name on the lid which they no doubt thought contained money. When they discovered that all it contained was my barrister's wig and some spare sets of bands that I wore with the wing collar, they threw the contents and the box down, no doubt in disgust. It had been raining heavily overnight and my wig was very muddy, so I had to take it home with me for my wife to give it a shampoo and set!

➤ On Saturday, 19 November 1977, we went with the children to the British Council Hall to see a concert performed by The Spinners. It is a British group consisting of four men, one of whom is a Jamaican, who played guitars and other instruments and sang Folk Music. The four men, Tony Davis, at 6 feet 7 inches the tallest member and leader of the group, Cliff Hall, the Jamaican but born in Cuba, Hugh Jones, 'the cheeky one' from Liverpool, and Mick Groves, who played jazz and skiffle, including the washboard, before joining the other three, were all extremely good and very entertaining. They were accompanied by a fifth man, John McCormick, on double bass. One song they sang was about an old woman who went to the churchyard to sweep up some bones. Some of the words went as follows: "She went to the cupboard to get a broom and as she opened the door ......" Here the lights all went out and there was a scream. Linda jumped into Joan's lap! A Krio woman sitting behind us shouted, "Watin dat!", meaning What's that! Then the lights all went on again, amidst much laughter at this simple but effective ruse! After the show the children all went backstage to meet the performers and have their programmes autographed by the four singers.

Two days later they gave a special performance for all secondary schools at the Annie Walsh Memorial School.

When we were next in England we bought two tapes recorded by the Spinners, and we still have them and play them occasionally to remind us of Freetown and their performance at the British Council.

➤ The British High Commission in Freetown gave a cocktail party at Runnymead, the residence of the High Commissioner at Hill Station. As it was near to Christmas, children above the age of twelve were included in the invitation, but the stewards were given strict instructions that children were only to be served soft drinks. Joan and I attended accompanied by Mary and John. The older children did not want to come, and Linda was too young.

At the party Mary and John met up with their cousin Mandy, and the three of them understandably preferred to sit together and chat rather than circulate with us among the adults. We kept an eye on them from a distance, and they appeared to be drinking 7-Up and eating peanuts quite contentedly. It was only many years later that we learned the full story. Mary was tall for her age, and was wearing a long dress, which made her look older than her years. The stewards refused to serve John and his cousin with anything stronger than Coca Cola, so Mary went alone to a steward who was standing with a tray of gin and tonic, and was allowed to help herself to three glasses without question. The three of them drank gin and tonic which we took for harmless 7-Up, and Mary repeated the exercise when their glasses were empty. When it was time to go home we found the children very happy and full of giggles, but took this merely to be their reaction to their first 'grown-up' party!

➤ After spending a few days in the Gambia, West Africa, doing a civil case, I got to Yundum Airport to catch a plane back to Freetown. Just ahead of me in the queue at the baggage weighing-in was a tall, slim Irish man called Paddy who travelled frequently on business between Freetown and the Gambia. At that time there was a severe shortage of Irish potatoes in Freetown, and Paddy was taking two sacks back with him. Behind him was a very fat Asian gentleman whose baggage consisted only of a modest briefcase. Paddy was waved through by the airport official without any delay. When it came to the turn of the fat gentleman, the official took one look at him and told him he would have to pay for excess weight. "How can you say that," spluttered the big man. "You let that other man through with far more baggage without charging him anything extra. Why are you charging me more?" The airlines official replied, "Sir, you need two seats for yourself alone, it is not your baggage we are charging you for! Come to think of it, you alone weigh more than the last passenger and his luggage put together."

➤ January is usually a very dry month with Harmattan winds and not a drop of rain. But on 13 January 1978, and yes, it was Friday and the 13th, we suddenly had very heavy rain from 7.00 am to 7.30 am and it was still dark up to 7.45 am, most unusual for Freetown. I saw a neighbour leaving his home in Lumley during the downpour with his umbrella up, but the rain was so heavy it was coming through the umbrella. My neighbour saw me on my veranda and called up to me, "Pa, this nohto umbrella rain!" Whereupon he closed his umbrella and continued on his way, resigned to getting drenched. The BBC World News had announced that on Wednesday last Britain had suffered the worst gale ever recorded, as well as flooding. Ships were washed ashore and people had to be rescued from houses etc. It seems that the unusual weather had taken two days to reach us and it brought us rain in January!

➤ Freetown had had its own television broadcasting studio from the early 1960's but it was only in black and white, and the transmitter could only reach as far as the outskirts of the city. On 22 February 1978 the new transmitting station at Leicester Peak was formally opened which would allow television broadcasts to reach as far as Moyamba, parts of Bo, Kambia and Port Loko for the first time. Not only that, it was able to broadcast in colour. We were told we would receive in colour on channels 2 and 7, but personally I was able to receive on 2 and 8. The programmes we received were a mixture of local and imported. We received news broadcasts in English, Mende, Temne and Limba, children's programmes, discussion and interview programmes and sometimes drama, all produced locally, while also enjoying American series such as Westerns like 'Bonanza' and 'High Chaparral', and English series like 'The Forsyte Saga' and 'Edward and Mrs Simpson'.

➤ Great excitement hit Freetown early in 1978 when the Rothmans Aerobatic Team of six planes flew in from Monrovia where they had been performing. This team was formed in the United Kingdom in 1970, the world's first full-time civilian formation aerobatic team, and has given well over 1500 displays at that time at airshows all over the world.

On Friday, 17<sup>th</sup> March, I heard quite a commotion outside my office. The Rothmans Team had taken to the air above Freetown. This caused all the thousands of bats which lived in the famous Cotton Tree, a landmark in the centre of Freetown, and the trees around the City Hotel (before it was burnt down), to leave their roosts and fly around in the air. There were four planes in the display, and one of them broke away to do some aerobatics on its own. One of the men nearby said, "That one must be the professor!" Later on the other three planes joined in again, and someone else said, "They are annoyed because he is doing everything on his own!" Another man recalled seeing a pilot called "Ten Sense" who was stationed in Freetown during the war doing similar aerobatics.

The next day I had a good view of the planes directly above my boat, Antonia, when I was out fishing in the open sea. Several other boats went out from Aqua Club to get a grandstand view. On Sunday I took my whole family to Lumley Beach to watch the Rothman show. Lumley Beach Road was packed full with cars and there was a traffic jam. At 4.00 pm we were invited to the home of some close friends, the Davises, who lived at Wilberforce, to watch a repeat performance from their veranda, which faced the sea. It was quite different watching the show from the hilltop, and the formations could be seen much clearer. The colourful smoke they deliberately emitted left a picture in the sky of the various patterns they had formed.

One of the best things about the shows was that they were free, so everyone had a chance to see them. The children in particular enjoyed the spectacle of the Rothmans Team, and watched them at every chance they had. They saw the vultures that were always present gliding on the currents of warm air high in the sky above Freetown, and christened them "Western Filter" after a brand of locally made cigarettes, and adopted the vultures as their own aerobatic team.

➤ In the seventies a new kind of bookshop came to Freetown. Text books bought from the schools or from the normal bookshops were very expensive, which meant that even when parents had managed to pay school fees for their child, they had to find much more than the cost of the fees to provide the child with the necessary books. Then the 'Butu Bookshops' began to appear, so named because the second-hand books were displayed on pavements and a prospective purchaser had to 'butu', or crouch down, to examine them. Sometime the books took up all of the pavement and passers-by had to walk in the road to avoid stepping on them. The books were sold at a fraction of the cost of new books and were a blessing to hard-up parents and students. One such place opened up close to the Diocesan Bookshop in what was Oxford Street, so people would check first to see if they could buy a cheap copy of the book they needed, before going to look at the new books inside this shop. We had occasionally bought books for our own children that way, when they were unobtainable from the usual sources. We believed that these books came from students who had left school or moved on to a higher form and no longer needed them. There were rumours, however, that as these books became popular, because of their cheapness, a few pupils were stealing books to sell to the 'Butu Bookshops'. For this reason, we believe, there was a move to ban these informal bookshops, but they did perform a service in that sometimes a book would not be available in Freetown except in second-hand copies, sold by the 'Butu Bookshops'. In these cases the price would occasionally be higher than what the book would have cost new in the schools, but if the book was part of the curriculum and therefore necessary, parents had no alternative but to pay the higher amount.

➻ One Sunday morning it was raining when we left home to go to St Luke's Church in Wilberforce. We used an umbrella to get from the carpark to the church. When the Mass had ended it was no longer raining and we forgot to pick up our umbrella. Halfway home we remembered the umbrella and went back for it. We looked around where we had been sitting, but could not find it. On our way home again I said to my family, "Whoever picked up the umbrella must have said, "Nar God dae gee" (meaning "It is a gift from God"!).

➻ It was early on a Friday morning and a Lebanese whom I knew quite well had driven to a building materials shop in East Street in Freetown (now called Ecowas Street) to purchase a few items. He had parked his car close to the open doors of the shop front. He had some more business to do close by so he left his car and walked to the next place he needed to visit. Having completed what he needed to do there, he moved on to the next street and so on. By this time it was lunchtime, and the owners of the building materials store wanted to close for lunch, but could not do so as the car was parked too near to the doors to allow them to close. The shop-owner telephoned to the home of the owner of the car and spoke to the man's wife, telling her that her husband's car was blocking the front of his shop. The wife exclaimed, "So that is where he left it! My husband has been walking around town looking for the car as he couldn't remember where he left it! As soon as he comes in I will tell him to go immediately and get it." She apologised for her husband's forgetfulness.

Another story I heard similar to the above was of an Irish Catholic priest who had need to visit Bo from Freetown. He could not find anyone to give him a lift, so even though he did not like driving long distances, he drove his car all the way to Bo. He carried out the business he went for, and met with someone who was about to drive to Freetown, so he got a lift with him. He had forgotten that he drove his own car to Bo, and didn't remember until he was back in Freetown!

➨ On 6 October 1959 the Wilberforce Memorial Hall was burnt down in an accidental fire. Nothing was done with the site until the government decided to create a new City Hall, and the grand opening in 1978 was arranged to coincide with the anniversary of Republic Day, 19 April. The new City Hall consisted of a main foyer, a library, a theatre, the Siaka Stevens and William Wilberforce suites, and eight rooms to be used as offices. The Auditorium was named after Mr Daniel Theodore Akibo Betts, a former mayor of Freetown, who had worked hard to bring the new City Hall into being, but who sadly died on 28 December 1975 before the work was completed. This edifice was built by the Democratic Peoples Republic of Korea, whose Leader at that time was Comrade Kim il Sung. It was opened by the President, in the presence of the Mayor of Freetown, Dr June Holst-Roness, and various personalities from the Gambia, Liberia and Nigeria.

Outside the front of the building, on the main road which was previously Water Street, now re-named Wallace-Johnson Street, was erected a bust of the late Isaac Theophilus Akuna Wallace-Johnson, a popular Trade Unionist who was born in 1894 and died in a road accident in Ghana in 1965 at the age of 70. Joan reminded me that we stood by the roadside in Brookfields to watch his funeral procession go past. She remembered in particular the coffin which was most unusual. It was completely covered in small squares of mirrored glass, with a cross marked on the top of the coffin in golden glass squares. The bust of Wallace-Johnson, made by Italian sculptor Professor Pepe Romano, stands on a pedestal which bears the inscription, "Indomitable freedom fighter, vanguard politician, pioneer, trade unionist, fearless journalist and pan-Africanist". I have since been told that this City Hall was destroyed by the rebels in 1999.

➨ Around this time the head of the army, Brigadier J.S. Momoh (later to become President of Sierra Leone), had introduced the Sierra Leone Women's Army Corps. A nucleus of fourteen women were engaged in rigorous army training. Women had joined the army before this, but only in special positions such as doctors and nurses, and they all held officer status. From this date women were able to join the army as regular soldiers.

➨ On 14 June 1978 Sierra Leone officially became a One Party State. President Siaka Stevens was sworn in under the new constitution by Chief Justice C.O.E. Cole, O.B.E., O.R., (the former Ceremonial President, in effect and in fact, President for only two days). President Stevens was the founder of the All Peoples Congress Party, which became the recognised party under the new constitution. Nearly two decades later Sierra Leone reverted to being a multi-party state, and many new parties sprang up. At the time of writing Sierra Leone is still a multi-party state, and the Sierra Leone Peoples Party, which disappeared when the one party state was declared, is now prominent again. In fact President Ahmad Tejan Kabbah, who took office in 1996, is the leader of the SLPP.

➤ In Sierra Leone, some prospective members of parliament were quite well off and were prepared to go to some lengths to make sure of being elected, such as buying out the other candidates so as to be returned unopposed. This was in the days when Sierra Leone was a one party state and perhaps several candidates would stand for the same ward. A few people merely stood for election in the hope that another candidate would offer them a sum of money to stand down, so that that candidate would be elected unopposed.

It waş said that some supporters would do anything to make sure that their candidate won the elections. They would therefore prepare substitute boxes with names on them and secretly swap them with the official election boxes at the close of voting. The substitute boxes would be taken to the counting office, while the real boxes were taken away and destroyed. I have heard of occasions where, when the lights went out unexpectedly near the close of voting, the candidate would sit on his own box to prevent it being tampered with or swapped in the darkness, and would then accompany his box to the counting office.

A story once told to me was that two men were standing for the same seat. Both of them had bald heads. It was usual in Sierra Leone for candidates to be represented by a symbol or to have their photograph pasted on their box. For example, one candidate might have an umbrella as his symbol, while another had a box of matches and another might have a cutlass. In this particular story, one of the two candidates was really anxious to enter parliament and had done a lot to become friendly with the voters registered in that constituency, while the other, who did not expect to be elected, did not do so much. The supporters of the first candidate were advised to vote for "the bald-headed man". Little did they know that both men were bald, and the box belonging to the second candidate was the first to be seen when entering the voting booth. The second candidate was extremely surprised to find himself duly elected to a seat in parliament, while the other found that his efforts in canvassing his constituents had all been in vain. When the results were announced, "What! I won?" cried the candidate who hadn't expected to. "What! I lost!" cried the other candidate in disbelief.

➤ Towards the end of September 1978, after some particularly heavy rain, I was told that the Baffin River in Kono District burst its banks, sweeping through towns and villages. It was feared that up to two hundred people had lost their lives, the worst disaster of its kind in Kono history up to that time. I believe a bridge was later built across the Baffin River.

➼ On 1 November 1978 the President of Sierra Leone returned from the USA where he had been having talks with the International Monetary Fund and the World Bank. As a result of those talks Sierra Leone broke away from the pound Sterling and was pegged to the Special Drawing Rights (SDR). Up to that time, we could go to the Post Office in Freetown and buy a Postal Order for two Leones, send it to England, and it could be cashed in a London Post Office for one pound sterling. There was a rush on the banks to get Sterling just before this date, as people were afraid it would become hard to obtain. It was explained that the change to SDR would give "a flexible exchange rate" which would protect the currency against "the weakness of any other currency be it pound or the dollar". The new rate was LE 2.10cents against one pound sterling!

➼ A few days later, on Sunday 5 November 1978, an earth tremor, the first that I have experienced, occurred in Sierra Leone at around 1.00 pm. The whole house shook with the vibration. This tremor was felt in several areas as far apart as Bawbaw Beach and Cline Town, a distance of about eighteen miles. That night it rained very heavily and there was a thunder storm, even though we seldom had rain in November in Freetown. This was the only time to my knowledge that this has happened in Freetown.

➼ On 19 March 1979 President Ahmed Sekou Touré of the Republic of Guinea arrived in Sierra Leone on a four-day state visit. Traffic on the day of his arrival became chaotic – the roads that the presidential cavalcade would take having been closed hours before his arrival. The Guinean president had a very great reception from the public, and in particular from the large Foulah community in Freetown who originated from Guinea. The Foulah men all turned out to see their Head of State. They wore long white gowns, white skull-caps and white slippers with pointed toes. President Sekou Touré, accompanied by President Stevens, was also dressed in a white flowing gown and white hat, and waved a white handkerchief. I have never seen so many people dressed all in white as I did that day. The next day President Sekou Touré visited the City Hall and passed in front of my chambers in Gloucester Street. Again there was a tremendous acclamation from the public.

Groups of Foulah musicians, some playing the nyayaru (guitar) and others the hordu (flute), and yet others the lala (a shaker or rattle which is L-shaped with round discs cut from a calabash threaded on the short part of the L), and other instruments such as the balangie (xylophone), were performing as they followed the cavalcade to the City Hall. The Yelibas sang praises of Sekou Touré and Siaka Stevens in the Guinean tongue as they walked in front of the musicians.

Sekou Touré died on 27 March 1984 in America where he had been flown for treatment following a heart attack. He had been president of Guinea since 1958, twenty six years in office as President. Friday, 30th March, was declared a public holiday in Sierra Leone to mark the funeral of Sekou Touré.

Ahmed Sekou Touré was descended from Samori Touré, a national hero in Guinea who had fought against French rule up to the time of his capture in 1898. (I have written more about Samori, otherwise known as Samodu, in my book 'Sawpit Boy'). Guinea was a French colony until 1958, when French President Charles de Gaulle offered Guinea autonomy with a Franco-African community. Sekou Touré, who came to political prominence through his activities as a trade unionist (as did Siaka Stevens in Sierra Leone) preferred complete independence and broke away from France. The French withdrew from Guinea, destroying all civillian archives and military equipment as they left. Much later Sekou Touré and the French were reconciled, to the extent that in the late 1970's the French President Valéry Giscard d'Estaing visited Guinea. On 3rd April 1984, the seventh day after Sekou Touré's death, a military coup d'etat took place lead by Lansana Conté. President Lansana Conté is still the leader of Guinea at the time this book was written.

➤ We had another visit to the theatre on 30th March 1979. It was for a performance of "Joseph and his Amazing Technicolour Dreamcoat" written by Tim Rice and Andrew Lloyd Webber (well-known writers of musicals in London), held at the British Council Hall in Freetown. It was performed by the Music Society of Milton Margai Teachers College, and our good friend Kitty Fadlu Deen, a teacher of music, played the piano and also did the choreography. It was very well done and enjoyed by all, and we were sorry to see it end!

➤ For many years the bridge that connected Juba to Lumley was narrow, hardly any wider than the lorries that used it, for one way traffic only. Every year, it was said, there were three fatal accidents on the bridge, as well as some that were less serious. A new bridge was needed, and during the construction work more accidents happened to the workers. Some of the workers said that a sacrifice was needed to prevent any more accidents, such sacrifice to include the slaughter of a cow, a sheep and a goat, and food prepared. This was done and the workers and their families gathered to eat, and a generous portion of the food was offered to the spirits of the bridge. After this work on the bridge continued with no serious incidents, and the new bridge was duly opened on 18 April 1979 and named Wallace-Johnson Bridge. I believe that the number of serious accidents at the bridge have much reduced, but whether this was due to the sacrifice, or because the bridge is much wider and stronger with two lane traffic and footpaths for pedestrians, I am unable to say. Everyone soon got used to the improved bridge, and I for one would look across at the old bridge and wonder at how dangerous it looked.

➼ In April 1979 the Minister of Finance in Sierra Leone thought a good way to raise funds would be to allow motorists to buy number plates for their vehicles carrying their initials. These special number plates cost two hundred Leones and soon began to appear on private cars belonging to businessmen around Freetown, such as EAB 1, MMH 1, and one person even had his full first name, NADIM 1. However, this led to some confusion when a man whose initials were VP wanted to have them on his number plate, as the plate VP 1 already existed as the first vehicle belonging to the Vice President. In another instance, the licence plate HMS 1, belonging to a Lebanese friend of mine, was objected to by the British High Commission as it could be read as belonging to Her Majesty's Service and they asked for it to be withdrawn. After two months the scheme was cancelled and all the special number plates with initials were withdrawn.

➼ When I was a member of the Historical Society of Sierra Leone, in 1979, I was able to track down the building in Ascension Town in Freetown where the famous warrior Bai Bureh was held after his arrest in 1898 and before he was sent on exile to the Gold Coast, now Ghana.

Bai Bureh was believed to have been born around 1840, the son of a Loko war-chief. His mother was thought to have been a Temne woman. He was known as Kabba Lahai or Kebalai, and under that name had been an ally of the British in an expedition to the Sambakke country in 1892. In 1886 he was made chief of Kasse and given the title of Bai Bureh. 'Bai' means Chief in Temne.

During the Governorship of Sir Frederick Cardew, K.C.M.G. (Knight Commander of the Order of St Michael and St George), there was an uprising in the then British Protectorate of Sierra Leone, which was established in 1896, due to the imposition of the 'Hut Tax' as a means of raising funds to cover the cost of administering the Protectorate. An annual tax was levied in the Protectorate of ten shillings on houses with four rooms and five shillings on smaller houses, to begin on 1st January 1898. Towns with twenty houses or less were to be exempt from paying tax. The people in the Protectorate objected to this. They did not understand why they should be made to pay for houses they owned.

A proclamation was published on 18th January 1898 prohibiting the importation of arms and ammunition into the Protectorate. This made the people feel that there was a reason for that, and they feared an outbreak of violence.

Various chiefs and people sent a petition to the District Commissioner at Karene for submission to the Governor, requesting the abolition of various clauses in the bill and the reduction of the Hut Tax. Among the signatories was Bai Bureh, who later led the Temne uprising against his former allies in

1898 in the Port Loko area. Further letters and petitions were sent by the same people, including an appeal that they asked to be forwarded to Her Majesty Queen Victoria in England.

Bai Bureh and many of the other chiefs, did not intend to pay the tax. The Government was determined to enforce payment and started collection of the tax in Port Loko in February 1898. The people had been warned by the Chiefs not to pay and some were charged and then sent to Freetown for imprisonment for offences such as Inciting others by threats to defy the law, Refusing to collect the House Tax, and Obstructing a Police Officer in the execution of his duty.

The following incident seems to have brought matters to a head. One Lance Corporal Stephen Williams was given a letter from District Commissioner Sharpe to deliver to Bai Bureh asking him to collect the tax. The letter was brought back unopened. The Lance Corporal later said, when giving evidence before the Royal Commissioner, that he was turned back without seeing Bai Bureh. Sharpe, however, said that although the letter was returned unopened, the Lance Corporal gave him a message from Bai Bureh that he had heard that "Captain Sharpe was coming to take his head off and that he, Bai Bureh, would not sit quietly and let a warrior like himself come and take his head off." It is has been said (in a report "The House Tax and the Temne Rising of 1898" by C. R. Morrison) that "It was this inflated message the invention of Williams which gave rise to all the trouble and the destruction of so many lives".

An English major, Tarbet, with a group of forty six Frontier Police and many carriers set out with the District Commissioner to arrest Bai Bureh. The forest was full of hidden warboys loyal to Bai Bureh. On the road to Karene a crowd gathered around the major and his men, jeering and mocking them, and eventually the Frontiers opened fire. After some shots on both sides, the warboys withdrew.

Bai Bureh was experienced in war, and his warriors had built stockades out of palm trees, near to the road but concealed from view, from behind which they could fire on the Frontier Police. In the following clashes the British suffered considerable losses of officers and men. The casualties in this area, however, were chiefly those of war. Bai Bureh's men were disciplined and he did not allow them to attack missionaries or traders. A reward of twenty pounds was offered for the arrest of Bai Bureh. This was later increased to fifty pounds by a letter from the Secretary for Native Affairs, J.C. Ernest Parkes to Chief Alimamy Bambo Lahai of Tonko Limba.

An Englishman, Thomas Chadwick, who was employed as an agent for G. B. Ollivant and Co., had introduced the use of carrier pigeons in Sierra Leone to get the first news of caravans of goods coming into the country from the north. He lent his pigeons to the Government so that news between the District Commissioner in Karene and the Governor in Freetown could be passed quickly, covering the sixty miles in one hour, instead of a long journey by foot. These messages were passed daily, and part of one such note read as follows: "..... This is our last pigeon and pigeon papers are required."

At the end of April 1898, in the Sherbro, Mende and Gallinas areas, attacks began without warning on all Europeans, Krios (Creoles), the people they employed and all associated with them. Let me tell you briefly of the Poro involvement in the 1898 War. Those who planned the uprising used the power of the Poro Society to keep their plans secret, making the groups of people swear an oath, with the choice of obedience or death. When everything was ready, messengers were sent around from village to village carrying a burnt palm leaf, the Poro signal for war. In these areas there was widespread slaughter and destruction, and European and American Missionaries were killed among the rest, as happened in Rotifunk.

In the Mende area most of the taxes had been already paid before the uprising. The people there had heard of the success of Bai Bureh and his men, but their intention was much wider. They wanted to drive out the British and all aliens such as the Krios, and regain control of the country for themselves.

Let us now go back to Bai Bureh's story. After months of fighting, in October 1898 Bai Bureh sent a message to the Muslim leaders in Freetown expressing his earnest desire for peace. The Muslim leaders forwarded this message to Sir David Chalmers, Her Majesty's Commissioner in Freetown, who had been sent out to investigate the cause of the unrest. He in turn wrote to Governor Cardew telling him of Bai Bureh's wish for peace. Cardew's response was that as the patrols and Frontier Police were still being fired on and war-boys were still gathering in Bai Bureh's territory, the only term was that Bai Bureh must surrender unconditionally. Cardew increased the reward for Bai Bureh's capture to £100. Bai Bureh, in turn, is said to have offered £500 for the capture of Cardew.

Many curious tales were told of Bai Bureh. It was said that he was no ordinary person, but could walk among people unseen, or appear as an elderly woman or even as an animal. Some of his followers believed that bullets could not kill him.

Bai Bureh surrendered in November 1898. There are unofficial reports that Bai Bureh came out of the bush and gave himself up voluntarily, and other reports that he was captured by an officer. It seems quite possible that Bai Bureh surrendered but that the British Officer in charge of the troop of men to which Bai Bureh gave himself up, took to himself the credit for the 'capture'.

During Bai Bureh's detention in a Freetown jail, Lieutenant H.E. Green, attached to the 1st West African Regiment, drew a sketch of him from life. This sketch was published in The Illustrated London News in December 1898, and has since been reproduced many times. It shows in profile a tall man with a white, pointed beard and strong, determined features, wearing a native cap and seated on a box. This is the only picture I have ever seen of Bai Bureh. It seems strange to think that after more than a hundred years, Lieutenant Green's drawing is still familiar to many people in Sierra Leone, while Lieutenant Green himself is little known. If this picture had not been drawn, we might today have no idea of what Bai Bureh looked like!

Sir David Chalmers presented his report to the British Parliament. Governor Cardew and Chalmers had not seen eye to eye, and Cardew wanted the opportunity to put his own views on the uprising, so he went to England for this purpose. Major Nathan acted as Governor in Cardew's absence. The Secretary of State, Chamberlain, warned that Bai Bureh must not be treated as a felon, and urged Nathan to release him if possible. After spending some time in prison in Freetown, Bai Bureh was moved to a house in Ascension Town in Freetown, near to the place where King Prempe of Ashanti in the Gold Coast was being held as a political prisoner.

Nathan decided against returning Bai Bureh back to his own chiefdom, which could be seen as a sign of weakness rather than of generosity. Bai Bureh was deported, along with Paramount Chief Nyagua and Bai Sherbro Kpana Lewis, on 30 July 1899, to the Gold Coast, now Ghana. Bai Bureh was allowed to return to Sierra Leone in 1905. He went back to his own chiefdom of Kasse where he was reinstated as Chief. He eventually died in 1908.

Some years ago a primary school in Freetown used the following song to teach their small charges the story of this great man:

Bai Bureh was a warrior
He fought against the British
The British made him surrender
Then he hollered Kottoh, mamu
Ah Kottoh, mamu, he hollered Kottoh, mamu
Ah Kottoh, mamu, he hollered Kottoh, mamu

The word 'Kottoh' means 'brother' in Temne, and 'mamu' means 'I beg', a plea for mercy.

In April 1978 my wife and I went to a cocktail party given by the Managing Director of Blackwood Hodge and his wife – Malcolm and Connie Davis - in honour of a visiting Director of the Company. I met an elderly lady of about seventy who was called Mrs Lee. Whilst talking to her she told me she was the daughter of a British army engineer who was in Sierra Leone during the laying of the railway in 1898. She further told me that her father had been involved in the Mende uprising of that year and had been bitten on the leg by a crocodile whilst attempting to swim across the Ribbi River. This was to retrieve canoes that the Warboys had taken and left on the other side, so that the Frontier Force could also cross the river.

❖ If anyone knows any more details of this story, I would be very happy to hear from him or her.

On 17th February 1977 President Siaka Stevens opened the new Port Loko District A.P.C. Headquarters. It was built through self-help and was named the Bai Bureh Memorial Hall.

From 15th to 17th July 1983 I attended the Sierra Leone Studies Symposium held at Fircroft College, Birmingham, where I met Dr Walter Marcus Jones, Christopher Fyfe, Laurens van der Laan, David Malamah Thomas, David Fashole Luke and Ted Cooper. We were all staying on the college campus, in the small rooms normally occupied by students during term time. The sessions took the form of a paper being presented by its author, then time was allowed for questions and discussion, with a chairman to keep order. Dr Marcus Jones chaired the first session.

On the second day I chaired a session at which two papers were read, Archeology in the Republic of Guinea presented by Keith Ray, and 1898 Revisited by Dr John Davidson. I found this last paper particularly interesting. Among other things Dr Davidson said that "The rebellion represented the near unanimous rejection by the Sherbro and Mende people of Sierra Leone government authority." He further said, "The rebellion was neither as widespread nor as total as has been suggested. ... parties of warriors spread disturbance over a wide area, but not over the whole of Mende country. ... Poro played an important part in the rising, but there is no evidence to suggest that it played a crucial role in its planning and co-ordination." It seemed to me that Dr Davidson was saying that the Mende uprising was completely unconnected with the Bai Bureh uprising against the Hut Tax.

My friend Ted Cooper presented a paper on 'The establishment of the Institute of Public Administration and Management, Freetown, 1977 - 1982'. During the symposium copies of my book 'Sawpit Boy' could be purchased from Adam Jones. He is the author of 'From Slaves to Palm Kernels - a History of the Galinhas Country (West Africa) 1730-1890', published in 1983 by Franz Steiner Verlag GMBH, Wiesbaden, and presented a paper on "Museums - a Neglected Source". I still have a copy of 'From Slaves to Palm Kernels' signed by the author.

A full account of the Hut Tax War of 1898 is given in Christopher Fyfe's book, 'A History of Sierra Leone', published in 1962 by Oxford University Press. See also 'Eminent Sierra Leoneans (in the Nineteenth Century)' published by the Department of Information for the Sierra Leone Society, I think in 1961, at a price of four shillings, 'Historical Dictionary of Sierra Leone' by Cyril P. Foray, published by The Scarecrow Press Inc in 1977, and 'Topics in Sierra Leone History' by Arthur Abraham, published by Leone Publishers in 1976. The Chalmers Report, in two parts, on the insurrection of 1898 was presented to Parliament in England in July 1899.

➳ I had to visit England to advise an English firm trading in Sierra Leone. I was picked up from the airport by a company car, on a cold and frosty Sunday morning in November 1979, and taken to my hotel in Mayfair, just one minute's walk from Regent Street. At night I went for a walk along Regent Street to see the Christmas lights. They were put up for the first time after a gap of seven years. I then strolled along Oxford Street, but found the lights there not very impressive. There were just a few laser beams in red and green pointing from one end of the street to the other.

I had several business meetings over the next few days, but also took advantage of being in London just before Christmas to do some shopping in my spare time. I bought some presents for my family and friends, and decided to treat myself as well. I bought a new rod, Alvey reel and some Rapala plugs. Later on I bought a Daiwa 6000 reel which had a meter to measure how much line was let out. This was the envy of my fishing friends! After finishing the business I came for, I returned to Freetown, via Banjul, glad to return to the warmth.

My son Michael told me the following four stories:

At the diamond mines in Yengema, the diamond dealers would go by truck to the village every morning to collect the diggers and take them the eight miles to the site. Some of the workers would prefer to wake up very early and walk all the way to the mining area every day, and the employers could not understand this. After a short while some of the walkers would stop turning up for work, and eventually the bosses discovered the reason for the energy of a few of the diggers. As they walked along the road they might just catch a glimpse of something shining by the side of the river which ran parallel with the road in places. If they were lucky the diamond they found would be big enough for them not to have to work for a while, or even set up in business for themselves.

A man called "Bitter Kola" by his co-workers held a lot of control over the other diggers, which he kept by telling the men stories of the various devils of the area. If a man stopped turning up for work, Bitter Kola would tell the others that the man must have done something wrong and the devil had caught him. Then Bitter Kola joined the ranks of the men who were walking to the site in the early morning, in the hope that he too would be lucky to find a large 'stone'. He did this for a while, but being unsuccessful in finding anything, he gave up and returned to coming to work in the truck. The other diggers, who did not like Bitter Kola's bullying style, said that the devil had eaten him, didn't like the taste and spat him out again.

➻ The local Town Chief knew that money was being made from diamonds and thought of a way to get a share of it. The diamond dealers had built roads leading from the villages where the diggers lived to the mining sites. The Chief levied a tax on the diamond dealers for every time their trucks travelled over the roads, even though the dealers were responsible for the roads being built at their own cost. In this way the Chief got rich and built more houses in the village.

➻ Various heavy machines of different kinds were used in the mining works. One day the diamond dealers advertised for a welder to work on the engine of the big Caterpillar but found it difficult to find a man who was suitable for the work. Men would apply saying that they knew about all kinds of welding, but when put to the test, it was found that they knew very little. Then a very small man with "kobbo foot" (badly bowed legs), turned up for the job. At first the boss was sceptical that the man would be able to do the job, but the little man said he was just the right man for the job and he would show them why. The "kobbo foot" man jumped up onto the Caterpillar and clamped his bowed legs around the engine. He was then able to swing himself around upside down and was in an ideal position to work underneath the engine without any undue strain. He was given the job.

➤➤ Not all of the employees showed the same level of skill and intelligence as this man. One man had climbed up to reach a thick metal pipe that needed to be cut at one end. He shouted out a warning when the pipe was nearly cut through and was about to fall. He then realised he had another problem, the pipe he had cut through was the one he was sitting on and he was sitting on the wrong end. He was lucky to be rescued in time by other workers before the pipe fell, as it would have taken him with it.

If the above story seems absurd, how about this one that was reported in a Freetown newspaper, We Yone, in May 1978:

> "Twelve acres of land planted with rice have suddenly become a huge garden of flowers , in a mystery that has baffled the people of Sembehun village – seventeen miles off Bo. [Bo is the second largest town in Sierra Leone.]
>
> Farmers of the sprawling village woke up one morning last week to find that the rice which they planted several months ago, has turned out to be blossoming flowers.
>
> Agricultural officers in Bo have also described this as a mystery."

A mystery indeed, but is it likely that a bag full of flower seeds was mistakenly supplied instead of rice? The farmers who planted the seeds must have thought they were just a new variety of rice! I remember reading a similar story of a farmer who planted black-eyed beans, but when he came to harvest his crop he found they were 'APC beans'. APC stand for the All Peoples Congress political party, which was in power at the time this story took place. Their symbol was the rising sun with a semicircle of rays around it, and the bean that grew had similar markings, hence the name.

# Chapter 5

# In the Eighties

On Saturday 1ˢᵗ March 1980 the price of petrol was increased from LE 2.25 to LE 3.00 per gallon. At that time the Leone was about LE 2.25 to one pound sterling. (In 2002 the Leone was about LE 3,200 to one pound – a great drop in value). This increase in the price of petrol was reflected in taxi and poda-poda fares which all went up. This resulted in riots in the East End of Freetown, and some Road Transport buses belonging to the government were damaged. To control the situation the government put a ceiling on fares charged by taxis and poda-podas.

The next development was a strike by all taxi and poda-poda drivers on Wednesday, 5ᵗʰ March, because they said that if they couldn't put their fares up they would be making a loss. They were not a charity, and needed a profit, however small, to run their businesses. This meant that very few people were able to get to work, and the Courts and schools closed early because tear gas was being thrown in central Freetown by the S.S.D. (Special Security Division, formerly the I.S.U. – Internal Security Unit). I picked up Linda from school, then drove up to Fourah Bay College to collect my older daughter Mary. On my way back I was stopped and told that a road block had been set up lower down the hill near Model School. I was obliged to turn around and go all the way around Mount Aureol by way of Kortright and Leicester and down to Lumley.

Later that evening we heard that the petrol station near our house in Lumley had been barricaded with empty petrol drums and that there was a disturbance of some kind with the S.S.D. on the scene. The street outside our house was deserted, then we heard a noise and saw smoke. When we investigated we found that an S.S.D. man had fired a teargas canister just outside our gates, although we could not see anyone on the road. We rushed around closing doors and windows to keep the smoke out. Joan peeped out through the front door to find out what teargas smelt like, but soon came back in again! The next morning we searched for and found the empty gas canister. I measured it and found it to be two and a half inches long and one and a half inches in diameter. We marked it with the date it was fired and kept it on the room-divider as a souvenir.

I was told that a construction company bus was burnt down that evening by the rioters. However, burning vehicles is not an uncommon occurrence anywhere when there is a riot on, and this applies to Sierra Leone as well.

The following day there was no public transport whatsoever. We kept all our children at home, which was a good thing because I heard later that tear gas was thrown into some schools, including John's school.

Rumours were circulating that the angry taxi and poda-poda drivers planned to stop all private cars on the roads the next day. Quite a few people decided to stay away from work and spend the day at home. A few members of the Aqua Club decided to spend the afternoon there and that included me. I had been in touch with the club and knew the bar was not open as the barmen had not been able to get there, so I took my own whisky and soda!

On Saturday, 8th March, the government announced new rates for fares and this time passengers and drivers alike accepted the changes. After a week of tension when Freetown was almost brought to a standstill, things began to return to normal. Shops were opening up as usual, whereas for the past few days the traders had only opened in the morning and just one doorway, which was easily shut if trouble should start.

From around this time taxi drivers began the practice of taking as many passengers as their vehicles would hold. You could stop an empty taxi and give the driver your destination, and on the way he would stop and pick up other passengers going to different places, so your journey would be crowded and possibly much longer than you expected. This was, I submit, because of the high cost and frequent shortages of petrol experienced by taxi and other drivers.

At a time of petrol shortage, some enterprising hawkers would buy petrol from the petrol stations and then stand by the roadside selling the petrol in gallon containers to people who were willing to pay extra to save themselves the inconvenience of joining the long queue of cars at the petrol pumps. Some of the more unscrupulous hawkers would try to increase their profits by mixing kerosene and petrol, kerosene being much cheaper. Some hawkers sold kerosene with a little red colouring added to give it the pink shade of petrol, and just add a sprinkling of petrol on the top to give the right petrol smell. It is small wonder that the cars would stall after a while.

➡ The anniversary of Republic Day in Sierra Leone, 19 April, was a public holiday. Father Liam O'Sullivan, a lecturer at Fourah Bay College, had arranged to take a party to visit the site of Mrs Melville's home, where she had written her book "A Residence at Sierra Leone", first printed in 1849, a copy of which is in my library. We are told by Christopher Fyfe in his book "A History of Sierra Leone," (published by Oxford University Press in 1962) that Mrs Melville was Scottish and had come to Sierra Leone in 1840. She was newly married, and her husband Michael Melville was Registrar of the Mixed Court in Freetown. At first they lived in Gloucester Street in Freetown, then moved to the hills above Freetown to Smith's Hill. The house was later bought by a Mr Heddle and became known as 'Heddle's Farm'.

We went by car as far as Father O'Sullivan's home at the Fourah Bay College campus, where we met up with the rest of the party, including the British High Commissioner Mr Michael Morgan and his wife, and continued the rest of the way on foot. We followed winding footpaths lined with enormous trees that had grown undisturbed for generations. We finally arrived at a clearing which gave a marvellous view down the hill to the sea. Of Mrs Melville's home only the foundations and a few low walls remained, made of red laterite stone, but it is easy to see how she would have involved herself so much with the flora and fauna of the area, surrounded as she was by nature. After a short visit we returned down the hill to Father O'Sullivan's home, where we had refreshments before going home at the end of a very interesting day.

➤➤ Father O'Sullivan taught mathematics at Fourah Bay College, of the University of Sierra Leone. My eldest son Jamal did a degree in Geography at this university, after going through St Edward's Secondary School where he did excellently in all subjects except mathematics, which he just passed without excelling. In his prelim year in university Jamal had no choice but to include mathematics as one of his subjects. After that year he could be more selective. He chose to drop mathematics and this pleased Father O'Sullivan. I met Father O'Sullivan at a dinner party, and he told me, amongst other things, "When Jamal gave up mathematics it was a great relief to both of us!" It was a relief to me as well because Jamal would have more time to devote to what he enjoyed and was good at, rather than something he only did because he was obliged to.

➤➤ One day at my office I had a surprise visit from Professor Norman Sherry, an author, who is a Fellow of the Royal Society of Literature, etc. He was in Freetown gathering information on the time that Graham Greene spent in Sierra Leone. Professor Sherry was the official biographer of Graham Greene, and had been visiting the City Hotel, one of the places where Graham Greene had stayed. While Professor Sherry was there someone had pointed out my chambers to him, in Gloucester Street opposite City Hotel, and told him that I had the biggest collection of old Sierra Leonean newspapers in the country.

The Freetown newspaper, The Weekly News, reported in 1935 that Mr Greene had arrived in Freetown and was travelling to Monrovia in Liberia overland and that he planned to write a book of his travels. He was accompanied by his cousin Barbara Greene, and his book was subsequently published in 1936 under the title 'Journey Without Maps'.

I remembered seeing Graham Greene when I was just a boy in primary school, in 1942. I was in Standard 2 at St Edward's Primary School in Howe Street (on the site where Santanno and Spiritus Houses now stand). I remember him as a tall, thin man wearing white shorts and a white shirt, when he came to visit the Catholic Mission which ran the school. Nearly everyone in Freetown, even the schoolboys, had heard the name of

Graham Greene. He wrote a novel set in Freetown called "The Heart of the Matter" which was published in 1948. The book was made into a film of the same name, with a famous actor, Trevor Howard, playing the part of the central character, Scobie. Elizabeth Allen played Scobie's wife, Louise, Peter Finch was the priest, and Wilson was played by Denholm Elliott – all well-known actors.

The film was made in Freetown, and I actually watched some of the scenes being filmed, particularly the scene where a dead man (actually a dummy) was thrown down a steep gutter which ran from street level down to the sea, filmed at Sawpit where I lived. Scobie is shown leaving the Police Station in Freetown at the beginning of the film. This imposing three storey building with stone steps leading up to the main entrance in fact housed the police station and the Law Courts at that time, but is now used solely as the Law Courts. There are two reclining figures above the entrance, facing in opposite directions. The Law Library is housed there, as well as the Robing Room, which held tall lockers where each of the lawyers who appeared in the courts could keep their wigs and gowns.

I also saw Trevor Howard one evening at the reception area of the Odeon Cinema. It was quite some years later that I saw the film, and realised that the ending had been changed a little from that of the book.

Professor Sherry subsequently visited my home and spent some time going through the Freetown newspapers for the relevant years, and he succeeded in finding several mentions of the writer. An official from the British High Commission arranged a showing of the film "The Heart of the Matter" in his home, and we attended with Professor Sherry. We met with him several times during his short stay in Sierra Leone, both socially and to assist him with his researches. Some years later, in 1989, the first volume of Professor Sherry's biography, "The Life of Graham Greene, Volume I: 1904-1939" was published in the United Kingdom. I was happy to see my name in the Acknowledgements in this volume.

A second volume covering 1939-1955 appeared in 1994, after the death of Graham Greene, in April 1991, at the age of 86. The sheer size of these books may appear daunting to the average reader, but do not let this put you off as I strongly recommend them. They are very entertaining and full of interesting detail, and tell of Graham Greene's time in Sierra Leone. The third and final volume will be published to coincide with the centenary of Graham Greene's birth and covers 1956-1991.

➤➤ Another film that was made in Sierra Leone many years later with Sierra Leonean actors is "Wanbone en Dem Pekin". It is the story of the adventures of three children when one of them is put under a spell by an evil dwarf, "Wanbone," who is in the pay of a smuggler, "Mr Big".

➤➤ The last year or two of the Seventies in Sierra Leone was spent largely in preparation for the holding of the Summit Meeting of the Organisation of African Unity, or OAU, founded in 1963. This conference was held annually, and the meeting for July 1979 had been held in Monrovia, Liberia. Sierra Leone was to host the 17th OAU Summit in 1980. It was usual for the outgoing Chairman to be present to hand over to the new Chairman, the Head of State of the host country. The previous Chairman had been President Tolbert of Liberia. On 12 April 1980 President Tolbert was assassinated in a military coup. Master Sergeant Samuel Doe became the new Head of State. This produced a slight awkwardness, but was resolved by having a former Chairman, President Leopold Senghor of Senegal, perform the handing over ceremony. Samuel Doe did not attend the meeting in Freetown, but sent his Foreign Minister, Baccus Matthews, to take his place.

A calypso style song had been written about the OAU, stating that "President Tolbert go hand over to Papa Shaki" (Siaka Stevens), but it had to be dropped after President Tolbert's assassination.

There was also a jingle heard frequently on the radio and television to make the people aware of the forthcoming summit meeting of the heads of member states in Sierra Leone, which went as follows:

"OAU for you, OAU for me, OAU for you and me, OAU for we."

This jingle was soon discontinued because the people began to sing the song but changing the letters OAU to IOU. Everyone was aware of the large amounts of money borrowed and owed to the various foreign companies who were carrying out works on such things as street lighting and telecommunications necessary to allow the country to host the summit meeting in an appropriate manner.

Donations were collected within Sierra Leone but also many of the wealthier member states made donations either in cash or kind. Many road improvements were carried out, which included the widening of Freetown Road, Lumley, where we lived, involving the loss of a ten feet wide strip of our land and the rebuilding of the wall facing the road. On the other side of the road a two storey wooden house was demolished to allow for the widening. The level of the road was raised about two feet, which was accomplished by bringing load after load of red laterite which was dumped on the road, levelled and rolled and then covered in tarmac. This was carried out on one side at a time, while traffic was allowed to pass on the other side. The work was carried out in the dry season and our house was covered, inside and out, by the red dust. Friends visiting us at that time would say, "My sympathy for the dust", as they entered.

The next step was to install street lighting. Up to this time very few roads had lights, but now all the main streets within Freetown, and all the routes that would be used by the visitors had street lighting. This was of particular benefit to us because one of the lamps erected on the central division in Freetown Road, Lumley, now a dual carriageway, was just a few yards from our house.

A modern conference centre was built at Aberdeen, equipped with the latest in telecommunications, next to the Bintumani Hotel. This was to help the visiting politicians remain in touch with their governments, and enabled the visiting press to get their stories home to their various news agencies and newspapers. A new hotel was built at Lumley Beach, called the Mammy Yoko Hotel.

Let me digress for a moment and tell you very briefly about a talk I gave at a Rotary meeting around this time about Mammy Yoko. Yoko was born around the middle of the nineteenth century and first came to notice for her beauty and gracefulness as a dancer when in the Sande Society, and she later set up a Sande society of her own where she trained many girls in the domestic sciences. Her first marriage was short-lived, and she then married a chief from Taiama. After his death, she married again to her late husband's close friend, Chief Gbanya of Senehun. Chief Gbanya found that Yoko was very diplomatic and made use of her as his emissary in his dealings with the British. As such she became well known to Governor Rowe. When Chief Gbanya was dying, he asked the Governor to make his favourite wife, Madam Yoko, chief in his place. After the death of Chief Gbanya, his successor was Movee of Senehun, but we are told that Governor Rowe recognised Madam Yoko as successor to Chief Gbanya.

Madam Yoko's time as chief spanned a very difficult period in the Protectorate of intertribal wars and slave dealing, culminating in the Hut Tax war of 1898. Madam Yoko paid the taxes and remained loyal to the British. When the government moved their District Headquarters to Moyamba, Madam Yoko built her new town there, Senehun having been destroyed in the Hut Tax War. After ruling as Chief for twenty one years, Madam Yoko committed suicide in 1906, by taking poison. Just before her death she had told her attendants that she had enjoyed to the full all that life had to give her of love, fame, wealth and power, and that now that old age was approaching she had nothing more to look forward to. Madam Yoko died in her mid-fifties without children, and she was succeeded as Chief of Moyamba by her brother Lamboi.

Sir Harry Luke, A.D.C. to Governor Leslie Probyn, said of her, "Most important of all the chiefs was Madam Yoko of Gpa-Mendi. By sheer ability and force of character this resolute little woman had built up in the formative years of the country the biggest Chiefdom in the whole of the Protectorate." However, Professor Arthur Abraham, a Sierra Leonean writer, in his book, "Topics in Sierra Leone History", published by Leone Publishers in 1976, said of her, "Madam Yoko's power was limited, and she could not hold together or control all the sections of a state created by war ...... those who were technically her sub-chiefs just ignored her and carried on their own affairs. ...... Madam Yoko's power was upheld by the colonial administration which elevated her to the position, and did not rest in customary constitutional law. ...... Yoko knew where the source of her authority lay, and was therefore unflinching in her loyalty to the administration. ...... Dr Hood, the District Surgeon for Ronietta District, who was also acting District Commissioner during the collection of the house tax, reported that 'the majority of her sub-chiefs are not loyal to her, and pay little attention to her orders until my assistance has been rendered'."

When the first Sierra Leone Museum was opened near the Cotton Tree in Freetown on 10th December 1957, a silver statuette of the late Mammy Yoko was displayed. It had been presented to her for her services to the British Government in 1906, just before she died.

To return to the OAU meeting; in spite of building two new hotels, still more accommodation was needed and a whole village of bungalows was built at Hill Station for visiting Heads of State. This complex included a large restaurant and casino, known as Bacardi's, a swimming pool and tennis courts.

The OAU Summit Conference opened on 1 July 1980. While previously many people had wondered at our choice of area to live, Lumley not being looked on as a prime residential area, we were now envied for living on the route to be taken by all the VIP's on their way to the conference centre. Luckily the day was a public holiday, so we were able to spend a lot of time on our front veranda watching the procession which started at 3.00pm. Delegate after delegate, about fifty of them, passed in front of our house. The Heads of State all travelled in white Mercedes Benz cars, mostly closed, and two police motorcycle outriders and a police car with wailing siren preceded each. A further police car with security men sitting out of the back door windows with only their legs on the inside and revolvers at the ready, followed behind each delegate's car.

'Pa Shaki', the President of Sierra Leone, travelled in an open car with the hood partially closed behind him because it was drizzling. I stood outside our gates and took a photograph of him as he passed within three feet of me. Freetown Road, Lumley, was lined with local school children waving flags. The girls were wearing dresses made with green material on the top, white in the middle and blue at the bottom, as the colours of the flag of Sierra Leone. The boys wore red shirts (the colour of the All Peoples Congress, the only party in the country at that time) with long white trousers. There were groups of women dressed in 'asheobi', that is, dresses or native costumes all made from the same material, a common practice in Sierra Leone for a special occasion, such as a wedding, when the ladies wished to identify themselves as belonging to a particular group.

The crowds cheered as the cars went past, but more so when President Sheku Touré of Guinea, which shares a border with Sierra Leone, went by. President Jawara of Gambia was warmly welcomed. Southern Rhodesia had held elections just a few months previously. The country was given a new name, Zimbabwe, and a new Prime Minister, Robert Mugabe, on

18 April 1980, and Sierra Leone welcomed him with open arms. The Ceremonial President of Zimbabwe was Reverend Banana, but he did not attend the conference. Among the special visitors to the summit meeting was the United Nations Secretary General, Kurt Waldheim, who was attending as an observer.

Three new large vehicle ferries had been ordered from Japan for the journey, which was about two miles long, across the Sierra Leone River between Freetown and Lungi where the International Airport was located. Unfortunately the ferries did not arrive until it was too late for them to be used to ferry the delegates across to the airport.

The OAU conference closed on 4 July 1980, and it was said to be the best and most enjoyable so far held. The Organisation of African Unity became the African Union as from July 2000.

➡ A few years before, Emperor Haile Salassie of Ethiopia was driven in state past our house when being taken by President Stevens to visit Lumley Beach. We also saw Princess Pahlavi of Iran when she visited Sierra Leone, and just missed seeing President Fidel Castro of Cuba, who was driven past our house one Sunday afternoon when on a short, surprise visit to Freetown, and we had gone to the beach that day! Our grandstand view was spoilt, however, when Aberdeen Bridge was finally built. This gave a shorter route from Freetown to the Conference Centre and the hotels at Lumley, so we no longer saw the V.I.P.'s going and coming to and from the beach road. Thus the saying, "When Aberdeen get bridge" for something that is not likely to happen, could no longer be used, and people fell back on the other popular phrase for the impossible, "When fol get teet" (meaning, 'When chickens have teeth').

One thing that did not change and which we watched every year from our veranda was the Myohaung Day parade held each January. Sierra Leone had taken part in World War II and had sent troops to fight in several places and finally at Myohaung in Burma, where they distinguished themselves (written about in greater detail in my book "Sawpit Boy"). One year we saw everyone assembling and heading for the war cemetery in Regent Road at Lumley, where prayers were said in memory of those who died. The usual practice was for the army, navy, boy scouts, girl guides and others taking part in the march to follow the army band from the cemetery down Regent Road and into Freetown Road, where they would all disband at the bottom of Spur Road. On this occasion we listened for the band coming but heard nothing. We saw the would-be marchers milling around, and then they all dispersed. We called to a soldier passing our gates and asked him why there was no march-past, because we were all disappointed. He replied that the army band had been sent up to Kenema to play at another function, forgetting that the Myohaung Day Parade was to take place that Sunday, and so there was no music to march to. The parade was normally held with much ceremony, with the band in ceremonial uniform, the drummer with his leopardskin, and the drum major leading the way tossing his baton in the air and catching it. Apparently the army officers felt that a "dry-march" (ie one without a band or other music) would not be appropriate.

➡ In the middle of October 1980, something strange happened. My clerk typist, Rosaline Conteh, who worked for me for years, told me of a dream she had had about me. She said she saw me as an old man, living in London on retirement, and that even my youngest child had left school and was grown up by that time. I did not take this dream seriously at the time, and put it down to her condition (she was pregnant at the time). It was not until years later, when I was writing this book, that I recalled her dream, which by then had come true. Is it possible that the future was revealed to her in a dream?

Rosaline was my typist and she would also go to Court to file a Writ of Summons or other papers or to the Registry to file agreements, conveyances and other documents. She worked for me faithfully for about eighteen years and I came to rely on her. In the early years she was never questioned and was allowed to carry out these duties without hindrance. Later, during the trials following an abortive coup, it was necessary for every clerk attending Court to carry an identity card with a photograph signed by the barrister/solicitor for whom they worked. I had a picture taken of her outside my chambers, wrote on the back that it was a picture of my clerk and stamped it with my Notary Public seal. She would show this to the usher on duty at the court to be allowed to enter the building. I still have the picture of her with my endorsement as a memento.

➡ The Mayor of Hull in the United Kingdom visited Freetown in October 1980 for a special ceremony with the Mayor of Freetown, Dr June Holst-Roness, for the twinning of the cities of Hull and Freetown. Hull has a special significance for Sierra Leoneans because it was the home of William Wilberforce, who was also Member of Parliament for Hull, in England, when he led the campaign for the abolition of slavery, which succeeded just a few days before his death. Wilberforce Street in Freetown and Wilberforce Village were named after this great man, and I hope they will remain as permanent tributes to his memory.

➡ Towards the end of October 1980, I heard that the lecturers at Fourah Bay College were on strike for better pay and conditions. This strike went on for a while. About a week later, I went home from the office for lunch as usual, collecting my children from school on the way. Again as usual in those days, I had a nap after my lunch. At about 3.45 pm I left home to go back to the office. I noticed that the roads were all deserted of cars, but there were people in clusters along Sanders Street and Siaka Stevens Street. All the shops were closed, and there were stones and broken bottles in the streets. When I arrived at my chambers I found everywhere closed, and my secretary and messenger had locked themselves in the secretary's office.

They told me of tear gas everywhere, and that the students had come down from Fourah Bay College in their pyjamas with their faces painted black. I closed the office and went home soon after.

I was told afterwards that the students had marched down to State House to see the Acting President, to find out when their lectures would resume. I was further told that the police, fearing for their own safety, fired tear gas on them, so the students ran riot, damaging cars and other property. Some students were arrested. The next day, Friday, a friend of mine told me he had been walking along Siaka Stevens Street and saw a government car with police outriders being stoned by some people. The outriders were ducking and swerving all over the place to avoid the stones. As usual, the shops all closed down, expecting further trouble. The matter was soon resolved, the lecturers resumed their lectures and the students went back to their studies!

➡ Soon after this incident, the Irish Committee in Freetown gave a cocktail party to bid farewell to His Grace Archbishop T.J. Brosnaham, C.S.Sp., C.R., a Catholic priest who had come to Sierra Leone as Bishop of Freetown and Bo in 1952. In 1971 he was created first Roman Catholic Archbishop of Sierra Leone. The Master of Ceremonies at the party, to which my wife and I were invited, was a good friend of mine, Dr Ahmadu Fadlu-Deen. He studied medicine in Ireland (where he met his future wife, Kitty), and had a strong friendship with the Catholic priests. It is interesting to note that Dr Fadlu-Deen was, and still is, a devout Muslim who later became an Alhaji.

➡ One day Linda came home from school at St Joseph's Secondary School with a black button pinned on her uniform. I asked her why she was wearing it and she told me it was because she had been speaking Krio in the playground. In an attempt to improve the girls' spoken English they were forbidden to speak in anything else whilst in the school's grounds. After a day or two I noticed Linda was not wearing the button anymore. She explained that the girls were allowed to enforce the rule themselves and when she heard another girl speaking in Krio Linda passed the button on to her. Most of the schools, as far as I am aware, had similar schemes to encourage the use of English while at school to improve fluency.

In November 2002 I heard of an announcement by the Minister of Education in Sierra Leone to the effect that the Government had banned the speaking of all vernacular languages within the compounds of all learning institutions. This has provoked an outcry among many Sierra Leoneans who see this as an insult to their own native tongues. There is nothing to stop them speaking in their own languages when they are away from school! My wife has told me that after studying French at school for four years she achieved only enough knowledge to pass her end of term examinations. She wished that some scheme had been in place at her school to enforce the use of what had been taught, if only for an hour, instead of forgetting all about it until the next lesson.

➤➤ I spent several years gathering materials for my first book. During this time I acquired a large collection of old Sierra Leonean newspapers (filling a whole store) which I used to glean information and assist my own recollections while writing the book. I also tracked down and interviewed many people about their own memories of people, events and places. The book was eventually called "SAWPIT BOY" and was privately printed in England in 1980. The books were shipped to Freetown and arrived on Monday, 30 March 1981 in a container belonging to my cousin-in-law, Sabah Shoueri. On Sunday, 5 April 1981, we gave a reception for fifty people in the garden of our home to launch the book. Professor Cyril Foray (a classmate of mine) was Master of Ceremonies, and the Lebanese Charge d'Affaires, Mr Abul Husn, officially launched the book. Mr Abul Husn took an interest in the history of Sierra Leone, and was made an honorary member of the Sierra Leone Historical Society, of which Mr Lenga-Kroma was president and I was vice president.

Cyril Foray was at that time Head of the History Department of Fourah Bay College and Public Orator for the College. Cyril, who hailed from Bo in the Southern Province of Sierra Leone, had a long and distinguished career, both in politics, where he served as Minister of External Affairs, and in education. Having studied history at Fourah Bay College and the University of California, he became a lecturer of history at Fourah Bay College and eventually served as Principal of the College. He twice served as Sierra Leone's High Commissioner to the United Kingdom, and during this time supported the Old Edwardians Association in London. Cyril was born in 1934 and died in Freetown on 31 July 2003. He was one of my closest friends from the time we sat together in class at St Edward's Secondary School, which was then located at Brookfields, where St Joseph's Secondary School now stands. He was a man of great intellect and humour, and our conversations would range from Latin tags and quotes from Shakespeare to politics, and back to the escapades of our young days. His obituary, with his photograph, appeared in The Times of London for Thursday, 21st August 2003.

'Sawpit Boy' was reviewed in the magazine West Africa of 8 June 1981 and had a three-page write-up, as well as a mention on the front cover. It also was reviewed in some of the Freetown newspapers, such as The Daily Mail, The Tablet and We Yone.

On the same day I was invited to be patron at a Thanksgiving Service held by the Lumley Hunters Society at St Marks Church, Lumley. Due to our party that day I was unable to attend, but sent a donation.

Later on, when I decided to move to England, I gave my whole collection of newspapers to Fourah Bay College, enough to fill a lorry. My law books were donated to the Law School in Freetown. These donations caught the attention of the local press, such as the Concord Times of 12 March 1997.

➼ On Christmas Eve it was usual for the family to come to us for dinner. At 11.30 pm we would all leave to go to Midnight Mass at the St Luke's Garrison Church. In 1981 the mass was celebrated by an English priest, Father Veal. After mass I wished the priest a happy Christmas and said, by way of joking, "I notice you are living well these days. With Fathers Lamb, Veal, Corry and Biere you are never short of food and drink!"

After the service we would return to the house briefly to see that all was well, then join a family gathering at the home of one of my cousins for pepper soup, and then on to Cape Club or Atlantic Club, or in more recent years to Alex's Beach Bar. All these clubs are along the beach at Lumley. When we got home we would go in very quietly so as not to wake up the children, and put all their presents around the Christmas tree in the sitting room before going to bed at about 4.00 am. This did not prevent us from getting up early when the children woke up.

➼ On Boxing Day 1981 we went to Tokeh beach. I went by boat with Joan and Mary, while John and Linda went with my cousin Choukri and his wife Toni by road. The purpose of our visit was to see a small plane that had crash-landed on the beach at Tokeh. It had been piloted by an Englishman whose name I didn't know, who was bringing it to Sierra Leone to sell. I was later told that the plane had come down in the sea and been dragged ashore by the villagers. The plane never flew again, but it was purchased by a Lebanese businessman who had a beach house at Tokeh Village. He had a concrete slab made outside his house and the plane was mounted on it. Visitors would go to see it without charge. Children loved to play on it and to sit in the pilot's seat and imagine themselves flying.

➼ Talking of children reminds me of the time my daughter Linda went with the geography class of her school, St Joseph's, by Road Transport bus to Kent, a village along the Peninsula, on a field trip. The bus was supposed to be back at the school compound at 6.00 pm, but when it got to 9.30 pm and there was still no sign of it I got out my car and drove with my son John along the coastal road as far as Sussex, looking for the bus. By this time I was very low on petrol and had to turn back. My wife had rung the nuns who ran the school for news but no one knew what had happened and the parents had all gathered at the school waiting to collect their daughters. Eventually, at about 10.30 pm, the bus stopped just outside our house at Lumley and Linda got out. The bus, with about sixty girls on board aged between eleven and thirteen, was being towed by a Road Transport breakdown lorry with a winch that was holding the front wheels of the bus clear of the road. We were so glad to see them back safely, and the first thing we did was to phone the school to let the other anxious parents know that the bus had broken down but was on its way with the girls all safe.

➡ On 18$^{th}$ May 1982 the Queen Elizabeth II liner, which used to ply the Atlantic between the United Kingdom and the United States of America, docked at the Queen Elizabeth II Quay at Cline Town in Freetown. It was carrying 3000 troops and crew who were on their way to take part in the Falklands War between Argentina and Britain. I drove up to Fourah Bay College with my family so that we could look down at the Quay and see the huge vessel. Like the Canberra, the Red Cross boat and others, this liner had called to take on water, food and fuel for its journey to the Ascension Islands where the British task force was gathering, to be within easy reach of the Falkland Islands. I was told the story of a soldier who had fallen overboard from the Q E II and no one on board had noticed the incident. The soldier had managed to swim about fourteen miles back to Freetown, and was admitted to the Hill Station Hospital.

A few weeks later, on 10$^{th}$ June 1982, I gave a talk at the Rotary Club of Freetown about the history of the Falkland Islands. The club had received a letter from the Rotary Club of Noroeste in Argentina explaining their position regarding the Falklands. This letter had been sent to all Rotary clubs all over the world. We went on holiday that year and stayed in Gillingham in Kent. While we were there we went to nearby Chatham to see the return from the Falklands of the vessel 'Endurance'. It had been on duty in the Antarctic when the war broke out and had been painted bright red to make it easily seen against the ice and snow. There had been no time to repaint the ship before sending it into service, and it was still red when it came home to Chatham Dockyard.

➡ In the 1980's Sierra Leone adopted a two-tier currency exchange rate. The official rate in January 1983 when purchasing foreign exchange was Le 2.27 to one pound sterling, while the commercial rate was Le 3.75 to one pound sterling. In theory, the commercial rate was the one businessmen had to pay when ordering goods from abroad to sell in Sierra Leone. The official rate was to apply in all other cases, but in practice school fees for children abroad was paid for in sterling purchased at the commercial rate. The immediate effect of this was that prices almost doubled, for example a gas cooker, which was sold at Le 1,480 at that time, became Le 2,280. This was understandable, as the traders would have to pay far more to replace their stock.

➡ By a letter dated 10$^{th}$ March 1983 I was invited by the Chairman of the Committee of Management of the City Council of Freetown (equal to the office of Mayor that had been suspended) Dr J.C. Oju Mends, O.R., J.P., C.O., M.B., CH.B.(B'Ham), D.T.M. & H. (Liverpool), D.PATH. (Lond.), F.R.C.P.(Edin), F.W.A.C.P., to join the board of the Disaster Relief Fund. My wife and I had been invited by a Lebanese doctor friend of ours to a dinner at the Chung Hua Chinese Restaurant given by the nurses of the Connaught Hospital. The nurses, hearing of my expertise at raising funds at Rotary, asked me to conduct an American Auction for three bottles of spirits, and I was able to raise quite a large sum of money. Dr Oju Mends had been present at the dinner and thought that I would be a useful fund raiser for the Disaster Relief Fund which had plans to raffle a car. The money raised would be used to compensate various citizens who had been victims of incidents such as fire destroying their homes.

➤➤ The Freetown Dinner Club was founded in 1944. Sir Ernest Morgan (a Sierra Leonean) conceived the idea of businessmen meeting every month in an exclusive club for dinner and general discussion. The idea was put to the City Council and accepted, and so the Dinner Club was formed with sixteen founder members and one secretary, divided equally between Sierra Leoneans and non-Sierra Leoneans. The first dinner was held at the City Hotel. Prospective members had to apply and be approved by the committee, and then wait for a vacancy before being allowed to attend meetings, as membership was limited to a set number. The Junior Dinner Club was started by Mr Hugh Clarke, also a Sierra Leonean. This information was given to me by Dr S. Broderick, who was ninety years old at the time and still a regular member of the Dinner Club.

In August 1983 I was invited by the Dinner Club as official Sierra Leonean guest and a Mr Brust of Standard Bank was the non-Sierra Leonean guest. By this time the club was meeting at the British Council at Tower Hill. As a guest I was called upon to make a speech after dinner.

➤➤ It would be remiss of me not to tell you of the tension that existed in Freetown at this time. Even though everything seemed peaceful, people were on the alert for trouble. On Monday, 28th January 1985, all the shops along Kissy Street suddenly closed around 11.30 am. This soon spread until most of the shops in Freetown were closed. I enquired as to the cause of the closure, but no one seemed to know what had happened. I found out later that a lorry carrying a container along Kissy Road (leading to Kissy Street) did not have the container well secured and it started to shift on the truck. The lorry driver shouted for people to get out of the way. The apprentice on the lorry jumped out and started running. Seeing this, the people nearby also started running. Others joined in, not knowing why, until there was a huge crowd running through the street. When the shopkeepers saw the panic they rushed to close their shops. When the market women saw the shops closing, they too cleared their wares and left hurriedly. Mothers ran to collect their children from the various schools.

My staff and I stood outside my office in Circular Road watching all the people scurrying by. We asked various people what was going on, but no-one could tell us with certainty, but most of them thought that it was some political trouble. There were many rumours at this time, some relating to the retirement of Sorie I. Koroma, the Vice President, and others involving the head of the army, Major General J. S. Momoh. Since I could see I would be doing no more work that day, I closed up my office, sent my staff home, collected my daughter from her school which was already half empty, and went home to Lumley for the rest of the day. It shows that there was an air of expectancy of political trouble that could erupt at any time if one minor incident concerning a lorry could close down most of Freetown!

Two months later there was a riot by the students at Fourah Bay College and the car belonging to the Principal, Professor Cyril Foray, was burnt down. The students then came on the rampage down into Freetown. The wife of the Vice Chancellor was a medical doctor, Dr Olayinka Koso-Thomas, and her surgery was in Circular Road just a few doors away from my chambers. Her car was parked outside her surgery and was badly damaged by the students. I closed my office and got into my car with my secretary Rosaline, who I was giving a lift home. My car was surrounded by a gang of schoolboys, who had joined the students in their protest. Some of them climbed on the bonnet, while another of them grabbed my watch off my wrist. As I started to drive away the boys threw stones at the car and cracked the front windscreen. The radio aerial was broken, and the car was dented in several places. On my way out of Freetown I noticed many other cars with cracked or broken windscreens. The police were out firing teargas all over town, and some main roads were blocked by students. When I arrived at my daughter's school, St Josephs at Brookfields, I found the girls were all locked inside the classrooms for their safety, and the teacher only let Linda leave the classroom when she saw me waiting outside.

The cracked windscreens and dents stayed on the cars for a long time. Inflation had made spare parts very expensive, so many people delayed repairing their cars in case there was more unrest and the cars were damaged again.

Dr Olayinka Koso-Thomas wrote a book entitled 'The Circumcision of Women' which was published by Zed Books Ltd in America and the United Kingdom in 1987. I have a copy which Dr Koso-Thomas signed for me in March 1991.

➡ Power cuts had long been a normal part of life in Freetown, but towards the end of the 1980's they became much more prevalent. We would go for weeks at a time with no electricity, and then the power would come on for just a few hours. When this happened the small boys who lived next door would shout out, "Light don cam, light don cam!" and dance around.

It was normal for me to sit on my front verandah facing the street after dark, and watch the traffic go by. To amuse myself, as we could not watch television or listen to our record player, I would count the number of cars passing by that only had one headlamp alight. I was surprised to find that it was quite a large number! Sometimes a friend would drive past and catch sight of me, and stop and join me for a while.

We were fortunate that by this time we had a gas cooker, which operated on bottled gas. There is no piped gas in Sierra Leone, but the bottled gas was usually available from the petrol stations. When a cylinder became empty, we used to send our gardener, with the empty cylinder in a wheelbarrow, along to the nearby petrol station about a hundred yards away where he would pay to exchange the empty one for a full one. Then gas became scarce! It was only available from the depot at Kissy, so every two weeks I had to go to Kissy – a few miles from my office in town - and queue for half a day or so, if I am lucky, for a bottle of gas. Most times I would take my messenger with me, pay for the gas and collect my numbered ticket, and leave him there with my ticket to wait, giving me the opportunity to go back to my office and do some work. I would go back and pick him up later in the day, and sometimes found that he was still waiting for the gas!

One day we visited our good friends Tungie and Arthur Stuart, and the discussion turned to the topic of the day - the shortage of gas. Some time previously we had given them a gift of a fondue set, which uses spirit to heat the oil which cooks the meat or fish. Tungie told us how useful she found the fondue set as she used it to cook when she did not have gas for her gas cooker. She told us that she used omole, a locally distilled potent spirit, sold by the distillery at Wellington. Tungie demonstrated its use by boiling some water to make tea. The spirit burnt very well without smoke or fumes or blackening of the pot being used, and so we learnt a way out of a gas shortage dilemma.

Another thing that would become scarce at times was petrol. It was sometimes possible to have a 44 gallon drum filled at the refinery at Kissy, which I would do in preference to what some people did, which was to park their cars and leave them overnight in a long queue at a petrol station which was believed to be getting a delivery the next day.

Around this time, a lawyer friend of mine was always to be seen with a large briefcase, even if he was just going to the Aqua Club on a Sunday afternoon. Eventually someone asked him why he always carried his briefcase even when he was not working. My friend opened his briefcase, took out an empty gallon container, and said, "Just in case there is petrol to be had in one of the petrol stations!"

Inflation had taken hold in Sierra Leone and the amount of Leones to the one pound Sterling had increased dramatically. There were plans to print notes of larger denominations, but in the meantime it was necessary to take a plastic carrier bag with you to the supermarket to carry sufficient notes to pay for the weekly shopping. The banks were running short of money and it became the practice to ask your bank for more money than you needed to withdraw from your account, in the knowledge that the cashier would tell you that you could only have perhaps a quarter of what you asked for.

# Chapter 6

# The Reverend John Newton

Newton, a village just after Waterloo in Sierra Leone, was, I believe, named after John Newton, an Englishman, born in July 1725. He did not live in the village, indeed it was not established until long after Newton had returned to England. Several books have been written about him.

After an unhappy childhood in London (the only child of his mother who died when he was six; his father quickly remarried), Newton became a seaman apprentice under his father, who was the captain of a merchant navy vessel, and learnt how to navigate a ship. He was later press-ganged into the navy, but when the captain learned that John was the son of a now retired merchant navy captain, John was made a midshipman. He deserted some time later, was captured and returned to his ship, where he was punished by being beaten in front of all the crew. During a voyage, when anchored off Madeira, the navy captain took by force two seamen from a merchant ship. John begged to be transferred to the merchant ship in exchange, the captain agreed, and John Newton found himself on board a ship engaged in the slave trade bound for Africa.

Eventually John met a Portuguese slave trader named Clow who was a passenger on the ship. John asked if he could work for Clow, and in 1745 he landed with Clow on Banana Island in Sierra Leone. Clow then went on to Plantain Island where he set up his headquarters, and he and Newton were the first white men to inhabit the island. Clow would take slaves in exchange for goods brought from England and elsewhere. For over a year John was ill-fed and ill-treated, and virtually a captive of Clow and his African wife. Eventually another white man set up business on Plantain Island and John was able to work for him instead of for Clow. He was transferred to his new master's factory on the Kittam River, a hundred miles or more from the Plantain Island. In February 1747 a ship came to anchor and the captain asked for John Newton as his father was trying to find him. John joined the ship and left Sierra Leone.

After a voyage lasting over one year, during which time John Newton was noted for his blasphemy and unwholesome way of life, the ship ran into a severe storm which lasted many days. The whole crew made great efforts to save themselves and their ship, until one night, exhausted after working on the pumps for hours to reduce the amount of seawater in the hold, John Newton said, "If this will not do, the Lord have mercy on us." The storm blew itself out after some hours, leaks were patched up, and a day or two later they knew they were safe and nearing home. John Newton later dated the beginning of his conversion from the time he spoke those words in 1748.

Back in England, Newton signed on as Mate on The Brownlow, a slave ship, and sailed to the Sierra Leone River to buy slaves. The ship then went on to Carolina in the USA to sell the slaves. On his return to England he proposed to Mary Catlett, his sweetheart, who was the daughter of his mother's old friend who lived in Chatham in Kent, and they were married on 12 February 1750 in St Margaret's Church, Rochester, Kent. John's father had been appointed by The Hudson Bay Company as Governor to Fort York in Hudson's Bay, and he wrote to John asking him to go with him, but his father's ship had sailed before John reached London. John's father later got cramp while swimming in Hudson's Bay and died from drowning.

Newton then got his first command, of the Duke of Argyle, a slave ship engaged in the 'Triangular Trade'. This involved taking goods to Africa to barter for slaves, taking the slaves in turn to the New World, North America, where the slaves were sold and goods bought with the money which were then brought back to England and sold. Newton wrote in his journal that the slaves were lying on shelves "Close to each other, like books upon a shelf". He estimated a third of the slaves died in the Middle Passage, the journey from Africa to America.

Newton got a new ship called 'The African', launched in April 1752. As captain, Newton acted as Minister at the Sunday services for the crew and got great pleasure and satisfaction from it. He returned again and again to Sierra Leone to buy slaves. In Peter Tucker's book "The Tuckers of Sierra Leone 1665-1914" published in 1997, we are told that between 1750 and 1754 John Newton was captain of a slave ship and purchased 105 slaves from Henry Tucker and his son at Sherbro. He also purchased camwood and ivory, popular in those days. Newton also purchased slaves from his old master, Clow.

In November 1754 'The African' was due to set sail again from Liverpool in England with Newton as captain, but two days before leaving Newton had a fit and was unable to leave, and the ship sailed with another captain. Newton was then 29 years old, and never went to sea again. He worked as a Tide Surveyor (Customs Officer) for several years before thinking of being ordained as a Minister of Religion in the Anglican Church. He was refused ordination several times before finally succeeding and moving to Olney in Buckinghamshire with his wife Mary when he was 39 years old. While at Olney, John Newton would occasionally preach in London before people such as Lord Dartmouth, John Thornton, and the Wilberforce family, old friends of Newton.

In 1767 Newton met William Cowper, who moved to Olney to be near Newton. Together they wrote the collection of hymns which were published as 'The Olney Hymns' in 1779, largely due to John Thornton, a wealthy merchant, who made all the arrangements with the publisher and then personally purchased and distributed one thousand copies. This collection of hymns has sold hundreds of thousands of copies in England and America, and the best of the hymns can still be found in modern hymn books. Newton wrote 280 of the hymns and Cowper wrote 68 of them. Besides the most famous, 'Amazing Grace', Newton wrote 'Glorious things of Thee are spoken', 'One there is above all others', 'Begone, unbelief; my Saviour is near', 'How sweet the name of Jesus sounds', among many other hymns which can still be heard in churches today. William Cowper is remembered as a poet as well as for writing hymns, one of which, 'God moves in a mysterious way his wonders to perform', is surely quoted today as often as when it first became popular.

In 1779 Thornton offered Newton the living of St Mary Woolnoth in London. Although he would miss the country life he was used to, Newton accepted the position and transferred to the city after fifteen years at Olney. One day in December 1785, Newton received a letter from a young man requesting "some serious conversation", in secret as he was a Member of Parliament and his face was well known. This was William Wilberforce. The young Wilberforce, born on 24 August 1759, was a prominent member of society, always to be seen at fashionable parties and in the gambling clubs. Wilberforce explained to Newton that he felt something was missing in his life, and giving up gambling and trying to make his life more meaningful did not seem enough. Newton advised him to remain in politics and to keep his wealthy society friends, and gave him a copy of "An Authentic Narrative ...", an account of Newton's early life and experiences in the Slave Trade which he wrote in 1762. Newton was full of remorse for his participation in the Slave Trade, and introduced William Wilberforce to his friends who opposed slavery, and brought him into close contact with John Thornton, whose son Henry was later to be closely associated with Wilberforce in the fight to abolish slavery. There was also a connection by marriage, as William Wilberforce's aunt, Mrs Wilberforce, was John Thornton's sister. Many people looked on slavery at this time as an "economic necessity".

On 22 May 1787 twelve men, none of whom were well-known socially or politically, formed The Society for the Abolition of Slavery. William Wilberforce was asked to direct their proceedings. Wilberforce said much later that the most important influence in leading him to what was the greatest work of his life was his first "serious conversation" with John Newton.

Newton wrote a pamphlet, "Thoughts upon the African Slave Trade", confessing his own part in the Trade. The Abolitionists printed and circulated 3,000 copies, and Newton was called to give evidence before the Privy Council in 1788, of the nine years he had spent in the Slave Trade.

The Abolitionists had established a colony for freed slaves in Freetown, Sierra Leone. John Newton was made a Director of the Sierra Leone Company because of his former knowledge of the country. Discussions were held on sending missionaries to the new colony, which resulted in the Church Missionary Society being formed in 1799 with John Newton on the Committee.

Mary Newton, John's beloved wife, died of cancer on 15 December 1790. John Newton served the church at St Mary Woolnoth's in London, until he died, blind and feeble but devout to the end, on 21 December 1807. He was buried there beside his wife, but in 1893 their remains were removed due to the construction of Bank Underground Station, and were transferred to the churchyard at Olney.

John Newton wrote his own epitaph, and I quote it in full:

JOHN NEWTON, Clerk
Once an infidel and libertine,
A servant of slaves in Africa:
Was by the rich mercy of our Lord and Saviour,
Jesus Christ,
Preserved, restored, pardoned,
And appointed to preach the Faith
He had long laboured to destroy.
Near sixteen years at Olney in Bucks:
And twenty-seven years in this Church.

Much of the information on the life of John Newton was obtained from 'An Ancient Mariner – A biography of John Newton' by Bernard Martin, who had access to John Newton's journal and private papers, first published in 1950 by William Heinemann Ltd and issued in paperback by Wyvern Books in 1960.

In 2002, when visiting Clapham to attend a meeting of the St Edward's Secondary School Old Boys Association, my wife and I paid a visit to the Holy Trinity Church on Clapham Common. Outside the church on the south side is a plaque commemorating the Clapham Sect placed there in 1919. Most of it can still be clearly read, although it was slightly damaged in the Second World War. It reads as follows:

Let us Praise God
For the memory and examples of all the faithfull
Departed who have worshiped in this church, and
Especially for the under-named
Servants of Christ .......... Called
THE CLAPHAM SECT
Who in the latter part of the XVIIIth and early part
Of the XIXth centuries laboured so abundantly for
National righteousness and the conversion of the

Heathen, and rested not until the curse of slavery
Was swept away from all parts of the British Dominions.

| | |
|---|---|
| CHARLES GRANT | HENRY THORNTON |
| ZACHARY MACAULAY | JOHN THORNTON |
| GRANVILLE SHARP | HENRY VENN Curate of Clapham |
| JOHN SHORE Lord Teignmouth | JOHN VENN Rector of Clapham |
| JAMES STEPHEN | WILLIAM WILBERFORCE |

"O God we have heard with our ears and our fathers have declared unto the noble works that Thou didst in their days and in the old time before them."

Most of these names are familiar to anyone who has read the early history of Freetown, and it sent shivers down our spines to know that we were walking on the same pavement trod by these great men on their way to worship all those years ago.

In the porch is a Blue Plaque unveiled by the High Commissioner for Jamaica in 1985, which reads:

Greater London Council
William Wilberforce
And
"The Clapham Sect"
Worshipped in this Church.
Their campaigning
Resulted in the
Abolition of Slavery
In
British Dominions
1833

Within the church can be found the Thornton Chapel, and there is a column in the north-east gallery commemorating John Thornton. In 1994 the Wilberforce Centre was opened in what was formerly the Lady Chapel. For those interested, there is a booklet available called "Holy Trinity Church, Clapham Common, published by the Parochial Church Council, Holy Trinity Church, Clapham Common, London, SW4, updated in 1995.

A village within Freetown, Sierra Leone, has been named after William Wilberforce, as well as a street in the heart of the town. Fort Thornton, where State House now stands, was named after Henry Thornton, a rich banker and member of the Sierra Leone Company and also of the Black Poor Committee, which had been formed to assist former slaves in England. Another name strongly associated with the abolition movement was Lord Barham, after whom Barham Road in Freetown was named.

Whenever I hear the hymn "Amazing Grace" in church in England it takes my mind back to Sierra Leone. That hymn is one of the favourites in Freetown (and also in America) and I am giving the words of this hymn in full to close this chapter.

## "Amazing Grace" by Reverend John Newton

Amazing grace! (How sweet the sound)
That saved a wretch like me!
I once was lost, but now am found,
Was blind but now I see.

'Twas grace that taught my heart to fear,
And grace my fears relieved;
How precious did that grace appear,
The hour I first believed!

Through many dangers, toils and snares,
I have already come;
'Tis grace has brought me safe thus far,
And grace will lead me home.

The Lord has promised good to me,
His word my hope secures;
He will my shield and portion be,
As long as life endures.

Yes, when this flesh and heart shall fail,
And mortal life shall cease;
I shall possess, within the veil,
A life of joy and peace.

The earth shall soon dissolve like snow,
The sun forbear to shine;
But God, who called me here below,
Will be forever mine.

When we've been there ten thousand years,
Bright shining as the sun,
We've no less days to sing God's praise
Than when we'd first begun.

# Chapter 7

# The Law and Lawyers

Anyone wishing to practise law in Sierra Leone, before the School of Law was established in Freetown, would need to have been called either to one of the four Inns of Court in England, namely the Inner Temple, Middle Temple, Grays Inn and Lincolns Inn, or to King's Inn in Dublin, Ireland. The four English Inns of Court are established in buildings near to the Royal Courts of Justice in London, and were founded in the thirteenth century, thus making them nearly eight hundred years old.

It is not the custom for a barrister to call another barrister 'Mr', even if he is not acquainted with him. To comply with this tradition, I call my colleagues in the legal fraternity by their first names if they are very close friends, or by their surnames if I do not know them quite so well. People who are not in the legal profession may address a barrister as 'Mr'. In England it is the custom for barristers not to shake hands with each other, although in Sierra Leone we do not strictly follow this rule.

We followed the English pattern of wearing wigs, gowns, wing-collars and bands when appearing in the High Court and upwards, but not in the Magistrate's Court or lower. A barrister's gown has a tippet hanging behind the left shoulder. This is nowadays just a small, oddly shaped piece of material, to represent the remnant of the scarf or band of material to which originally in the early days the lawyer's hat was fastened (not his wig), so that it could be taken off the head and allowed to hang down behind.

We each had a locker in the robing room in the courts where we kept our court attire, usually in blue bags. A red bag is given by Queen's Counsel to a barrister who has appeared with him and done exceptionally well. A Queen's Counsel (Q.C.) is a barrister who has been appointed by the Queen, on nomination of the Chief Justice, as counsel to the crown, who takes precedence over ordinary barristers. He wears a silk gown, instead of a stuff one, hence a Q.C. is often referred to as a 'silk'. He can only appear in court with a junior barrister in attendance.

Sierra Leone had three Q.C.'s, Berthan Macaulay (Senior) M.A., LLB, and Johnny Smythe (now deceased, formerly a gunner in the R.A.F. in World War II, and a Prisoner of War after being shot down over Germany), and John Anthony Roberts. This last was called to the Bar in November 1969 and practised in England. He registered in Sierra Leone in August 1975. John Roberts was also called to the Bar in Jamaica, Trinidad and Tobago, Bahamas, and St Kitts and Nevis. He has been made a freeman of the City of London and of Atlanta in the U.S.A. He is a product of St Edward's Secondary School in Freetown, as I am. Like some other Sierra Leoneans he joined the Royal Air Force, and served for ten years in various parts of the world in several capacities, including pilot and air traffic controller. His many interests included boxing, cricket, football and sprinting. He is also interested in music and is an expert organist. His wife, Eulette, is from the West Indies. John Roberts became Britain's first black Q.C., in 1988, and the first black Member of the Bench at Grays Inn. He also became the first black Head of Chambers, and drives a red Rolls Royce.

When John Roberts was sent by the British Foreign Office to the Virgin Islands in 1992 to act as Judge of the Supreme Court to clear the backlog of legal cases, he met Mr Justice Ephraim Georges. On learning that John Roberts came from Sierra Leone, Ephraim Georges asked him if he knew an old friend from his own law student days, one Farid Anthony. John Roberts told him that he knew me very well, and put Ephraim and me in touch with each other after a gap of around thirty years. I learnt that Ephraim's sister-in-law lives just a few miles from me, and when Ephraim's daughter came to England on holiday and stayed with her aunt, she came to visit me in Gillingham, Kent.

There can be no more Q.C.'s in Sierra Leone as the country is now a Republic and its judicial system is completely independent of England.

Probably the most famous Sierra Leonean lawyer in the years prior to Independence was Sir Samuel Lewis. He was born on 13 November 1843 and became one of the leading citizens of Sierra Leone. In January 1867 Samuel Lewis was admitted to the Middle Temple in London. He entered chambers in Paper Buildings at the Inner Temple the following year and was called to the Bar in 1871. (Many years later I, too, had a connection with Paper Buildings when I became a 'Door Tenant' whilst practising in Sierra Leone, and when I eventually came to England I joined 2 Paper Buildings. A previous building on that site was named after Sir Robert Sawyer, one time Attorney General to Charles II in the 17th Century.)

Sir Samuel Lewis's career at the Bar was long and illustrious and covered three decades. He successfully appeared for clients in the Gambia, Nigeria and the Gold Coast (now Ghana), as well as Sierra Leone. For many years he also held a seat on the Legislative Council.

In 1895 he became the first mayor of Freetown. He was re-elected in 1896 and again in 1899. He was the first African to be knighted, in the New Year Honours list of 1896. I have some bound copies of the Sierra Leone Weekly News dating from 1889 to 1892 where I read accounts of some of Sir Samuel Lewis's cases, and was impressed by his eloquence and expertise. I was interested to learn that the Court Hall where he appeared was in a three-storey stone building in Water Street in Freetown, with prisoners' cells on the ground floor. The first floor held cells for debtors and Europeans, and the Court Hall was on the top floor. This building was in use from 1816 until the First World War started in 1914.

Sir Samuel Lewis died in London in 1903 at the age of 59 and was buried in Acton cemetery.

I was called to the English Bar on 26 November 1963, which meant that I was now qualified to practise in a Court of Law. This phrase, being called or admitted 'to the bar', comes from students only being allowed to sit in the back or public area of the Court until they are qualified, when they are allowed to come forward to the rail or 'bar' to present their case before a judge as a fully fledged barrister.

I travelled to Sierra Leone on the new M.V. Apapa at the end of the following January and enrolled at the Sierra Leone Bar on 12 February 1964. At that time there was only one other Lebanese lawyer in Sierra Leone, Shakib N.K. Basma, LL.B., O.R. (Order of the Rokel), the first Lebanese lawyer in West Africa. He was called to the Bar at the Middle Temple on 17 July 1962 and enrolled at the Sierra Leone Bar on 16 October 1962. A few years later we were joined by another Lebanese lawyer, Edmond Michael from Bo (now deceased), and more have qualified since then. In fact, the son of the late Edmond Michael has qualified as a lawyer at the relatively new School of Law in Freetown.

During my secondary schooldays some friends and I adopted a Latin phrase as our motto: 'Fiat iustitia ruat caelum' – 'Let justice be done even though the heavens fall'. When I was studying law I was taught to go by the various rules of advocacy, amongst which were honesty, industry, courage, judgement and eloquence. I have tried to keep these in mind during the many years of my practice.

In England a lawyer will study to become either a barrister or a solicitor, taking the examinations set out by either the Bar Council for barristers, or the Law Society for Solicitors. A client would consult a solicitor, who would in turn, if necessary, instruct a Barrister to appear in court. In Sierra Leone the legal system is fused, and barristers could also practise as solicitors and solicitors could practise as barristers, hence we could all put "Barrister and Solicitor" on our letter-heads.

The hierarchy of the courts in Sierra Leone was as follows:-

The Tribal Court – this had a qualified magistrate helped by three assessors who knew the laws of that tribe to advise the magistrate. Lawyers were not allowed to appear and minor matters only were heard in this Court. There were also the Magistrate Court, Supreme Court, Court of Appeal and finally Privy Council in the United Kingdom. This continued after Independence until 1971.

On 19 April 1971 Sierra Leone became a Republican State and cases no longer went to Privy Council in UK. The Courts were rearranged and the hierarchy became: Magistrate Court, High Court, Court of Appeal, and Supreme Court. The Tribal Court still exists as the lowest court.

During the first few years of my practice, I had on occasion gone to The Gambia to act on behalf of clients, and was registered to practice in The Gambia on 27 January 1970. However, a Notice, P.N. No. 11 of 1976 relating to The Courts Act Cap. 36, was passed through parliament. This prevented lawyers who were not resident in the Gambia from appearing, other than in the Court of Appeal, without the express consent of the Chief Justice and the Bar Association. This Notice was made retrospective as from July 1970. At this time, 1976, the three judges who made up the Gambian Court of Appeal were two from Sierra Leone and one from Ghana. Much later I did my pupillage in London and obtained a certificate to practise as a barrister in England and Wales.

➡ In Sierra Leone it is frequently said (I hope in jest) that "Lawyers are liars". In fact Shakib Basma would always quote an epitaph which he found somewhere which goes as follows:

"Here lies a lawyer, laugh if you will,

He lied for his living, He lived while he lied.

When he could lie no longer he lay down and died."

Another legal epitaph which I found states:

"Here lieth one, believe it if you can

Who, though an attorney, was an honest man."

I also came across this quote from "The Beggar's Opera", which ran as follows:-

"A fox may steal your hens, sir,

If lawyer's hand is fee'd, sir,

He steals your whole estate."

I have, however, always considered myself to be an honest man.

Years later I came across this joke in England: Three lawyers were walking along the pavement one cold winter's day with their hands in their pockets. A passer-by commented, "How strange to see lawyers with their hands in their own pockets for a change!"

It is always necessary, of course, to choose one's words carefully when speaking in court as they are recorded. Later on I came across a passage in a book by Neil Boyd, "Father in a Fix", which said that spoken words cannot be unsaid, and compared them to toothpaste, which once out of the tube cannot be squeezed back in again. I agree with that in toto. For instance, a witness once said, when taking the oath, "I swear to tell the truth, the whole truth, and nothing of the truth, so help me God." The judge suddenly looked at the witness and made him take the oath again. The judge could not tell if it was a genuine mistake on the part of the witness. The lawyer hadn't realised what had happened until the judge pointed it out.

In another case, told to me by Shakib Basma, Counsel had exhausted all his verbal skills to impress the Trial Judge with his views, but the Judge was not impressed. Counsel asked, "My Lord, I trust you are following me?"

The Judge replied, "It is not following you, it is getting back home that worries me!"

➡ Sierra Leone has had a military government on occasion, the first time was in 1967. After a meeting, the Bar Association sent a resolution to the military government stating that it should hand over to a civilian government. The regime's response was to demand that the lawyers show cause why they should not all be locked up. The lawyers refused to show cause, and we were all summoned in a body to be detained. Joan and I had planned to play badminton with some friends in our garden early that evening, but instead I rushed home and told Joan what had happened. I packed a small suitcase in case of detention, and left with a colleague, Roland Harding, who came to pick me up. He later became a judge. I left my wife to explain to our guests why I was called away, and the badminton party did not take place as nobody felt like playing under the circumstances.

At the Ministry of the Interior we found a large gathering of lawyers assembled, and armed soldiers everywhere. One soldier pointed his rifle at me and I pushed it aside, saying, "Don't point your rifle at me!" We were standing on the steps waiting for what would happen next. By this time, the doctors had given notice that if the lawyers were detained, they would all come out on strike in sympathy. Eventually we were all ushered into a large room where we found the military Head of State. He didn't say very much but looked around the gathering. His eye fell on a face that looked foreign, and he asked the lawyer, "Where do you come from?" The lawyer, Roger Candappa, replied, "Ceylon." Without more ado, the Head of State ordered the lawyer, "Twenty four hours, back to Ceylon!" (Ceylon is now Sri Lanka.) Candappa had been in Sierra Leone for a number of years, both as magistrate and later as a practising barrister, and led chambers shared by two other lawyers, Emile Thompson Davis and Shakib Basma. He had the largest law library in Freetown. We were all eventually allowed to leave, and most of us walked across the road into the Paramount Hotel, where we headed for the bar to have a last drink with our friend Roger Candappa before he left the country the next day.

Within a short time the next part of the story had been invented and passed around. It was said that the Head of State, after ordering the deportation of my colleague, looked around the company and spotted another pale face, my own. The story went further that he said to me, "Where are you from?" and my reply was, "Sawpit". The Head of State reputedly ordered me, "Twenty four hours, back to Sawpit!" Another white lawyer stood beside me, Shakib Basma. I made my own addition to the story that he too was asked, "Where are you from?", and Shakib answered, "Kissy Street, Sir!" The Head of State then said, in my version, "Take him to Kissy Crase-Yard!" (the local mental hospital). The story about me continued that a few days later the Head of State was driving in Freetown and caught sight of me near the Law Courts, and sent two soldiers to bring me to him at his office. The punchline came when he demanded to know why I had not gone back to Sawpit. His Deputy, the joke went on, started laughing and explained to the Head of State that in fact I *had* gone back to Sawpit, it was the street I was born in just down the road from the Law Courts!

The funniest part of that story, for me, was when my son Michael came home one evening and said that he had just heard a female politician repeat the story of my 'deportation', adding that she knew it to be true because she was present at the time! That joke has been told so many times over, I suspect that by now many people believe that I was in fact "deported to Sawpit".

➤ Every year towards the end of September, the Assize Service would be held in Freetown at St George's Cathedral. This was attended by all the legal profession and their families. The Judges and barristers, wearing their wigs and gowns, would march in procession from the Law Courts in Siaka Stevens Street to the Cathedral in George Street.

Whilst the service was going on I noticed a man was bowing whenever the name of Jesus was mentioned. He was also bowing when the name of Satan was mentioned during the preaching. At the end of the service, when we had dispersed outside, I asked the man why he bowed when the name of Jesus was spoken and also bowed at the name of Satan. He replied, "Man can't tell!" I hurried away to join my colleagues. We all returned to the Law Courts, where the Chief Justice held a reception for lawyers and their wives and other invitees.

➤ One of my early cases, in fact in 1967, was to defend some crew members of a British merchant ship, before a magistrate, Mr Donald Macaulay (who later became a judge), at Magistrate Court No. 1. The ship was delayed in Freetown for the investigation and trial to be completed. They were accused of stealing some articles from one of the Arches of the ship, but were subsequently acquitted and discharged. The four lawyers who defended the merchant seamen were Ken During, Shakib N K Basma, Henry Joko Smart and myself.

➤ This reminds me of an incident which happened in the 1970's. I was doing a case in the Gambia. One night I had just arrived back at my hotel on my way back from a restaurant when I saw an argument going on between some British sailors, a Gambian taxi driver and a Gambian policeman. I walked over and called the policeman aside and asked him what the problem was. He told me that the taxi driver had taken the sailors from the hotel to a night-club, and later back to the hotel again. The dispute had arisen because the taxi driver wanted to charge for the time he spent waiting at the night-club, whilst the sailors only wanted to pay for the journeys between the hotel and the night club and not for the waiting time, as they had not asked him to wait. It was only by chance that they took the same taxi for the return journey.

It looked to me as if the argument would go on for some time, as apparently there was a misunderstanding between the sailors and the taxi driver, caused no doubt by the language difference, so I asked the policeman how much money was involved. The amount he told me did not warrant the time being wasted by all concerned, so I went with the policeman and gave the driver the amount he was asking for. The driver was now satisfied and left quietly, and I went up to my room. The sailors wondered what had happened to make the driver leave so suddenly in the middle of an argument, as all the conversation between the policeman, the driver and myself had been carried on in Krio. A few minutes later there was a knock on my door, and when I went to answer I found the sailors outside. They explained that they were in port for a short while from H.M.S. Hermione and that the policeman had told them why the taxi driver had gone away. They wanted to buy me a drink in appreciation of my intervention, and insisted I went downstairs with them to the bar. We had a few drinks together, and before we broke up they invited me to visit the ship the next morning, which I was happy to do.

The next morning I went to the ship, and was greeted by the sailors who were watching out for me. They took me on a tour of the ship and we had another drink together in the mess. Before I left they gave me a pair of cufflinks which were five-sided and bore a crown on top and the ship's emblem of a tree with what I believe is a dove, and the name "H.M.S. Hermione" underneath, done in blue and gold.

Some years later, on 21st June 1983, I heard over my office radio that Chatham Dockyard in England had been closed down as a Naval Base and H.M.S. Hermione pulled out on that date and fired the last naval shot in farewell to the Dockyard. I looked down at my shirtcuff and found that by chance I was wearing the cufflinks given to me by the sailors of H.M.S. Hermione.

I wore those cufflinks with pride for many years until 1998 when I lost one of them. I had collapsed at Bromley South railway station in England and been taken to hospital. I was transferred on to a hospital in Wimbledon, and when my family were finally able to track down my clothes and briefcase that had been left behind at Bromley hospital, one of my cufflinks was found to be missing. I still keep the remaining one as a souvenir of my meeting with the sailors of H.M.S. Hermione in the Gambia so many years ago.

➤ The presiding judge was falling asleep in court whilst I was on my feet defending my client on a criminal charge after the prosecution had closed its case. Getting fed up with the judge falling asleep and waking up a few minutes later only to close his eyes again in the next few minutes, I devised a ruse during my pleading. I made as if I was talking but only went through

105

the motions without making a sound. The judge said to me, "I can't hear you Mr Anthony." I replied, "I have been speaking loud enough for even those at the back of this large court to hear, and I can't speak any louder." Prosecuting Counsel then realised what I was doing. The judge must have thought that he couldn't hear me because he kept dozing off, but he did not say so. All he said, which was my intention, was, "I am adjourning this case until tomorrow morning." Prosecuting Counsel said (with a wink), "That is the best thing under the circumstances." That was the only time this had happened to me!

➤ Shakib Basma liked his clients to think of him as being very busy with many important cases on hand. On this particular occasion, his clerk told him there was a smartly dressed gentleman waiting to see him. After keeping him waiting for a short while, Shakib picked up his telephone and then asked his clerk to show in the distinguished stranger. As the gentleman entered his office, Shakib was speaking into the telephone. Without stopping his 'conversation', Shakib gestured to his visitor to take a seat. After about ten minutes of talking into the telephone about "settling out of court for £50,000 ... that other case I have settled for £20,000 ... in the case of Bangura I was able to get him off against all the odds ...", Shakib brought his discussion to an end and put down the receiver. He turned to the new 'client' and apologised for being so long on the telephone but explained that he was very much in demand due to his constant success in court. Shakib then said to him, "And now, what can I do for you?" The so-called client said to Shakib, "There is nothing you can do for me. Your phone is out of order and I just came to repair it!"

Later I used this story as the basis for a sketch in a Christmas concert at the Freetown Aqua Sports Club.

➤ The court in Freetown was in session. Two men with a ladder came in and marched up to the bench (where the judge sits). One of them said to the judge "Excuse us, we have come to take the clock down and take it away for repairs as it is losing time." Whereupon, without waiting for an answer, they set their ladder, made of two long bamboo sticks with rope tied between them for the rungs, against the side wall of the court. One of them climbed up, removed the clock from the wall, climbed down again, and the two of them left the court. They were never seen again, nor was the clock. It turned out they were thieves who thought that to steal right from under the very nose of the court would give them extra credit among their own kind. And so it did in fact. They were not wrong!

Some years later this story was told to me again, but as having happened in the Gambia before the then Chief Justice, Sir Philip Bridges. It is funny how a story like that does the rounds! Did it happen in Freetown or the Gambia? It doesn't matter where, the story is told again and again.

➤ A lawyer was defending a Lebanese businessman in a Court in the Provinces. As usual, the first question he asked the client was for him to state his name and address. The Lebanese trader said, "You eat kebbe* and tabouleh** nar me house yesterday, you sleep nar me house yesterday night, and now you ask me me name en address?  Na the same as yesterday!  If na so you da forget quick I go get another lawyer."

➤ I was defending another Lebanese trader on a charge of reckless driving. He had hit the new bridge at Aberdeen in Freetown, causing slight damage. The trader lived some thirty miles from Freetown and needed to close his shop every time he had to appear in Court.  The case was adjourned several times for various reasons without even starting, and each time the trader came to Freetown, losing valuable business.  At long last his case was heard and he was found guilty and fined the sum of LE 2,000, whereupon the trader took out his wallet and placed some money in front of the Magistrate saying "Here is LE 10,000.  Every time I come to Court I get for close me shop and loss business.  Noh call me here egain.  Any tem I hit the bridge take LE 2,000 and noh call me here egain until the money finish!"  The Magistrate was speechless!

➤ I defended a client on a criminal case, and after some eloquent pleading I was able to get my client off.  A few days later I heard some information about my client which made me doubt his truthfulness.  I saw him shortly afterwards and asked him, "Did you really commit that crime or not?"  He replied, "I thought I did, until I heard you defend me.  Then I was convinced that I had not done it!"

➤ I was reading the local daily paper one day, sitting in court waiting for the judge to arrive.  I started laughing uncontrollably just as the judge made his entrance.  He asked me what was so funny, and I replied that my laughter was directed at what I had just read in the obituary column, and I told him what it was.  It read "In memory of ——— ——— who died on — —— - ——, at the age of 120 years.  He left a wife, five children, 16 grandchildren and 35 great grandchildren.  He fought in two World Wars...."  The part that had caused my amusement was the bit at the end which read "His sun went down whilst it was yet day"!  I wondered how old he would have to have been to reach the evening of his life.

➤ The man in the dock was found guilty, and the Judge sentenced him to six months in prison.  The man then said to the Judge, "I also sentence you to six months in your chair", and was led away by the officers of the Court. At the end of the day the Judge tried to rise from his chair, and to his surprise found he could not get up.  After several fruitless attempts he remembered the words of the man he had sentenced to six months in

---

\* A Lebanese dish made of ground meat and broken wheat mixed with spices and either fried or baked.

\*\* Tabouleh is a salad with all the ingredients chopped very finely and mixed with broken wheat, usually eaten with lettuce leaves.

prison. He sent for the man and said to him, "I have reconsidered my verdict and have relented. I release you from your prison sentence." The man replied, "Thank you, my Lord. I also release you from your chair." The man left the Court a free man, and the Judge found to his relief that he too could get up from his chair and leave the Court. I have not found out if this is a true story, but is it impossible?

The above story is a popular one in Sierra Leone and can be heard on various occasions with small variations but it is doubtful if it is true.

➡ On Friday, 13 June 1975, I went to the Law Courts to the chambers of the Chief Justice, C.O.E. Cole, and took the oaths for Commissioner for Oaths and for Notary Public. I received two certificates, which were framed and hung in my office. As a Commissioner for Oaths I could witness a document sworn by the maker to be used in Sierra Leone. As a Notary Public I could witness documents that were to be used abroad. I had a seal made in England for each of these appointments. That evening we had a small party at home for about twenty guests to celebrate my appointment.

➡ I was in Kambia District in the North on a case for a client. The lawyer opposing me spoke for about one-and-a-half hours and examined three witnesses. My cross-examination of them was very brief. In the end, I submitted on behalf of my client that he had no case to answer. The magistrate agreed with me and discharged my client. Just outside the court my client turned to me and said in Krio, which I translate here into English: "I paid you to talk plenty for me and you said only a few words, whilst the other lawyer was talking a lot." I said to him, "Did you pay me to talk a lot, or to get you off? I got you off, what more do you want?" The client had expected a lot of legal argument from me, and felt that he had not got his money's worth because I was able to get him off the charges against him with a simple submission of no case. He ignored the fact that I had travelled seventy miles each way to appear in court, and had to listen carefully to the other lawyer's case and the evidence offered by the other side, before making my submission.

This attitude, however, is not restricted to Sierra Leone only. Many years later I made an application in an immigration matter in England, and got a successful conclusion much quicker than the client had expected. I called the client to my office and passed on the good news. Although pleased with the result, the client asked me whether, since the matter was over so soon, I could refund some of the fee!

It would seem that some clients are only impressed by the volume of words, and not by the knowledge and skill that can bring about the desired result by the quickest available method.

➡ A Lebanese man in Freetown had a small altercation with the police about parking his car in a prohibited area. The police told him he should move his car. The car was not obstructing traffic so the man saw no reason why he should move it. He said to the policemen, "If the President himself told me to move the car I would not do it." The Lebanese man was charged to court, and he came to see me in my chambers to ask me to act for him. I agreed to do this, on the condition that he would take my advice and do what I said. When the case came up in court and the charge was read, I advised my client to plead guilty. The court was packed with journalists hoping to see the Lebanese man humiliated for daring to say he would not obey even the President. As my client had pleaded guilty to a traffic offence, the prosecution did not bother to address the court. The magistrate fined my client a small sum and the case was over. It took less than ten minutes. My client went home relieved, but the journalists who had waited all morning for the case to come up, left disappointed, as they had hoped to be able to report a story involving the defiant use of the name of the President.

➤ This year, 1978, a good friend of mine, Manilius Garber, was elected Chairman of the African Bar Association. The Law Conference had been held, with great success, in Freetown, but unfortunately I was unable to attend as I was on holiday with my family in England.

➤ In September 1978 a new legal appointment came into effect in Sierra Leone. Nasiru D. Tejan-Cole took the oath of office on 25 September 1978 to become the first ever Director of Public Prosecutions (D.P.P.) in Sierra Leone, nearly sixteen years after being called to the English bar on 27 November 1962. This post made Tejan-Cole directly responsible for the prosecution of criminal cases in court and for the appointment of lawyers from the prosecution office to try those cases. Nasiru D. Tejan-Cole was enrolled at the Bar in Sierra Leone on 21 November 1964.

That same month, September 1978, brought the sad news of the death of a colleague of mine, Alexander B. Cotay. He was older than I was by twenty years, but we were good friends. He was the editor of the first newspaper in the Protectorate, The Observer, published in Bo from 1949 for six years. Cotay was also the first Sierra Leonean High Commissioner for Sierra Leone and the Gambia in London in 1959 for one year. He was called to the Bar in England in 1964 and was enrolled at the Sierra Leone Bar on 10 April 1965. He held a degree in journalism, and for two years he was the editor of "Debates in Parliament". Cotay was appointed police magistrate in 1967, moved on to become senior police magistrate, and at the time of his death was principal police magistrate, a post he held for seven years.

These two Sierra Leoneans deserve to be remembered for their places in the history of Sierra Leone.

Another prominent family in the legal history of Sierra Leone is that of Fashole Luke. Justice Sir Emile Fashole Luke was a Justice of the Supreme Court in the 1960's, and he was Speaker of the House of Representatives from 1968 to 1973. He died on 5th January 1980 at the age of 84. His son

Desmond Edgar Fashole Luke was born in Freetown in 1935. He attended St Edward's Primary School and Prince of Wales Secondary School in Freetown. He later studied in England and got a Master of Arts degree at Oxford University, as well as becoming an Oxford Blue. He also gained a Bachelor of Arts Honours degree from Cambridge University in 1959. He was called to the Bar in 1962, I believe, and set up private practice in Freetown. He entered politics in the 1970's and was appointed Minister of External Affairs and later Minister of Health. Desmond has served as Chief Justice of Sierra Leone during the presidency of Ahmed Tejan Kabbah. His elder brother, Egerton Fashole Luke, is a well-known doctor in Freetown. Their cousin, Eben Livesey Luke, obtained an Honours degree in Law in England and was called to the Bar in June 1956. He set up private practice in Freetown and became President of the Bar Association. He later became a judge and was appointed substantive Chief Justice towards the end of 1979. He was awarded the O.R.S.L. in 1978. As brilliant a family as anyone could wish for!

➤ One day in Freetown I defended a woman who was charged with stealing a small outboard engine. It was a Preliminary Investigation, which means that, above a certain amount, the magistrate can, if he or she finds that the investigations carried enough evidence, commit the case to the High Court for a full hearing.

At the end of the Preliminary Investigation I submitted to the magistrate as follows:

"Your Worship, take a look at this feeble woman. She is frail and cannot be said to be strong enough to have lifted this outboard engine and climb over a high wall while carrying it, as is the prosecution's case."

The magistrate looked at the woman and agreed with my submission. He thereupon said he found no case for her to answer and dismissed the case. My client then asked me if she was free to go and could she take the engine with her. I said yes she was free to go and that as the case had not been proved against her it followed that she had not stolen the engine and could take it with her. To the surprise of the court, and myself, the woman walked up to the exhibit, picked up the engine, put it on her right shoulder, and walked casually out of the court without any sign of strain. Both the magistrate and myself were bereft of words!

➤ In November 1980 I went to London from the Gambia for a case which was due to be heard at the Privy Council. I was met at Victoria Station by an English friend, who drove me to the Cumberland Hotel in Oxford Street, where my client had booked a room for me. The following day I went to the Privy Council and was introduced to a solicitor whom I instructed on behalf of my client, and handed all the paperwork to him and briefed him on the details of the case. The Deputy Registrar of the Judicial Committee of the Privy Council then took me upstairs to see the layout of the Privy Council Court, a court I had never been to before. The purpose of my trip to England being completed, I reported to my client in the Gambia by telephone, and then had a few days to spend doing shopping before returning to the Gambia.

I was due to return on the following Thursday. I booked in my luggage at Victoria Station before taking the train to Gatwick, as we could in those days. I paid quite a large sum in excess baggage, having done some early Christmas shopping. At 2.00 pm I was at Gatwick waiting for take-off. After a long delay the passengers were informed at 10.00 pm that our pilot had been involved in a road accident on the way to the airport. Their efforts to find a standby pilot had been unsuccessful, and so we were all taken to the Hickmet Hotel nearby for the night. We had free dinner and drinks and hotel room for the night and finally left Gatwick on Friday at 11.00 am.

By evening I was in Gambia and having dinner with my client at the Palm Grove Hotel where I was due to stay overnight. I was due to fly home to Freetown on Saturday, but the plane did not turn up. I spent the day visiting my sister and her family at Barra Point. The next morning, Sunday, I left the hotel at 4.00 am to go to Yundum Airport at Banjul. I travelled first class to Freetown, after paying further excess baggage in Dalasis, and got home at 10.30 am the same morning, it being only a one hour flight from Gambia to Sierra Leone.

➠ On 30 July 1981 a coup d'etat took place in Banjul, Gambia. The President, Sir Dawda Jawara, leader of the Peoples Progressive Party, was visiting England at the time to attend the wedding of Prince Charles and Lady Diana Spencer. Sir Dawda announced that the rebels were holding only the airport and the radio station, and that he was returning to Gambia to put down the rebellion. Sir Dawda flew to Senegal, which surrounds the Gambia except for its coastal area, and Senegalese troops entered the Gambia. By 11.00 am it was announced that only the radio station was held by the rebels. The leader was one Kukoi Samba Sanyang, who carried out the coup with the aid of the paramilitary Gambian Field Force, which consisted of only 400 to 450 men. Gambia had no other army and no airforce, but had a police force, some of whom supported the Paramilitaries. Sanyang formed the short-lived National Revolution Council with a committee of twelve men. When the rebellion was put down Sanyang was found to have escaped, but many of the paramilitary rebels were caught, along with some civilians.

Later that year I was asked to go to the Gambia, with some other barristers and judges from Sierra Leone, Ghana, Nigeria and England, to prosecute the coup-makers in the treason trials. Mr Justice Marcus Cole, a judge from Sierra Leone, was appointed as judge. Sierra Leonean barristers included Berthan Macaulay, QC, at that time practising in chambers in England, Albert Metzger, Solomon Berewa (formerly Attorney General and Minister of Justice, now Vice President of Sierra Leone), D. Robbin-Coker,

Ebun Thomas, and George Gelaga King who was appointed as a special judge. From England came Desmond de Silva, (now QC and Head of Chambers at 2 Paper Buildings) and John Causer. Jyeke Dako (a former Director of Public Prosecutions in Ghana) and Nathaniel Mills came from Ghana.

Our hotel and other bills were paid by the Gambian Government and we were each provided with a chauffeur-driven car. I was booked in to the Atlantic Hotel in Banjul. Our first task was to go through the case papers of the various accused persons to determine the various charges. These ranged from treason to far less charges for civilians who had simply taken the opportunity offered by the unsettled situation to indulge in looting.

At first I appeared in the Law Courts building in Banjul, an old Colonial style construction with wooden floors and wooden louvered windows. During this time the Chief Justice was Sir Philip Bridges, an Englishman, before whom I had appeared in another case the previous year. Sir Philip did not preside over any of the treason trials, as far as I am aware.

Outside of my working hours, the stories I was told were varied, and I can only tell a few here.

The rebels were able to arm themselves very well. The government had a very strongly built armoury with thick concrete walls and a strong iron door with a large padlock. The rebels shot the padlock open. Probably the government had no inkling that a coup would take place.

The civilians who joined the coup-makers were issued with guns and some of them had never fired or even handled a gun before. One of these, a young man, shot himself in the foot trying to find out how his gun worked. Another is said to have used the muzzle of his gun to scratch his head while his finger was on the trigger, and blew his brains out.

Another story I was told concerned the British SAS (Special Air Service). The rebels were holding captive the wife of the President and her baby. A message had been got to the President's wife that she must persuade the rebels to allow her to attend the hospital with her child because the child was in need of medical attention. A rebel guard accompanied her inside the hospital where a small group of SAS soldiers were waiting. An SAS soldier took the baby from the mother and pushed the child towards the armed rebel, who, taken off guard, dropped his weapon to catch hold of the child. The SAS soldiers were then able to arrest the rebel and return the President's wife and child to the safety of her family. The rebel was later charged with treason.

One evening at the Atlantic Hotel where I was staying, I was called over to a table where my fellow lawyer Ebun Thomas was sitting with an Englishman. I joined them for a drink, and was interested to learn that the Englishman was no other than Robin White of the BBC African Service, who had been invited by Ebun for dinner. Unfortunately I could only stay for half an hour as I had to join a friend and his wife for dinner at his home.

One thing that struck me was that electrical power failures occurred quite often while I was in Gambia. The Gambia Utilities Corporation, the GUC, supplied electricity. I noticed that during such failures a lot of candles were used, so I dubbed the Corporation 'Gambia Uses Candles'! Little did I know that Freetown would later become notorious for power cuts.

The Gambian government engaged a barrister friend of mine, Albert Metzger, as a special judge in the treason trials in the Gambia at the same time as I was engaged as a special prosecutor. All the foreign lawyers engaged on the treason trials were allowed first class tickets to go home every second weekend to see their families. In Freetown Albert and I were very friendly and on first name terms and would visit each other's chambers frequently. One weekend he and I found ourselves travelling home together on the same plane, so we sat together. During the flight I asked Albert if he knew where Sierra Leone airspace began. He said to me, tongue in cheek in a joking manner, "Remember in the Gambia I am a judge and should be addressed as 'My Lord'." I never said another word until I was sure we were over Sierra Leone waters, and then I said to him, "Albert, we are now over Sierra Leone waters and in Sierra Leone you are not a judge. Until we get back to the Gambia can I call you Albert?" We both burst out laughing.

A retired judge from Freetown, Mr Justice C.O.E. Cole, was appointed a special judge to preside over the court at Kannifing in Banjul. I appeared before him quite often in the treason trials. One morning in court I was prosecuting an accused on a charge of 'going armed in public' (the usual charge for those not directly connected with the coup but who carried guns). I found myself distracted by an unusual sight. A large green praying mantis had landed on the wig of the presiding judge whilst the defence lawyer was arguing his case. It was about three inches long with a triangular head and bulbous eyes on either side of the triangle, the point being its chin. It sat upright with it forelegs in a praying position, hence its name. I debated within myself how to draw this 'landing' to the attention of the judge. After waiting a minute or two to see if the mantis would leave the judge's wig voluntarily, and seeing that it had no intention of doing so, I stood up to address the judge on that point. As if it knew what I was going to say, the praying mantis flew up and left the court by way of the window! I sat down and the case continued. The judge asked me later why I had stood up to speak and then changed my mind so suddenly. He was amused when I told him why, because that was the first he had known that his wig had attracted a praying mantis and had been a landing ground.

I worked as Prosecuting Counsel in Banjul for a contract of three months (including the month of December but I went home for Christmas and New Year). During this time I had a meeting with the President and presented him with a copy of my book 'Sawpit Boy' – a combination of autobiography and history of Sierra Leone. In February I was asked to renew my contract with the government by the then Solicitor General, Mr Wallace Grant (who had bought a copy of 'Sawpit Boy' and had brought his young children to visit me to meet 'a live author')!

Although I was asked to do a further three months, I agreed to do only one month.

This time I stayed at the Palm Beach Hotel which was sited on the beach a few miles outside Banjul. During this time I had a driver during the day, but the car was left with me for my own use during the evening. My wife joined me for the last week of my contract.

Sir Dawda Jawara decided to protect himself and his country from further civilian-led coup attempts by disbanding the Gambian Field Force and setting up the Gambian National Army. Possibly Senegal encouraged this as it did not want to have to take responsibility for the security of the Gambian government. This proved to be his downfall, however, as a coup carried out by the army some years later was successful and Sir Dawda was deposed. This coup was led by Captain Yaya Jammeh, who has ruled the country since then.

➡ I was defending two Afro-Lebanese brothers in the provinces in a civil matter, and Shakib Basma was on the other side, against me. Shakib, as usual, was making his point with gusto, and raising objections to almost everything I said in court. My clients did not like what they felt was Shakib's fighting manner to me personally, and during a break in the proceedings they said to me, "When Mr Basma leaves the court shall we beat him up to teach him a lesson?" I had hard work explaining to them that Mr Basma was only doing the best he could for his clients, and that he and I were good friends outside the courtroom. Luckily my clients were both acquitted, which helped to cool down their aggressiveness.

Shakib and I appeared on opposite sides several times, often in the Provinces. I had a client whose case came up before the Magistrate in Kambia, and after the day's hearing was over Shakib and I met up to have a meal and a drink together at a local restaurant. The next morning at court my client met me with angry words. "Why did I see you last evening so friendly with Mr Basma when he is acting for the people who are against me. I thought you were on my side!" he said. So once again I had to explain ....

➡ The following story started when I went to defend a Lebanese in Kychom in Samu Chiefdom in the Northern Province. The name Kychom means "a place to rest".

My client had been charged with having two drums of petrol in his store, which at that time was illegal except for those who traded in petrol. The drums were seized and were to be used as evidence in court. When the case came up the prosecution asked the magistrate for permission to open the drums to prove that the contents were petrol. The magistrate approved and the drums were opened. The prosecution was surprised not to be met with unmistakable petrol fumes; on the contrary, there was no smell at all. The contents were tested, and tasted, and found to be fresh water and not petrol! There was nothing more for me to do but to request that the magistrate dismiss the charge against my client, which he had no alternative but to do. But the excitement was not over for the day.

I left Kychom by car with my client and his two Lebanese friends, who happened to be my friends as well. We were on our way to the home of my client, where I had left my car that morning, when we saw a number of young men blocking the road. We were forced to stop, and a Freetown newspaper reported the next part of the story.

The Unity Independent newspaper of the next day, 1st July 1968 carried a headline in bold letters on the front page, "LAWYER IN KYCHOM ATTACK." It went on to tell the story of when I was travelling by car with three other Lebanese, clients of mine, and we were attacked by a gang of about twenty unknown youths. Luckily for me the gang concentrated on the three businessmen and took little notice of me, so I was able to escape with the driver of the car back to Kychom and raise the alarm. Kychom is a town a few miles from Kambia, capital of Kambia District in the Northern Province of Sierra Leone. The three men were beaten up and robbed and held prisoner for a few hours. On their release they went to Kambia Government Hospital were they were treated and later returned to their homes. In the meantime I had travelled by "pampam" (a small launch with an awning) to Freetown with the wife of one of the three victims. By the time we had arrived in Freetown and the authorities had been notified, it was too late and the culprits had all disappeared.

➡ In the Magistrates Court in Freetown, after a submission by the defence lawyer which was upheld, the magistrate addressed the defendant in English, as was usual as English was the language of the court and indeed the official language of Sierra Leone. The defendant was not fluent in English, and spoke mainly Krio (a local form of broken English spoken all over Sierra Leone), and so an interpreter was needed to explain the magistrate's remarks to him. The magistrate said: "In my opinion I agree with the defence lawyer that you have been made a scapegoat in this case," and waited for this to be interpreted in Krio. The interpreter, doing his best, said to the defendant, "The magistrate say that that goat way escape nar you yone", meaning "The goat that escaped belonged to you". The interpreter could not understand why the magistrate was so annoyed that he drove him out of court.

➡ Early one Saturday morning, after a rather rollicking night at the Tropicana Night Club, owned in those days by two Lebanese, the Isaac brothers, a lawyer friend of mine, Shakib Basma, had to appear in the magistrate's court on a minor issue for a client. Shakib duly armed himself with a bottle of Ammonia Sulphate to enable him to be awake and alert. Throughout the proceedings Shakib would take small sniffs from the bottle with the plastic cap only partially removed. His client was duly discharged on submission that the prosecution had not made out a case against his client. The prosecution officer suspected that the outcome of the proceedings was determined by the juju in the bottle, and appealed for a sniff to enhance his prowess. Counsel Basma duly obliged, but removed the cap wholly from the bottle, and told the prosecutor to take a deep sniff, which the prosecutor did, thereby inhaling the full blast of the ammonia. The result, needless to say, was that the prosecutor was knocked off his feet. When the prosecutor had recovered a little, Shakib said to him, "The juju na Syrian man juju, e noh fit Sa Lone man!" (The 'medicine' is for Lebanese only, it is not suitable for Sierra Leoneans).

➳ In those days when I was practising, I used to smoke very large cigars. In fact I couldn't smoke a cigarette because it is so small it would fall out of my mouth! It was one of the Isaac brothers, Salim, who said to me that my cigars were like 'mattah pencil', meaning that they were so large they looked like pestles. (In Sierra Leone the mortars stand about two feet high and are used for breaking up rice and preparing other foodstuffs, and the pestle used is about five feet long!) I laughed out loud at his witticism. Salim and his late brother Romanus were my good friends and would drop in to my office in Gloucester Street from time to time.

➳ I had just left the robing room one day after hanging my wig and gown in my locker, and was walking along towards the steps leading down to the street when I met Shakib, who was laughing as he walked past me. I said to him, "You must have won your case or heard something funny in court." He told me that he had overheard part of a conversation between two Sierra Leonean lawyers. One was tall and the other was short, and they had just appeared in court against each other. Shakib recounted that the tall counsel had said to the other, "Listen, I can put you in my small pocket." The short lawyer answered, "If you put me in your small pocket, there will be more sense in that pocket than in the whole of your head!" The conversation sounded so funny it made me laugh too as I made my way to my car.

I smiled again as I caught sight of the notice on the opposite side of the street to the Law Courts. It should have read "No Hooting", but during the trials of those accused of an attempted coup, some clever fellow had added an 'S' before the "Hooting".

➳ Shakib was defending a Lebanese client in the Magistrates Court in Freetown. It was the month of Ramadan, the month of fasting for Muslims. Devout Muslims will obey the law of fasting during the hours of daylight to the extent that they will not drink water or even swallow their own saliva. Shakib's client was Muslim, and was fasting. During the hearing of his case in Court, he was becoming uncomfortable as he could find nowhere to spit out the saliva that was filling his mouth. At length he decided the only thing to do was to leave the court quickly, spit, and come back again. The

Magistrate saw him leave hurriedly, and ordered the police to go after him and bring him back. The police did as the magistrate said, and the poor Lebanese man found himself surrounded by policemen, who took him back to court. Shakib had to explain to the magistrate that his client was not trying to run away but as it was Ramadan, his client had a mouthful of saliva that he had had to dispose of, and he had intended to return to the court immediately even without the police escort!

➠ A businessman was appearing before a magistrate on a charge of driving a car recklessly. At the end of the case the magistrate said, "I find you guilty as charged and fine you £50.00." The businessman, whose education was limited, said to the magistrate, "£50.00 noh too much? Less me small bit!" (Isn't £50.00 too much? Go down a little bit.") The magistrate answered in Krio, "You tink say dis nah fish markit?" (Do you think this is a fish market?) To which the businessman replied, "Las week you go nar me shop en when ah charge you £20.00 you ask me for less en ah less you. Wen ah ask you for less me you noh gree." (Last week you went to my shop and when I charged you £20.00 you asked me to reduce it and I did. When I ask you to reduce, you will not agree.)

➠ Can a driving licence be valid for forty one years? It was reported in one of the Sierra Leone newspapers nearly twenty five years ago that a man driving a vehicle with a foreign licence plate was involved in an accident with another car. The police were involved and as the man could not produce a local driving licence, he was charged. In the magistrates court the driver produced a United Kingdom driving licence valid until 31 December 2018. The court was flabbergasted. The man explained that his licence was issued at a cost of £5.00 sterling when he was doing a course in England, and was valid until he reached the age of 65. The British High Commission confirmed this story and the man was acquitted!

➠ In December 1976, Albert Metzger, Dr Abdulai Conteh*, (who were President and Secretary respectively of the Sierra Leone Bar Association), and I went to Monrovia, Liberia, to represent the Sierra Leone Bar Association at the Second Judicial Conference of Liberia. Although a bridge had been built across the Mano River between Sierra Leone and Liberia and was opened earlier that year, we all preferred to fly directly to Monrovia as it was much quicker. We stayed at the Ducor Intercontinental Hotel. The Chief Justice Mr C.O.E. Cole was also there representing the Bench. There were Judges and lawyers from all over West Africa, and a representative from the Bar of the United States of America. Liberia was founded in 1822 when the first group of free black people arrived there from the United States. The capital was named Monrovia in honour of the fifth President of the United States of America, Mr James Monroe. The

---

* Dr Abdulai Conteh is at the time of writing Chief Justice of Belize.

motto on the emblem for the Republic of Liberia is "The Love of Liberty Brought Us Here".

The theme of the Conference was "The Role of the Judiciary in a Developing Country". The opening ceremonies began on Monday morning when we assembled at the Centennial Memorial Building. All the delegates, wearing their robes, then marched in procession to the E.J. Roye Memorial building, which was the Headquarters of the ruling party in Liberia at that time, the True Whig Party. Prayers were said and the Chairman, Counsellor Toye C. Barnard, read the opening address. After a break for lunch, the first session commenced at the Hall of Justice of the Supreme Court of Liberia. The motto of the Liberian Supreme Court is "Let Justice be Done to All Men". Later on we attended a cocktail party on the sixth floor of the Temple of Justice given by the Chief Justice of Liberia, His Honour James A.A. Pierre.

The conference continued the next day, Tuesday. During the break we had lunch at the home of one of the Liberian Counsellors. In the evening we were all invited to dine with the President of Liberia, William R. Tolbert, at the Executive Mansion. We ate in a large elegant room with a mirrored ceiling, which gave me a rather odd feeling to see all the plates of food upside down! I sat between two Liberian Judges, and the meal was very good, a mixture of African and European dishes. The food was served with wine followed by liqueurs and cigars.

The following day, during the break between sessions, we were invited for lunch to the home of Arthur Hickson, Senior Vice President of the Bank of Liberia for Development and Industry. I had known Arthur many years before when we were boys and had played together in Freetown. It was an unexpected pleasure to meet with him again after such a long time! The afternoon session of the conference was chaired by Mr Justice C.O.E. Cole of Sierra Leone. The main paper was about the independence of the Judiciary, and when I was called upon to comment my speech included the fact that, "It was mainly a moral issue. If as lawyers we cannot be swayed then it was a good basis for future judges; a strong bar makes a strong judiciary." This was very well received by the audience, and I got a big round of applause! One big loss was that Albert Metzger had to return to Freetown as he was to appear in Court in a murder trial. The day was rounded off with a cocktail party at the residence of the Ambassador of the Ivory Coast, Mr J. Georges Anoma.

On the final day I missed part of the closing session because I had to catch the plane back to Freetown. My only expenses for the trip were my return ticket and spending money, as the lawyers in Monrovia insisted on paying my hotel bill. I left Monrovia by car to travel the thirty miles to Robertsfield Airport. I was accompanied all the way by an escort – a liaison officer – and the car had flashing lights to get us through the heavy traffic with no hold-ups. On the plane to Freetown I met a close friend,

Rudolf Dworzak, and others who were returning to Freetown after playing for the Sierra Leone cricket team in a tournament in Nigeria. We talked about cricket, and he told me that Nigeria came first, we came second, Ghana was third and Gambia fourth. It was a pleasant journey to finish off what had been a very enjoyable and satisfactory conference in Monrovia.

➤ When we transferred to England I joined chambers in the Inner Temple to update myself to be able to practise as a barrister in England and Wales. My son John said he would come to visit me when he finished work so I gave him the address. He decided he would not write it down but would remember it by word association, as being connected with book. He arrived at the Inner Temple in due course and asked the Usher for directions to "2 Chapter House". The Usher shook his head and said there was no such place. John tried again, with "2 Page Buildings?" The Usher again shook his head, so John explained his word association memory aid. The Usher started reeling off all the buildings in the Inner Temple. When he got to "Paper Buildings" John said, "That's it. That's what I'm looking for!" The Usher pointed out to John which way he should go, but as a parting comment told him, "Next time, please write the address down!"

➤ When travelling around England I would, if the opportunity offered, have a look at the local Law Courts. I had this chance in Oxford, and was interested to see lots of Coats of Arms on the walls, each with the date and name of the High Sheriff for that year. The plaques were colourful and varied, but to my surprise one particular coat of arms appeared at least eight times, although the names were different. This showed crossed swords, one of them broken at the tip, on a pale blue background. Then I saw a notice that explained it, which read as follows:

"Above are The Coats of Arms of those High Sheriffs of Oxfordshire who are entitled to bear Arms. The other High Sheriffs are commemorated by the blue plaques displaying the Crossed Sword of Justice and the Blunted Sword of Mercy, the 'Curtana'. The Curtana is also known as 'King Edward the Confessor's Sword'."

# Chapter 8

# Some Krio Customs, Traditions and Proverbs

A visitor to Freetown might be surprised at the number of English-sounding names he encounters among the Krio population. There are several reasons for this. In the early nineteenth century apprentices would often take the name of their European master. Another reason is that those who were baptised might take the name of the Missionary who baptised them. A third way that this came about emanated from a promise by the Church Missionary Society to name a child at the institution after anyone who donated £5.00 or more for the upkeep of that child. Thus the names of Williams, Nicol, Richards, Pratt, Crowther etc became quite common in the former colony.

➤ Freetown has many pleasant and interesting customs and traditions. Any special occasion requires a lot of food and drink to satisfy the friends and relations gathered together to help a family celebrate. I will give you a brief summary of some of the customs I know of.

The special cooking in memory of the dead is known as "Awujoh", a word of Yoruba origin, or "cook". This is done forty days after the death, the day the spirit of the deceased is said to leave earth. It is done again one year after, and then, if the relatives can afford it and wish to honour their dead relative it is done again on the 10th year anniversary and major anniversaries. Light snacks are served first, such as abohboh, made of blackeyed beans, akara, fried plantains and sweet potatoes, rice pap, and olelleh, made of peeled and ground blackeyed beans mixed with palm oil and steamed. Later more food is served, like foofoo (made from cassava) with bitter leaf sauce and crane-crane sauce, jollof rice, fried chicken, rice bread, cake and ginger beer.

A small portion of food is cooked separately without salt for the ancestors. At some point a small hole is dug in the compound near the house and an elderly relative will kneel beside the hole and pray to the spirits of the dead. A small amount of water or alcohol is first poured into the hole. This libation, whatever it may be, is referred to as "pouring cold water" for the dead, who are presumed to be thirsty. Then a portion of the special food is put into the hole and covered up. Some friends and relatives will have gathered to watch this ritual, and they will then try in fun to take a morsel from the leftover food for the ancestors, as this is supposed to bring good luck.

Yuba (vultures) are believed by some to be the reincarnation of the ancestors of the Krio families. It is forbidden to shoot a vulture in Sierra Leone (possibly because vultures are scavengers and clean the town from the bodies of animals that have been run over and left by the roadside). If there is an Awujoh the vultures are bound to turn up, attracted by the preparation, usually out of doors, of the meat that is going to be cooked. They will quickly dispose of the entrails and any discarded parts. If an Awujoh takes place and no vultures appear it is considered bad luck. The late Ebenezer Calendar wrote a song about the vultures – "Yuba no get paper but e know when e forty days", meaning that the vulture has no education to read a calendar but will always turn up for the Forty Day ceremony or 'cook'.

After the Awujoh people are offered small parcels of food to take home, things like bread, drinks, akara, etc. All leftover food is given away at the end of the day as nothing should be kept for the next day – charity being part of the ceremony.

The Naming ceremony or "Pull nar door", also called 'Komojade', a Yoruba word meaning 'bringing out the child', is another important ceremony. A female child is brought out when it is seven days old, and a male child is brought out on the ninth day. If there are twin babies they are brought out on the eighth day. This, of course, would refer to a child being born at home to a Krio family. The ceremony would be held on the day the child was brought out of its mother's bedroom for the first time and introduced to the outside world. The mother would usually leave her room for the first time on the same day. It was usual for a woman to keep to her bed for a week or more after childbirth (even in England), unlike the present day. The infant was taken around the house by an older woman relative and told, "This is the kitchen, this is the parlour" etc., then out into the street and shown the immediate neighbourhood. The woman then brought the baby back to its home and told it that there was no place like home and that wherever it went in life it could always return home.

Friends and relatives would be invited, and a priest would say prayers, and one of the family would annouce the child's names. Food was then brought out, consisting of rice bread, beans and akara, and other light refreshment. It was traditional to also set out small saucers containing salt, pepper, water and sugar. Muslims who can afford it slaughter a lamb at the same time the child's name is announced to the gathering.

In some areas when twins are born they are taken from house to house around the village and someone will carry a 'fannah' (a kind of large flat, round, woven tray used to winnow rice), in which people will put gifts of money to help the family with the extra expense of having two babies at the same time.

An engagement or 'Put-stop' (literally putting a stop to a girl marrying any other suitor) has some charming customs. The young man will come to the home of his intended bride accompanied by some of his male relatives. The relatives knock on the door. The parents of the bride then ask what they have come for. The reply is, "We saw a rose in your garden and have come to ask permission to pluck that rose". One of the bride-to-be's parents then asks, "If we give you the rose will you cherish it?" The Groom's relations reply positively. The bride-to-be is kept hidden, while different girls are brought forward by the parents of the chosen girl, with the question, "Is this the rose?" The suitor rejects them all. Then the girl he wants to marry is brought out last. The suitor's relatives clap and dance, crying "This is the rose" and "Hibbi, Hibbi, Hooray." Then the visitors are all invited into the house and prayers are said, then food and drinks are served.

As plans for the wedding commence, the mothers of the bride and groom decide what material they will choose to wear on the day of the wedding. Samples of this material are then sent round to all their female relatives and friends, so that they may buy the same material, usually from a Lebanese shop. The Lebanese traders were always happy when material from their shop was chosen for the 'ashoebi', as they were certain to sell a large amount. The ladies were usually free to choose their own styles, but the material had to be the same.

About a week before the Krio wedding the two families will get together. The groom's family will bring gifts with them, usually two calabashes containing among other things, peppers and a needle, symbolising the hope that the future bride will be a good cook and housewife. Food such as abobboh, beans akara, fried plantain etc, would be served, and also four red and four white kola nuts would be brought out, then broken in halves and passed round.

The bride is known as Yawo, while mother of the bride is known as Yawo Mammy. The groom is Okoh and his mother is Okoh Mammy. Marriages were sometimes arranged by the parents of the couple concerned, and sometimes a bride-price was paid by the parents of the groom to the bride's parents. This amount could be demanded back if the marriage failed due to the fault of the wife.

My wife and I attended a Krio wedding a few years ago and Joan made herself a dress from the 'ashoebi' material to wear at the party at the home of the bride's family. A few months later we were invited to a cocktail party given by some European friends and Joan thought she would wear that dress again as no one at the party would recognise it. Halfway through the evening a voice behind Joan said, "I know where that dress came from!" An Englishman who had been at the wedding and had left Sierra Leone shortly after to return to work in England, had come back to Freetown on a short visit and by chance turned up at the same party!

➡ Courtesy is very important in Sierra Leone. When approaching a stranger with any query, for example, to ask directions, it is incumbent on you to greet the stranger with 'Good morning' or the appropriate phrase for the time of day, before getting to the point of the conversation. This applies even with someone you know very well. It is always expected that you find time to greet the other person and enquire about his health before getting to the gist of the matter.

A custom that I have only come across in Sierra Leone is that it is bad manners to use your left hand when giving or receiving. If a Sierra Leonean for some reason has to offer or receive something with his left hand, he will say, "Excuse my left". My wife found it very strange when a lady apologised for handing her something with her left hand, as in England, and in the whole of Europe, the left hand is not considered as being inferior to the right. From then on Joan tried to remember to comply with the local custom so as not to offend unintentionally.

It is possible to insult someone without actually using words. If, during an exchange of words, one party were to draw his breath through his teeth with a hissing sound, i.e. "suck teet", the other would take this as an insult.

One custom of speech in Sierra Leone is to say to a man, "Blow you nose," if he had inadvertently left his fly unzipped. A very bad insult usually used when someone asks a personal question you do not want to answer, is to put one finger on your nose and say, "Ask me nose!" Perhaps this is the equivalent of the English phrase, "Mind your own business"?

If someone tells you he is going to "do Mammy Coker", he means that he is going to do a piece of work privately during working hours to earn a bit of extra money without his boss knowing. It also applies to small jobs taken on outside his normal working hours.

When something particularly happy or fortunate happens to someone, even perhaps in the middle of the year, his friends may wish him "Happy New Year", irrespective of the date, because it is seen as the beginning of a time of change for the better.

An older person is never called by his first name. He is either 'Mr ......' to be formal or is called 'Uncle' if he is a family friend, as a sign of respect for his age. This applies also to women who are called 'Mrs ......' or 'Auntie'.

➤ Francis Bacon said, "The genius, wit and spirit of a nation are discovered in its proverbs". The Krio language lends itself easily to proverbs, and they are rich and varied. For instance, if one Krio makes a promise to another, he is reminded of the proverb that 'promise nar debt', meaning that a promise is like a debt that has to be honoured. Another proverb commonly heard especially where there is litigation between two people is, "Law nar lek biskit, oosai yu noh day expect am, nah day e kin broke." Translated into English this means, "Law is like a biscuit, where you do not expect it is where it will break," or it is not possible to tell the outcome of a case until it is decided. Another proverb says, "Wata way nar yu yone noh go run pass yu" meaning literally, "Water which is yours will not run past you" or, something that is meant for you will come to you. "Hab ope pan dieman soos" or as the Englishman says, "Waiting for dead men's shoes", means that you are likely to wait a long time for a person to die for you to take his place or possessions.

A more obvious one is "Born me I feber you," meaning "You are my parent and I resemble you". "Orange tik nobar bon lem" translates to "An orange tree will never bear a lime", possibly "Like breeds like" is a close English equivalent. "Kapu sens noh kapu book," means common sense gained from experience is more important than knowledge gained from books. "Ihe same rain way fodom pan bitters way make e bitter, nar de same rain fodom pan sugar cane way make e sweet" (the rain that falls on the bitter leaf to make it bitter is the same rain that falls on sugar cane to make it sweet), can mean that a single event can have different effects on different people.

"Elephant head nohto pickin load", translates to "an elephant's head is too heavy for a child to carry", meaning that it takes a mature man to deal with an important task. A proverb which is alike in meaning is "One finger noh bah pick coconut", you cannot pick a coconut with one finger alone, you need to use your whole hand. Another version of this is "One finger noh bah pick los (head lice!), meaning that several people working together can achieve more than one alone, and it can also mean that it takes two to quarrel. "Belful lek tiffman wef" means that the wife of a thief is always well fed.

"We two don wer wan foot trossis", translates into 'we are each wearing one leg of the trousers', and means that there is a quarrel between the two people concerned. "Teet and tongue sef can make plaba" (even teeth and tongue can quarrel) means that even close friends can quarrel sometimes. "Tell fren tru noh pwell fren" means that telling a friend the truth does not spoil the friendship.

Other proverbs commonly used in Sierra Leone are: "Nah trouble mek monkey eat pepper," meaning that a person has to bear his lot when he has no other option. "Nar rain make sheep en goat meet nar wan under-cellar" means that trouble can bring unlikely companions together. "Monkey work, babu eat", means that one person does the hard work and another reaps the benefit. Another saying with a similar meaning is "Hastings drink, Waterloo drunk". "Babu lek for hallah den go gi am watchman wok", means that the baboon likes to shout so he is employed as a watchman, or, speaking derogatorily, a noisy person is suitable to be employed as a watchman.

"Cow way noh get tail nah God day dreb im fly", in English "A cow that has no tail will have the flies that bother it driven away by God", means that when nature fails, God will help. "Troki wan box but e an short", or in English, "the turtle wants to box but his arms are too short", can be likened to "The spirit is willing but the flesh is weak." "Ose tight so tay, fol go lay egg", translates to "No matter how small a house is, a hen will find a place to lay its egg". "Next world noh go tan so" means "Heaven or the afterlife will not be like this". This is said by someone who feels he has been taken advantage of and he can do nothing about it. If you ask someone to "Ge me haf" (give me half), you are not asking to be given half of what he has but only a small, unspecified, amount, leaving the owner to decide how generous he wants to be. A saying which does not need interpretation is, "Eat until you are tired, sleep until you are hungry." "Wey short man tote honey, all man go lick", means that when a short man carries a pan of honey on his head, everyone is able to reach it.

"If blen yai man say e go stone you nar becos e tinap pan stone", means literally that if a blind man threatens to throw a stone at you it is because he is standing on one. This suggests that a weak person may make a threat if he knows he has the means to carry it out. "All kondoh lay im belleh nar gron, yo noh no oose wan im belleh de hart am" (all lizards lay with their bellies on the ground, you cannot tell if one of them has stomach ache).

A proverb that will have meaning for almost everyone is "'If a bin know' nah im kin always lef las", or "'If only I had known' is always the last thing said".

One thing that is common to all children wherever they may be is that they do not listen to their elders. In Sierra Leone such children are described as 'tranga yase' meaning 'strong ears' or 'will not heed advice'. One can sometimes hear the children singing the following song:

"Me mama say mek ah noh commot,
Me papa say mek ah sidom nar ose
But wen me paddy cam we go Lumley Beach
Motor car go broke me wase.
Tranga yase noh good oh, tranga yase noh good oh"

Loosely translated the song says: my mother told me not to go out, my father said I should stay at home, but when my friend came we went to Lumley Beach, and I was hit by a motor car and suffered a broken bottom; not listening to advice is not good.

Another song frequently heard in Freetown went like this:

"King Jimmy* around the waterside,
Lovely fish, you get them everyday,
And if you want to get some bonga fish
You better take a walk to the waterside
King Jimmy bonga sweet - Foofoo noh day fityai okra soup."
Goderich get Funkia mina -
Lumley get Barakuta

---

* King Jimmy was a Temne Chief responsible for the burning of Granville Town in 1789, after giving the settlers three days warning to leave, in retaliation for the burning of his own town by sailors from a British ship. He died seven years later. The song refers to the part of the Freetown waterfront area named after him.

Murray Town get catfish
Congo Town get .........

The okra plant is related to hibiscus. It has a long stem with a yellow flower similar to the hibiscus flower. The okra grows directly from the stem and is a very popular vegetable in Sierra Leone. It is a green pod with small seeds inside and is either cooked whole, or sliced very finely to make 'draw soup'. It grows quite high but when it is bearing okra the weight of the okra makes the stem bend over. This led to the song which goes as follows: -

"Okra tink e langa pass im master
But wan day, wan day e mus butu before am,
Well nar day now, nar day now, nar day now,
Well nar day now, e sabi but e noh no."

Roughly translated this means that the okra plant thinks it is taller than its owner, but one day it will bend lower than the owner, the okra thinks it knows better than its owner (because it grows upright at first) but it does not.

A different song about okra goes as follows:-

"Okro soup en soke farinyah
Lili peppeh en lili sol
For match yesterday bonga."

This means 'Okra soup and soaked farina, with a little pepper and a little salt, will be as tasty as the bonga you had yesterday'. Bonga is a fish that has very many bones and is usually sold dried for use in palaver sauce, such as cassava leaves or potato leaves, etc.

One of the popular local songs was "Faiya, Faiya". People who only heard it and did not see the name of the song written down, usually think that the song says "Fire, Fire", as I did, until one day we invited Ebenezer Calendar, who wrote the song, to play for us at Lumley. He sang the song, accompanying himself on his guitar as usual, and then explained that the song was about a man who was in love with a married woman whose husband was called Faiya and who was on his way home. The song goes like this:-

Faiya, Faiya, Faiya, Faiya, Faiya day cam (twice)
I went to see my loving girl, my loving girl I love so well,
Faiya, Faiya, Faiya, Faiya, Faiya day cam.

Another popular song written and sung by Calendar was 'Welcome to Sierra Leone Double Decker Buses'. In 1951 double decker buses were introduced to Freetown for the first time by the Road Transport Department. The first driver of the double deckers was Mr Abdulai Bah, who then trained other drivers. These buses ran between Cline Town and, I think, Congo Cross. After the first consignment of six buses, no more double deckers were imported to Sierra Leone.

126

Calendar was one of the very popular figures in Sierra Leone and was often called upon to play and sing at Krio weddings. In fact he worked for a time in his younger days as a carpenter for Alimamy Bungie the famous undertaker. He would work all day on the coffins, and in the evening would go with Alimamy Bungie's men to sing at wakes. He was small in stature, and would wear colourful costumes for his performances with his maringar band. His songs were widely known and sung by young and old. Calendar, who had a Jamaican father and Sierra Leonean mother, died in Freetown in April 1985 at the age of 73.

Salia Koroma, born in 1903, was also a very well known musician. He sang mostly in Mende and accompanied himself on his accordian. Songs such as 'Ganene Bimbe' became very popular.

I was given a copy of an album of Sierra Leone Music by the German Ambassador in Freetown containing music by the above and also the Famous Scrubbs and His Band, Ali Ganda Carnival Star Orchestra singing the 'Freedom, Freedom Sierra Leone' Calypso and others. 'My Lovely Elizabeth', not contained in this album, was a very popular record in the 1960's and was written and sung by 'Rogie' (Rogers).

# Chapter 9

# Devils, Witches and Juju

Sierra Leone has its own mythology of spirits and "devils". The term "devil" in Sierra Leone does not necessarily mean something evil, as some devils are helpful and good-natured. Certain carvings made of soapstone were dug up by farmers tilling their land. These figures, usually about twelve to fifteen inches high, and most often in the shape of a man sitting with his knees drawn up, were called Nomoli by the Mende people. Some were fertility figures probably buried in the farms to bring a plentiful harvest. The genuine Nomoli figures are very old, and we have not been able to trace their exact history. We would be happy to learn more of the origins of these interesting figures. A picture of a Nomoli figure can be seen on the front cover of Christopher Fyfe's book, 'A Short History of Sierra Leone', first published in 1962 by Longmans.

The "Ronsho" is a "devil" that is reputed to be good for the person to whom it belongs. It is believed to stand no more than two feet high, taking the form of a small man, some even say a small green man. The Ronsho is said to live in the 'under-cellar' of the person it is attached to. When a house is built a little way above the ground, the area between the floor of the house and the ground is known as the 'under-cellar' of houses in Freetown. No one would live there as it is too low – only three or four feet high. It is said that if you own a Ronsho you might become a rich man on money brought your way by your Ronsho. Perhaps this is very similar to the Leprechauns in Ireland who can show you the way to the pot of gold! I have yet to see a Ronsho myself! I give here below a quote from a book by an unknown author entitled 'West Africans Who Made History' from the chapter about Mr A.B.C. Sibthorpe (A.B.C. stand for Aaron Belisarius Cosimo). Mr Sibthorpe had twice lost his writings and personal property by fire, the first time deliberately and the second by accident.

> 'He (Sibthorpe) thanked the neighbours for saving his house, and muttered sadly that the gods were against him. The natives with their local superstitions said that Sibthorpe must have disobeyed the laws of the fire devil Ronsho, for it was believed that anyone suffering loss by fire twice was in the power of Ronsho.'

When I was going to school there was a belief amongst schoolchildren in Freetown that finding a 'Thunder axe' would make the finder wealthy. The belief was that during the rain season, an extra loud clap of thunder during a storm resulted in the fall of a Thunder axe to earth, and anyone finding this would be rich. I have never yet found a Thunder axe, and perhaps that is why I am not rich! I wonder if the schoolchildren in Freetown today still keep their eyes open for a Thunder axe when they are out after a bad storm!

➼ If you were travelling at night on the road from Wilberforce to Adonkia, a few miles outside of Freetown, you might be unfortunate enough to meet up with a tall, thin woman, covered from head to foot, wearing native dress and carrying a bundle on her head. She was popularly called "Jenet Bundle", and is reputed to kill or maim passers-by who spoke to her. Children would scatter when told "Jenet Bundle is coming", and parents could get their offspring to behave well with threats of what Jenet Bundle would do to them if they did not do what they were told.

➼ In the village of Lumley, near Freetown, a woman was kicked by a cockerel and died shortly after. The story went round that the cockerel was a "witchbird" and that the woman must have offended someone who sent the "witchbird" to deal with her. I was later told that the medical cause of the poor woman's death was tetanus.

➼ A story reported in one of the local newspapers tells of a snake that was about fourteen feet long that gave chase to a magistrate in his parlour. The magistrate had to shut himself in his bedroom while his servants tried unsuccessfully to kill the snake with sticks. In desperation the magistrate telephoned to a Lebanese friend nearby, explaining what was happening, and asking him to come with his gun. The Lebanese man arrived and shot the snake seven times before it died. It was said that the same snake had previously made an attack on another magistrate in the same town a few days earlier, but the snake had mysteriously disappeared when attempts had been made to kill it. Wagging tongues said "these attacks may not be unconnected with cases pending in Court".

➼ A local newspaper reports stories of witches and witchguns. Witches may be male or female in Sierra Leone. A person may feel he is under threat of attack by 'witchgun', that is, someone wants to injure or kill him by supernatural means. A witchgun, and the shot from it, cannot be seen or heard, but the person so shot, it is believed by some, would sicken and die, regardless of medical treatment. The person feeling threatened in this way could go to a 'medicine man' who would give him a potion to protect him against the effects of a witchgun. The witch firing the witchgun need not be anywhere near the victim.

Some people claim to have a personal magic so strong that if they were shot at the bullets would merely bounce off without doing any harm. A few bystanders have claimed to have seen these people shot without suffering any injury.

Can it be that legends including "Jenet Bundle", the "Witchbird" and the "Witchgun" came about through incidents that some people cannot explain easily in natural terms and so supernatural causes were attributed to them?

Perhaps someone with more information than I have can explain these phenomena.

➤ The Human Baboon is also something of a phenomenon in Sierra Leone. One often hears of a 'baboon' attacking a human being, but this 'baboon' can speak in the human tongue! One story involved a palm-wine tapper, who was up a tree to check if the 'bullie' (gourd) was full. Suddenly a baboon climbed up the tree behind him, caught hold of his foot, and told him in a local language that he had been caught by a baboon. The palm-wine tapper had his cutlass with him as usual, and chopped at the hand of the human baboon, forcing the human baboon to retreat back down the tree, where he and his two companions, all wearing baboon skins, long trousers, and palm leaves on their heads, ran off into the jungle. The palm-wine tapper raised the alarm, and he and the villagers followed the human baboons into the bush, but were unable to find them.

This activity, like the 'Borfima' mentioned in another chapter, and other undesirable practices, was something the Government was trying to stamp out.

➤ Some years ago, I believe it was in 1981 or 1982, it was said that a phantom lady went around Freetown kidnapping schoolgirls. She would approach a young girl on her way to school, and by some ruse get the girl to take hold of something wrapped in a piece of paper. The girl would lose all power to resist and would follow the woman quietly. The woman would then remove whatever gold jewellery the girl was wearing and then abandon her. The girl would come back to her senses after a while and be able to find her way home. It would appear that the girls robbed in this way had been hypnotised. This brought to mind the Jenet Bundle story, except that in these cases the girls were only robbed.

➤ I have a piece of beach land at Mamah Beach on the peninsula road leading from Freetown. Next to the boundary of my land, on the beach just above high water line, was built a tiny hut made of bamboo and thatch. Some of the villagers would visit it from time to time and leave offerings of food and drink, presumably so that the "sea devil" would look kindly on them. This may well have been one of the more benevolent of the devils, as stated above.

We walked along the beach towards the village and came to a kind of stockade at least seven feet high and beautifully made from wicker and straw, with intricate designs woven into it. It was densely made, there was no point at which you could see through the fence. We later discovered that this was a Poro bush.

➤ Kasilla is the name of a devil who is said to control the sea around Bonthe on Sherbro Island and is feared by the local people. Sherbro Island is in the south of Sierra Leone, and on one side of it is the Atlantic Ocean and on the other the Sherbro River. Lights can be seen at night at sea and on the river, as if belonging to a launch, but no launch can be seen and no sound is heard. Sometimes the lights could be seen going at great speed up the river towards Mattru Jong, then the lights would disappear and reappear very quickly at a completely different place. When these lights are seen, some people believe that Kasilla is around.

If there were accidents on the river and people were drowned or injured, it was thought that Kasilla was responsible, so from time to time the people of Bonthe would 'pull sara', that is to make an offering, to the sea devil to appease him. A lot of food would be prepared and cooked on the beach at Turners Peninsula (named after Governor Turner, 1826). Some of the food was put into a boat and the boat was pushed out into the river. If the food disappeared the people believed that Kasilla had taken it and was pleased with them.

More details on this can be found in Peter Tucker's book, 'The Tuckers of Sierra Leone 1665-1914. I have also heard about Kasilla from some good friends of mine, Farid and Wilhemina Hassib, who both come from Bonthe and have on occasion seen strange lights at sea that cannot be explained as no boats were in the area.

When in October 1977 my son Jamal had to go to Bonthe to prepare his dissertation on coastal geomorphology for his degree, he was given a letter of introduction by Anwar Hassib to a Lebanese trader there who would put him up and help him. I told Jamal before he left Freetown to watch out for Kasilla!!

I understand that a launch built in the 1940's by a Lebanese businessman to carry goods and produce around Bonthe was called 'Kasilla'.

➠ The Gongoli is a masked devil. The mask is that of an ugly man, much larger than life, and the whole body from the head down is covered in raffia in long strips, very densely hung so that the clothes of the man inside cannot be seen. The only part of the human inhabitant of the costume that can be seen are his feet, usually clothed only in socks, with no shoes, and his hands, which are usually also covered by long socks. He avoids going anywhere near fire, for obvious reasons. The Gongoli likes to keep his identity secret, and if spoken to will reply in a deep, disguised voice that no one could recognise. The only person who would know his identity is his "minder" or controller, who is dressed in ordinary clothes and walks beside him to keep him under control and sometimes accepts the offerings to the Gongoli on his behalf. Sometimes the Gongoli goes from house to house alone, collecting a few coins here and there as he dances his way along. At Christmastime he would sing "Happy Chrismes, me no die oh". For New Year he would just change a couple of words, "Happy New Year," and so on.

One day a passer-by shouted, "Gongoli, Gongoli, you don ketch fire, you grass clothes deh burn." The Gongoli, believing that he was on fire, did not wait to check his costume but made a dash for the nearest water, which happened to be the wharf at Sawpit, throwing off his heavy mask as he ran down the steps leading to the sea. He dived into the water to put out the supposed fire. A crowd had gathered to watch, as to see a Gongoli discard his mask and run for his life was a most uncommon scene.

➨ I have written elsewhere in my book "Sawpit Boy" about the 'kaka devil', a man dressed in sacking and with a pot of live coals on his head. He rubbed coaldust all over his body and had a rope tied around his waist, the end of which was held by his 'agba' or controller, the implication being that without this restraint he might run amok. The agba would sing as they danced through the streets, "Kaka debul day cam oh, Tuma yengeh ah yengeh tuma".

➨ One of the most often seen masked 'devils' in Sierra Leone is the Bundu Devil. The devil is a woman and belongs to the Bundu Society, which is for women only. The Bundu devil is all in black, a black wooden mask and a long black raffia gown, very thick so that nothing can be seen of the person beneath except for her feet. The Society's purpose is to train young girls in the art of womanhood, with respect to being a good wife and running the household. When the young girls leave the Bundu Bush (the secret place where the training is carried out, by women alone), accompanied by the Bundu Devil and other women in normal native costume, they are dressed only in grass skirts and their bodies and faces are painted white, with a substance that is easily washed off. As the society is secret and for women only, we know very little about it and can only say what we see when the girls appear in public. The Sande Society is also for women.

There is a similar society for men called the Poro Society which is widespread in Sierra Leone, not exclusively Mende. Under certain conditions women can belong to the Poro as well. The Mende language has no 'r', so the Mende people refer to the Poro as Poi. The Soko Society is for Temne men. There are also a number of hunting societies, which all have their own masked 'devils'. The hunting society 'devils' are often called 'odeh' which is a Yoruba word meaning 'masked devil'. 'Eke Murray' was an area near the Albert Academy Secondary School, which nearly 150 years ago used to be a sacred and prohibited bush for the Egugun devil. Nowadays much of the traditional meaning of the masked devil has been lost and it is merely a sign of local festivity.

'Juju' is quite a different thing from the various devils. It involved using 'magic' of one kind or another to put a curse on someone or to bring about or prevent a particular event. It can take the form of a small packet of red cloth with cowrie shells attached to it, and it is said to contain a spell prepared by the medicine man.

I came across an account in a Sierra Leone newspaper of an instance where the threat of juju was sufficient. A female student at a college had hung her dress out to dry after laundering, and the dress was stolen. The usual enquiries by the police brought no result. The young lady resorted to threats, parading the hostel saying that she would put juju so that the person who took her dress would die within three days, and that anyone who wore it would also die. The next morning the student awoke to find her dress was hanging just where she had put it! In this case, juju worked.

I tried it myself on one occasion, when our laundry was disappearing from our own clothesline at home. It was happening frequently so I made up what looked like a juju and hung it on the clothesline, hoping it would deter the thieves. It seemed to work for a couple of days and the washing was safe. The third day the clothes were hung out as usual, but this time most of the items went missing and the 'juju' was found hanging low down on the fence. We could not understand why the thief was apparently no longer worried by the juju, but it was explained to me that if the thief were to urinate on the juju it would lose its power. Presumably this was what had happened, and so we threw the 'juju' away and took to hanging out the washing on the veranda!

Another newspaper report was of a young lawyer who had been entertaining two young ladies, only to find when they had left that some money was missing. Threats of police investigation brought no reaction, so the lawyer decided to resort to the juju man. The juju man asked for objects belonging to the suspects, and incanted the magic words over them. His magic wand pointed to the object representing one of the young ladies. The lawyer approached the girl and demanded the return of his money. Unfortunately she had already spent some, but she returned the rest of the amount. Let us hope that both the lawyer and his visitor had learnt lessons from this incident.

One case where the medicine man seemed at first to have got it wrong was in the case of an English lady known to my wife. This lady told Joan that her jewellery disappeared from her wardrobe and she suspected a member of her domestic staff of stealing it. A medicine man was called in, but after a few minutes meditation the medicine man stated that the jewellery had not been stolen but was still in the house. The lady, all the same, sacked the person she suspected of theft. It was quite some time later that the water heater in the lady's bathroom stopped working and she called in a plumber to look at it. He climbed up on a chair to reach to the top of the appliance. He then called out to the lady of the house that he had found a packet on top of the water heater, pushed back against the wall out of sight. It was the missing jewellery! It would seem that the medicine man was right after all. The jewellery had never left the house. The thief must have hidden it there in the hope he would be able to retrieve it later, but had no opportunity to do so.

One kind of medicine man is one who uses a pot to catch a guilty person. When called to a house or compound where a theft has occurred, the medicine man will ask for all the suspects to be assembled. If one suspect is not available, someone else can stand in for that person. The medicine man will go to each of the suspects in turn with a small empty pot which he will hold against the naked stomach of each suspect in turn. When he reaches the guilty person the pot will stick to him and remain in place without being held. The usual result is that that person will then confess. This system is said to work the same way if an absent person is guilty; the pot will fasten itself to the abdomen of the substitute for that person. The person whose goods have been stolen will be satisfied with this result. Some people have tried to explain this phenomenon by saying that a guilty person would be very scared when the pot-man reached him and this would make him draw in his stomach muscles, creating a vacuum which would make the pot stick to him. If this were so, it does not account for the times when a stand-in has been caught by the pot, when the stand-in may not even know the person he is substituting and whether or not he is guilty.

The fear of the unknown played a great part in boosting superstition. A large tree had fallen in Freetown as the result of a storm, and some of the poorer people were busily cutting off the branches and carrying them away to use for firewood. A large part of the root of the tree was still in ground. The next morning when the people returned to cut more firewood from the fallen tree, they found that it was standing upright! In their fear they rushed home and brought back all the wood they had taken from this tree the day before. What they failed to understand was that when sufficient branches had been removed to lessen the weight of the top part of the tree, the remainder of the tree was able to return to an upright position.

# Chapter 10

# Hunting

My hunting days began when I was living and doing business in Mambolo in the Northern Province. I bought a second-hand single barrelled shotgun and had it licensed. I used to go shooting after I had closed my shop. Once I went at night with a Court Messenger, who was appointed to accompany the Paramount Chief in his travels. This time I had a carbide headlight. This was a hunting lamp which I wore on my head much in the way a coal miner in England would do, but without the helmet. The lamp had a rubber tube at the back which was connected to the container attached to my belt on my left side which held the carbide. If I remember rightly, when I was ready to light the headlamp I would add water to the dry carbide in the container, which I sealed. The gas from the carbide and water would pass through the tube to the lamp, which I then lit with a match.

Another use for carbide which I learnt later was to sprinkle it (without touching the carbide by hand) on the ground outside our chicken house to keep away snakes.

We walked the whole night looking for animals or birds, but we were not successful and we returned home about 5.00 am.

Back in the late 1950's my cousin Choukri and his father Christo Courban (my first cousin Salma's husband) were on their way from Kambia when their journey was delayed because of the unusually high level of the river due to heavy rains. The Mange ferry was unable to operate, so my relatives came to Mambolo to stay with me until the level of the water had subsided enough to enable them to cross over and continue their journey to Freetown. This ferry took only about three cars, and was operated by two cables stretched from one shore to the other across the river. One cable was high up, and the ferry was attached to it by two pulleys, one at each end of the ferry. The other cable was lower, near the level of the water, and the ferrymen would catch hold of the lower cable with wooden hooks and pull the ferry across the river. Some people would make a living by arriving early at the ferry-crossing in their old vehicle, although they had no intention of going over the river, then selling their place in the queue to someone behind them who was in a hurry.

I introduced my uncle and cousin to my then father-in-law, who invited Uncle Christo to stay with him, whilst Choukri stayed with me and my family.

The next evening Choukri and I went out hunting in his father's car, and finding nothing better for the pot we shot a monkey. We had been told the flesh of a monkey was very good to eat, similar to chicken. We went home and started to prepare the creature for cooking, but when we looked more closely at the animal's hands we decided that it was so much like a human being that we could not bring ourselves to cook it. We did not want to throw it away, so we took it to the nearby village of Ropolo and gave it to a family, who were happy to receive it and gave us a bully of mampama (a calabash of palm-wine) in appreciation. This we gladly accepted and took it home with us. We chilled it in my kerosine-operated fridge and enjoyed it later that night in the light of my kerosine pressure lamp.

I never shot a member of the monkey family after that day, and was confirmed in my decision by the words of our youngest daughter Linda some years later. She had been walking with Joan through some woods near our house and saw a family of monkeys, a mother, father and three young monkeys. Linda said to me, "They were just like us!" I was even more convinced when I saw some chimps in captivity and watched the mother feeding her young at her breast, just like a woman with her baby. In Sierra Leone if it rains when the sun is shining, children will sing "Rain cam, sun cam, baboo day bon pikin nah bush" (meaning, when rain and sun come together, chimps will be having their babies in the jungle).

Luckily for Choukri and his father, the waters of the river subsided a few days later and they were able to return to Freetown. We were sorry to see them go as we had enjoyed their company and hearing all the news of the capital.

A few days later I went out for a stroll through the town in the evening. I passed the shop of Mr Huballah, a Lebanese trader who had a shop opposite my own. He had a family of small children, mainly boys. (Much later I met the sons again in Freetown when they were grown up and doing business for themselves, and Hussein Huballah and I became friends.) It was dark and as there were no street lights I switched on my torch. I noticed a man following behind me, making use of the circle of light from my torch. This was not the first time that this particular man had taken advantage of my light by walking close behind me, and I became irritated by him. I stopped walking to let him go by, but he stopped too. This happened several times so I thought up a way to discourage him from walking behind me so as to see his way by my torch. The road through Mambolo was a dirt road with a few potholes here and there. I spied a pothole ahead and raised the beam of my torch a little so that the man behind me would not catch sight of the hole. When I got near to the hole I switched off my torch and side-stepped the hole. The eyes of the man behind me had become used to the light of my torch and in the sudden darkness he could see nothing and stepped straight into the hole and fell over! I decided it was time to return home quickly. That man never followed me again, so my strategy worked!

On another occasion I met a crowd of people near the slipway and went to see what was going on. What I saw, for the first and only time, was a huge manatee or seacow, a mammal at least ten feet long which must have weighed a ton or so, that had been caught in the river. Some of the local people, mis-hearing the man who knew what it was called, said it was a 'man-eater'! It had thick dark grey skin, with short bristly hairs all over. There were flippers where its front legs would have been but it had no rear limbs. Its tail was flat and rounded. The manatee rears out of the water to suckle its young at its breast with its flippers cradling the baby, and it is reputed that this has given rise to the legends of mermaids. The sailors of old who reported this must have been very short-sighted, as the manatee is one of the ugliest creatures you can find. The manatee lives in rivers and coastal regions, preferring to be where the water is warm, and eats up to fifty kilograms of water plants in a day. Some people were busily cutting it up into large chunks and I saw that the flesh was red, more like meat than fish. Somehow I didn't fancy any of it, so I continued on my walk.

Some friends from Freetown, namely Allie Abess and Frank Isaac, came to spend a week with me in Mambolo. On the Sunday we hired a small launch and went with two or three more friends to spend the day on an island a few miles down-river. We took rice, meat and all the ingredients for plassas with us, together with all the pots and pans, and planned to cook our meal and play football. No sooner had we lit a fire and set the pot to cook, than the tide came up and put out the fire. We moved everything further up the island and lit the fire once more. Once again the water rose up very quickly, and again we moved even further from the water. After repeating this process three times, with our lunch nowhere near being cooked, we gave up and piled everything back in the launch. We returned to Mambolo where we continued our cooking over a wood fire in our compound, successfully. By this time we were very hungry, and so enjoyed the food immensely.

Besides running my shop and going hunting, I also found time to play football for the Mambolo team against teams from the Kambia area. I was the only Lebanese player, although there were two or three Afro-Lebanese playing for other towns in the Kambia District, and though I say it myself, I was a pretty good player. I can remember being carried shoulder-high after an away match against Kasiri, when my defence against the Kasiri players had been crucial to our success.

In the year 2000 I heard that oil was discovered in the Great Scarcies River between Mambolo and Kasiri. If this is true it will take more people to the area and business will escalate, as there will be a demand for more building materials, provisions, launches and 'pampams'. Retailers would need more goods to sell, tailors would be required to sew more clothes.

More and improved medical facilities would be required, reliable water and electricity supplies would be needed. With more salaried workers in the area there would be more money to spend, and in turn more food, for example rice, palm oil, vegetables and fish, would be in demand. I can only hope that the oil proves to be in abundance and that prosperity will eventually come to the area and hence to the whole country. Some years ago it was said that oil was found in the Sherbro region, but although there was much speculation nothing so far has happened to my knowledge.

➼ When I first returned to Freetown after qualifying as a barrister, I lived in a flat in Freetown with my wife and children. I used to go hunting sometimes at the weekend with some Lebanese friends. One Sunday Melik Sabrah, Farouk Blell, Mounir Hassanieh and I, set off early in the morning by car to Mile 47, hunting as we went along. We killed several game birds on our way, stopping the car for a few minutes when we saw something promising to shoot. After one such stop, we all got back into the car. Farouk and I were sitting in the back. Usually we would break our shotguns and lean the barrels of the guns against the open windows so that the barrels were pointing outwards and upwards. Farouk was unintentionally holding his loaded shotgun with the barrel pointing towards me, as he stooped down to pick up something from the floor of the car. I reached out and pushed the barrel away so that it pointed to the rear of the car, away from me, and said "Never point a gun, loaded or unloaded, at anybody." I had hardly finished speaking when there was a sudden blast as the gun went off and blew out the rear windscreen of the car. Mounir, who owned the car and was driving, stopped the car short and we all sat in stunned silence for a while. At last we all got out to survey the damage and get rid of the tension that had gripped us. Farouk was white and shaking from what was so nearly a tragedy.

Eventually, we all decided that we would call it a day and return home. We all took the cartridges out of our shotguns and returned them to our belts. Mounir suggested that Farouk should drive the car for a while to help him regain his composure. Farouk got into the driving seat and we all piled into the car, having put all the guns into the boot. As he turned the car to go back the way we had come, he backed into a tree that had refused to get out of the way! Farouk felt he did not want to drive anymore as he had had troubles enough for one day.

I told my friends that I did not want my wife to know anything about what had happened that day, because I knew she would be worried and would not want me to go hunting any more. It was about a decade later, when I had given up hunting, that I told my wife the story of what had happened that day.

➼ Melik, Farouk and I would sometimes cross over the Sierra Leone River by ferry from Kissy to Lungi. We would drive thirteen miles to a small village called Babara on the bank of the Little Scarcies river where we would leave the car in charge of Mr Sampha Kamara who ran a small shop and used to work with Melik's uncle. We would hire a 'pampam', a small launch with an awning and a small 8 h.p. outboard engine, and go hunting along the river. It was not unusual for us to kill several game birds and the occasional crocodile. From the launch we could see rice farms along the banks, and if the rice was nearly ready for harvesting the farmers would build raised platforms above the rice and small boys would stand up there watching for birds. When they saw some they would let fly stones with their slings to drive the birds away. This was necessary, because a flock of birds could eat a lot of rice in a short time. In fact I remember my watchman being injured on his back by a stone from one of the boys using a sling to frighten birds away from the farm next to our garden in Lumley.

It was along this river that I saw a palm-nut vulture for the first time. I had not seen one before and I asked Melik what kind of bird it was. He told me it was called the 'banga bird'. When I got home later that night Joan and I looked it up in Birds of West Central and Western Africa by C.W. Mackworth-Praed and Captain C.H.B. Grant and found that Melik was right, it was called the palm-nut vulture (palm nut being 'banga' in Krio). It is not really a vulture although it looks like one. It is a large black and white bird with a pearl-coloured bill, and can be found wherever large numbers of oil-palms are grown.

On our way along the Little Scarcies river (in fact a misnomer because overall it is wider than the Great Scarcies) we saw a large launch with an inboard engine which was loaded with palm kernels. It must have carried about a hundred bags each weighing about a hundred pounds. Passengers were sitting on top of the bags of kernels and a few more sat on the front where it was cooler. This reminded me of when I worked as a storekeeper for the SLPTC (Sierra Leone Produce and Trading Company), dealing in palm kernels and coffee.

On our return to Babara we would find that the shopkeeper's wife had prepared a meal of rice and stew for us with the money we had left. We would always leave behind with her some game birds that we had shot, but if we were lucky enough to get a crocodile we would take it back to Freetown where the skin would be taken to a craftsman who would make it into handbags. The crocodile is supposed to be the biggest reptile, and therefore a cold-blooded creature, unlike humans.

➤➤ When travelling 'upline' (as the Provinces were known in the early days of the railway) by road to do a case I would leave very early in the morning, taking my driver Mahmoud with me. Mahmoud and I had been friends for many years, we had been boys together. His father had sent him to the Lebanon for a while when he was very young, where he learnt to speak Arabic. We would usually stop when we reached Waterloo and buy some cassava bread soaked in nutoil with fried fish and perhaps some parched groundnuts as well to eat on the road.

Mahmoud and I would take it in turns to drive, so that neither of us became too tired. I would usually take my shotgun with me, as often we would see game birds in the trees or bushes near the road as we went along. I took turns with Mahmoud to shoot, and we shared whatever we killed for the pot. It was Mahmoud's turn to shoot, and he was cautiously stalking the bird, which was perched in a low tree about forty yards from the road. He walked slowly and quietly with his eyes fixed on the bird. He approached so near to the tree that I asked him, "Are you going to shoot, or do you mean to knock the bird off its perch?" Suddenly Mahmoud disappeared. He had fallen down a deep hole, but was saved from injury by the gun falling across the hole and resting on the two sides, with Mahmoud still holding on to it. I went over and gave him a hand to come up. When he was once more on firm ground, I took the gun from him and found to my dismay that the barrel was bent, so that was the end of our hunting for the rest of the day.

After returning to Freetown, I found that I could still fire the gun, but my aim had to be adjusted to allow for the slight curvature of the barrel. That meant that when a game bird was sighted directly ahead of me, I had to aim slightly to the right! This elicited comments from my hunting friends that I was aiming badly to the right, only for them to be amazed when I brought down the game bird. Eventually I took the gun to the workshop at the Sierra Leone Army barracks at Juba, where they were able to straighten the barrel for me.

➼ One morning, in January of 1976, I left home at 6.30 am with Mahmoud, to drive up to Bo to do a case. It was completed successfully the same day, so by afternoon we were on our way back to Freetown. Passing through a small village I saw large quantities of various fruits for sale, so we stopped to buy. Citrus fruits are at their most plentiful at that time of year, and I was able to buy six dozen large oranges at ten cents a dozen, and grapefruit, picked from the tree while I waited, at twenty cents a dozen. I bought several very large pineapples at thirty cents each, pawpaws (papayas) at five cents each, and a big bag of sweet potatoes and some 'chinese', a small root vegetable something like the Irish potato, for one Leone. In those days one Leone was equal to ten shillings sterling, and ten cents was the equivalent of one shilling. When British currency changed to decimal, ten shillings became fifty pence.

Fruit and vegetables were usually much cheaper bought up in the provinces than in the markets of Freetown, due to the fact that the produce had to be brought to Freetown by lorry and transport costs were quite high. My children were always eager to see what I had in the boot of the car when I came back from one of these trips.

As well as being my driver for a time, Mahmoud was also a very good butcher, and if I had a live sheep or goat that I wanted prepared for the pot I would send for Mahmoud and he would come and do the necessary. He would never ask for payment, but I would always give him some part of the animal to take home with him. Sometimes if I was having a barbecue for some friends in the garden, Mahmoud would come and take charge of the pig or sheep being barbecued, often bringing with him a young boy to turn the handle of the spit.

One day the boy he brought to turn the spit was too small to reach up to turn the handle all the way round, and it would swing back again. We had to send the small boy home because the pig was being cooked on one side only! Mahmoud had to roll up his sleeves and do the work himself, but he consoled himself by taking the best of the crackling!

# Chapter 11

# Elections and Politics

In 1961 when Sierra Leone achieved Independence the Sierra Leone Peoples Party (SLPP) was in power, led by Sir Milton Margai, MBE (received in 1943), who was a medical doctor. Sir Maurice H. Dorman, an Englishman, had been Governor of Sierra Leone from 1956 to 1961. At Independence he became Governor-General until 1962. Elections were held in 1962 in which the SLPP retained power. In that same year the first Sierra Leonean Governor-General was appointed in the person of Sir Henry Lightfoot Boston. In 1964 Sir Milton died and his half-brother, Sir Albert Margai, succeeded him as leader of the SLPP.

Further elections were held in 1967 in which the All People's Congress (APC), led by Mr (later Dr) Siaka Probyn Stevens gained a slight majority of one seat over the SLPP. The APC was prevented from taking power when the head of the Sierra Leone Army, Brigadier David Lansana, declared Martial Law. The senior officers of the army, believing that Brigadier Lansana intended to declare the SLPP leader, Sir Albert Margai, as Prime Minister, overthrew him and took power themselves. Lieutenant-Colonel Ambrose Genda was declared Chairman of the new National Reformation Council (NRC) and he was recalled to Freetown to take office as Head of State. Before he arrived, however, he received further a message to disembark at Las Palmas and await further orders. Colonel (later Brigadier) Andrew T. Juxon-Smith succeeded Genda as chairman of the NRC and Head of State. William Leigh, Commissioner of Police, was appointed Deputy Chairman and Commissioner for External Affairs under the NRC. The Governor-General, Sir Henry Lightfoot Boston, was relieved of his duties by the NRC and he went to England, where he died two years later, in January 1969. His body was returned to Sierra Leone where he received a State Funeral including a 21-gun salute. He was buried at Kissy Road Cemetery near the grave of his wife, to the sound of the Last Post played by trumpeters of the Sierra Leone Military Forces.

In 1968 the NRC was overthrown by junior army officers, who formed the ACRM (Anti Corruption Revolutionary Movement). They recalled Brigadier John Bangura from Guinea to head an interim government leading to civilian rule. In a matter of a week or two Mr Siaka Stevens was appointed Prime Minister as leader of the APC ruling party. This was the first time any African nation had returned to civilian rule after a military coup, and the civilian government was greeted with great joy. Sir Henry

Lightfoot Boston had been invited to return to his post as Governor-General, but he was too ill to leave England. Sir Banja Tejan-Sie, who was Chief Justice from 1967, was appointed Acting Govorner-General. In September 1970 Sir Banja was appointed substantive Governor-General, a position he held until April 1971. When Sierra Leone became a Republic Sir Banja retired from politics and went to live in England, where he died in London on 8th August 2000. His body was taken to Freetown and given a State Funeral.

The APC came into power in 1968 with a very small majority but with a lot of popularity among the people. During the next few years some SLPP members decided to 'cross-carpet' – that is, to cross the floor of the House to the Government benches and join the APC. At the next election the APC had a much greater majority, and this led eventually to the declaration of a One Party State, with the APC as the only party, in 1978.

To bring the story up to date on some of the main participants in the events above, I propose to give a brief account of some of them.

**Sir Albert Margai** was educated at St Edwards Secondary School and was also a lawyer belonging to the Inner Temple, so he and I had three things in common. I knew him quite well and he would always wave if I was on my veranda in Lumley when he passed our house on his way home to Juba. [As a schoolboy Albert Margai was given the Bronze Cross and the Gilt Cross by the Scouts Association for helping Edward Hamelburg (later Father Hamelburg) in saving the life of Father Mulcahy, well-known Principal of St Edward's Secondary School, during a school outing to Lumley Beach. Father Mulcahy had gone into the sea to help the boys get to shore after a sudden storm blew up. Father Mulcahy became tired after some time and Albert and Edward went to his help.] As Minister of Finance in the SLPP government, Albert Margai was responsible for the introduction of decimal currency – the Leone – to Sierra Leone in 1964. He was knighted in 1965. In 1966 Sir Albert became unpopular by trying to introduce a one party state. After Brigadier Lansana was overthrown following his declaration of Martial Law, Sir Albert was detained by the army officers for a few days. When the civilian government came into power in 1968, Sir Albert went into voluntary exile to Britain. He died in 1980.

**Brigadier David Lansana** was the first Sierra Leonean to be appointed Force Commander of the Sierra Leone army, prior to independence this position was held by a British army officer. He too was a personal friend of mine and we would exchange visits. When Brigadier Lansana declared Martial Law in 1967, the fear held by his senior officers that his intention was to impose Sir Albert and the SLPP on the country may have been fuelled by the fact that David Lansana's wife was sister to Paramount Chief Madam Ella Koblo Gulama. Madam Ella had been Minister without Portfolio and a member of Albert Margai's cabinet, among other positions she held. After the NRC government was formed, David Lansana was

143

given a diplomatic posting to New York. In 1968 the civilian government charged him in connection with his actions in 1967, and he was convicted and sentenced to five years imprisonment. Some time after his release in 1973, he was arrested again on a separate charge of treason. He was found guilty and executed at Pademba Road Prison two years after his previous release.

**Lieutenant-Colonel Ambrose Genda** was technically Head of State for four days, but did not arrive in Freetown in 1967 to take up the leadership of the NRC. He was appointed Ambassador to Liberia for one year, and then become Sierra Leone's High Commissioner in London in 1968-1969. He also served as Ambassador in Moscow for a year, before settling in London. He died in London in July 2001.

**Brigadier Andrew T. Juxon-Smith** was in London in 1967, having completed his army training at Sandhurst. He was staying at the then British Council Hostel at No. 1 Hans Crescent, Knightsbridge, with many other students from Sierra Leone and other countries, when he was recalled to Sierra Leone to take up the leadership of the NRC. Juxon-Smith was a disciplinarian who insisted on punctuality. People made a point of getting to work on time, because Juxon-Smith would get his secretary to telephone any department, especially in the mornings, to check on who was at their desk on time. When the NRC was overthrown, Brigadier Juxon-Smith was arrested and charged with treason. He was convicted and sentenced to death in 1969, but was reprieved a few years later. After his release he opened a shop in Sanders Street in Freetown, then went to live in America where I am told he became a Reverend. It was rumoured that Juxon-Smith claimed his leadership of the country did not last for long because he came to power by a coup instead of waiting to be chosen for leadership by the people. I believe that Juxon-Smith died in the United States about 1997.

**William Leigh** was a Flight Sergeant in the RAF during the Second World War, and then joined the Colonial Police Service where he served in Ghana before being appointed to the Sierra Leone Police Force in 1948. He was the first Sierra Leonean to hold the position of Commissioner of Police, in 1963. When the NRC took power he came Deputy Chairman and Commissioner for External Affairs. William Leigh was charged with treason with other members of the NRC. He was convicted and sentenced to death but was reprieved and released three years later. He was discharged from the police force. William Leigh had been a client of mine and his wife Sara ran a hairdressing salon next to my office in Westmoreland Street in the 1960's.

**Brigadier John Bangura** was the first Sierra Leonean army officer to be trained at Sandhurst in the United Kingdom. Brigadier Bangura was arrested in 1967 but released in the same year and sent to Washington as a diplomat. He left his post in Washington and went to Guinea with the hope of overthrowing the NRC. The NRC was overthrown by the junior officers of the Sierra Leone Army and Brigadier Bangura was recalled to Freetown. He headed an interim government and in a very short time the country was returned to a civilian government under the leadership of Siaka Stevens of the All Peoples Congress. In 1971 John Bangura and other senior officers were arrested and charged with treason for trying to overthrow the government. He was convicted and sentenced to death, and executed with three other senior officers at Pademba Road Prison in 1971.

**President Dr Siaka Probyn Stevens** was born in Moyamba on 24 August 1905. He was educated at Albert Academy in Freetown (which was founded in 1907 by the Evangelical United Brethren). His middle name 'Probyn' was given to him by his father in honour of Governor Sir Leslie Probyn, whom his father respected. Siaka Probyn Stevens joined the Sierra Leone police force, where his first assignment was dog catching. He reached the rank of first class sergeant and musketry instructor. He then worked for fifteen years in connection with the Delco (Sierra Leone Development Company) railway linking Pepel with the iron ore mines at Marampa and during that time became stationmaster. He was co-founder of the United Mine Workers Union. After various trade union appointments he went to Ruskin College, Oxford, in England, where he continued to study trade unionism. He was elected to the Legislative Council in 1951 and became the first Minister of Lands and Mines. He was a member of the SLPP, but broke away to form the "Elections before Independence Movement" in 1960 with people such as S. I. Koroma, C. A. Kamara-Taylor and S.A.T. Koroma, which later that year became the APC (All Peoples Congress). He went to England in 1961 to put the demands of the APC for elections before Independence. While there he was served with a warrant granted in the Court in Freetown for his arrest on charges of libel, sedition and conspiracy. Siaka Stevens returned to Freetown in the company of a senior police officer who held his passport until they reached Freetown. On 18th April 1961 the executive members of the APC, including Siaka Stevens, were arrested. He and others were released on 18 May 1961, after the Independence celebrations, which started on 27 April, were all over.

Siaka Stevens was the leader of the opposition party in parliament. In 1964 he was elected Mayor of Freetown. He won the parliamentary elections in 1967, but due to the military take-over he did not assume office until 1968, when he became Prime Minister. He received the degree of Doctor of Civil Laws (Honoris Causa) at the inauguration of the University of Sierra Leone in 1969, and became Chancellor of the University four years later. Before that, in 1971, he became President of the Republic of Sierra Leone and remained in office until handing over to Major-General Joseph Saidu Momoh, Force Commander, who was elected in a simple Yes/No ballot in 1985. Major-General Momoh had been a nominated Member of Parliament as head of the army since 1974. During

Siaka Stevens' years in power there were several attempted coups, followed by treason trials and executions.

Siaka Probyn Stevens died in Freetown on 29 May 1988, and was given a state funeral on 12 June 1988. Although Siaka Stevens started his years in power being extremely popular, in later years he became very unpopular with most of the public, who gave him several derogatory names including Monica (coined from the words 'money' and 'car', said to be two of his favourite things), and 'Pas ah die' meaning 'Over my dead body'. This last was his answer when asked when he would retire from office, but in the end he retired in 1985.

**Major-General Joseph Saidu Momoh** was Force Commander of the Sierra Leone Army from 1971. President Siaka Stevens appointed him Member of Parliament and Minister of State a few years later. In 1985 President Stevens retired from the presidency and named Joseph Saidu Momoh as sole candidate to succeed him and he was duly elected as President.

In March 1986 it was announced that an attempted coup had been foiled. More than 60 people were arrested, but not all were charged. A month later Francis Minah, first vice-president and lawyer, was arrested and charged with treason. He was found guilty at all stages of the Court system and was executed in October 1989, along with five others. Other death sentences were commuted to life imprisonment.

In 1987 an eight-sided coin was produced to the value of one Leone with the head of Dr Joseph Saidu Momoh on one side, together with the motto, 'Unity, Freedom and Justice', and the Sierra Leone coat of arms on the other. The Doctorate in Civil Law (D.C.L.) was awarded to him by the University of Sierra Leone. Dr Momoh also held the title of Grand Commander of the Republic of Sierra Leone, the Order of the British Empire (Military Division) in 1971, and the Order of the Rokel in 1974.

President Momoh set up a commission to review the one party constitution, which recommended a return to a multi-party system. A new constitution was approved by Parliament and ratified in 1991. One saying of his that is called to mind and is likely to be remembered by most who heard it during a speech President Momoh made in Kailahun is, "Education was a privilege, not a right." President Momoh lost power to Valentine Strasser in 1992. Ex-President Joseph Saidu Momoh died in the Republic of Guinea on Sunday, 3rd August 2003. He was given a State Funeral in Freetown, Sierra Leone, and was buried at Kissy Road Cemetary on 24 August 2003.

In March 1991 (while President Momoh was still in office) a large band of rebels calling themselves the Revolutionary United Front (RUF) and led by a Sierra Leonean called Foday Sankoh attacked Sierra Leone from Liberia. Foday Sankoh was a former corporal in the Sierra Leone army who had spent seven years in prison for his part in a former attempted coup. The RUF was engaged in a programme of terrorism and destruction in the provinces, and attempts by the government to defeat them militarily or to come to a successful peace agreement had so far ended in failure. When Johnny Paul Koroma became Head of State there was an alliance between the AFRC and the RUF, and Foday Sankoh was sworn in as Second in Command in absentia in July 1997, being held under house arrest in Nigeria at that time. ECOMOG, the military wing of ECOWAS (Economic Community of West African States) sent troops to Sierra Leone, mainly Nigerians, to try to put down the coup.

To cut a long and complicated story short, ECOMOG forces were finally able to overcome the AFRC in February 1998, and President Kabbah returned to Freetown from Guinea where he had been since May 1997. Foday Saybana Sankoh died in hospital on 29th July 2003 while held in custody by the International Tribunal set up to try war crimes in Sierra Leone.

**Captain Valentine Strasser** was a member of the Sierra Leone Army serving with a contingent that had been sent to the Provinces to contain the rebel disturbances.

At the end of April 1992, members of armed forces occupied the presidential offices of President Joseph Saidu Momoh and took control of the radio station. I was not in Freetown at that time and can only relate the story as it has been told to me, which was as follows: Captain Valentine Strasser led a delegation of junior members of the army and went to Freetown with the intention of confronting President Momoh to complain that the soldiers had not received their pay for several months. The soldiers, I was told, found that President Momoh and his aides had left and gone to Guinea, so they took control of the city. The National Provisional Ruling Council was formed and Captain Valentine Strasser was appointed their leader, making him the youngest African Head of State ever at the age of 28.

In January 1996, Strasser was deposed by Julius Maada Bio. The Advisory Council set up in 1992 was dissolved to make way for national elections in February and March 1996 for a return to civilian government. Captain Strasser lived in England for some years after being deposed, but now lives in Sierra Leone.

**Alhaji Ahmad Tejan Kabbah**, was born in Pendembu, Kailahun District and attended St. Edward's School in Freetown and later attended University College of Wales in the United Kingdom. He studied law at Grays Inn, London, and has a B.A. in Economics. He worked for the United Nations Development Programme (UNDP) for over twenty-one years. He was their Resident Representative in Uganda, Tanzania and Lesotho and was transferred to U.N. Headquarters in New York where he attained the high post of Director of Administrative and Management Services, prior to his retirement and return to Sierra Leone in 1992, when he was appointed Chairman of the Advisory Council set up by the NPRC. He has been a member of the Sierra Leone People's Party since 1954.

International observers from all over the world arrived in Sierra Leone to attend the elections in 1996, after four years of military government. These elections were afterwards reported to be the freest and fairest ever to have been conducted in the region. Thirteen political parties contested the elections, and the SLPP was declared to hold the majority number of seats. In the Presidential election, Alhaji Ahmed Tejan Kabbah, leader of the SLPP, was elected President of Sierra Leone for a four year term. The House of Representatives is made up of sixty-eight elected members and twelve Paramount Chiefs, making a total of eighty members.

In May 1997 a military coup took place carried out by the Armed Forces Revolutionary Council (AFRC). The junior officers released Major Johnny Paul Koroma from prison to be their leader and Head of State, and President Kabbah went to Guinea until February 1998.

Rebel attacks on Freetown followed, in violation of various peace agreements, but on 18th January 2002, after demobilisation and disarmament of combatants, President Kabbah declared the rebel war was over. In 2001 he was awarded the order of Grand Commander of the Republic of the Gambia by the Gambian Government.

In May 2002 elections were held again and Alhaji Ahmad Tejan Kabbah was elected for a further term, with the SLPP holding the majority of seats in Parliament.

# Chapter 12

# Freetown Aqua Sports Club and Fishing

Freetown was fortunate to have an active water sports and social club called the    Freetown Aqua Sports Club, of which I twice served as Commodore (what would be known as President in other less aquatic clubs), in 1980-81 and 1989-90. The club emblem was a Bullom boat with a triangular sail in blue on a white background and could be bought at the club as a car badge.   Water sports included power boats, sailing boats, wind surfing and swimming.   There were also two squash courts and a football field, a fairly large swimming pool and a paddling pool for the toddlers.  The club had a pump with a hose leading down to the sea, which pumped up seawater for the pools.   This was occasionally inconvenient because it was only possible to fill the pool if the tide was high enough to reach the inlet hose.  In the meantime the tiled pools were scrubbed clean by the boat boys.

The bar and chophouse (a separate bar serving food) were under cover so they could be used the whole year round, with stools along the bar and chairs and tables as well.   On the wall above the bar counter were two large boards listing all the Commodores, with their relevant dates, who had served the club since its inception.   The whole area for drinks and food could be closed off with big sliding glass doors when it rained.  For a time there were fruit machines as well.  The club was quite a few feet above sea level, with a low cliff facing the sea.   There were raised flower beds all along the edge of the cliff to prevent people walking too near the edge, and the beds were mainly planted with roses with thorns, kept trimmed, which was an extra deterrent to the children.   To get to the beach you had to either walk down the slope to where the boats were parked, or use the flight of steps that went straight down to the sand from near the bar. Children were encouraged to swim in the pool rather than from the beach because of possible danger from boats coming in or going out.

It was strictly a membership club.  The gate leading to the large carpark was kept closed, with a gateman on duty to open to members when they showed their passes.  Members could take in guests for a small fee, but each guest was only allowed three visits.   Thereafter they would need to apply for membership if they wanted to continue using the club.  A new member would be proposed and seconded by a committee member, and this would then be voted on at the monthly committee meeting.   The number of members was restricted and there was usually a waiting list.

Any increase in membership had to be first approved by the committee and then confirmed at a General Meeting.

The club was run by a committee of about eight unpaid volunteers who were elected at the Annual General Meeting. Apart from the Commodore and Vice Commodore there were members responsible for powerboats and sailing boats, membership, the chop house, house and grounds, the bar, and entertainments or social events. Some one would help out by taking minutes at the meetings, but that person was not usually a voting member. In the early days of the club a Bar Book was issued to each member and was kept behind the bar. A sum of money was deposited and entered in the book, and drinks and food taken would be entered in the book until the money ran out, when a further sum would be deposited. This was to make it difficult for non-members to use the club, as they would not be able to purchase anything. As the club expanded this system was discontinued as it was too time-consuming.

Some of the members owned their own speedboats or sailing boats. Speedboats had boat sheds or open parking. The sailing dinghies of various sizes were parked in the open near to the slipway for launching boats. Club members would pay rent for the spaces occupied by their boats, as well as annual membership fees. Later on when wind surfing became popular, special sheds were built to accommodate the wind surfers. The club became popular as a drinking club as well, where members would go for a drink after their day's work.

There was a time, however, when due to an administrative error and some forgetfulness, the application for the renewal of the club's bar licence was not made in time, and this resulted in no alcohol being sold at the club for three months. It said a lot for the friendly and sociable atmosphere that the bar continued to be reasonably busy during that time. A great many Chapman's were drunk, consisting of a mixture of 7-Up, orange juice and Angostura bitters!

Freetown Aqua Sports Club was started in 1967, with Peter Bartlett, the Manager of Aureol Tobacco Company, as the first Commodore. I joined a year or so later. After I had been a member for some time I decided that I would get a boat. My first boat was a small wooden one with a small outboard engine that I bought from an Englishman who was a lecturer at Fourah Bay College in Mount Aureol, Freetown. The boat was low in the water and quite small. My wife is not a swimmer and not very confident in small boats. After only one trip she complained that she did not feel safe sitting so close to the water! I used to go on short fishing trips, but soon realised that if I wished to take my family with me I needed to get something bigger.

In 1975 I sold the wooden boat and ordered a new eighteen feet Fletcher fibreglass speedboat with an 85hp engine from A Genet & Co Ltd, costing 8,000 Leones (equal to £4,000 at that time), including all interior fittings. I had to have a trailer specially built by Souham Haroun, a Lebanese friend of mine, in readiness for its arrival. It was an exciting day in February 1976 when I went to the club with my wife and family to see the new boat for the first time. It was delivered to the club by lorry and all the boat boys joined in lifting the boat from the lorry onto the trailer. The boat had a steering wheel like a car and a covered section at the front with seats inside, but my family usually preferred to sit in the open on the long seat at the back. We discussed what we should call it, and my wife suggested Antonia, being a feminine form of Anthony, and so Antonia it was called. We had an official launching, but I wouldn't risk letting anyone break a bottle on the bow of my new, spotless boat. Our first trip out was just a short trial run to Lungi and back, running at half speed of 3000 r.p.m. to break in the new engine. Later at the bar I ordered two bottles of champagne to toast the new boat. My family was, not surprisingly, unanimous in preferring Antonia to the small wooden boat I had before! Later on it was necessary to register all boats used for sports fishing so I had to get a licence. The cost of the licence was relative to the size of the engine. I had to pay Le 50.00 per year, and my boat was numbered SF22 (SF for Sports Fishing) which I had to paint on the bows.

➟ When a businessman, Paddy Warren, newly arrived in Freetown, he was told about the Aqua Club at Murray Town and he became a member. When I met him there he said to me, "The people of Freetown are very friendly. I had not been here long when everyone seemed to know my name, and said to me 'Paddy, how are you' wherever I went." I had to disillusion him by telling him that 'Paddy' in Krio meant 'friend', and what they were saying to him was 'Friend, how are you'. He could only laugh at his mistake.

Paddy soon took a great interest in the club. He became very involved in the running of the chop house, thinking up new ideas for the menu and helping to organise evening events when dinner would be served, often consisting of a barbecue with a variety of salads and other dishes. He built a clay oven so that the club could have fresh bread baked on the premises.

One item that the chophouse sold became very popular with the children. The club sold a lot of hamburgers and from time to time the crumbs of burger left on the hot plate would be scraped off. Some children loved this and Joseph, the chef, used to give it to them free of charge. When it was discovered there was a rush to get what became known as "nasties", a burger bun with the scrapings, the chophouse started charging ten cents each for them (the equivalent of one English shilling or five new pence, at that time). This charge did not detract from its popularity.

Paddy owned a large catamaran, called 'Scats', which he would anchor just outside the club because it was too big to come up the slipway. He had bought the boat in England and sailed it to Freetown with a Sierra Leonean who worked for him as crewmember. I am not sure whether he also had a European friend travel with him. The club took a great interest and pride in Paddy's journey and news would be passed on as to how he was advancing. A party was held in the club to welcome them when they arrived. Paddy bought some beach land at Whale Bay and weekends would usually see him setting off on his 'cat' to relax and fish.

Soon after I bought the Fletcher, the club held a fishing competition that I decided to enter. I went out in my boat with an English friend, Martin Nott, who was a businessman in Freetown, and is now a Catholic Parish Priest in the United Kingdom, ordained in 1990. We spent several hours trolling. Eventually, as it was getting near the time for us to return, we reeled in our lines, only to find a very small fish on one of them which we had not even known was on the line until we pulled it in. We put on all the speed we could muster and went back to the club with our catch, which consisted of just the one fish, which measured all of nine inches long. Others had caught large barracudas and groupers, the largest being a 40lb barracuda caught by Paddy Warren, but we decided to bluff it out and walked up from the jetty to the clubhouse carrying the fish between us, my friend holding the tail and I the head! In the end we did better than some people with respectable catches, for we got the booby prize for the smallest fish caught – two bottles of Martini each.

The following weekend we did very much better. I took Martin and another friend, Dr Dave Wright, an ear, nose and throat specialist, and we spent the whole afternoon at sea. We caught four large barracudas amongst us. The last fish caught was bitten in half by an even larger fish as it was being reeled in, so it was more accurate to say we brought in three and a half fish! We each took home one whole fish, and I took the bitten 'half' home as well to show my wife and children to demonstrate the dangers of swimming in deep water.

A few months later there was another fishing competition – the Johnny Walker Competition. My fishing partners were again Martin Nott and Dave Wright. There was a prize for the biggest fish caught of two bottles of Black Label Whisky, which at that time cost all of seventeen Leones per bottle, a lot of money in those days. There was a similar prize for the largest number of fish caught by each boat. Dave called our attention to the time, so we belted back and arrived outside the club at 6.28 pm - the weighing in closed at 6.30 pm! There was no time to lose so, without waiting for the boat to be drawn up the slipway, Martin and Dave each jumped into the sea holding a large barracuda. Martin managed to get to shore and the fish he was carrying was weighed in time. Unfortunately, Dave lost his fish on the way to shore. Thus the only catch registered for our boat was the one Martin carried in, but this was not good enough to win us a prize. However, we did win the booby prize again, for which Dave qualified by catching a large fish out at sea and then losing it in shallow water near the slipway. This prize was a further two bottles of Black Label, which we hadn't expected to win, and if he hadn't lost the fish we wouldn't have won anything anyway, so this loss turned out to be our gain. We carried a hanging scale with us and had weighed the two fish in the boat. Some of the other entries weighed more than ours would have done even if we had not lost a fish. We left the boatboys* diving for the lost fish, and they managed to find it at 7.00 pm - too late for the competition, so we let them keep the fish.

Many years later, when on a visit to Freetown in 2002, I met up with Dave Wright again and reminded him of the time he let go of a large barracuda during the fishing competition. "Let go of it!" he cried, "So would you have done if it had bitten your fingers!"

Martin and I often went fishing together in my boat, and he recently reminded me of the time when he had to jump overboard twice in one afternoon. It was a Bank Holiday and we were spending it at sea, trolling or doing bottom fishing with the engine switched off. When we were ready to return to the club, I pulled on the cord to start the engine. Somehow I managed to let go of the cord and it fell into the sea. Martin, ever helpful, jumped overboard and retrieved the cord. I made a second attempt to restart the engine and the result was just the same as before, including me letting go of the cord. Once again I asked Martin to recover the cord. He did so with some reluctance, but retrieved the cord again and as the sea was on the ebb he was washed towards the boat and climbed back aboard. Martin said that if I were so careless as to let go of the cord a third time I should have to jump in myself! Luckily for me the engine started at the third attempt, and I kept tight hold of the cord.

My friend Dr Dave Wright had a boat of his own, a large sailing boat, and I would occasionally go fishing with him. It was then I learnt the warning, "ready to tack", that he would shout out to me when he wanted to change course. The huge boom would swing over towards me, causing me to duck quickly to avoid a nasty knock.

As well as fishing competitions the club held regular races for sailing boats. These were usually held once a month on a Saturday afternoon, and my son John sometimes acted as crew for a friend of mine, Ted Cooper, who had a sailing boat. They did very well, and John still has more than one pewter mug he won during those days. As sailing boats were dependent upon the wind they used a different set of rules when meeting up with another boat at sea to what applied to motor boats. With motor boats, of which I can speak from experience, it was necessary to pass other motor boats with their green lights adjacent. The green light was on the left, or port side of the boat, and the boats would always pass each other on that side. The starboard side of the boat would have a red light. The

---

* It was usual in the club to call the men who worked at launching and bringing in the members' boats, 'boatboys' to distinguish them from the boat-owning members.

reason for this is that the captain of each boat knew which way to turn his boat to avoid a collision with another boat going in the opposite direction.

Other boats were not the only things we had to watch out for. As banana plants only bore fruit once, the discarded trunks were sometimes thrown into the sea and would travel quite a long distance in the water. As they are very heavy when laden with water, they could damage a boat if you were to collide with one of them, so we always kept a wary eye open for drifting banana trunks.

➤ Events which were very popular with the children were the swimming galas held two or three times a year. They were usually sponsored by one of the airlines, such as KLM (Dutch) or UTA (French), and the airline would supply prizes for the winners of the races. In addition, after the gala was over, there would be a cheese and wine party for participants and parents (the parents got the wine, there were soft drinks for the children). The cheese and wine would have been specially flown in by the sponsoring airline, usually accompanied by fresh grapes and other fruit, not easily available in Freetown, and these occasions were very enjoyable.

➤ Some of the Lebanese men would gather to play backgammon, or rather, the Lebanese version of the game known as 'tawleh' (meaning 'table'), 'tric-trac' or 'Shesh-besh', which means 'Six-five'. The rules are different to backgammon as usually played in England, and it seemed to be part of the game when moving the seeds to slam them down on the board with a resounding clatter that could be heard from some distance away. Sunday afternoons were the most popular time to play, and it was not unusual to see people like John Hawa or Malik Yanni come into the club with their boards under their arms. Sometimes two or three games would be going on at adjacent tables at the same time. The game was played for the love of it, and no money was involved in the games at Aqua Club.

➤ One day at Aqua Club when my youngest daughter was just a few months old, I was standing at the bar having a drink with a friend while my wife was sitting at a nearby table with baby Linda. Linda had got to the stage of being able to sit up alone without support, and my wife had put her to sit on the floor. Suddenly she slowly toppled forward until her nose rested on the floor, which made her cry. My friend and I cried out together, "Wate man fordom e bruise e nose". This phrase was a reference to a type of yellow plum which, when it fell from the tree, got bruised, and so came to be generally known as 'Wate man fordom e bruise e nose', meaning in English 'White man fell down and bruised his nose'. My wife Joan was not amused as she did not get the joke, having never heard of that particular plum.

➤ I used to go fishing regularly miles out from shore, sometimes alone. As I sat waiting for a bite, 'pontus ubique et ubique caelum' was a Latin phrase that would often come into my head at these times; translated it means 'the sea all around and the sky all above'.

I started to bring home bigger fish, sometimes barracudas five or six feet long, perhaps the smaller mackerel or snapper. When freshly caught their colours are bright and shiny, but they soon fade. On some occasions I caught a Jack (a fish to be reckoned with known for its fighting prowess, commonly called 'cowreh' in Sierra Leone). One weighed as much as thirty-eight pounds! It had red flesh and I didn't like it much cooked on its own, but made into fishballs and cooked in a stew to eat with rice, it was very tasty. However thirty-eight pounds of fish makes a lot of fishballs, so I shared it with my neighbours.

On Saturdays I would usually go out fishing with friends. On one particular Saturday I took a relative with me with two other friends. When we were far out at sea trolling for barracuda, my relative, let us call him Hassan, announced that he needed to pay a visit to the Gents. As my speed boat did not contain a toilet, I told him to hang over the side of the boat near the back, which he did. The sea was a little choppy, and we suddenly noticed Hassan was no longer with us. We heard cries of "Help, stop the boat," from behind us, and looked round only to see Hassan bobbing in the water behind us surrounded by the mess he had created. I stopped the boat and threw a line overboard. Hassan seized it and tried to come back on board, but I stopped him. "You need a wash," I told him. "Just hold on to the rope and we will tow you for a while. When you are clean you can come aboard." We proceeded to do just that, and after a few minutes of "washing" we allowed him back on board. The experience seemed to put Hassan off fishing, for he never came with me again.

Quite recently I was going through some old accounts of the Bai Bureh Uprising of 1898 and came across a paragraph about a British officer that made me think of my relative Hassan:-

> "This officer had some curious experiences in Africa. While employed in the Royal Niger Companies Police, he lost a field gun in action and was made to pay for it. On another occasion at a fire in Freetown, **he fell down a cesspit in mess kit and had to be hurled into the harbour before he was allowed indoors to change.**"

➡ Sam Courban, a lawyer cousin of mine, is the second son of one of the twenty-eight first cousins I have (or had, as sadly most of them have now died). One Saturday Sam and I, with some friends, went deep-sea fishing in my boat. We were trolling with several rods, each with a line running far behind the boat but at different lengths so as not to let them tangle with each other. I was the only one to have a line with a meter to tell me how much line I had let out.

I was the lucky one to get a fish on my line, and as I reeled it in we could tell it was a large one due to the bending of the rod! When it was right up to the boat I lifted it up on the line and called one of my friends to gaff it, that is to lean over the side of the boat with a large hook with a handle, and hook the fish securely by the gills so that it can be lifted into the boat. When the live barracuda, measuring about six feet, was lying on the bottom of the boat, we quickly pushed an empty glass bottle into its mouth to prevent it from biting anyone. This was our usual practise when we caught a fish, irrespective of its size, as a safety precaution. The 'safety' precaution, however, had a small danger of its own. On one occasion, having caught a large fish, I shoved a bottle in its mouth as usual, only to have the fish fire it back at me when I turned my back. The bottle caught me on my left hip but caused no damage. I quickly replaced the bottle, but this time made sure that it was firmly in place!

The bottle incident was not the only time that I was struck by a flying object while out in my boat. There was one occasion when I was bending over to do something or the other when I received a sharp blow on my bottom. I looked round to see who was responsible for this, thinking it was the doing of one of my friends, only to find that a flying fish had done it! It was one of several flying fish that suddenly appeared flying above the surface of the water near the boat, presumably being chased by mackerels, and several of them landed inside the boat. I took them home with me, being my only catch of the day (if I can say that I caught them when they simply threw themselves into my boat!). We cleaned them and had them for supper, and found them very tasty. I never acquired them quite so easily or cheaply again, but after this would sometimes buy them from the local fishermen.

About a year later Sam bought a bigger boat than mine, and we sometimes went fishing in his boat. Sam made use of the priest, a heavy rounded stick like a truncheon, to hit the fish on the head to kill them, instead of putting a bottle in its mouth.

One afternoon when Sam came with me in my boat, he brought his pistol with him and was doing target practice out at sea. He would fire at some object floating in the sea, perhaps a banana tree or a bottle or a piece of driftwood. The shell case of the bullet would fly out from the back of the gun, and one of them hit me on my bare chest as I was standing just behind him. The casing stuck fast on my chest with a sizzle, and when I pulled it off it left a burn mark on my skin. I always kept a first aid box in the boat, so I was able to put some soothing cream on the small round wound on my chest. I took the shell home to show my wife and children and told them what had happened.

➻ Another friend I often went fishing with once caught what felt like a large fish, and we hoped it was a large barracuda as it was very heavy in the water. My friend struggled with it for nearly an hour and eventually brought it near the boat. All my offers of help were turned down, understandably, as my friend said he wanted to bring the fish to the boat unaided. When at last he got it to the side of the boat, I got ready the gaff to bring it in, but alas, my friend was destined to be disappointed. Come to

156

think of it, I was disappointed as well, for when my friend pulled it out of the water we found that the 'fish' had turned into a plastic bag full of water, which was very heavy. After so much fighting to bring the 'fish' in, and spending nearly an hour only to bring in a plastic bag, our mortification was great. We continued fishing, hoping this time to bring in a real barracuda or mackerel, or whatever, so long as it was a fish!

➡ When out with a good friend of mine, Dzul Iscandri, on another occasion, we saw what looked like a small patch of haze in the distance. I asked Dzul what he thought it was but he couldn't tell, so we turned the boat towards it. After ten minutes fast driving we were near enough to see that in fact the haze was caused by two whales spouting water out of their blowholes as they played together. I turned the boat through 180 degrees and drove away at top speed, putting as much distance as possible between them and us. The boat's bow lifted above the water and the stern, where Dzul was sitting, was low as we planed. We looked back to see the whales pumping out the water which had caused the haze we had seen from afar. Had it not been for the risk of the boat being overturned by the whales for their sport, we would have stayed to watch them.

As well as the occasional whales, enormous manta rays wider than my boat could sometime be seen jumping flat out of the water, and landing back on the sea with a belly flop. These mantas were big enough, if you were unfortunate, to jump up from under your boat and lift it out of the water, most likely overturning it. On a few occasions we also saw dolphins, sometimes in quite a large group, and watched them jumping gracefully out of the water in synchronised pairs as if performing for us.

Another fish that my fishing friends and I tried to catch, without success, was the sawfish. This fish is a member of the ray family. It has a long flattened head and an elongated snout like a long blade with a row of large teeth along each side. This 'saw' can be as much as six feet in length and constitute one third of the total length of the fish. Sawfish are bottom dwellers, and strike from side to side with the snout among a school of fish to kill or maim their prey. I understand the sawfish can also use this offensive weapon to cut large pieces of flesh from bigger fish. It is probably a good thing we never did catch one, because it would have been too big for us to handle, being as long as my boat and weighing far more! I bought the saw-teeth from two of these creatures from the local fishermen, one being very large, which I somehow lost in Freetown. The other is only thirty inches long and has forty-six teeth, and I still have it in my home in England, together with a snakeskin from a boa constrictor that is over ten feet long.

A sea creature very common in the waters of Sierra Leone is the cuttlefish. I have never actually seen one, but the cuttle-bone, its internal shell, can be found in abundance on the beaches. It is four to five inches long and pointed at one end, and full of a white substance that can be easily ground to powder and used for bringing out the shine in metals. It is also used for caged birds to sharpen their beaks on. We used it ourselves, ground up to powder and fed to our ducks mixed in with their normal food, when the shells of their eggs were not strong enough.

➤ We did several types of fishing from the boat. We would most often troll for fish, which means that we would use rods and lines with lures with one or more hooks which would be allowed to run out at varying distances behind the boat. The reason for this is to make sure that the lines do not snag on the engine, and also do not tangle with each other, because usually each person in the boat would have his own line out. I would always carry spare lines so if a friend did not have his own I would lend him one. The boat would be run at a very slow speed so that the lures in the water would look like small fish. The thinner the line used, the more experience is required for 'playing' a fish to avoid breaking the line. A lot of fun can be had in bringing in a large fish, weighing about 50 pounds, on a thin line intended for a smaller fish.

We would hope to catch barracuda (torpedo-shaped predators thought by some to be more dangerous than sharks), mackerel, and jack when trolling. Mackerel swim faster than the barracuda, so when we were fishing for mackerel I would run the boat a little faster. Sometimes when a fish had been pulled in close to the boat it would try to dislodge the hook and often would swim under the boat, making it necessary to turn the boat so that we could get the fish on the side to pull it up.

Fishing with a line and rod is not without its dangers. One friend went out in his large sailing boat and whilst trying to throw out his line on a rod, he caught - his own head! Wearing a hat might have helped. This incident, however, did not spoil his enthusiasm for fishing.

Another method would be bottom fishing. For that we would stop the boat, switch off the engine, and perhaps even anchor if the tide was running. I had a fish-finder instrument on the boat, which would show if a shoal of fish was under the boat. We would use what in Freetown we called a 'boota' (in English a 'boulter'), being a long line with lead weights attached, which would have shorter lines with hooks on them tied to the main line at intervals.

I would sometimes do bottom fishing with my friend the late Lionel Miller, another lawyer. We would sit at our ease and enjoy the peace and gentle motion of the boat, discussing the events of the week whilst waiting for a bite. Quite likely we would catch snappers or groupers this way. These fish tended to stay nearer to the bottom of the ocean. One afternoon we were relaxing in this way when a sudden breeze caught Lionel's hat and blew it into the sea. It floated a few yards from us and out of the blue a seagull that had been following the boat swooped down and sat on it, as if it were a nest in the middle of the sea. We turned the boat and picked up Lionel's hat, after shooing the bird away. Luckily, the hat was only wet!

Perhaps the bird brought us luck, because on our way back to the club we had a bite and caught a large barracuda, four feet ten inches long and weighing thirty-eight pounds!

Some of my friends preferred underwater spear fishing, for groupers or snappers, but they would usually check the sea for the presence of the Portuguese man-of-war, known locally as "wata-bosin". This was a large jellyfish which was quite common and would leave red weals on the skin if you were unlucky enough to come in contact with it.

➤ I made good use of my boat and went to various places with my wife and children. There were places that could be reached quicker and easier by boat than by road. For instance, one Sunday in February 1976 I took Joan and my three youngest children by boat to Kambia. My eldest daughter Rahme, generally known as Margaret, was studying nursing in England at that time, and Jamal and Michael were studying for degrees at Fourah Bay College up Mount Aureol.

My friend Dr Mike Rekab (a dentist) went in his speedboat Maramy, accompanied by the American Ambassador Mr Samuels, Mr Janneh, a Member of Parliament, and his security guard, and Alusine Hajallie. Mr Hajallie's brother-in-law, Rafik, travelled in my boat. We left Aqua Club at 9.00 am and it took us one hour twenty minutes to reach Kychom, where we dropped the American Ambassador, Mr Janneh and his security guard. We tied up next to what was thought to be the biggest launch made in Sierra Leone, with an inboard engine and a large awning. It was owned by Paramount Chief Yumkella of Kychom and was called, I think, M.L. Kychom. It was used for carrying goods and passengers between Kambia and Freetown.

The two boats then continued up the Great Scarcies River to Kasiri, just ten minutes away, to the home of Rafik. His wife, Kadija, had prepared lunch for us all and was very nice to us. We had an excellent meal of both African and Lebanese dishes. We had Jollof rice and crane-crane sauce with rice, both African. We also had Lebanese mehshe, which is rice and ground beef wrapped in cabbage leaves, shish-kebab and salad. After visiting some friends, we left Alusine and Rafik at their homes in Kasiri and went on in the two boats to Rokupr. On our way we passed Mambolo, and I showed Joan and the children where I used to live, and told them of the manatee I once saw there. I also told them that there was a rice-mill at Mambolo, which at the time I lived there was operated by Pa Charles, Mr Tucker and Mr Morrison. The locally-grown husk rice was cleaned and supplied to the mainly Lebanese buyers in Kasiri. The bags of cleaned rice were stacked roof-high in their hundreds in the stores and outside the shops ready for shipment to Freetown.

My children were delighted to see a pelican on the river bank, and numerous other birds as we sped along the river. Suddenly my engine stopped and I found I was out of petrol, the ten gallon tank I started off with at Aqua Club was dry. I connected up the smaller tank which contained five gallons, but the engine would not start at first, due to an overflow of petrol. Mike turned back to see what the matter was. By this time we had drifted on to a mud bank but we pushed the boat off again with a long cane which I kept in the boat for use in such circumstances (man can't tell!). The engine soon started (after the overflow had dried up). We continued up river, and I drove in the wake left by Mike's boat Maramy, where the water was smooth. As we passed small villages we saw the women washing their clothes on the river bank, and they waved to us as we went by.    We arrived at Rokupr at 4.00 pm.

We caused a sensation when we arrived, as two speedboats were seldom seen arriving together. We went to see Allie Mullah at the Rokupr Trading and Transport Company Ltd, but he had gone to supervise the building of a Mosque, a self-help project. Before returning I showed my family where I used to live when I had a shop in Rokupr some years before after moving from Mambolo. I lived in Rokupr for about eighteen months, before transferring to a different part of Sierra Leone – Kailahun in the Eastern Province, where my father, brother and sister were living. After filling up with petrol we left Rokupr at 4.20 pm and it took us twenty-five minutes to reach Kychom, where Mike picked up the American Ambassador, then he led the way back to Freetown. On our way we passed Bailor, and I showed my wife and children where the launches used to stop for the night. I knew the place quite well because when I lived in Mambolo I used to travel by launch to Freetown and we would tie up at Bailor and sleep on board the launch until morning, so as to arrive in Freetown before mid-day.

As we continued on our way the sea became quite choppy and we had to reduce speed to about twenty knots. We arrived back at the Club at 7.15 pm – exactly two hours. Our trip was much quicker going to Kychom for two reasons, one, the tide was in our favour, and two, the sea was very calm so we were able to travel at speed. The whole family had enjoyed their day out. We were all ready for an early night and slept like logs.

➼ One Sunday in April 1976 I went to the Aqua Club at 7.00 a.m. in order to launch my boat, as the tide was going out and the water would be too low to launch at the time I wanted to set out. I found that there was no electricity for the boat winch. I left the other boat owners waiting at the club while I drove to the Electricity Department at Falconbridge in Freetown to see if anything could be done. The manager of the power station, Mr Labor, promised to give the club power for two hours, but later decided to give Aqua Club power for the day. Freetown had frequent power cuts because there was not sufficient electricity for everybody. Power would be shared, different areas having power at different times of the day, but it was sometimes possible to arrange for a particular area to have power out of the scheduled time for a particular occasion.

Back at Aqua Club the others and I launched our boats and anchored them in shallow water, and then went home for breakfast. I collected my cousin Choukri Courban and went to the club where we were met by Mr Paul Cole-King, a UN expert on museums, who went with us to the Banana Islands, which was due south of Aqua Club. He wanted in particular to see and photograph the old grave of Captain Reid, who died at the Bananas in 1712. The Banana Islands consisted of three islands, namely Dublin, Ricketts, and Meheux which got its name from Jean Meheux, a French trader, who settled there for several years. The nearest town on the mainland is Kent.

We anchored in 'Dead Dog's Bay' to have our lunch. This name had been given to one of the bays in the islands by Anne Beasley, wife of Mike Beasley, an Englishman who was manager of the Sierra Leone Brewery at that time. She had gone fishing there with her husband one weekend and seen a dead dog floating in the water. She named the area Dead Dog's Bay, and that name has stayed with the boat-owning fraternity until this day.

In the afternoon we wanted to land Mr Cole-King on Dublin Island and wait for him while he explored the cemetery, but the tide was high and choppy and we could not land. This also meant that Mr Cole-King could not swim ashore, with or without his camera, so he had to stay on the boat with us and we fished for the rest of the day. Choukri caught a barracuda, and another barracuda got away, just as we had brought it near to the boat for gaffing.

➤ I drove in to town on the morning of 6 September 1976, and everything looked as normal. At 10 o'clock I received a call in my chambers from the manageress of Aqua Club telling me that the club had been hit by a tornado in the early hours of the morning and many of the boats and boatsheds had been damaged. At that time I was the committee member for House and Grounds so I drove straight out there. The damage was severe but very limited. The carpark and club house were untouched, as were the first few boatsheds, where, luckily for me, my own boat was kept. Further on, everything was a shambles. Some of the sheds had their roofs blown off, while other roofs had blown down and collapsed on to the boats themselves, damaging them very badly. Some speedboats were parked in a long open shed. One speedboat, bigger and higher than those around it, took the weight of the roof and saved some of the smaller boats from major damage. A few of the sailing boats were blown over on their sides, but sustained only minor damage. They were parked in the open, and that saved them, as most of the damage to boats was caused by the falling and collapsing roofs. Apparently a whirlwind had suddenly blown in from the sea, passed along the boat-shed area of the club, and then turned back out to sea. It lasted only two minutes, but did many thousands of Leones worth of damage. In those days the Leone was two to one pound Sterling.

In 1980 the weather again did damage at the club. On Wednesday 6<sup>th</sup> February the wind blew very strongly for the whole day and night. The sea was very choppy. It was low tide when I got to the club, but as the tide came in the water was very rough with waves breaking with violence on the rocks, a sight that was unusual at Aqua Club. Some of the people out wind-surfing had to be helped in to shore by sailing boats.

The next day I went to the club and found one of the catamarans smashed against the rocks. As Boat Member at that time I had warned the owner of that boat that he should keep an eye on it and be ready to move it to safety in the lagoon nearby. He insisted that his anchor chain was very heavy and it would take a lot to lift it. Famous last words!! Another 'cat' had broken its anchor chain, but luckily the owner had left a watchman on board and he was able to throw out another, larger anchor which held the boat just twenty feet from the rocks. Paddy's 'cat' survived the storm as it was firmly anchored.

➡ Sometimes on Sunday I would go in my boat with my family to join a group of friends at Bawbaw Beach, some miles along the Freetown peninsula. Two very good friends, Dr Ahmadu Fadlu-Deen and Badamassi Mahdi, an engineer, jointly owned a few acres of beach land and had built a beach house there. Nearly every Sunday my family and I would go to Bawbaw Beach, sometimes by car and sometimes by boat. The first time we went by car, I followed the instructions given to me by Kitty, Ahmadu's wife. It consisted of counting the number of bridges that we drove over starting from Goderich village, and to turn off when we had gone over twelve bridges. At the entrance to the road leading to their beach land Kitty had tied a red cloth on one of the trees, showing us where to turn off. This worked perfectly and we found the place without difficulty.

When I went by boat the children on the beach would all swim out to the boat to be taken for a ride. If I caught a fish on the way there, it would be taken on shore, cleaned and cooked immediately and added to all the various dishes set out for lunch. It was usual for a large group of friends to gather there for the day, and each family would bring food which would be set out on the tables and shared by us all. The group consisted of many different nationalities – Sierra Leonean, Chinese, Asian, Lebanese, English, Canadian, American, Vietnamese and more, so the food was also varied and always delicious, the more so for being eaten in the open air, and my barracuda found its way to nearly every plate!

The children would all play games on the beach or swim, while the adults relaxed, swam or played bridge. Sometimes someone would bring a guitar and we would have a singsong. In the afternoon around 4.00 pm we would always have an English style tea, with cups of tea and coffee, and various types of cake, brought by the wives. When it was time to go, if I had come by boat I would have to swim out to it because the tide had come in and the boat was now in deep water. I would bring the boat as far in shore as I could, to load up my family, and because of this I bought a flat-bottomed inflatable dinghy with four oars capable of taking six people. When we had got all the people and bits and pieces back to the boat, we would deflate the dinghy and that too would go in the boat. We would return by sea to Aqua Club where we had left our car. Those days were special and are still fresh in the minds of all my family and friends.

Before going home we had to wash the boat down with fresh water, inside and out, and flush out the engine, something we did every time we took the boat out. This was to wash away all the salt. The hose pipe was connected directly to the engine by a special connector and the tap opened. Fresh water flowed through the hose and would circulate through the engine and come out through two holes at the back of the engine. After ten to fifteen minutes I would taste the water to see if it was still salty. When the water tasted fresh I knew the engine was properly flushed and so I disconnected the hose.

➼ Soon after buying the Fletcher I made a trip to England with a Lebanese friend, Ahmed Jaward, who wanted to do business with an English friend of mine. When the business was concluded, we had time to do some shopping and I decided to buy some life jackets to be kept in the boat. Ahmed came with me and helped me to carry them, as six life jackets are bulky for one man to carry! I also bought a hooter. It was a very loud one and had to be attached to a cylinder of gas. It worked by simply depressing a button on the top, and I mainly used it to attract the attention of the boatboys near the slipway so they could have the trailer ready for me to bring up my boat.

A few days after our return to Freetown I went out in my boat fishing with the same friend. When we set out the weather was very good, the sun shining and the sea very calm and as smooth as glass as if stationary. It is always good, however, to remember that the weather can suddenly change, as the following lines remind us:
"Though the weather is fine, and the winds blow fair,
Sudden changes may well come to pass,
Then let not security dull prudent care,
But watch well the range of the 'glass'!"
('Glass' here means barometer.)

We had been fishing for about two hours without catching anything when suddenly it started getting dark and a wind sprang up, and then rain began to fall. We donned our life jackets. (Was it coincidence that the first time the life jackets were used I was with the friend who helped me to choose them and carry them back to our hotel in London?) Within minutes the rain was so heavy that we could hardly see the front of the boat, so I had to guide the boat by means of a mariner's compass or aqua meter. This compass was specially made for boats and it tells the direction you are going. Suddenly Ahmed saw some lights and shouted, "Look, that must be land over there." I turned the boat in the direction he was pointing but could hardly see anything, but in a few minutes I too saw the lights he was referring to. Being more used to the sea, I knew immediately that those lights were not on land. I cried, "Land my foot, that is a ship coming towards us and it is too close for comfort!" I quickly swung the wheel away from the lights that were bearing down on us, but not in time to avoid the wake of the large ship as it swept passed us. We were tossed here and there by the waves, but the boat was a good one, having what we call a "deep V" hull, and we were safe enough. I think my friend was really not a boatman, however, for he seldom came fishing with me again, although we remained good friends and met frequently.

➤ One year we had great excitement at the club because the Whitbread Multihull round-the-world yacht race was going to have Freetown as one of its ports of call, and it was planned that they would all come in to Aqua Club to anchor. At that time Dr Michael A. Rekab, a dentist who practised with Dr Rolv Holst-Roness, was the club commodore and I was one of the committee members, and some changes and improvements were planned. Mr Jack Stoll of the sawmills at Panguma, north of Kenema in the Eastern Province, generously donated timber to build some offices that would be used during the race for banking facilities for the visitors. Mr Stoll had lived in Sierra Leone for well over thirty years, of which twenty years were spent in Panguma.

Improvements were made to the chophouse, which provided hamburgers and snacks on a regular basis, and full-scale meals from time to time when the club had a dinner and dance. We had visions of seeing Freetown Aqua Sports Club on international television, radio and world-wide newspaper coverage. Then the blow fell. The yacht race was re-routed and the yachts would not be coming to Freetown after all. Everyone was very disappointed, but at least the club had the benefit of a brand new wooden chalet which was used for committee meetings and manager's office.

➤ In 1981 whilst I was Commodore of the club (with Rudolf Dworzak Snr as Vice Commodore), the telephone on the bar 'gave up the ghost'. I placed a notice on the telephone reading 'OUT OF ORDER', to prevent people wasting their time trying to get through. Whilst sitting at bar the next day a strong breeze sprung up and blew the notice off the telephone and on to my lap. The members who were present with me at the bar that evening, including Amy Dworzak, now Amy Cobb, have never let me forget the time my private parts were so publicly labelled 'Out of order'!

➤ My children all spent quite a bit of time at the club and got to know the workers quite well. One young man had been set to clean the beach of all the rubbish brought in by the tide. One day my son John discovered that this young man would empty the leaves that he had cleared behind the rocks on the beach when the tide was out. John asked him why he did that, as when the tide rose again it would bring all the leaves back and leave them on the beach.  His explanation was that if the beach was clean the manageress of the club would find him another job helping the boat boys push the various speedboats in and out of the water and he preferred cleaning the beach to pushing heavy boats.

➤ The story above reminded me about an incident with our gardener at home in Lumley.  We had tall canna lilies in red and yellow lining the path to the front gate and all around the badminton court.  The flower heads would fall off when they died, and as there were so many of them the gardener was kept busy sweeping up the dead ones.  One day we went out into the garden to find all the canna lilies had been cut off about a foot from the ground and there was not a flower to be seen.  We called the gardener and asked him why he had done it.  He told us, "The flowers fall and make the paths look dirty and I have to sweep them daily.  With no flowers the place will stay clean!"

➤ In the early days of Aqua Club, as we all called it, an evening of food and fireworks was usually planned for Guy Fawkes Day, 5 November.  The food would be a barbecue with burgers and sausages and jacket potatoes.  The fireworks would be let off on the beach by some adults, with the children watching from the grass near the clubhouse where they could see everything but were in no danger.  This went on for some years but then firework displays were banned by the authorities after a panic had followed a particularly noisy Fifth November held at Hill Station Club when people living nearby had mistaken the bangs for gunshots.

➤ Every year the club had a Christmas party for the children of members.  Father Christmas would always attend, arriving by boat or by car, depending on whoever was planning the event that year.  One of the members would dress up as Father Christmas (on one occasion played by me), and would arrive at the club with bulging sacks of gaily wrapped presents.  Each child would receive a gift from Father Christmas, which had been secretly handed in to the club in advance by the parents, with a value limit set by the club to avoid jealousy among the children.

It was also usual during the 1980's for the Club to put on a variety show at Christmas time, and many of the members took an active part in producing or performing in the show.  The bar area was converted into the stage, and the audience sat on chairs placed on the grass in the open air.  One year I wrote (and acted in) a series of comic sketches with a legal flavour.  One such play was called "The Deaf Client" and went as follows: The client was accused of using the "V" sign against someone, thus provoking a breach of the peace, and was charged to court.  She consulted a barrister, a Mr S.A.B.Y. Book, Q.C., M.A., Ph.D, B.Cal, etc. (played by a good friend of mine – Zed Bahsoon).  On his signboard, after his name and degrees it read:  "Aqua Chambers, phone 30268 (when in working order): Hours of business 8.30 to 9.30 am.  Lunch 9.30 am to 5.00 pm.  Afternoon 5.00 pm to 6.30 pm."  The lawyer advised the client to plead deafness and whatever the magistrate said to her, she should make as if she could not hear him and say "Eehh?" In court she acted perfectly and said "Eehh?" to everything that was said to her. Mr S.A.B.Y. Book then explained that his client was deaf and used sign language, giving several examples. He explained further that the "V" sign simply meant "well done". The magistrate (played by me) then said, holding up three fingers, "Does that mean 'Very well done'?"

In the end the magistrate acquitted her. The barrister thanked the magistrate, and as he left the stage with his client he told her to come to his chambers to settle his fees. The final scene showed the lawyer in his chambers asking the client to pay her bill, at which she looked at him and said "Eehh?" He repeated the question again only to elicit the same answer, "Eehh?" It then dawned on him that she had learnt the lesson he had taught her only too well and was using it to her benefit. He was left with no alternative but to drive her out of his office! The moral of this story is, never teach a client to say anything untruthful in court when it may be later used against you!

I also acted as Compere to the show and introduced each act with a bit of 'patter'. In the lead-in to the sketch about S.A.B.Y. Book, I mentioned that he wrote many books and that I picked up one called 'The Study of Aerodynamics in Ancient Times', only to discover that it was all about kite-flying! The audience was in stitches, which put them in a good frame of mind to enjoy the sketch that followed.

Another sketch that I did was entitled 'The Sunken Ship'. I wore a long Arab gown, a white skull cap and a long grey beard. My only props were a blackboard and a piece of chalk; I drew a rapid sketch of the sky and sea, and gave it the title The Sunken Ship. The children in the audience shouted out, "Where is the ship?" to which I replied, "You can't see it because it has sunk and it's under the water!" It went down well and produced a laugh, to fill the gap while the stage was got ready for the next playlet.

Other years the members put on a pantomime, as well as a few sketches. I can remember 'Cinderella' and 'Sleeping Beauty', both produced with as much attention to costumes and scenery as to acting, proving the members had many hidden talents. A printed programme was usually produced for these performances. 'The Victorians' was produced by a club member, Sandy Laskey, an American, and the programme contained the following instructions to the audience: "1. Ladies, please remove your hats. 2. Smoking 'seegars' is prohited. 3. No spitting. 4. You are requested not to throw peanuts at the pianist." Food was served in the interval, and on this occasion was prepared by another member, Chic Courban, my cousin, who was a very good cook. All the members gave their services free of charge, and any profits from the entrance fees were donated to charity.

I also remember a special performance by the Tabule Theatre called "Dis Man Na Debul" (This Man is a Devil). Tickets would be sold for these shows, and just before Christmas, donations would be made from the money raised to local children's charities.

➽ An occasional event at the club was an evening of special food cooked by a member or members. It was a very cosmopolitan club and sometimes a member could be persuaded to prepare some special dishes of his own country's cuisine. Thus we had a Lebanese night, arranged by Salim Sabrah, an Italian night organised by Daniella Bundo, and a Spanish night with paella, although I cannot now remember who did the cooking. Another Lebanese meal was laid on by a member, Zain Ibrahim, a good friend and fellow fisherman who owned a business on the main road at Congo Cross. These meals were always very popular, and the club tried to provide appropriate music and wine to accompany the food, to give an authentic atmosphere.

➽ During my second tenure of office as Commodore, in 1989/90, the Royal Yacht Britannia paid a short visit to Freetown. If I remember correctly it was on its way to Nigeria where it was to meet Prince Charles and Princess Diana. The club was informed of the visit by the British High Commission, and we were happy to throw the club open to the members of the crew for the length of their stay, a facility which they were happy to make use of. A reception was held on board the Royal Yacht on the second day of their visit, and as I was Commodore of the Aqua Club, my wife and I were invited. Being English, my wife was particularly happy to attend, and so was I. We thoroughly enjoyed being taken over the yacht and shown the various apartments the Queen and her family used when on board. We were even shown the engine rooms, which were so spotlessly clean you could have eaten your lunch off the engines. At the end of the visit, the band from the Royal Yacht Beat the Retreat on the quay whilst the guests stood along the rails of the ship to watch. A memorable evening.

This brought to mind the club's invitation a few years before of the USS Thorn, an American ship on a visit to Freetown. The crew was allowed free use of the facilities of the club during their stay, and in return for this the ship's band performed at the club one evening.

➽ Whenever any of us took our boats out from the club, we always wrote on the blackboard in the winch house where we were going and the time we intended to be back. This was a simple precaution and was meant to avoid search parties setting out unnecessarily before the estimated time of arrival was past by an hour or so. I assisted in several searches for boats that were late returning to the club.

On one occasion, a small speedboat carrying four Lebanese friends of mine was late back and several boats went out that evening to look for it but with no success. Several club members with boats arranged to meet at the club early in the morning to continue the search. Most of the members thought that they would most likely find the missing boat around Banana Islands, a favourite fishing area, or anchored somewhere due to a broken-down engine, which could happen to any of us at any time. I had looked at the tide book that morning, and also made enquiries from the boat boys where it was likely that the flow of tide would have carried the boat. From the information gathered I, with two other members, took my boat out towards the Guinea shore in the opposite direction to where the other searchers had gone. After travelling for about twenty five minutes one of my companions said he could see a boat in the distance but could not tell who was in it or what type of boat it was. I looked as well but it was too far away to see clearly. We decided to go and find out. After travelling for about twenty minutes at full speed we could see people standing up and waving to us. When we got nearer we saw that it was the boat we were looking for. The engine had conked out. The boat had been in water too deep to use the anchor effectively, and so it had drifted, but not as fast, due to the anchor being towed through the sea behind them. I took my friends into my boat, fastening a rope to their boat so I could tow it behind me. My wife had given me a flask of hot cocoa and some brandy, in case I was lucky enough to find the missing mariners. They were all very grateful for the brandy, which they passed from hand to hand, to warm themselves up, but declined the cocoa, saying the brandy did a much better job.

When we got back to the Aqua Club, we found it was full of the relatives and friends of the missing men waiting anxiously for news. A big cheer went up when they saw that we had them all safe and sound. The other boats returned one by one, disheartened by not having found them, but were happy to see the missing members safely in the club. A few minutes later we all dispersed to our various homes or workplaces.

➤➤ I particularly remember one Wednesday afternoon when I went out fishing with two of my friends, Rudolph Dworzak (Senior) and Mike Rekab (who has been Commodore of the Aqua Club twice), both boat-owners themselves. When we set out from the club the sea was very calm like oil. We trolled for a while and caught nothing, then we anchored off Tokeh and Rudi (that is Rudolph) and Mike did some diving and spear-gun shooting underwater, and got three groupers and two jacks. At 6.30 pm we were on our way back to the club when our small tank ran out of petrol. We changed over to the large tank, but the engine would not start – the battery went flat for some reason or the other. We then changed over to the small spare engine. This ran for a few miles, then it too conked out! This happened on the seaward side of the Cape, a mile or so from the club, and we were drifting towards the rocks, where still could be seen the remains of a cargo ship that had been wrecked there many years before. Try as we could, we could not get the engine started. By this time a breeze had sprung up and the sea had become very choppy, so we dropped anchor.

As it happened a canoe was passing by with two fishermen on board. We waved to them and they paddled up to us. One of them was a big, strong man who was, we discovered, a policeman off duty who knew me, who was attached as security guard to a Judge of the Appeal Court. We told him our predicament, and asked him if he could go and get help for us. He told us not to worry, they would take us in themselves. But it is true that troubles do not come singly. When we tried to pull up the anchor we found it had got caught on the rocks. I found an empty plastic gallon container in the boat, cut the anchor rope and tied the container on the end to act as a marker buoy, so that we could come back the next day to try and retrieve the anchor.

We were not sure the two men would be able to tow us on their own, but as they insisted we threw them a line. They tied it on to the stern of the canoe and they started paddling. The sea was rough with white heads, and the men were sweating with their efforts. It took us over two hours to get round the point and in to Cape Club beach, a trip we could have done in five minutes had the engine been working. It was funny to see two men with paddles in a small canoe about seven feet long, towing a speedboat a lot larger than itself with three men in it. At the Cape Club we borrowed a battery from a Spanish friend, Pedro Zerpa Zerpa, who was at that time the Honorary Consul for Sierra Leone to Las Palmas, and got back to Aqua Club in just a few minutes. We turned the tables and towed the canoe with its two occupants back to Aberdeen where the men had been heading when they came to our aid. The men were warmly thanked, but they refused to accept any reward for their efforts. They said they were simply glad to be of help to fellow fishermen in need, and felt that we would have done the same for them if they had lost their paddles! This was true enough because on several occasions we had towed in fishermen when they were in difficulties. We would never leave a speedboat, sailing boat or canoe out in the open sea without going to their aid. For instance, one Saturday afternoon I was out fishing with my wife and some friends near Cape Point when we saw two Frenchmen who were clinging to their overturned kayak. We took them into my speedboat, kayak and all, and took them in to Lumley Beach near the Mammy Yoko Hotel where they worked as chefs.

Let me return to the story of the policeman who helped us. By the time we got back to Aqua Club it was 11.30 pm, the club was closed and the staff had gone home, apart from the watchmen. This meant that we had to bring the boat up the slipway ourselves, using the hand winch, but with three of us it was not too difficult. The next day I returned the borrowed battery, and waited to hear from Mr Cole, the fishing policeman, as to whether he had been able to retrieve my anchor.

Two days later Mr Cole called at my chambers. He had not been able to free the anchor, but he brought me a gift of two wooden paddles for my boat! He and I became friends, and he would often call on me in my chambers in Gloucester Street, opposite the City Hotel, whenever he was in town. Sometimes he would come in his police uniform. Unlike England, lawyers in Sierra Leone do not mind the police calling on us in Chambers in their uniforms. (Incidentally, we heard some years later, after we had come to England, that City Hotel had burned down.) Occasionally we would go fishing together in my boat. The following Saturday I took my boat out for a short while to look for my anchor but couldn't find even the marker I had left. My friend Rudi, an engineer, very kindly presented me with an anchor he had made for me himself.

➥ A Sierra Leonean lawyer friend of mine was a member of the club and also had his own speedboat. One Saturday in November 1975 he had been out fishing with another Sierra Leonean friend of his, and they did not come back at the expected time. When he was about an hour overdue, two or three of the members who had not yet gone home and who were also boat owners launched their boats to go out and search for him. The search was abandoned after about an hour as it was getting dark, and they planned to set out again in larger numbers in the morning. On Sunday morning I got a telephone call telling me what had happened, and I set off for the club. Some other members and I launched our boats to go and search, but to no avail. In the evening the presidential helicopter took off and searched the area but also in vain. On Monday morning it took off again and this time was able to spot the lost boat. The Commodore of the club, who at this time was Rolv Holst-Roness, a dentist, was directed by the helicopter pilot as to where the missing boat was, and he launched his speedboat and went out to tow them in.

On Tuesday evening I met my lawyer friend at the club, and over a drink he told me of his ordeal at sea. He said that they had had a good day fishing on Saturday and caught about six dozen small snappers, but by Sunday evening they had had to throw them all back in the sea as they had begun to smell! They had no food with them and only a gallon of water, which they soon finished in the heat of the day, so they were both hungry and thirsty. Actually, if they had known about it, they could have chewed some of the raw flesh from the fish which would have given them enough moisture to keep them going – raw fish contains fresh water, not salt water.

He also told me about the deprivation of his companion, who was a heavy smoker and was well stocked with cigarettes, but had run out of matches. In his desperation he put a cigarette in his mouth and pointed it up to the sun and said, "If only the sun could light my cigarette!"

There had been a bad storm in the early hours of Monday morning and we had been concerned for the safety of the missing mariners, but in fact the storm had been over the land and they were unharmed.

There was another time when I came close to being lost at sea, with a Hungarian friend. He worked with the National Workshop in Freetown, and he used to borrow a boat with a 60 hp Johnson engine, belonging to a friend of ours. We set off for an afternoon of fishing, and luckily decided not to go too far out at sea but to fish around Government Wharf. We switched off the engine and dropped anchor, to do some bottom fishing. After catching a few fishes we decided to raise the anchor and move on. We started the engine first, according to my custom, and then drew up the anchor, but when we tried to put the engine in forward gear, the lever would not move forward. We tried it in reverse and it went easily. We tried the forward gears again, but failed. The only way left for us was to troll backwards with the gear in reverse. We had to move slowly because when going backwards the water tended to come in over the stern. So we trolled backwards all the way to the Aqua Club, much to the amazement of the members who saw us coming in.

# Chapter 13

# At Home in Lumley

In 1966 we started building a house in Lumley Village, not far from Lumley beach. This village was originally called Pa Sandi, but in the early nineteenth century was renamed after Lieutenant-Colonel Lumley, Acting Governor. Up to now some of the older generation still refer to the village as Pa Sandi.

The design of our house was originally planned to be on pillars, which in fact was how it was built, but walls were later added to the ground floor between the pillars to make two garages, store rooms, servants' quarters and so on. The floor of our living accommodation was floated on top of the pillars, and then the outside and dividing walls were built up. The roof was put on before the windows and doors were installed, because the indoor work could then continue during the rains that lasted for over four months. In Sierra Leone there is a tradition among builders regarding completing the roof of a house. Like so many other houses in Sierra Leone, the roof was made of corrugated iron sheets. Ours was quite a large house so the roof took quite a while to complete. But the day the last corrugated iron sheet was nailed in place, the workmen who were working on the roof refused to come down until I had provided food for them. I knew of this custom beforehand and had bought rice, palm oil, fish and other ingredients and taken them all out to the site with large cooking pots in readiness for the ceremony of "bringing the workers down". When the food was ready I called the workers down and work stopped for the rest of the day whilst we all enjoyed the food. Although there was still a lot of work to be done, finishing the roof was a major milestone.

The sand used in the building had been delivered to the site in tipper lorries. These lorries would be driven out to one of the authorised beaches to be loaded up. The driver would then deliver the sand to the person who had ordered it. It was not unusual for the drivers to take on passengers whilst going back empty to the beaches, to earn a little extra money. On one occasion a driver had picked up some people who said they wanted to go to Adonkia, a village on the Peninsula road. When he reached the point they had paid up to, he stopped and waited for them to get out. Most of the passengers climbed down from the vehicle, but two men thought they would go a further distance without paying any extra, and just crouched down in the truck thinking they would not be seen. Unknown to them the driver could see them in his mirror, and shouted out, "Adonkia, Adonkia".

Still the men did not get out, and just crouched lower and remained quiet. The driver was in a hurry to move off, so thought of a way to 'assist' his passengers to alight. He reached down and pulled the lever that raised the front of the truck to empty out the sand. In this case, his unwanted passengers slid down the slippery truck and found themselves in a heap on the road. The driver continued on his way.

At last the house was finished and we moved from central Freetown to the outskirts. We had a large garden with many mature trees. There were several citrus trees - two orange, one grapefruit and one lime. The common variety of orange grown in Sierra Leone can be ripe and sweet even though it is still green in colour. The girls selling oranges in Freetown would make patterns on them whilst peeling off the outer green skin with a knife. When you bought an orange the girl would cut a small slice off the top so that you could suck out the juice.

In addition there was a berry tree, a Bathurst plum tree and a 'chook-chook' plum tree. The Bathurst plum was small and sweet. It had a bright red skin and a large single seed, and in fact there was very little fruit to eat. The 'chook-chook' plum was much larger and was often eaten with salt while it was still green and sour, ie not yet ripe. The flesh was still firm and crisp, and when cut would show thorny fibres within the fruit (chook-chook means thorn). When ripe the plum would become yellow and the flesh would be soft and juicy, but the fibres would still be there.

There were three varieties of mango trees in our garden. One was called 'rope-rope' mango, because the flesh was stringy, another was the cherry mango, and the third variety was the Guinea mango, which is the kind most often seen for sale in Europe.

Do you know why the mango is so called? Two men were travelling somewhere in Sierra Leone long ago. There were no houses nearby, only trees. The men were hungry and tired and lay down to rest under a tree, one saying to the other, "Empty bag nobar tinnap," meaning "An empty bag cannot stand up." One of them looked up and saw unfamiliar fruits hanging above them. He said to the other, "If we eat this fruit and it is poisonous we will die. If we do not eat this fruit, we may die of hunger anyway. So it is better to eat the fruit and take a chance." They ate a lot of the fruit as they were very hungry, then they lay down again. When nothing happened to them they looked at each other and one said to the other, "This can make man go," meaning they now had strength to continue their journey. From then on the fruit became known as 'mango'!!

One of our mango trees was very large and grew in the centre of the garden. One day Joan was trying to find our gardener and searched around the compound but couldn't find him. Then she heard a rustling noise above her head, and looked up to find the gardener right up at the top of the mango tree, where the biggest and best fruit could be found. On being asked what he was doing up in the tree, he replied nonchalantly, "I just came up to look at the view!"

We had two African apple trees, which bore small bell shaped fruits that were bright pink on the outside and white inside, and very sweet and crisp to eat. They would become soft and rubbery a day or two after being picked, if not kept in the fridge, which would explain why I have never seen them on the supermarket shelves in Europe. The type of apple familiar in Europe, known in Sierra Leone as 'rose apple', does not grow there. Our 'apple' trees would sometimes bear fruit in abundance, and then we would pack them in lots of several dozens in plastic bags and baskets and take them to our friends. We would also take a big bowlful and put it on the bar at Aqua Club for people to help themselves.

Another tree we had was the 'bobby-water'. There were two varieties of this fruit, one smallish and purple, the other green and about the size of an orange or bigger. We had the green variety, and when picked at just the right time the flesh was sweet and succulent. If picked a little too soon it would have a white juice which looked like milk (hence the name "bobby water" in Krio which translates to "breast milk" in English). This milk would stick like glue to your lips and teeth if the fruit was picked before it was quite ripe. This fruit is also known as "star apple" because when cut across the centre of the fruit, the section containing the seeds formed a star shape within the circle of the fruit.

Halfway down the garden grew a cashew nut tree. The nut that most people are familiar with grows at the end of a red or yellow fruit that is very juicy. The cashew nut itself has a thick casing which contains a kind of acid that is very strong. If one is foolish enough to try to bite through this casing the acid would run on the lips and chin, which would seem harmless at the time but by the next day a rash would appear which was quite painful and which took quite a few days to clear up. My wife can testify to this because the first time she ate cashew nut fruit she had not been warned!

Just near the back veranda and steps grew a large pawpaw (papaya) tree. It was a male tree and so did not bear fruit, but we had not yet got around to cutting it down. Our water tank stood on top of the cement roof of the back veranda. One day it developed a problem and we had a constant flow of water from the overflow pipe which overhung the pawpaw tree. The water poured out over the top leaves of the pawpaw tree and from there down to the lower leaves like a cascade. This happened during the Dry Season so the birds were attracted to this unusual birdbath. We were surprised and fascinated to see how the larger birds such as the bulbuls used the top leaves for their bath, and the smaller birds like firefinches and sunbirds used the lower leaves. For a few days, until we reluctantly had the overflow repaired, our back veranda was a bird-watchers paradise.

We had female pawpaw trees as well, some of which would produce very large fruits weighing a kilo or more. The fruit is delicious and is very good for the tummy, especially when eaten in the morning for breakfast. The fruit had other benefits too. My wife would use the skin as a meat tenderiser. Placed cut side down on a piece of steak, the skin would soften the meat ready for frying in an hour or so. I am told that the skin is also good for healing wounds.

We planted a hedge of small pitanga trees, a fruit that looked like a miniature tomato but was very tasty. The seed inside was very large for the size of the fruit, so there was not really very much to eat. The pitanga is high in vitamin C and calcium. It is also known as the Barbados cherry or Brazilian cherry. We had an avocado pear tree which gave us a good supply of pears for many years. They were the type known in Freetown as 'butter pear', green skin on the outside and the flesh inside a yellow-green colour. We planted a second tree, which grew well and produced two avocado pears in its first season. These pears were extremely large and weighed about a kilo each, I have never seen avocados that size before. Unfortunately the effort seemed to have exhausted the tree, because it died before producing any more. When we moved to England we were disappointed to see that the avocados on sale were very small and not as tasty as those we were used to.

Soursop and sweetsop also grew in our garden, but the most plentiful trees in our garden were coconut trees – eighteen of them. Men who traded in coconuts would come to us to buy. These men would arrive in the morning and climb the trees with a withe to pick the coconuts. They would then sit down in the garden and peel off the outer green shell with a sharp cutlass. The nuts would be counted and paid for and bagged, then the men would take a poda-poda (local transport – privately owned mini-buses which would operate along recognised routes with frequent stops taking passengers inside and all manner of goods packed on the roof) into Freetown. The jelly coconuts would be picked while they were still young, which meant they would have more than a pint of delicious coconut milk, while the flesh of the coconut would be just a thin layer of white jelly which could be scooped up with a spoon. If the coconuts are left on the tree until the outer green husk becomes brown and withered, the coconut inside would have very little milk and the flesh would be the hard white nut Europeans are familiar with. It is the milk of the coconut that turns into the flesh of the nut if left on the tree long enough. Our trees yielded about 2500 coconuts each year. The milk of the coconut is also referred to in Sierra Leone, and most places where coconuts grow, as 'coconut water'.

When a customer wanted a coconut the seller usually asked him, "Jelly or strong one?" The seller can tell which is which. If the customer asks for jelly, the seller would cut off a small section of the top to enable the customer to drink the milk. The seller would then cut the coconut in half and use his cutlass to separate the soft jelly from the shell and so that it can be eaten, usually by hand. A strong coconut is cut in two, and the seller again uses his cutlass to separate the nut from the shell. The customer would leave the empty shells for the seller to dispose of when he had finished his day's business.

At some parties, including ours, coconut milk would be served in the shell with a dash (or two) of rum, to be drunk with a straw.

Another benefit from the coconut trees was the presence of the palm swifts, which would make their nests underneath the leaves and could usually be seen swooping around in the air in a flock.

Some years later I brought back from the Gambia two 'roni' nuts to plant in our garden. Over the years they grew up to be very large palm trees but very different from coconut trees in that the trunk was much thicker and the leaves, while attached to the tree in the same way, grew in a fan shape and were used for weaving baskets. Another difference was that the nut, instead of having one section inside like the coconut, had three small sections. The year we left Freetown the trees produced flowers for the first time and have been supplying the nuts quite plentifully ever since.

One very wet and windy evening we had an English friend come to visit us to say goodbye as he was leaving for England the next day. During general conversation our friend commented that in spite of the strong winds we sometime had in Sierra Leone, the coconut trees would sway and bend but very rarely fall. We agreed with him, but two days later when strolling around the garden we found one of our coconut trees had fallen! In the twenty-five years that we lived in that house and garden in Lumley, that was the only one of our coconut trees to fall.

The fallen tree was a source of great entertainment to our children. Half of the root was still in the ground and the first few feet of trunk touched the earth. From there it rose gradually upward so that where the leaves grew was about five feet above the ground. The children would sit astride the trunk and ride it as if it were a horse, or walk along it as if it were a tightrope, and when they reached the top they would slide down the leaves to the ground. It also served as a hiding place and a play tent. Over the next few years the tree continued to grow. Its trunk dropped gradually lower until it was flat along the ground while the head of the tree grew up straight thus forming a right angle. Eventually it started to bear coconuts again!

Linda was only about three years old when the coconut tree fell. She invented a companion who became quite real for her. It was a fairy called Pompom the Giant, who could be very large or very small as it pleased him (or Linda) and he lived in the roots of the fallen coconut tree. Later, as Linda began to grow out of her fantasy friend, she said he had moved out of the garden and gone to live in the mountains along the peninsula road. For some years, however, the rest of the family continued to tease her about Pompom the Giant!

As soon as we finished building the house, the next thing we did was to build a badminton court in the garden. It was usually possible to play badminton out of doors during the dry season because there was seldom a strong breeze to interfere with the flight of the shuttlecock. We found the dimensions of the court in a book and carefully painted the lines on the cement, and put up a net. Friends would sometimes come in the early evening for a game before it got dark, or on a Sunday. Near the badminton court was a large grassy area where we played croquet. I had first played croquet on a weekend at Cumberland Lodge in England organised by the Inner Temple in October 1962 when I was a Law student. I enjoyed it so much that when I had a garden of my own I bought a croquet set so that I could invite my friends to play.

On one particular Sunday we had invited a small group of friends and family for lunch. Some of us played badminton, while others played croquet or backgammon (Lebanese style), and when the grown-ups stopped for a rest and a drink in the shade, our children took over the badminton court. Linda was still only three years old, and the other children would not let her join in, saying she was too small. They were playing doubles, Jamal and John playing against Michael and Mary, and Linda was left out. We had a break for lunch, and everyone went upstairs to the dining room. Some of our friends had taken their plates out to the veranda, and one of them called us to see what our youngest daughter was doing. Linda was all alone on the badminton court, going through the motions of a very energetic game, serving and then running as if to return the shot. She had no racquet or shuttlecock, and no opponent that anyone could see, but she was enjoying her game. We left her to play until she got tired and came up for lunch.

We also built a small swimming pool for our children, and sometimes friends would bring their own children to join in the fun. It was built above ground with the walls three feet high, which prevented any toddler falling in, and was filled with fresh water from a tap at one side. After a few years the pool became too small for the children so we converted it to a "baffa", a small open-sided hut. We made an opening in the wall of the pond facing the house, put up a framework of metal pipes and thatched it with coconut leaves. Much later we improved upon this and built pillars and gave it a roof of red clay tiles. This became the area where often the wives would gather to play scrabble while the menfolk played croquet or badminton.

If we had a barbecue lunch, we sometimes asked my friend Souham Haroun to come and cook the pig for us. He was an expert at barbecued pig, which would be so well-cooked that the flesh would almost fall off the bone, and was so tasty that everyone was coming back for more. After the meal, when most of us were not feeling so energetic, the Trivial Pursuit board would come out and we would make up teams and play on into the evening. We had electricity installed in the baffa so we had lights and could plug in a tape recorder or radio, and a fridge so that the cold drinks were close at hand.

When making the new roof for the baffa, the metal pipes that were welded together as the support for the original roof were cut off from the pond wall at the base of each pipe and moved to a new site a few yards away. This formed a good framework for climbing plants and we grew passion-fruit over it. After one or two rain seasons the whole framework was covered as if with a living green roof which would be dotted first with the beautiful flowers, then with the bright yellow fruit. The fruits are round and small, and filled with a sweet pulp full of small black seeds. We used to collect the pulp from a bowlful of passion-fruit and add some water, then put it through a sieve to remove the seeds. It made a very tasty and refreshing drink. (Lime juice and water, with sugar added to taste, was another drink we made from the garden fruit.)

The passion-flower is an evergreen climber native to South America, named by Spanish priests who saw in the flower the symbols of the instruments of Christ's Passion. The purple corona filaments represent the crown of thorns. The five stamens are the five wounds of Christ (in both hands, both feet, and in his side) and the three stigmas are the three nails (one in each hand and one nailing both feet together). The five sepals and five petals symbolise the twelve Apostles minus Peter (who became the Head of the church) and Judas (who betrayed Jesus). I do not understand the last part as there were twelve Apostles, not ten. I can understand why Judas could be left out, as he was the one who betrayed Jesus for thirty pieces of silver. "Quid non mortalia pectora cogis, Auri sacra fames" (Virgil) - To what dost thou not drive the human heart, oh accursed hunger for money? Judas was not there to go and spread the Word with the other Apostles after Jesus ascended into Heaven. I do not know why St Peter, who was an Apostle and became the first Pope, was omitted.

I now grow passion-flowers in England and find the flower to be identical to the ones in Freetown. Unfortunately, although the fruit is quite plentiful it is orange in colour when ripe and usually it is not very pleasant to taste so we make no use of it. However, in 2003 we had a very hot summer and found the fruit ripened and was good to eat.

There is a romantic 'language of the flowers' whereby many flowers have a special meaning; to name a few, 'secret love' for gardenia, 'single blessedness' for bachelor's buttons and 'beauty always new' for the rose. We had all of these flowers and many more, including bougainvillaea in purple, pink, orange and white, allamanda or yellow bells, porcelain rose, mare's tails and Pride of Barbados. We had large clumps of lobster claws, so called because of its red waxy flowers in the shape of lobster claws. We were never short of flowers for the house.

There were hibiscus shrubs in several different colours and types, but we seldom used them as cut flowers as the blooms dropped after one day. One kind that was really spectacular was the blushing hibiscus. In the early morning the flower was pure white, and throughout the day it would gradually change colour until by evening it was deep pink.

For a while we had moon flowers growing on the railings of the front verandah, a creeper rather like the convolvulus but the flowers were white and huge and opened only at night, hence the name 'moon flower', when they gave off a lovely perfume. Another creeper grew on the fence behind the house with heart-shaped leaves and lovely flowers with a delicate tracery in violet. It was called Dutchman's Pipe from the shape and curve of the carpel.

One of the trees we planted ourselves was a breadfruit tree. We bought it as a very young tree, about six feet high, and brought it home in the car with the top sticking out of the window. We planted it down near the end of the garden and it grew very quickly. Before long it began to bear fruit, and we needed a long pole to be able to reach them. The breadfruit looks like a green football and is very good to eat, but is always cooked as you cannot eat it raw. We would fry it in slices, add some cheese on top and pop it under the grill for a minute, or just spread a little butter on it. Alternatively it can be cut small like chips and fried, used in stew instead of potatoes, or even roasted whole in the ashes of a fire. We found the breadfruit tree very useful over the years.

There is a belief in Sierra Leone that if you have a fruit tree that does not bear fruit you can help it by cutting the bark of the tree and inserting a penny into the cut. You must then tie a strip of white cloth around the tree. This is said to make the tree bear fruit freely. I never tried this method myself, but would be glad to hear from anyone who has tried it and found that it worked!

As for bananas, we had several varieties which we planted and which grew into huge clumps and outnumbered the coconut trees. A banana tree only bears once and then dies, but several small plants will have started to grow around the roots of the old tree by the time it has produced fruit - anything up to a hundred bananas or more from one tree. The flower comes up from the centre of the plant then bends over to one side. As the large, dark red, leathery petals fall off one by one the tiny bananas are exposed. These grow larger over the course of a few months, and when they are large enough (but still green, ie unripe) they are cut down. Some people would simple hang up the whole stem as it was cut from the banana plant, and remove the bananas for eating as they got ripe. We usually cut the hands of bananas from the stem and kept them in a carton until they ripened. There were some varieties that would remain green even though they were ripe, but the kinds we had in our garden would all turn 'banana yellow' when they were ripe, except for the red banana. This tree would grow quite tall and, in our garden at least would not produce as many bananas as the other kinds. The fruit itself had dark red skin and the bananas were short and stubby. Banana leaves could be used as an umbrella if it suddenly started to rain as the leaves were very large and waterproof.

We occasionally tried to grow plantains but without much success. The plantain looks like a banana but much larger. It is usually boiled, or fried in slices in palmoil and served with pepper sauce made with palm oil, quite delicious.

➡ In 1974 I took the family into town to see the film 'Oliver', a musical version of the Charles Dickens story, 'Oliver Twist'. We all enjoyed the film, but by the end Linda was beginning to feel unwell. We went home and gave Linda some Junior Asprin before she went to bed. By morning she had developed some spots, and Mary was not feeling too well either, so we took the two of them to see the doctor. The diagnosis was chicken pox, which meant keeping them both home from school as it is infectious. The spots were very itchy so we bought calamine lotion to dab on. The spots spread and became so plentiful that Linda and Mary looked liked Bundu girls, as the lotion dried out to a white powder on their faces and body. This went on for a couple of weeks, and just as they were getting over it, John came out in spots. A few bottles of calamine lotion later, we thought it was all over, when Michael developed a rash! It was chicken pox again! Michael suffered more than the others, as the disease is more painful when you are older. The only child in the house to escape it was Jamal, but he had caught it when he was very young and so was now immune.

➡ We had a table-tennis table and occasionally I challenged a few of my friends, including Dr Arthur Stuart (who was a very good player and most times beat me), to a game, though more usually it was used by the children. My two oldest sons, Jamal and Michael, invented a game of their own using the stoppers from soft drinks bottles. They would collect enough of each kind to make a 'team', and then would play perhaps 7-Up against Coca-Cola or something similar. They each had a favourite stopper to use to move the other stoppers, in a similar fashion to Tiddlywinks, until one or other of them scored a goal by flipping a stopper between the chalk-mark goal posts. The rules of football were loosely applied. This game used to engross the boys for hours, and the table-tennis table was used for this far more often than for table-tennis. When my youngest son grew big enough he too would play this game, with whichever of his brothers would play with him. We had a dartboard, and would on occasion hang it up on the wall of our veranda and challenge some friends to a game. I found it necessary to hang a sheet of hardboard behind it because of all the holes we were making in the wall! The hardboard got hit more often than the dartboard!

Our large garden was a constant source of interest, surprises and entertainment for all the family. Just before the rain season started in earnest, the flying ants would appear. If this happened during the day, it was possible to see the column of flying ants coming up from a tiny hole in the ground in their thousands. The birds gathered in the air above the hole and would swoop around collecting beakfuls of the ants. The ants only had wings for a very short time, seemingly just to help them up out of the ground, and then the wings would drop off and the ants became little wriggling termites. They were more of a problem if the flying ants hatched out at night, because they would be attracted by the light to the open windows of the house and fly inside in large numbers. We were then left to sweep up piles of wings and termites from the tables and chairs and floors. We decided it was time to put mosquito netting on the doors and windows. For the doors, I had wooden frames made that slid across the doorway from the outside, and for the windows I designed smaller frames that fitted on the inside, with a small flap on hinges that would lift up so that we could reach through to open and close the windows. The whole of the frames on the windows could be removed for cleaning when necessary.

The right hand boundary of our garden, looking at it from the street, was a small stream, which was completely dry during the dry season but would start to flow soon after the first rains. On the second year of living in our house in Lumley we noticed a pair of shining blue kingfishers had made a nest in a hole in the bank of the stream during the rainy season. They lived there right through the rains, laying their eggs and raising their young. They would fly in and out during the day, either to catch fish in the stream or to go further afield. Once the riverbed had dried up the kingfishers would disappear, and we would not see them again until the next rains. This happened every year that we lived in the house. Where they came from or where they went during the dry season we never found out. Whether it was the same pair we couldn't tell, but we looked forward to the visit of the kingfishers every year.

The smallest kingfisher to visit us was also one of the most colourful. One afternoon we found a pygmy kingfisher sitting quietly on the floor in a corner of the sitting room. Joan carefully picked it up while one of the children ran to get an empty birdcage which we had not used since our pair of love birds died, probably of old age. Joan set the kingfisher carefully on the perch and we all gathered round to have a close look at the rainbow-coloured bird. It was no more than three inches from beak to tail with vivid blue upperparts and orange-red on the underparts. There were purple patches on the sides of the head, and tiny stripes of green and black on top. The bill was bright red, as were the feet. After a few minutes we carried the cage out into the garden and left the door open. We moved away and watched as the tiny bird flew safely away. After this we quite often saw a pigmy kingfisher sitting on the clothesline.

Frogs were abundant in our garden during the rain season, because of the nearness of the stream. One frog would start to croak, and then all the others would join in. The croaking would go on for a few minutes and then, as if there was a conductor conducting the whole assembly of frogs, they would all stop together and silence would reign for a few minutes. Then one croak would be heard and they would all start again. This went on through the night during their breeding season.

The most attractive frogs were the tiny tree frogs, which could be found sitting on leaves of the plants on our front veranda, or even on the wall. They have tiny round pads on the tip of each toe, which act as suction pads. They are bright green frogs, only an inch or two long, but appear in regency stripes, mainly pink or gold, running from head to tail.

Another visitor to our front veranda was a large toad. One day Joan noticed one of the plants seemed to be dying and went to have a closer look. She found that a large toad about five or so inches long had dug a hole in the soil in the pot, uprooting the plant, and was sitting there in the shade, probably because it was cool and regularly watered. Joan put the toad back in the garden and replanted the flower, only to find next morning that the toad had returned. After several tries at moving it, she gave up and left the toad to repose in its chosen home. Talk of 'trangayase'? (Strong-headedness).

A creature that was occasionally found in the garden and held great fascination for us was the chameleon, belonging to the lizard family. They were probably present quite often but were not easily noticed, possibly due to their habit of changing colour to match their background, and also because they lived in trees. The first time my wife saw one was when it fell from an orange tree with a thud on to the cement path just in front of her. The chameleon moves quite slowly with a hesitating gait, as if testing the ground to see if it can take its weight before taking the next step. Their range of colour went from yellow through green to grey, and if startled, would change as you watched. They had a knack of making their bodies very thin, almost flat, and then puffing themselves out. Their feet are also unusual, having two toes on one side and three on the other on each foot, spread out like hands so they can grasp a branch. Their tails can also be used to hold on to the tree. They have got long thin tongues that suddenly shoot out of their mouths to catch an insect. The most remarkable feature of the chameleon, however, is their eyes, which can swivel around in all directions independent of each other, so that one eye can, for example, look forward while the other one looks backwards.

Sierra Leone is very rich in wild life and my wife, Joan, discovered the joys of bird watching. As a Londoner she was used to seeing only two types of bird on a regular basis, sparrows and pigeons, and now she was faced with birds in a variety of colours, sizes and types she had never even imagined. Joan started making lists of the birds she could see within the space of a month from our garden in Lumley, and sometimes got as far as fifty different birds. Some were very common and could be seen without making any effort. The Bronze Mannikin, for example, was a small brown and white bird and could be seen in our garden in large flocks on the ground when the grass seed was plentiful. Also common, but not in such large numbers, were the firefinches. The males are more attractive, being mainly red, and the females brown with red touches here and there.

Late one evening we heard the sound of what we thought was an owl coming from the garden. Joan went down in the dark to try and track it down to see what it was. She followed the sound and discovered that the creature was up in a mango tree just the other side of the stream. Apparently other people had also heard the noise and as Joan stood in the shadows a group of women collected under the tree just a few yards away. They were beating pots and pans to make as loud a noise as possible and shouting out curses in Krio to drive the creature away, and Joan learnt some new Krio phrases she had not heard before! The women believed that the call was that of a Kohkoh, a 'witchbird', which sucks the blood of small children in their beds at night. Joan came away quietly so as not to be seen.

Some people believe that this legend refers to a bat, possibly because of the stories of vampire bats. I have always held the theory that the Kohkoh is really an owl, and not a bat. Owls are also active at night, and the call of the owl is more like the noise connected with the Kohkoh. In support of my theory, just after this incident Joan saw a large brown owl settled in the shade high on a branch in a mango tree in our garden, and it could be found there during the heat of the day for several weeks afterwards.

It was possible to tell the season of year by which birds are found in the country. The cattle egret could frequently be seen during the dry season, occasionally in our garden but more often found where cattle were browsing, waiting to catch the insects disturbed by the cattle's feet. These birds were locally known as 'cow angels', and it was widely believed that they were the 'guardian angels' of the cows, which could not see them, which explained why the cattle always ignored the birds that would be almost under their feet at times. It was believed that people also had their guardian angels which could be seen by some animals but not by ourselves. Cattle egrets are white birds, but as the rain season approached they developed buff coloured plumes on the head and neck. As the rains set in the cattle egrets would fly north to breed, appearing again in the dry season.

A bird that always visited us during the rains was the allied hornbill, a large black and white bird with a huge whitish bill. It travelled in groups and could be seen in early morning or late afternoon, perching prominently on the coconut trees. It has a long call which would start slowly then, as the call got more rapid, the bird would get excited and stretch its neck straight up pointing to the sky, and the leaf would bounce up and down with the efforts it was making. The others in the group would answer, and the calls would go on for quite a while, then the whole group would fly away to entertain someone else.

Whilst I was supervising the clearing of some of the branches which had fallen into the stream running beside our garden during the rain season of 1981, I saw a snake about five feet or more long swimming in the stream only a few yards from me. It was a large cobra. When it saw me it stopped and reared its head, with the intention of spitting at me. It was either the cobra or me! I had my shotgun with me and fired one shot at the cobra, killing it before it had time to spit its poison at me. I had noticed that its tongue was round with a slit in it, and I supposed then that that was where the poison was emitted. I have since learnt from "West African Snakes" by G.S. Cansdale that the poison is in the fangs. If the poison gets in the eyes it can cause blindness if not washed out quickly.

I was reminded of the time when my wife was getting some potatoes out of a sack in the store under the front steps and felt a fine spray of liquid on her arm. She was confused as it was not raining and in any case the rain would not reach her in the store. Suddenly she noticed a large black snake slithering along the floor, and then realised what the liquid was. The cobra had aimed for her eyes as they usually do, but luckily for Joan the snake missed its aim as Joan bent over the potato sack at the precise moment that it spat. Joan didn't expect she would ever feel grateful to a bag of potatoes!

The only time Joan was bitten by a snake she was lucky in that it was only a grass snake. Our watchman was coming towards me from the gate to give me a message, and in his haste he knocked over a small cement plant pot. He quickly righted the pot, and laid the begonia that had fallen out back in the pot. Joan went to see that the flower was properly replanted, only to jump back in surprise when she was bitten on the ankle by a bright green snake. She wondered why the snake was still there, as usually a snake will wriggle away at top speed instead of staying to attack. Then she saw what was wrong. When the watchman had put the plant pot back in place he had unknowingly stood it on the snake's tail! A bite from a grass snake is harmless so Joan forgave it and lifted up the pot so that the beautiful emerald snake could go on its way, which it did very quickly.

Incidentally, a green mamba looks very much like the green grass snake, only longer, but is highly poisonous.

➤ I had a gardener with one leg shorter than the other due to an accident some years before, which made him limp. His name was Musa, which means Moses in English. One day I sent him to the local petrol station to buy some penetrating oil. He had apparently never heard of penetrating oil before so I made him repeat the words after me, and told him to go on repeating them until he got to the petrol station so he would not forget what to ask for. On his return, he reported to me that the petrol station did not have any. I asked him what he had asked for, and he replied, "Traiting pen oil, Sir". No wonder the sellers at the petrol station did not have any! It would have been surprising had they had any oil that straightened bent pens!

➤➤ Joan discovered a hole in the ground at the end of our garden. She wanted to know what kind of animal lived in the hole so she asked our gardener to set a trap that would catch the creature without harming it. He set up a contraption of bent twigs and bits of string at the mouth of the hole, and we wondered what we would catch. The next morning we found that a half-eaten mango from the tree overhanging the hole had fallen right at the entrance. The creature we caught was a Gambian Fruit Bat which had flown down to eat the mango. We had the opportunity to have a closer inspection of the bat. It had soft light brown fur with little white spots near each ear and under each shoulder. After a close inspection we released it unharmed. Although we had many bats in the garden, we usually saw them just as dark shadows flitting around the fruit trees at night and heard their squeaking. These bats are not vampire bats. We decided to dismantle the trap, and never did discover what lived in that hole!

One evening a young man came to the gates with an animal for sale. I asked him what it was and he said, "It is a shame-beef, sir". I called Joan to come and look at the creature, which was new to me, and she said it was a pangolin. She recognised it from having read about it in one of Gerald Durrell's books. The pangolin is a scaly anteater and is covered in scales that make it look rather like a large pinecone. It is locally known as 'shame-beef' from its habit of rolling into a ball with the scales on the outside when it feels it is in danger. It lives in trees and is an expert climber, which it immediately proved to us by climbing up the doorframe, using its tail to help it keep its hold. We bought the animal and called it Seamus (pronounced Shame-us so Joan thought it a suitable name for a shame-beef). We had a large wooden cage made for it with a wire-netting front, but it spent most of the day asleep as it is nocturnal, and would wake around 5.00 pm when Joan would feed it with ants nests from our garden.

We had quite a few species of lizard. It is not uncommon to see the lizard with his head incessantly bobbing up and down as if watching and waiting for something to happen. There were also lizards that lived only in the house, including the geckos that were pale pink and their skin looked almost transparent. They had suction pads on their feet and could often be seen in the evenings running up the wall to catch an unwary moth or other insect.

Monitor lizards were quite common and most days one could see them sunning themselves in our garden, only to lumber off when one approached too closely. While usually harmless, the monitor lizard (locally called iguana) has a long and powerful tail which it uses to defend itself by dealing a heavy blow with it at whatever is attacking it. We once had a dog that liked to chase them, but it would soon back off if the 'iguana' decided to stand and fight, having had an experience of the viciousness of the iguana's tail. They can run quite fast but without much grace. However, if they went into the river forming our boundary in order to get away, they would bring their legs close to their body and ripple through the water like a snake.

One day our gardener came running to me whilst I was playing badminton with my children and said in Krio, "Wan fox day nar wata." My children ran to the gate leading to the stream beside our house to see the 'fox', as it was unheard of to see a fox in Sierra Leone. To their disappointment, it turned out to be simply one of our 'forks' which had inadvertently been thrown away with the rubbish. Whilst the lighter rubbish floated away, the fork sank to the bed of the stream and our gardener had seen it and thought he would inform us accordingly. In Sierra Leone it is usual for the Lebanese to use the plural of the word 'fork' as the singular form can sound like a bad word.

I am not very good at cooking. One Shrove Tuesday my wife was busily making pancakes for all the family. I watched her cooking the pancake on one side, then tossing it in the air so that it came down in the frying pan with the cooked side uppermost. This tossing of the pancakes took my interest so I thought I would try it. When my wife had left the room for a moment, I put some batter in the pan and quickly cooked it on one side. I loosened it around the edges as I had seen my wife do, then gave the frying pan a flip to send the pancake up in the air so that it would turn over and I could cook the other side. Unfortunately for me, this was one instance when "What goes up must come down" didn't apply. I looked in the pan, and then on the floor, and finally looked up at the ceiling. There was the pancake stuck on the ceiling – I must have used a bit too much energy in my flipping! Finally the pancake fell down, just as my wife came back into the kitchen. She was not too impressed with my efforts to help, and I left the kitchen, beaten by a pancake! One good result from this episode is that my wife seldom asks me to help in the kitchen, so in my case out of bad came good!

When I was a young lawyer I had a healthy appetite. My English wife cooked palm oil stew twice a week with all the proper ingredients. A ruse that I developed to eat a lot without seeming to was to put more stew than was necessary for the rice on my plate. I then complained of having too much stew, and added more rice to even the balance. 'Unfortunately' I had then put too much rice and had to add more stew, and this continued until I could eat no more. My wife commented, tongue in cheek, that as I was serving myself I had no-one but myself to blame for getting it wrong! My own attitude was, "Before good chop pwell, leh belleh bos." Roughly translated this means, "Instead of leaving good food to spoil, eat until the stomach bursts". I, like the Corporation of Bedford in "She Stoops to Conquer" by Oliver Goldsmith (18th century), was famous for achievement at table.

Joan was good at cooking (although she didn't enjoy it), having learned to cook many Sierra Leonean, Lebanese and English dishes. I am a lucky bloke!

It is funny how the mind automatically assumes the bad and not the good. For example, when opening the door of the fridge one day, I felt something fall on my hand. I straightaway withdrew my hand, thinking it was a spider or some insect. It turned out to be nothing worse than a grape that had fallen from the bunch on the shelf in the fridge!

One of the memories that has stuck in my mind was going to Lumley Beach with my family in the early evening to watch the fishermen pulling in their catch. Whilst waiting for the catch to be brought ashore, we sometimes passed the time looking for the telltale airholes in the sand where the waves had just receded, which showed that a tiny shellfish was just below the surface. We would take home our little haul and cook them, usually just enough for each of us to have a taste, but they were very enjoyable, more so because we dug for them ourselves.

The fishermen used what is called a 'chain boat', which in fact is a very big canoe. The net they used was about five feet wide but many yards in length, and with a long rope attached to each end. One end of the rope would be left with some of the fishermen on the beach while the others set out in the boat with the net piled high inside. They would set off travelling in a large semi-circle, paying out the net, which had floats on the top and was weighted at the lower edge, as they went. Eventually, when all that was left in the boat was the rope at the end of the net, they would pull the boat back on shore. Two teams of men would start to haul in the rope, moving towards each other as the net was pulled towards the beach. The sea was not deep and the lower edge of the net dragged on the sand so the fish could not escape. The two teams of men would meet up and join into one, pulling on both ends of the net together, sometimes chanting to help them keep the rhythm of the pull. Some of the smaller fish would be caught in the holes of the net, whilst the bigger fish would be trapped as the centre of the net was finally pulled up onto the beach. It was always exciting to see what was caught. On one occasion a small hammerhead shark was caught in the net, a very unusual and curious sight. It had a head shaped like the head of a hammer with the eyes and nostrils at each end of the hammer. The one we saw was just a baby, but the hammerhead shark can grow up to eighteen feet in length. Like all sharks, the hammerhead has only cartilage, and no bones.

The market women who dealt in fish would be waiting with their large enamel bowls to buy the fish as soon as it was on the shore. Sometimes I bought fresh mackerel or mullet from the fishermen, or even a pan full of whitebait, the baby herrings that in Freetown we called minnows. If there were some kinni in the catch (baby barracuda) I usually bought some, as the young fish tasted even better than the adult fish. Our meal that evening would be fresh fried fish with chips and salad, all the more relished for having seen the fish caught just a short while before, with sometimes a few cockles found by us.

At times I enjoyed food that needed little or no preparation. I like gari with sardines. The gari is soaked in water to soften it and then the excess water is squeezed out. Add a tin or two of sardines in oil, chopped onion and a little chopped hot pepper, mix together and it is ready for eating! Parched groundnut and bread was another favourite of mine, as was honey with bread. A man used to go around the town with a large bowl of honey on his head, shouting, "Honey, honey," and I used to buy from him. My wife would sift the honey through a piece of muslin into bottles, because we would find the occasional bee in the honey.

For a while we were lucky enough to have our own bees nesting in the roof of our house. We saw a swarm of bees in the garden, and closed the doors and windows to keep them out of the house. We thought after a while that they had gone away, then realised that they had settled inside the edge of the roof, between the corrugated sheets and the cellotex ceiling, and could be seen flying in and out. There was a local superstition that to have bees in your roof brought you good fortune and prosperity. I am not aware that we were particularly prosperous while the bees were living with us, but we did not have any bad luck, unless you count a few bee stings as such.

We did once think of harvesting our own honey, and called the local honey-collector to get the honey out. He did not bother with any protective clothing. He just put a ladder against the roof and climbed up with a plastic bucket. He made a hole in the cellotex and put in his bare hand to draw out the honeycomb. We did not get very much honey; the man explained to us that we had called him at the wrong time and the bees had eaten most of it themselves. We asked him why the bees did not sting him, and he said that he simply talked to them while he was taking the honey so they allowed him to take it without attacking him. I thought this sounded very strange, but Joan told me that in England many beekeepers believed in talking to their bees and telling them if anything important, like a death, should happen in the family. Soon after we had taken the honey, the bees moved on to somewhere else. We did not know why, but when we next saw the honey-collector we asked him. He told us that it was usual to take the honey while the bees were busy making it, and they would just go on and make more to compensate for what was taken. In our case, they were eating the honey themselves, and it may have been the loss of it that made them move on to set up a new hive.

The only time we had a problem with our bees was when our daughter Linda was a little girl and was stung on her left hand in between her little finger and ring finger. We took out the sting and put some antiseptic on the puncture, and it seemed to give her no trouble. Some hours later, about eleven o'clock at night, we checked on her before going to bed. She was fast asleep, but her whole hand was swollen like a balloon. We quickly called our close friend and doctor, Arthur Stuart, who came immediately and gave her an injection. He told us that Linda had had an allergic reaction to the protein in the sting. The swelling subsided quite quickly and she had no further problem.

I heard of one lady, however, who was fatally attacked by bees. She was on her way to a wedding in a fashionable part of Freetown and was dressed up in colourful clothes and wearing quite a lot of perfume. Unknowingly she passed near to a swarm of bees and they attacked her. She received so many stings that the doctors could not save her and she died a few hours later.

Linda was playing draughts with her grandfather (my father) at our house in Lumley, one day when he was visiting us from his home in Kailahun. The board they were playing on was the usual size used in Sierra Leone, with ten squares across instead of eight as played in England, alternately black and white as usual, and was played with twenty pieces (men) instead of twelve each, set out in four rows of five men on each side. The rules in both games are similar, the main difference being that when seizing the other player's men you can move diagonally both forwards and backward in Sierra Leone, whilst in the English game a piece can only move backwards after being crowned. The move when seizing two or three of your opponent's pieces in one go and moving in a zigzag is called 'ben tail' in Krio. Also in the African game a king can move as many squares as it wants in any one direction, so long as they are empty, whereas in the English game even a king can only move one square at a time. I would sometimes play board games such as Ludo, Snakes and Ladders and so on with my wife and children, but if we were playing draughts my wife always preferred to play the Sierra Leone version as she found it more interesting. Sierra Leoneans are expert at this game and I have pitted my skills against them quite often and most times lost. I was interested in reading somewhere that the game of draughts is said to have been invented by the Egyptian god Thoth, along with dice and mathematics, amongst other things.

➤ We did quite a bit of entertaining, usually having a buffet lunch or supper for around thirty people, but now and again we would have something bigger which took much more planning. One year, in the seventies, we gave a party in late December for about a hundred people. I decided to give it a legal flavour by having the invitation cards printed to look like a legal Summons, as follows:-

EYP/75          1975          A No.1
IN THE SQUIRE'S COURT AT LUMLEY
Between:
FARID R. ANTHONY
AND
JOAN L. ANTHONY  -     APPLICANTS
AND
-     RESPONDENTS

IN THE MATTER OF THE END-OF-YEAR PARTY

YOU ARE HEREBY SUMMONED to appear before the
above-mentioned Court at 27, Freetown Road, Lumley, on
Saturday, 27th December 1975 at nine o'clock in the
afternoon and thereon from hour to hour on the hearing
of an application by the applicants herein.

AND TAKE NOTICE that after appearing personally you
shall be required to take active part in the End-of-Year
Party to the satisfaction of the Court.

AND TAKE FURTHER NOTICE that on failure to appear
as hereinbefore requested you will suffer forfeiture of all
benefits accruing therefrom, AND unless you give notice
of your inability to appear you shall be deemed to have
accepted.

All notices should be sent to the Registrar of the said
Court at 4, Gloucester Street, Freetown.

Dated this 1st day of December 1975

F. R. ANTHONY
J. L. ANTHONY
APPLICANTS IN PERSON

This Summons was taken out on behalf of the Applicants
herein whose address for service is 4, Gloucester Street,
Freetown. (Phone 26704 or 024 206).

Some of the guests who did not read the invitation properly, rang me at my chambers to ask what they had done for me to issue a Summons against them. I told them to read the Summons again more carefully.

We took on some extra staff for the night, having a barman from the Aqua Club run the bar for us as it was his night off. We arranged for two policemen to control traffic and sort out the parking. We had a whole pig being barbecued on one side of the badminton court, and a large barracuda six feet long (caught by me!) being cooked on the other side. We had borrowed some extra chairs and tables and these were set out in the garden. Food was served on trestle tables on the badminton court. Joan had a little outside help with the cooking, my cousin Nuhad having offered to prepare the Jollof rice, and her brother Choukri and his wife Toni cooked two large legs of pork in their oven for us. The rest of the food, consisting of kebbe, humous, onion flans, salads, chicken legs, etc., was prepared by Joan with help from our children.

Of the hundred people we invited, only a few could not come, and of those who did come, some brought an extra guest or two. We had taken great pains with the decoration of the garden, having paper lanterns with candles inside them hanging from the trees, and 'pan-lamps' (small kerosine lamps made from empty evaporated milk tins with wicks added) were scattered around our large garden. The party started at 9.00 pm and was really swinging by 10.00 pm. The last guests left at 4.00 am. Our younger children had stayed awake until 2.30 am, not wanting to miss the fun. Jamal and Michael, and three of their friends, helped us clear everything away from the garden, packing the borrowed chairs and tables in the store for safety, and by 5.00 am we all went to bed, exhausted.

The end of the year was crowned by my eldest daughter, Rahme, sending us a card to say she had passed her exams in England qualifying her as a nurse.

➤➤ It was usual on New Year's Eve for Joan and I to go to a party or dinner-dance somewhere. We always made sure there was a mammy-nurse at home with the children, as well as the watchman on duty outside. What we did not know was that the children would all stay up late listening to the mammy-nurse telling stories. The mammy-nurse had filed teeth – her upper teeth were each filed to a point. She had, we learned much later, a fund of ghost stories with which she regaled the children when we were not around. On this occasion, having put them in the right mood by telling them of the local belief that "die man deh grap" on New Year's Eve, that is, "Dead men rise from their graves", she told our youngest son John that the wailing that could be heard outside the window was a ghost calling John's name. John looked out of the window and couldn't see anything, but just in case, he was careful not to say anything, and kept away from the window after that. The belief is that if a ghost calls your name and you answer him, he will take you away! We were not told this story until years later, when our daughter Mary said that she is now sure that the wailing outside the window was in fact nothing more than some caterwauling cats out on the spree.

Linda, the youngest, was sometimes made to go to bed by the older ones who wanted to watch television late into the night but were not too sure that she would not tell us about it. One night Michael put an empty clothesbasket upside down on his head and then covered it and himself with a white bedsheet. He then went moaning through the parlour, to make Linda run away into her bedroom to go to bed. This strange sight, however, sent our dog berserk, as he was far more scared than Linda was. The next morning when the dog was let out as usual, he set off down the garden at top speed and we never saw him again!

We got another dog to replace the one we lost. This dog was mainly black but its eyebrows were brown. It would sometimes bark furiously with the hair on its back standing up, and it would be staring at something that we could not see, even though it was not yet dark. We called the watchman to look around, which he did, only to come back and tell us that he could see nothing. We were surprised that the dog continued to bark fiercely, but the watchman explained that any dog that looked like our new dog, which had beneath each eye a black spot, that looked like a second pair of eyes, was said to have 'four yai' (four eyes), and could see devils or spirits that were invisible to humans, hence the barking! We called the dog away from whatever he was barking at and he quietened down. We decided that if there was a spirit around it was probably not harmful to us, and in any case we did not see what we could do about it, so we left it in peace.

➤ We always had a few chickens about the place, and often chicks would be hatched, but there were always a few chicks lost to some predator or other. One thing we learned was that chickens are cleverer than we thought. One day we saw a hawk hovering around the garden, looking for something to pounce on. We saw the mother hen strutting around looking anxious, but saw no sign of any of the chicks. After a few minutes the hawk gave up and flew away to find a better source of food. The little brown hen looked around then gave a few clucks in fowl language. Suddenly ten fluffy yellow chicks appeared all around her. They had been crouching down in the grass to be hidden from the hawk, and were also hidden from us from where we had been standing watching on the back veranda overlooking the garden. My wife looked on that hen with more respect from that day.

Another time the hen was not so lucky. Sometimes a hawk would quietly settle in a tree until it saw a chance to attack, and one day I saw a hawk swoop down and rise again with a chick in its talons. The mother hen was so desperate to save her chick that she managed to fly up almost level with the roof of our house in her efforts to attack the hawk, before fluttering ungainly back to earth. Her efforts were unsuccessful.

We kept ducks as well as chickens, and started off with a pair of Muscovy ducks that we called, with little originality, Donald and Daisy. After a while we had ducklings. Occasionally we made wine for our own use, such as banana wine and mead, and at this time were engaged in producing ginger wine which contained, among other ingredients, pearl barley. After being fermented for the required time we sifted the wine and decided that we may as well feed the pearl barley to the ducks instead of throwing it away. The ducks all loved it, and Donald and Daisy seemed to be little affected, but a little while later we noticed the ducklings staggering around. At first we thought they were ill, and wondered what we could do to treat them, then suddenly Joan realised that they were simply drunk from scoffing all that alcoholic pearl barley!

Walking in the garden one weekend we noticed Donald, the big male Muscovy, had caught a live green grass snake about two feet six inches long. Donald was holding it in the middle and was trying to move his beak along the snake's body so that the head of the snake would be in his beak. The snake fought back and tried to bite the duck, but in vain. At last Donald the duck got the head of the snake into his beak and within a few seconds had swallowed the snake – live! This was the first and last time we saw this happen.

We only had a few Muscovy ducks so we did not get many eggs from them. Then I heard that someone was importing Khaki Campbell ducks that were good layers, so we bought twenty-two females and two males. They were delivered in a large carton, and when we took them out we found that one male had a broken leg, probably from being trampled on by the other ducks during the journey. Joan found a small flat piece of wood to use as a splint, bandaged it securely to the broken leg and let the duck loose with the others. In a couple of weeks Joan removed the splint and found the leg was healed. I bought the special food from the Feed Mill at Cline Town, consisting mainly of corn, that encouraged egg production. Twice a day Joan measured out the feed and added a little water to it and fed it to the ducks. Ducks will choke if given dry feed, and need to have plenty of drinking water available. Unlike the Muscovy ducks, the Khaki Campbells were all identical and entirely brown, whereas Muscovy ducks were a mixture of black, white and green, much more colourful, and each one looked a little different. We soon had a good supply of large duck eggs, more than we could eat, so we sold off the surplus.

➼ One day in Lumley, when I had just driven home from the Law Courts, someone I knew came to the gates of my house with a large white dog with black spots all over. He said to me, "Do you want this damnation," pointing at the dog, "I no longer want it." I looked at the big dog and then I called my wife to look at it as well. It seemed perfectly well and healthy, so we both agreed to take the Dalmatian and tried not to smile when the man said he would be happy to have the "Damnation" off his hands. He left and we then introduced our new dog to the other dogs we already had. The Dalmatian is not native to Sierra Leone, and our other dogs were mongrels. I suggested we should call it "Damnation" in jest, but my wife disagreed. She said we shouldn't laugh at the man for getting the dog's breed wrong and in any case she did not want to be heard shouting "Damnation" at the top of her voice when calling the dog in from the garden for his food.

➤  The whole family was having a quiet evening at home watching television, when suddenly we heard our front gate shaking frantically, and the Foulah tradesman who sat by the roadside selling his wares opposite our house started shouting, "Tiff, Tiff!" (meaning "Thief, Thief!"). We all rushed to the front veranda and looked out only to see an English friend of mine standing unsteadily in our carport. He had not bothered to loosen the chain or remove the open padlock, but instead had climbed over the gate, which was higher than he was, which prompted the cries of Thief. My watchman was standing there with his cutlass ready, but uncertain what to do next.

I asked my friend what the matter was, thinking perhaps he had been robbed, but he said, smiling, "My car has broken down coming down the hill from Spur Road, and I knew you lived nearby and would be the person to help me." I went down in my shorts and joined my friend, whom I soon realised had been 'celebrating' well before he got to me. I opened the gates and we set out to walk up Spur Road to where he had left his car. Sure enough the engine would not start, so I got in and let the car roll slowly down the hill and along the road to my house. My friend walked in front of the car waving his arms as if directing traffic, much to the amusement of my son John who was with me, and myself.

It was only necessary for John to help my friend push the last few yards to my carport when the car ran out of momentum. I parked the car for the night inside my gate, and I got out my own car and drove my friend home, knowing that in the morning he would be able to find a mechanic in Lumley, of whom there were several, who could get his car started. By the time I got back from my chambers the next day the car had gone. When I next met my friend, he told me that his car simply had a petrol blockage, which a mechanic had been able to clear in a few minutes.

➤  Although we usually had a watchman, and dogs as well, we were sometimes bothered by thieves. One morning we woke to find that a large ivory carving which stood on top of the television was missing. We realised that a thief must have climbed on to the veranda and reached through the guard bars on the open window to take the carving. Even though I now recognised the danger, that position was a good one for displaying my carvings, so I placed another one there. However this time I took precautions.  I bought a piece of strong chain and attached one end securely to the wooden base of the carving.  The other end was attached to a bracket on the wall on which stood a large speaker, behind the television.

A few nights later the whole household was woken by a crash and clatter from the sitting room.  We all rushed out of our bedrooms only to see the television face down on the floor.  The bracket had been wrenched out of the wall, the speaker was on the floor, and the chain attached to the ivory led to the window.  We found the ivory carving, still attached to the other end of the chain, outside on the veranda resting on the back of a chair.  We were just in time to catch a glimpse of the thief as he fell down the front steps in his haste to get away.  Dogs and watchman alike were the only ones to sleep through the commotion.  I retrieved the ivory from outside the window, and went back to sleep.  The next day I bought some decorative blocks and built an open-work wall between the front steps and the veranda, to make any future illegal 'visit' more difficult.

We were sometimes troubled with thieves during the day as well, if the gardener was not around and the dogs were sleeping.  We had several times lost a clothesline full of washing, and on one particular occasion my wife was alone in the compound and had a full line of clothes hanging out to dry.  She decided to keep guard from the back veranda with an air rifle in her hands - no-one could see she had deliberately not put any pellets in it.  After a while Joan went downstairs to see if any clothes were dry.  She took off the line the clothes that were dry, about half of them, and went back up the back stairs and through the house to the bedroom where she put them down on the bed.  She returned immediately to the back veranda to continue her guard duties, only to find that the rest of the clothes were gone!  Someone must have been watching for an opportunity and slipped into the garden as soon as her back was turned.

This has also happened to us in England – a common occurrence everywhere it seems.

# Chapter 14

# Flooding

In Sierra Leone the rains are very heavy and sometimes continue for days. I enjoyed the early rains, when the roads and gutters were washed clean. The air smelt fresh and was free of dust, so the views over Freetown from the hills were sharp and clear and everything looked nearer.

Our house was built on the main road in Lumley and the right hand boundary of the land, looking from the road, was a stream bed which was completely dry during the dry season, but which ran quite swiftly about two feet deep during the rainy season. It was called Babadori Stream. At least once a year, after a period of several days of heavy rain, the garden would be flooded. The water would run down off the surrounding hills and gather at the lowest point, which happened to be just where we lived. The floodwater would rise quickly to perhaps two feet deep and cover the fields opposite our house so it was no longer possible to see where the road was, and the current was always very strong.

One of the most common forms of public transport in Sierra Leone is the 'poda-poda'. This is a kind of mini bus with about twenty seats inside (though it often carries more people than that), and with a roof rack where the passengers' belongings are packed. These might be anything from a cloth bundle to a large enamel bowl of freshly caught fish. Poda-podas are always run by private enterprise, unlike the buses, which are owned by the Road Transport Department. Poda-podas did not have any timetable, but as there were many of them passengers did not usually have long to wait.

On one occasion a poda-poda was being guided along the flooded road by the 'apprentice' (driver's assistant who collects the fares). The apprentice was walking slowly backwards in front of the van and beckoning the driver on, when suddenly the apprentice completely disappeared. There were deep gutters on each side of the road, and the apprentice had fallen into the gutter opposite our house! The poda-poda stopped. After a few moments the apprentice reappeared a little further along and clambered back on to the road. He climbed back on board, and the poda-poda remained where it was until the floodwaters had begun to recede and the edge of the road was once more visible.

On another occasion a Volkswagen Beetle car, belonging to an Englishman and with his children in the back, had been lifted by the force of the water and would have been carried away but for the railings of the bridge. The bonnet of the car had passed through the railings and would have fallen through into the river and been swept away but that the top of the car was too high to pass through. I saw what had happened and went out to help the family to safety. Luckily for them the flood never lasted long, and the water soon receded. After a while when the floodwaters had gone down the car was pulled back on to the road. After a few minutes tinkering with the engine the car started, and the family was able to go on its way after such a scare.

If we had warning of the flood and saw the water rising, we would go down and open the big metal gates in front of the house, a span of eighteen feet, to let the water through. The bottom parts of the gates were solid panels, and if we did not do this the gates would buckle and break apart. Next we opened the double gates to the main garage, and then the door by which we left the garage to go upstairs to the house. We would then check as far as we could that everything that could get spoilt was put up on cupboards and tables out of reach of the water. We would then retreat back upstairs with the watchman and gardener and watch the progress of the flooding from the front veranda.

We were very lucky that the design of the house was such that the downstairs was only the double garage, store rooms and quarters for the watchman and gardener, so our own living area upstairs was never flooded. The double garage had similar gates to the main gates on the road, only smaller. When the flood water rose it would get into the garage, and when the level of water had risen quite high the weight of water would break open the wooden door to the side of the garage. The flood water would sometimes reach the level of the steering wheel inside the car, and a lot of drying out would be necessary before I could get it started, usually on the following day, by leaving the bonnet, doors and boot open. The floodwater left a mark on the walls of the garage. In the meantime, once the road was clear again I would hitch a ride with a friend to my chambers in Freetown, a few miles away.

The first year we lived in the house we were not aware of the annual flood and so had spent a lot of time and trouble planting vegetables in the end part of the garden, in raised beds as is the usual method in Sierra Leone. After the flood not only the plants but the beds themselves had been washed away! Nearer to the house we had planted some rose bushes in wine barrels cut in half and filled with soil. The flood water was so strong it lifted those barrels of soil and carried them right out of the garden and we never saw them again. As a result we built up beds with ball stones (laterite) cemented in place for planting flowers.

The wire netting fence at the bottom of the garden would be knocked flat by the water and had to be repaired. Also the water was very dirty and full of rubbish such as old shoes and plastic bags etc, and it would take a very long time to gather all of this and get rid of it.

For several years we kept Khaki Campbell ducks for the eggs, and on one occasion the flood broke the fence of their enclosure and the ducks were swept away. When the water had gone down we went to search for them but could see no sign of them, and we gave them up for lost. But the next day, lo and behold, they were to be seen coming up from the end of the garden in single file, two males and twenty-two females, and not a duck was lost!

The children would find the flood quite exciting, and afterwards would go round our large garden looking for small fish – mainly 'mango page' - that had been washed in from the stream and left stranded when the water receded. The live fish were thrown back into the stream, which was by now a raging river.

Although we lived in the house at Lumley for many years, the flood still had the power to take us by surprise. In 1991 we decided to leave Sierra Leone and go to live in the United Kingdom, where my wife originated, for a year or two. We packed some suitcases in advance with things we wanted to take and would not need again before we travelled, like photograph albums and warmer clothes. On the Saturday night we were going out for dinner, and decided that leaving packed cases in the living room was tempting providence (or helping thieves), especially as our watchman had not come to work that evening, so we took them downstairs and locked them in the store.

We arrived back home very late and went straight to bed, and were woken around dawn by the flood waters banging against the main gates. We threw on some clothes and rushed down to open the gates to prevent damage to them, and to check that our dogs were safe. In the turmoil we forgot all about our suitcases for a couple of days. When we remembered them and opened the store, they were standing in a puddle. Nearly everything inside was soaked. We had to start all over again, washing all the clothes and drying them, and taking photographs out of the albums and laying them out all over our large veranda to dry. We were very lucky that most of the photographs could be saved, although the albums were thrown away.

We had packed a box of photograph slides that were nearly thirty years old, and found the water had washed them clean, there were no pictures to be seen. This was a matter of some disappointment because they were pictures taken on the night I was called to the Bar at the Inner Temple in London and showed me in my wig and gown, and the friends who had gathered for the party we had had afterwards at our home.

I could go on forever with stories about the flooding in Lumley, but my stories are those of annoyance and inconvenience, because they didn't affect us very seriously as our living quarters were never touched by the flood waters. It has, however, made us sympathetic to those unfortunate people whose homes have been invaded by flood waters.

# Chapter 15

# My Watchmen and I

In 1964 I took my wife for her first trip up-country to visit my father in Kailahun.  The living quarters were behind the shop, and my father had a watchman to guard the premises.  Late that night when we were all fast asleep, my wife suddenly shot up in bed and grabbed hold of me, shaking me awake.  "What's that noise outside", she said.  I had heard the watchman passing by the window and knocking with his cutlass on a piece of metal pipe as he went.  I was so accustomed to this that it did not rouse me, but my wife was scared out of her wits.  I explained to her that the watchman would make a noise from time to time, both to show his employer that he was awake and doing his job, and to let any prospective thief who wished to do his "shopping" out of hours know that there was a watchman alert and on guard.

Later on when I built a house at Lumley, my own watchman would make a similar noise when patrolling the house and compound.  By this time my wife was accustomed to the racket and it would no longer wake her.

There were the occasional times when I didn't have a watchman for a night or two, so I devised my own method of making a noise like a watchman on patrol.  I rigged up a system of string and glass bottles, so that when I pulled the end of the string from my bed, the bottles hanging in the garage would clang together and make a noise as if a watchman was doing his rounds.  It was very effective!

➡ One particular watchman employed to guard my house in Lumley at night, would regularly fall asleep half way through the night because, as I found out later, he was also working during the day.  This meant that not only did he get two salaries at the end of the month, from me and from his day job, he did not need to pay any rent for somewhere to sleep.

Whenever I challenged the watchman that he was sleeping, he would jump up and vigorously deny that he had been asleep, he was merely resting!  I then devised several ways of proving to him that he was asleep and that I was aware of it.

One night I went down quietly whilst he was asleep and placed some cement blocks on each side of his head, and crossed a heavy board on the top with another block on top of it.  I then went back upstairs and called him.  He woke up with a start and tried to get up and hit his head against the block.  That night at least he did not deny that he had been asleep!

Another night about a week later I found him fast asleep as usual and this time I loosely tied his two ankles together, went back upstairs and called him. After a few shouts he woke up, tried to get to his feet and promptly fell over.

When the watchman settled down to sleep he would always place his cutlass, slippers and torch neatly beside him, and sometimes I would go down and remove them without waking him. In the morning he would come up and knock on the door and ask to have them back so he could leave. I would return them to him and it was understood between us that once more I had caught him asleep. One day he came up and rang the bell and asked for the return of his belongings. I told him, quite honestly, that I had not taken them. The truth of the matter was that a thief had come in the night and finding nothing better to hand, had stolen his cutlass, slippers and torch. The watchman never believed that I had not taken his belongings, and I did not see him again after that.

➼ I took on a new watchman and things went well until one night I was woken at about 4.00am by the watchman hammering on the front door and yelling and screaming. I opened the door in some fear, not knowing what to expect. The watchman told me a whole gang of thieves had come from across the stream that was the boundary of my land, and had broken into the store and stolen everything. I cautiously went down with the watchman reluctantly following me at a distance, ready to run back into the house. I found the door of the storeroom locked as I had left it. I opened it up and examined the store, then showed the watchman that everything was in its place and nothing was missing. He continued to insist that the gang of thieves had been there and asked could he spend the rest of the night in the parlour as he was too frightened to stay downstairs on his own! I refused as I didn't want to encourage him to take refuge with me every time he had a bad dream.

➼ I was not the only one to have problems with my watchman sleeping at night. This story was told to me by some close friends, Kitty and Ahmadu Fadlu-Deen:-

"We suspected our watchman was sleeping at nights, so Ahmadu decided to come on him unawares late one night when we returned from a late night party. The watchman was in a crouched embryonic position. He must have been in a light slumber because he heard Ahmadu's footsteps but cleverly decided not to jump up. He waited for Ahmadu to reach nearer and then lifted both his hands and looked upwards as if completing his prayers, said "Ah-min" and stood up. Ahmadu had to stop in his tracks and smile, inwardly acknowledging that his watchman had got away with it this time.

I have mellowed over the years where my watchmen were concerned, and if I met them asleep at night I would just wake them up, talk with them for a little, and then go back to bed.

➤ However, not all watchmen slept through the night. I remember one particular man, a quiet-spoken Foulah, who surprised me when I went down to check on things late one night. I found him sitting under a light near the garage with a needle and thread in his hand, busily working away at a piece of embroidery. I watched him work for a little while, and then asked him if he would do some embroidery work for my wife. He agreed, and my wife asked him to embroider a picture of a train engine on a pillowcase for our youngest child. That month he got an extra payment from us, one as a non-sleeping watchman and secondly for embroidery!

➤ Another watchman who didn't sleep, I have forgotten his name now, was a man who worked for us for a couple of years and then left, saying he had saved some money and was going back home. A long time later he returned, saying he was once more looking for work. He had been hardworking and honest when I employed him before, so I had no hesitation in taking him on again. He had been with us for less than a week when he came up and woke us in the middle of the night saying there had been a fire. My wife and I went downstairs with him and he took us to the room where he slept during the day. By the light of my torch I could see that the walls and ceiling were entirely smoke-blackened and were still warm. Where there had been a small wooden chest of drawers there was a pile of ash. In the centre of the ash was what looked at first like a flat aluminium plate and on second inspection proved to be an aluminium saucepan that my wife had given him to boil his coffee! The metal bedstead was still intact, but the mattress was also reduced to ashes. Upon further inspection from outside we found that the wall of the watchman's room which formed part of the back stairs was cracked from the heat.

In the morning we found that the wire mosquito netting which was on frames fitted inside the windows of our bedroom had been disturbed. We had a look all around the outside of the house, and found handprints and footprints on the wall outside our bedroom, and outside all the other bedrooms as well. The mosquito netting had been disturbed in all the four bedrooms, but nothing had been stolen, possibly because as the rooms were not being used there was nothing left lying about to be taken. One old handbag had been removed from the room overlooking the back stairs, but there had been nothing in it and we found the bag lying on the stairs. We sacked the watchman, because we felt so many events in the space of one night were too much for us, especially as the presence of a watchman was supposed to make us feel safe to sleep at night.

# Chapter 16

# Rotary in Sierra Leone

Rotary International, the parent body to which every Rotary club belongs, is based in Chicago in the U.S.A., and each Rotary club pays annual dues to Rotary International based on the number of members in that club. Rotarians cannot belong directly to Rotary International, they can only belong to their local Rotary club. Dues are also paid to the District Funds. Each Rotarian pays an annual subscription to his own club to cover these amounts. Clubs belong to a District, and the District Governor is expected to visit all the clubs in his District at least once during his year of office. This can be very wearing when the clubs are spread over several different countries, as is the case in Africa. In 1985/86 for instance, there were thirty-five clubs from eleven different countries in our District, 910, with a total of 1,200 members. District 910 is now District 9100.

Rotary was started in Chicago, Illinois, USA, in 1905 by a lawyer called Paul P. Harris. The first meeting consisted of four men, Paul Harris, Hiram Shorey, Gustavus Loehr and Syvester Schiele. Meetings were rotated among the offices of members, which is why the name 'Rotary' was chosen. In 1910 Rotary went International when a club was opened in Winnepeg in Canada, but it was not until 1922 at the Convention in America (Los Angeles) that the delegates voted to change the name from the International Association of Rotary Clubs to Rotary International. At the time of writing there are some 1.2 million Rotarians as members of about 30,000 Rotary clubs in more than 160 countries.

The donation of one thousand dollars to the Rotary International Annual Programs Fund qualified the person in whose name the donation has been made to be known as a Paul Harris Fellow. This donation need not be made all in one go, but can be accumulated, and when it reaches a thousand dollars then that person, whether a member of a Rotary club or not, is recognised as a Paul Harris Fellow. The Freetown Rotary Club has several Paul Harris Fellows. Paul Harris died in 1947, and Rotarians made donations in his memory to the Rotary Foundation amounting to $2,000,000.

The motto of Rotary is 'Service above self – He profits most who serves best.'

The objects of Rotary are fourfold. They are to encourage and foster:-
1.   The development of acquaintance as an opportunity for Service.
2.   High ethical standards in business and professions.

3. The application of the ideal of service by every Rotarian to his personal business and community life.
4. The advancement of international understanding, goodwill and peace through world fellowship.

This last rule is the reason why it is necessary for Rotarians travelling abroad to make up Rotary attendance by going to the local club in the country they are visiting. If a Rotarian is unable to attend his own club for the weekly meeting, he must make-up at a club in the area where he is visiting, be it home or abroad, if there is a Rotary club within reasonable travelling distance.

At every meeting Rotarians are reminded of the Four Way Test that they should apply in their everyday lives, by the current president calling on any Rotarian to read out the following:

1. Is it the Truth?
2. Is it fair to all concerned?
3. Will it build goodwill and better friendships?
4. Will it be beneficial to all concerned?

This Test was formulated in 1932 by a Rotarian in Chicago called Herbert J. Taylor for employees of his company, and adopted by Rotary in 1933.

The first Rotary club in Sierra Leone was inaugurated in Freetown on 26 August 1962. It was part of District 910 and was called the Freetown Rotary Club. The first president was Lucien V. Genet, and among the other Charter members were R. W. Butler, R. Holst-Roness, R. J. Olu-Wright, Tommy F. Hope, E. D. Morgan, B.A. Rawlings, Dr Kibon M. Aboud, John Akar and William F. Conton. The club met every Thursday at 1.00 pm for lunch in the Wilberforce Room at the Paramount Hotel in Freetown. The meal would be a choice of English or African food. A short prayer was always said, standing up, before the meal, carefully worded to be suitable to all religions as follows: "We are grateful for food and fellowship and may we be mindful of the needs of others". Two Rotarians would sit at a table just inside the door to collect payment for the meal as the members came in. This would always be a little more than the hotel charged the club, as another way of raising funds for charity. This duty would be performed throughout the month and then another two Rotarians would take over on a rota basis.

The meetings usually included a guest speaker, provided in turn by the members, or the member could choose to speak himself. The topics would range from the speaker's own business or personal interests or experiences to a proposed charitable venture – in fact whatever the speaker of the day might choose. If there was no speaker that week due to one reason or another, I was frequently called upon to fill the gap. If the speaker was not a Rotarian, his lunch was paid for by the club.

One such speech given by me involved a lot of Krio slang. After I had finished my talk, one Rotarian at the far end of the room said aloud,

"Spoken like a Sawpit Boy", referring to the street in Freetown where I had been born. Since then I have often been referred to as "Sawpit Boy". When, a few years later, I wrote my first book, about Sierra Leone and my early life, I chose my nickname "Sawpit Boy" for its title.

One lunch-time meeting each month was a business meeting with no speaker. Any resolution voted on needed to have a two-thirds majority vote of the Rotarians present before being passed.

The Board of Directors met once a month on the Tuesday preceding the last Thursday of each month, the club's business meeting. As fellowship is as important to Rotary as the charitable aspect, these board meetings were held in the home of each director in rotation, and the business part of the meeting would always be followed by refreshments provided by the host and some time for general conversation and friendship. A roster was drawn up showing which director would host each monthly meeting, but these dates could be changed if inconvenient and the director concerned could find another willing to swap with him. In the earlier days drinks would be served during the board meeting, but it was found that the serving of alcohol had a disruptive effect on the smooth running of the meeting, and it was decided to ban all drinks until all business had been dealt with. This resulted in the meetings going on later to allow time for eating and drinking. Anyone who wanted to leave without waiting for refreshments was free to do so, but generally speaking the Rotarians did not object to the later finish and stayed for the fellowship. I cannot speak for what the wives may have thought of this arrangement!

In Sierra Leone the average man or woman believes that Rotary "nar jentri-man club"; "nar dem 'big' man dem lib day" (meaning that Rotary is for rich or important people only), reported Jocelyn Belu-John, Editor of the Freetown Rotary Club Bulletin in 1976. This is as true today as it ever was, but the public must be aware that Rotary exists to serve the community.

Each Rotary Club has its own banner, and its design usually incorporates something common to the particular club or country that it is in. In the case of the Rotary Club of Freetown, the banner, which is slightly pointed and edged with yellow fringe, has a green background with the Rotary International emblem in the top left hand corner in yellow. On the right is a yellow palm tree, with the words Freetown Sierra Leone near the bottom edge. The emblem is a cogwheel in royal blue and gold, with six spokes and twenty-four cogs, and with the words 'Rotary International' inside it. A member of a club who is going abroad would take a banner with him to present to the club he visits, in exchange for one from that club. Our club had a large collection of banners from clubs all over the world, which had been sewn on large dark blue cloths which were hung up on the walls at every meeting.

When it was the National Day of any country, a toast to that country would be drunk at the weekly meeting. Toasts were also drunk to the home club of any visiting Rotarian.

The Rotary Club of Freetown had its own monthly bulletin, called at first 'Freewheel', but later it was called 'Roundabout'. These bulletins contained articles about Rotary, about Sierra Leone, and various things of interest, including jokes. Rotary International had a magazine called 'The Rotarian' which was circulated to every member of every Rotary Club.

A person who is interested in becoming a Rotarian is not able to just ask for an application form. A member of Rotary will invite him as his guest to attend two or three of the weekly meetings. After that, the host will ask him what he thinks of Rotary. If his answer shows him to be the kind of person that would make a good Rotarian, the host will propose him to the membership committee as a prospective member, without the guest knowing. If the committee approves, the host will then ask his guest if he wants to join. If he is agreeable, he will be inducted at the next weekly meeting. I was introduced to Rotary by a good friend of mine, John Hawa, who has a business in Freetown. In due course I was inducted as a member in 1974.

Rotary International often sends Rotarians around the world on charitable missions or Rotary business. It is expected that club members will offer hospitality to such visiting Rotarians, who are sometimes accompanied by their wives. It was usual in Sierra Leone for one Rotarian to invite the visitors to stay with them in their homes, whilst others would invite them for meals or on outings to places of interest. My wife and I have acted as hosts to such visitors several times and found those occasions very rewarding, particularly the visit of Dr Ken Hobbs and his wife Eva who came to Freetown as part of a West African tour in connection with the 3H programme (Health, Hunger and Humanity). I also remember William and Miriam Cable who stayed with us. Miriam Cable brought with her seeds of fast growing leucaena trees for replanting areas where trees had been cut down for firewood. These we passed on to Rotarian Dale Gilles, who was in charge of the Boys Society. One of the Society's projects was planting trees.

On 3 October 1978 the Rotary Club of Freetown was honoured by a visit from the President of Rotary International, Rotarian Clem Ranouf and his wife, for a day and a half. In honour of the important visitors, the President of Sierra Leone, Dr Siaka Stevens (who was an honorary member of the Freetown Rotary Club), allowed the smaller of his two personal helicopters to be used to bring the visitors from the airport at Lungi to the grounds of State House in Freetown. Many Rotarians had gathered there to welcome the President of Rotary. The helicopter first brought Mrs Ranouf and then returned to Lungi to fetch Rotarian Clem Ranouf. Joan and I went to Bintumani Hotel in the evening for a reception followed by a dinner.

Rotarian Clem launched an appeal for all Rotarians around the world to subscribe $15 each to a common fund to study diseases and their eradication. I, as chairman of the Fundraising Committee at that time, committed our club not to $15, but to £15 per head, that is Le 1,800 to be raised by me. This pledge was duly fulfilled. After dinner we were all entertained by the Sierra Leone Dance Troupe.

I remember the visit of another senior Rotarian from America who was visiting the clubs in West Africa to discuss a proposed health scheme. He was travelling with his wife, and when they arrived at Lungi Airport they discovered his wife's suitcase was lost. The lady had only her overnight bag with her, and was staying for two days in Freetown, including attending a dinner-dance. The members of the Freetown club decided to present her with a dress. There was a boutique, in the Paramount Hotel where Rotary meetings were held, which sold embroidered dresses made from gara (tie-dye) material. The seamstress took a selection to the lady for her to choose from. The selected dress fitted very well but was too long, and my wife, who was present, was fascinated to see the seamstress deal with the problem. She first got out her scissors and cut the hem to the desired length, then took out of her bag a candle and a box of matches. She lit the candle, and passed the hem of the dress quickly against the flame, running it through her fingers until the hem had been singed all the way round. This can only be done with synthetic material such as polyester, and has the effect of sealing the ends so the material will not fray. It also gives the hem a very slightly frilled look, which is very attractive on lightweight material. The visiting Rotarian's wife had a dress to wear for the dinner, and my wife learned a new dressmaking skill which she afterwards used herself.

I joined the Freetown Rotary Club in 1974 during the presidency of Rotarian David Stables in 1973/74, thereby becoming one of the forty or so members. Over the next few years I served on various committees and later became chairman of the fund-raising committee. I became president of the Rotary Club of Freetown for 1985/86, with Dr W.S. Marcus-Jones, a lawyer and lecturer in law at Fourah Bay College, as First Vice-President, and Dr. Alex Thomas as Second Vice-President. They in turn became presidents themselves in the following years. Elections were held every year to select a new president and committee members. Each Rotary International President adopted a theme of his own for his year in office. The R.I. President for 1985/86, Rotarian Edward Cadman of the Wenatchee Club in U.S.A., used as his theme 'You are the Key'. My own theme for my year in office underscored that, 'You are on Active Service for Rotary', in addition to 'You are the Key'. A club president need not take on a theme for his year, but I chose to. In my Presidential Address, among other things I wrote: "Are you a Backbone of the Rotary Club you belong to or are you merely a Jawbone (i.e. do you just come to eat and talk and do nothing else?).  The District Governor for that year was Rotarian Mike Asafo-Boakye of Accra, Ghana.

As President of the Rotary Club of Freetown, I attended the Annual Convention, which that year was being held in Las Vegas in America.  My wife came with me, and we set off to the Paramount Hotel in Freetown with all our luggage to get the special coach to the airport at Lungi.  While waiting for the coach to arrive, my wife commented on a huge cartoon of frozen raw fish that someone was taking with her to England.  When we arrived at Gatwick Airport in England, we simply got our suitcases and rushed for the bus to Heathrow where we were getting the plane to Los Angeles.  We caught it by the skin of our teeth, with everyone in their seats and strapped in ready for take-off, just waiting for us.  At Los Angeles, we changed quickly to an internal USA flight to Las Vegas, and were picked up at the airport by a stretch limousine, together with another Rotarian from Freetown, Farid Hassib, and were taken to our different hotels.  I think there were about 26,000 Rotarians from all over the world attending the Convention that year.

It was only when we were in our room in the Marina Hotel that we had time to look at our luggage.  My wife said her suitcase felt damp, and when she opened it there was a strong smell of fish!  We then remembered the carton of fish at the Paramount Hotel, and realised it must have been packed on top of my wife's suitcase all the way to England.  She had to spend her first few hours in Las Vegas washing her clothes and hanging them up to dry all over our hotel room!

The Convention was a mixture of meetings on Rotary business and entertainments to which the accompanying wives were also invited.  Among the events we attended were a rodeo, a musical performance with singer Tony Bennett and a dinner at Caesar's Palace, where some of the Rotarians were staying, including some from Freetown.   The Rotarians were scattered among the many hotels along the main street, and special buses were laid on to enable the thousands of Rotarians from countries around the world where there were Rotary clubs, to travel easily between the hotels and the convention centre.

The Marina Hotel where we stayed in 1986 has since been demolished to make way for the 5,034 room hotel called MGM Grand.  Farid Hassib, a businessman, and another member of the Freetown Rotary Club, Dale Gilles, who was in charge of the Boys Society in Freetown, stayed at Caesar's Palace, which was much grander than the Marina and had 680 rooms.  Caesar's Palace has now been extended and made even bigger, and has 2,456 rooms.

One of the main aims of Rotary is fund raising, such funds being used to help the community in various ways.  For instance, schooling is not free in many of the developing countries such as Sierra Leone, so Rotary would offer scholarships to some promising boys and girls whose parents were struggling to pay their fees. Other projects included the renovation of the Blind School in Freetown, construction of Gloucester Village primary school, a swimming pool for the Milton Margai Teachers Training College, and playground equipment for schools. Rotary also helped if there was a local disaster. For instance, I remember a large fire destroying several houses in Peterson Street in Freetown. A public committee was formed to help those whose homes and belongings were lost, and I was responsible for raising a large sum of money for the Rotary Club of Freetown which was handed over to the committee.

Talking of the Milton Margai Teachers Training College, I became friendly with an English Rotarian from my club, Bill Jackson, who taught there. He would occasionally go fishing with me, and one day he invited Joan and me to have dinner with him and his wife, called June. When we got to the dessert, it was served in glass dishes in a lovely smokey-brown colour and my wife commented on how nice they were. The Jacksons told us the story of how they had come by the set of dishes when they were working in Thailand some years before. They told us there was a glass-making factory in the town where they were staying, which would make glass designs to order. However, the factory was very short of the raw materials and asked customers to supply their own glass. Our friends supplied some empty beer bottles to the factory, showed the craftsman the design of dish they wanted, and in a short time collected a set of serving dish and six small bowls beautifully made and in an unusual colour!

Health was prominent in the minds of Rotarians, and our club would provide vaccines for diseases such as polio and measles. We also provided the expertise and funds to dig wells for villages that had no fresh water supply, to avoid the need for the villagers to walk miles for clean water. Many other projects were also carried out. For instance, the Rotary Foundation would offer educational awards for further education to young men and women every year. These awards were for one academic year and the awardee would study in a country other than his own. He or she was expected to be an outstanding student and to be an ambassador of goodwill of his or her country and to attend Rotary meetings in the country of study. Family members of Rotarians are not eligible for any of these awards.

Funds were raised in different ways. Dinner-dances were held with tickets being sold to the public. Raffles and sponsored walks as well as other events, were some of the ways of raising funds. I recall my wife and my daughter Linda taking part in a sponsored walk in 1980 that started at Hill Station Club and went on to Cape Sierra and back. They both raised a good sum of money for the Rotary Club of Freetown. There were many taking part as each Rotarian was supposed to either walk himself or find at least one other person to walk on his behalf.

Once a year a grand raffle would be held and tickets were sold all over the country. The first prize was usually a new car, followed perhaps by a refrigerator, and several further prizes to a total of around twelve, reducing in value until the last prize was normally two crates of beer. Most of the prizes were donated by businesses and individuals in Freetown, but the car and the refrigerator were always purchased by the club from the proceeds of the raffle, although the suppliers usually gave the club a very good discount. The draw for the winning tickets would be held on a Sunday afternoon on television, and the chairman of the fund-raising committee would be spokesman for the occasion. For the first few years Rotarians were allowed to buy tickets for the grand raffle, but after some of the larger prizes were won by Rotarians the rules were changed, disallowing Rotarians from buying tickets for the draw.

Nearer to home, the Rotarians would 'fine' themselves and each other at their weekly meetings for things in their everyday lives. For instance, when Rotarian Suru Davies was made a Right Worshipful Master of his Freemason's Lodge, he was first congratulated, and then fined! The fines were imposed by the Sergeant-at-Arms, and these fines changed from week to week. He might decide, after looking around, that all Rotarians with a blue tie should be fined, which would result in such Rotarians hurriedly hiding their ties in their pockets, in fun, but they would pay their fines with good grace when presented with the fines box. It was usual for a Rotarian to pay a substantial fine on his birthday, commensurate with the years of his age!

A raffle was held at each weekly meeting, the prize being presented by a member of the club in rotation. The choice of item rested with the member, but the value was fixed. For instance, a prize that I won which was presented by Rotarian Tommy Hope, was a small table bell with the Rotary emblem on the top, measuring about four inches in height, which I still have in a display cabinet in my house in England.

For the meeting in Christmas week we always had a choir perform for us instead of a speaker, and the meal would go on longer than usual. Some of us invited our wives to that meeting and a special Christmas lunch would be served, with paper hats for everyone to get them in the party mood. The club made two special collections among themselves, for the choir and for the staff of the hotel who had served their lunches all year. The manageress of the hotel was the guest of the club at the Christmas lunch.

In 1980 Rotary International celebrated seventy-five years since Rotary began. In that year a special dinner-dance was held in Freetown, and as well Rotary took the unusual step of launching some special postage stamps in Freetown in honour of the seventy-fifth anniversary. I remember I bought six sets of First Day Covers, which I still have.

There is a special Rotary song called 'Vive le Rotary' which was sung on special occasions, such as a visit from the District Governor. It is sung to the tune of a traditional folk song circa 1844, 'Vive La Compagnie' and the words go like this:

1. Let every good knight raise his helmet and glove
   Vive Le Rotary!
   To carry our message of service and love
   Vive Le Rotary!

   Chorus: Vive Le, Vive Le Rotary!
   Vive Le, Vive Le Rotary!
   Truth is our Right
   Love is our Might
   Vive Le Rotary!

2. When something is wrong, let us straighten it out
   Vive Le Rotary!
   For nothing is worse than a fear or a doubt
   Vive Le Rotary!

3. The grooming of a man is the duty we claim
   Vive Le Rotary!
   Let's carry on business with fame to our name
   Vive Le Rotary!

4. The man with a smile is the fellow we need
   Vive Le Rotary!
   Who loses himself in the shaming of greed
   Vive Le Rotary!

Approval always had to be sought from the District Governor if any area wanted to form a new club. Enquiries had been made from a few people who lived or worked in the Brookfields area if a new Rotary club could be set up in that area to serve the local community. Rotarian Suru Davies, a Sierra Leonean, was asked by the then District Governor to investigate this possibility. It was found that there were enough potential members in suitable categories to make the establishment of a new club viable, and Suru went ahead with the formalities. Eventually in 1984 a new club was formed called the Greater Freetown Club, which held its weekly meetings in the evenings for dinner at Brookfields Hotel. The first president was Rotarian Albert Metzger, BA, LLB (Hons), Barrister and Solicitor, who served for two consecutive years. Albert was a Commissioner for Oaths, a Notary Public, a member of the International Society for the Comparative Study of Public Law, and a Consultant on Narcotics Legislation in Africa. Within a short time a third club was inaugurated at Wellington, followed by two clubs in the provinces, Bo and Kenema.

Suru Davies, a Past-President of the Freetown club, later went to England with his family. His interest in Rotary is still very strong and he soon became a member of the Rotary Club of Hillside in Finchley, North London. By the year 2000/2001 Suru had risen to become President of the Hillside Club.

Attendance at weekly meetings was a requirement and not a matter of choice. If a member was absent without good cause for three consecutive weeks he was asked to resign. Having another club nearby with an evening meeting helped the members of the original Freetown club keep up their attendance, as it gave them a second chance if they were forced by circumstances to miss their own meeting. When attending another club's meeting a Rotarian would be given a 'make-up' card to present to his own club to register his attendance for that week.

If a member of one club wished to leave and join another Rotary club, he would have to resign from his own club and then apply to join the other club. Transfer from one club to another was not automatic, as each club was individual.

Up to the time I left Freetown, my club could boast of two Past District Governors – Rotarian Tommy Hope (now deceased) and Rotarian Sam Baxter.

Inner Wheel Clubs existed alongside Rotary. Some of the wives of the Rotarians of a club would get together to form an Inner Wheel Club. It too was an international body with rules and subscriptions to be paid. Only one female relative of each Rotarian was eligible to join. If the Rotarian's wife did not want to join but his grown-up daughter did, that was acceptable, but not wife and daughter. The Inner Wheel Club of Freetown was inaugurated on 6th February 1966, at the suggestion of the Rotary Club of Freetown, and the first President was Dr June Holst-Roness. My wife became a member of Inner Wheel quite soon after I joined Rotary, and in due course served as president of her club in 1981/82.

For some time women had been complaining about being banned from Rotary and eventually in 1989 Rotary International decreed that women would be allowed to join at the discretion of each individual club. The Freetown Rotary club agreed that women be allowed to join them, provided they filled the criterion of representing a classification of profession or occupation that was not already filled. For instance, more than one lawyer, male or female, would be allowed to join as long as he or she had a different speciality. For example, civil law, criminal law, matrimonial and so on were all separate categories, and a club was only allowed to have one member from each category.

A few secondary schools in Freetown had 'Rotoract' clubs, for instance, the Freetown Grammar School for Boys, Annie Walsh School for Girls, and Girls High School. The school would approach the local Rotary Club to say they have sufficient pupils of fourteen and above with an interest in forming a Rotoract Club. Rotary would then approve and help organise the club which, once set up, would be self-supporting but could always call on

Rotary for help and advice. Interact Clubs were for primary school children, no older than thirteen. Occasionally the Rotary Club would invite representatives of local Rotoract and Interact Clubs to attend a Rotary lunch meeting.

By this time I was classed as a 'Senior Active' member, having served for more than fifteen years, which meant that I was no longer required to be a member of any of the committees, although I could be one if I so wished. I believe that this classification no longer exists in Rotary, and members are either 'Active' or 'Honorary'.

When I left Freetown in 1991 there were three clubs in the Freetown area and two clubs in the provinces. Since that time, I have been informed, all the clubs in Sierra Leone merged into one due to the unrest in Sierra Leone. Many Rotarians left the country, and for the others conditions were such as to make it difficult to maintain individual clubs. They merged the remnants of all the clubs in an attempt to keep Rotary alive in that country. I understand that now there are two clubs in Freetown, the Freetown Club, which now meets at the British Council Hall due to the damage incurred by the Paramount Hotel where it used to meet, and the Greater Freetown Club, which still meets at the Brookfields Hotel, but at lunchtime instead of in the evening.

A few years after I left Sierra Leone, the Rebel war that was being carried on in parts of the Provinces reached Freetown, and many Sierra Leoneans were forced to leave the country. I spoke to Albert Metzger when he came to London, and he told me the story about travelling on a boat called "The African Queen" from the Queen Elizabeth II Quay in Freetown to Banjul, Gambia. The boat was packed full with about 800 passengers. Albert met with two other Rotarians, one a pharmacist and the other a medical doctor. In the spirit of Rotary, the doctor was very busy all through the sea trip attending the sick on the boat with very limited medical facilities. During the trip the passengers were ordered to lean to one side and then the other from time to time, to help the craft keep its balance through the very high and violent waves. Albert said, "I was ill for most of the trip which seemed like one long void in my life – a vacuum I want to forget."

In Banjul, Albert, the two other Rotarians and their families, and many other refugees stayed at the Fajara Hotel as guests of a generous and illustrious businessman, Mr Mohamed Jawara, a Gambian. Albert and the others listened to the news about Sierra Leone broadcast every night by various stations such as the BBC, Voice of America, Radio Vatican and Radio Gambia. The Sierra Leoneans discussed the troubles they had left behind them, always endeavouring to find answers to the problems. After this experience of being forced to flee from the land of his birth, and contemplating the daily news of the deterioration of his country, Albert wrote the following poem, as a variation of Rudyard Kipling's "If.":-

"The Devil's If

IF you can tell a lie and be proud of it,
IF you can amputate your enemies hands
And only for fun,
IF you can mix with murderers and bandits,
And yet profess to be a saint,
IF you can gamble all your illegal winnings,
And blame ill fortune for your losses,
IF neither your foes nor your friends
Are worse than you
And in moral turpitude you top them all,
IF you can think only demon's thoughts
And do only evil acts,
IF you can persecute and prosecute
Your friends and enemies alike,
IF you can kill and only as a pastime,
IF your bedfellows are destruction and demons,
IF wrong and right for you remain the same
Yours is the devil's and all that's in Him,
And which is more,
You'll be the devil too."

It was heartwarming to read a story about some very young Sierra Leoneans who had been victims of the war in Sierra Leone. These young people had been taken to the United States of America for medical treatment for their injuries, by six Rotary clubs in New York State. After their wounds had healed they were fitted with modern artificial limbs to replace those hacked off with machetes by rebels. The group live in Hospital housing with someone to take care of them, and the Rotary clubs concerned have continued to take an interest in these young people. Once again Rotary has held out its hand to those in need.

# Chapter 17

# Made in Sierra Leone

At the time of writing Sierra Leone is judged one of the poorest nations of the world, but need it be like that? The country has, amongst its riches, minerals such as diamonds, gold, silver, rutile (titanium dioxide), manganese, bauxite, chrome. Iron ore was discovered at Lunsar in 1929. Production began in 1933 at Marampa mine at Lunsar, and at one time Marampa was the biggest iron ore supplier to Scotland. The mines closed down in 1975. Crude oil has been discovered in Sierra Leone but to date it is not commercially exploited. Rubber is also found in Sierra Leone in small quantities. Sierra Leone was one of the first countries in West Africa to export timber, particularly mahogany, to the United Kingdom.

A poem – A Glimpse of Africa - written by Willie Mae D. Hargrave, in the book "African Primitive Life" by Carrie Guerphan Hargrave, published in 1944, agrees with me by saying,

"The treasures in its wealthy soil,
Silver, gem, stone and gold,
Come forth abundantly thru toil
Adorn its people brave and bold."

In the field of agriculture, Sierra Leone produces coffee, cocoa, palm kernels, piassava and kola nuts for export. The kola nut grows on a large tree, in pods containing eight or ten nuts. The nuts can be white, pink or red and are removed from the pod and are usually sold peeled. If the skin is left on they are known as 'kanda kola'. A kola nut can be divided into two halves with a black line marking where the halves join. The halves are not usually exactly equal either in size or shape. The kola nut can be used as a stimulant, and I found it very useful in keeping me awake when I was studying late at night. I also use it to settle my stomach after a large meal of palm oil stew and rice. It can help to keep hunger at bay, and can also be used as a dye. It is usual to share this nut if you are eating it whilst in company. You would offer a piece to your companion before taking a bite yourself. Kola has a bitter taste and not everyone eats it, it is an acquired taste.

Piassava is obtained from the midribs of the raffia palm, and at one time Sierra Leone was the leading country in the production of piassava, used for making brooms and brushes. Sugar cane, groundnuts, ginger, and fruits such as bananas, mangoes, pineapples and many others are produced for local consumption, as well as cassava (which originated in South America), sweet potatoes and other root vegetables. Rice is grown locally, but not in sufficient amounts to feed the population. The harbour at Freetown is said to be the second largest in the world, and fish such as barracudas, mackerel, snappers, groupers, herring and others are of the highest quality. Prawns, shrimps, lobsters, crabs and oysters abound, and were sold and exported by Sierra Fisheries Ltd.

Salad vegetables such as lettuce, tomatoes, spring onions and cucumbers grown in Sierra Leone can be bought in the markets. Various leaves such as cassava leaf, potato leaf and crane-crane are sold for the preparation of sauces. Beef is available fresh in the market, and pork and lamb, locally produced, can be bought in the markets. Palm oil, groundnut oil and coconut oil are sold by the bottle or by gallon.

From the 1960's onwards factories began to flourish producing all kinds of different items. One of the oldest was the Forest Industries at Kenema, now defunct, which used to make furniture such as dining tables and chairs, arm chairs of various types, beds, wardrobes and dressing tables, and smaller items such as lamps and whisky stools. There was a cement tile factory run by Salvador Arouni in King Tom, the clay factory making roofing tiles and bricks was owned by J. S. Mohamed (now deceased), a bucket factory, and a plastics factory that made tumblers, pegs, combs and other household items. Wheelbarrows were also made in Freetown. The shoe factory was run by Bata Shoe Company, and Ahmed Jaward, a Lebanese businessman, operated the mattress factory. Another company, Osman Thomas Sons & Brothers at Wilkinson Road also made mattresses. The Jute Factory made bags for loading produce for export. Wooden planks and boards were produced for building purposes. The paint factory made both oil- and water-based paint in various colours. The glass factory, owned by a Lebanese called Philip Bulous, imported sheets of glass that could be cut in different sizes for windows. They also coated the glass with silver nitrate to make mirrors.

A Nigerian man by the name of Adenuga, who had lived in Sierra Leone for many years, was very enterprising and made records of local music and sold them to the public from his small shop in Goderich Street.

At the Wellington Industrial Estate could be found the Sierra Leone Brewery, which made Star and Heineken beers, and the non-alcoholic Maltina, and Wellington Distillery Ltd which produced Diamond Gin and Queen Elizabeth Gin, Duncan Whisky, Brandy, and a very good liqueur called Afrikoko. They also produced spirits in a single tot plastic packet called Totapak. A company called Natco (from National Confectionary Company Ltd) produced biscuits and sweets. The Tutik factory bottled mineral water, so called because the stream of pure water bubbled up between two trees - 'tu tik' in Krio. They also made margarine, icecream, jam, as well as shampoo.

Aureol Tobacco Company Ltd made a wide range of cigarettes and tobacco products, including State Express 555, Western Filter, High Life, and Sierra, both plain and menthol, and imported Lucky Strike. These sold well because the import of foreign cigarettes had been banned, except by special licence. Smokers were allowed to bring in the normal allowance of duty free cigarettes and tobacco, and were given one month in which to use them, after which they became illegal. A smoker in possession of foreign cigarettes might be asked to prove that he or she had returned to Sierra Leone within the last month. The company encouraged people in the Northern Province to grow tobacco, which they would then purchase.

Sugar was produced at the Magbass Sugar Refinery, set up by the Chinese and later taken over by a local businessman. Both moist or granulated sugar and cube sugar were made, and these were very popular in Sierra Leone. There was a cocoa factory owned by my cousin Samir Courban, also a lawyer, which produced Gold Mountain Cocoa Powder for the local market and exported the cocoa butter for use in cosmetics. Seaboard (West Africa) Ltd made Life Flour. A.J. Seward made non-prescription tablets, Vaseline, perfume, pomade and Baboo-bone ointment. They also made Saturday Night Powder and Bint el Sudan, both talcum powders. Their premises were in Battery next to the Cable and Wireless offices. This company was bought out by the late Mr Joseph Bahsoon of City Pharmacy, but later closed down. Another member of the Bahsoon family sold freshly ground coffee, and Turkish coffee, drunk mainly by the Lebanese in very small coffee cups, at his shop in Kissy Street. H. Jaber also made ground coffee. Mr Hedjazi sold ice-cream. Abess Bahsoon ran the 7-Up Factory which made 7-Up, Pepsi-Cola, Soda water, Tonic, Ginger Ale and other soft drinks. The Freetown Cold Storage Company Ltd made Sprite, Pepsi Cola, and others. A company was set up by the Ministry of Social Welfare to make Benimix, a baby food. The Sierra Leone Produce Marketing Board produced palm oil from their oil mills, both for home use and export.

The Sierra Leone Refinery imported crude oil, and by means of fragmentary distillation produced petrol, diesel, kerosine, cylinder gas and other products, including washing up liquid.

Another factory product was Whitex bleach, and the plastic containers it was sold in were also made in Sierra Leone. A business called the United Paper Company (Unipac) imported huge rolls of soft tissue paper and made them into toilet rolls. An Asian firm called Shankerdas made plastic conduit pipes for electric cables, among other things, and sold gin, whisky, rum and brandy in small plastic packets called Peg-a-pak, similar to Totapak made by Wellington Distillery mentioned above. There was a foam factory called Foamex, owned by Mr H. Huballah, a Lebanese born in Mambolo in the Northern Province, which made sheets of foam in different thicknesses, from a few millimetres to a few inches for use as mattresses. Sierra Leone Knitting Mills Ltd made underwear and other clothing.

Shotgun cartridges were made in Freetown by the Sierra Leone Cartridge Factory. It was started by President Siaka Stevens with Mr Eccles James. Later Mr J. S. Mohamed became a partner and managed the business. Katema Sawmills made pre-fabricated buildings. Balani Industries made various pharmaceutical products.

Chalk and blackboard dusters for use in schools were also made locally by a company called Patmadeens Industries. The shareholders of the company were Mr M. Badamasi Mahdi, a Sierra Leonean civil engineer, Dr V. Patel, an Indian lecturer in chemistry at Fourah Bay College, and Dr Ahmadu T. Fadlu-Deen, a Sierra Leonean medical practitioner with keen business ideas. The fourth member was Mr Rex Cowan, a Sierra Leone businessman who was responsible for the marketing and distribution of the products. The felt for the blackboard dusters was imported, and the handles of the dusters were made from waste wood from the Forest Industries Co-operation. After some time this company was forced by circumstances to close down.

There was a factory that made 'Wan Tem Kratch' matches. The boxes were decorated with series of pictures such as 'African Masks', 'Afro Music', which showed African musicians playing different types of local instruments, and 'African Culture' showing craftsmen such as wood carvers and weavers, etc.

Omole, an illegal spirit distilled in secret from palm-wine and sugar, was made by various people. This drink was very strong and brought about the saying, "E don drink omole" to describe someone who was drunk and talking nonsense. Later the making of this drink became more respectable and legal when Wellington Distilleries, owned by Duncan Gilbey and Matheson, began purchasing it to purify for use in the production of gin and vodka, although the omole makers were still banned from selling it direct to the public. A company called James International began to make Sassman, also a very strong spirit which people would buy and drink neat. The company then advertised that the spirit was better if drunk with a mixer, such as ginger ale.

Choitrams & Co Ltd bottled wine called Kono Plane and Kio. Another Asian company, Daswani, imported wine in barrels and bottled it for sale, but I have forgotten what the wine was called.

On a much smaller scale, the women used to make soap in long bars for laundry use, locally known as 'soda soap'. Black soap was made in round balls and did not look very attractive, but was very good for the skin. Starch was made from cassava and sold in the markets. Flower pots were made from cement and painted, and sold by the roadside. Metal coalpots and cutlasses were also made and sold, and even 'shekabulehs' were made by the local blacksmiths. The shekabuleh was a gun with a long barrel used by the hunters in the provinces, which could fire nails, small pebbles or anything that was loaded into it. Flat wooden spoons were carved and sold - from the smaller ones used for cooking to the large ones, called 'kpata', used for beating the clothes when doing the laundry at the waterside and for the gara dyeing. Native brooms are made by taking the central rib from palm leaves and tying them up in a bundle. These are very effective, and my wife still uses one in England to sweep the stairs. Rugs were made locally from raffia. Rope of various thicknesses was made from local plants grown in the provinces.

The most important local craft was producing tie-dye or 'gara' material, using at first imported cotton damask material, then later more modern synthetics. This material was used to make the traditional African gowns, as well as tablecloths and napkins and bedspreads. The dyes used at first were indigo (blue) and later kola (brown), then as imported dyes became easily obtainable the colours and patterns became much more varied. Other crafts include making baskets from the leaves of various types of palm tree, and making wooden carvings.

These wood carvings ranged from small animals to coffee tables carved in the shape of elephants carrying a flat board on their heads, from Bundo mask lamps to 'Gongoli' masks. I have some walking sticks which are carved with male or female figures, and just below the handle is some open-work with a small wooden ball inside that rattles as you walk with the stick. The balls were carved inside the walking sticks from a single piece of wood and were not inserted afterwards. I also have several elephant coffee tables, smaller elephant ashtrays and carved African heads.

Ivory tusks were also carved, sometimes left as a complete tusk with pictures carved along it, or perhaps made into lamps or small animal carvings.

'Country cloth' was also produced, using cotton grown in the provinces. Cotton, or kapok, was also gathered from the famous Cotton trees. A very useful item made from bamboo and the leaves of the palm tree was worn like a hat but was circular and wide enough to protect the head and shoulders from rain. They were cheap to buy and left both hands free, unlike an umbrella.

The tailors are very skilled at sewing and embroidering the traditional garments, using electric or treadle sewing machines, sometimes two or three tailors working in a space so small there is no room to pass between the machines. They are also good at copying European styles, and a lady need only to show them a picture of the style she wants for them to produce the identical style in a very short time.

Gold was mined in Sierra Leone and made into very fine filigree jewellery by the goldsmiths in Freetown.

Many local musical instruments are made in Sierra Leone from a variety of materials. The balangie, a form of xylophone, is a row of varying lengths of bamboo with small gourds fastened underneath, to give different tones when struck by the players with small wooden hammers.

There are many kinds of drums, including the 'talking drum', which is held under one arm and has leather strings attached to the skin stretched over the top of the drum down to the skin at the bottom. These strings when pressed with the arm can change the tone of the beaten drum, so making it possible to use the drum to send messages, as was done in the olden days.

The shegureh is a small gourd with a long, thin neck. A net is made with cowrie shells or beads woven into it and fitted over the gourd, with long strings attached which are held in one hand. The other hand shakes the gourd rhymically so that it is struck by the cowrie shells, which create a pleasing background to the music. This instrument is usually played by Mende women, and is often an accompaniment to singing.

Another instrument is the kongoma or kondi. I bought one of these myself for one Leone in 1975, from a shop next to my chambers in Gloucester Street in Freetown which sold a variety of African crafts including wooden and ivory carvings. The kongoma is made out of a gallon tin container, which had probably contained cooking oil. The screw-on top is removed, and a round hole nearly one inch in diameter is punched in each side about halfway down. The front is replaced with a thin piece of plywood. Across the front is fastened a row of eleven or twelve flattened umbrella spokes of graded lengths. Two metal rods are attached to the tin underneath the spokes, and between them a third rod is fastened on top of the spokes, which causes the spokes to bend slightly outwards. When the ends are pressed the kongoma can give all the notes of the tonic solfa. On the top of the tin container is a piece of metal shaped like a fish tail with little flat diamond-shaped bits of metal hanging all around the edge. The bottom of the kongoma is held against the stomach of the player, and he plays the ends of the umbrella spokes with his thumbs, shaking the kongoma at the same time to make the bits of hanging metal jingle.

I still have the kongoma, and quite recently it was played by a Sierra Leonean doctor friend, accompanying a Sierra Leonean teacher on the trumpet and an Indian magistrate friend playing the drums. The resulting music was charming to the ear.

I remember a man called Aman who made his own banjo from local materials and walked the streets of Freetown during my youth, playing as he went along. I never saw him stop and ask for money, and I guess he played for the sheer enjoyment of the music. Some people said of him that he was not very bright mentally, but was harmless.

Most of these industries and crafts have been disrupted or discontinued because of the civil war that was draining our country and hurting our people. Hopefully now that the war has ended Sierra Leone will begin to climb back to what it was before and even better.

➼ Cooked food and snacks, known as '**Mumuyereh**', were available along the streets of Freetown, and most of the items were also available in the large towns in the provinces. Sometimes the traders, mainly women and girls, would set up a pitch by the roadside with large enamel bowls with food of one kind or another covered with a clean cloth or plastic sheet. Other traders prefer to walk with their wares, crying out in a sing-song voice what they are selling, similar to the cries of old London. I remember the man who was selling small cakes who strolled along singing, "Ah get the **cake**, the sugar boku" (boku means plenty, from the French - beaucoup). Another would cry, "Ah get the **akara**". These were made from ground rice mixed with mashed banana and fried in small balls. "**Binch Akara**" was made from black-eyed beans, soaked and the skins removed, then ground up fine and fried in the same way. This akara is sometimes sold with a bread roll, opened up and the akara put inside and then sprinkled with hot pepper sauce.

**Abala**, made from ground rice, and **Oleleh**, made from ground black-eyed beans, mixed with palm oil and a little pepper, are wrapped in banana leaves and steamed, and are sold in small warm parcels. The two kinds are kept separated in a large calabash lined with clean sacks, and covered to keep them warm. Abala is a favourite of mine, whilst Joan prefers Oleleh. We have been able to get these two tasty foods in England, but somehow they do not taste quite as good when they are not wrapped in banana leaves! **Agidi**, which is white, is made from corn and has no palm oil, but is cooked in the same way, steamed in small banana leaf packets.

**Groundnuts** were sold roasted in the dry season, or boiled in their shells during the rains. I believe this is because during the rains the roasted groundnuts quickly go soft and taste stale, so the groundnuts are sold boiled instead. **Gramantine** (or tiger nuts) are, I believe, imported, and were not always available. So, I believe, is **Akparoro**, another nut that is also sold cooked, boiled in their husks. **Congou** (or bangles) are made from groundnuts with a bit of pepper. **Groundnut Cake** was familiar to my wife when she first saw it, but she called it peanut brittle, peanuts broken up and mixed in sugar syrup cooked and then poured out to set hard, when it is broken into pieces. Rice pap is cooked at home and then the trader, usually a girl, would walk through the streets with the large bowl on her head. When a customer wanted to buy she would lift down the bowl and measure out a serving into a plastic beaker. She would wait for the empty beaker, then continue her walkabout. When she passed a public standpipe she would wash all the dirty beakers ready for use again.

**Kanya** is made from groundnut and sugar mixed with either ground rice or gari ( dry ground cassava), and is sometimes called 'block' because it is packed into a small mould and then turned out into a small 'block'. **Coconut cake** comes in two types, either grated coconut mixed with flour and sugar and baked like biscuits, or the coconut is chopped into small pieces and mixed with syrup, and put in small rounds to set. **Banana chips** are very tasty, made from green bananas, and so are **plantain chips**, both sold in small plastic bags. Plantain slices are also fried in palm oil in thicker slices and sold, with pepper sauce, as are sweet potato slices. (Plantains and sweet potatoes are available in England, so we often cook these ourselves.) One of Joan's favourites is **peppermint**, made from sugar with peppermint essence, worked until it is white and sold in small bite-sized knots of sugar. **Puffcake** is made from sugar and flour and fried in small balls. **Doughnuts** are nothing like the ones known in England, they are fried in small, crunchy pieces and usually sold in a cone-shaped twist of grease-proof paper.

**Roast meat** is sold warm on bamboo skewers. **Roast cassava** is bought straight from a coal-pot which burnt charcoal, from women who cook it by the road-side. During the rain season **boiled mangoes** are sold, usually the rope-rope variety picked when semi-ripe. **Corn-on-the-cob** is roasted on the coal-pot, or sometimes boiled in the husk and sold warm from a covered basket. **Cassava bread and fried fish** is locally called '**record and pin**', the cassava bread being the record as it is round and flat, and the fish is the pin because it is fried with the head on and so is pointed. This last is a speciality of Waterloo market, a few miles from Freetown, where you could find dozens of women side by side all selling the same food. In my schooldays the 'record' was about half an inch thick and five inches in diameter for a penny. Nowadays it is small and thin – about one-eighth inch thick by about two inches in diameter, and I hate to think how much it costs. **Cow 'kandah'** (cow hide) is sold fried in small pieces. **Breadfruit** is also cut in slices and fried.

# Chapter 18

# Miscellany

In the Eastern Province of Sierra Leone in days gone by when leopards were common, it was the practice among the Mende people for women and children to walk in front of the men when travelling through the forest. No, it is not because a man wants to look at his wife's 'toomba' (bottom)! The reason for this was from fear of an attack by a leopard, as these animals were noted for their habit of allowing the first people to pass by safely and then attack from the rear. Thus the habit developed of women walking in front of men. I was told that another habit is for a man to lie in a hammock (usually tied between two trees) and not a woman, the reason being that a man in a hammock can respond to any attack instantly.

➤ Another practice, mainly in the provinces, is that of 'call name'. In the villages in the provinces, a man who could afford it might have several wives. Another man might persuade one of the wives to commit adultery with him. If the husband suspects that his wife has been unfaithful he beats her to get her to confess the name of her lover. If she does, the husband approaches the lover and asks for financial compensation for the damage done to him. If the lover refuses to pay up, a summons may be issued by the village Chief for 'call name', and the wife is called to publicly admit her shame and name the culprit who is then fined. The amount of the fine takes into consideration the costs due to the court, and the remainder of the money is then paid to the wronged husband. It was not unknown for a husband to encourage one of his wives to have an affair with another man and then 'confess', in order for the husband to get the financial benefit. I do not know if this still occurs.

➤ When I was very young I remember some of my mother's Lebanese friends would like to visit her to drink Turkish coffee from small cups. The coffee was finely ground, almost like flour, and a lot of sediment was left in the bottom of the cup. When they had finished drinking, one of the ladies, who was versed in the interpretation of coffee grounds, would take their cups and quickly turn them upside down on the saucers. She would then pick up the cups one by one, and 'basr' (an Arabic word), that is, tell the fortune of the lady who had drunk from that cup. She would look at the patterns left by the sediment and recognise some shapes, perhaps a boat or a dog or maybe a person. These pictures all had meanings, and from these the lady would predict some events in the future of that person. This pastime was very popular among Lebanese women, and some of them were looked on as being particularly adept at this. In England, before the advent of teabags, some people practised reading the future in tealeaves.

➤ In 1965 I paid a visit to my father and sister Mary in Kailahun where my father had a shop. My sister said she had a present for me, and I wondered what it could be. I was both surprised and pleased when she gave me an object made out of silver and ivory which she told me was a snuff box which had been given to her that had belonged to a Paramount Chief. It measures about fourteen inches long and is in three pieces, ivory in the middle and silver at each end. The larger end has a pattern of crowns engraved in the silver, with a moulding in silver in the same shape as the crown measuring two and a half by two inches on the top. The lower silver part is also moulded but has no engraving. There is a simple design of lines and circles carved into the ivory on both sides, so that whichever way you look at it, it is the same. It has a silver chain twenty six inches long. This snuff box is hanging in my house in England. I have seen pictures of others that have small spoons attached that were used for taking out the snuff. Snuff was placed between the lower lip and the lower front teeth. I have seen a similar snuff box in the Sierra Leone Museum in Freetown near the well-known Cotton Tree.

➤ On a recent visit to my cousin George Farrah in England, we met his nephew John Farrah, and we all fell to discussing the old days in Sierra Leone when George's father, also called John, was a young man living in Segbwema. The Mandingo people who tended cattle nearby would sometimes lose a cow due to a marauding leopard. They would call on my Uncle John to help them and he would set off with his shotgun. A trap would be set up baited with a piece of strong-smelling steak to attract the leopard. My uncle would sit concealed, with his double-barrelled shotgun cocked, patiently waiting for the leopard to appear. If he was lucky the leopard would come for the meat, whereupon it would be shot.

➤ A story told to us by George's nephew, John, was of him as a young lad living with his parents in Kono in Sierra Leone. He would record from the radio the music and time signal on BBC for the six o'clock news. He would then put his tape recorder near the open window on another day and play it back as loud as possible about ten minutes before six o'clock. Passers-by, thinking that their watches were wrong, would change the time, much to John's amusement. This young man became more serious as he grew up, and did his Ph.D. in Vascular Technology in England and now works in various laboratories.

➤ Did you know that Harford School for Girls, founded around 1900 and named at that time Moyamba Girls School, was the first secondary school for girls in the provinces? When it was decided to amalgamate the girls boarding home at Shenge with Moyamba Girls School, the name was changed to the Lillian R. Harford School for Girls. It became a secondary school in 1944 and so remains to this day and is popularly known as

Harford School, and is the sister school of Albert Academy in Freetown. Old girls of the school included Mrs Rebecca Stevens, wife of the late President Siaka Stevens, and Mrs Mabinty Koroma, wife of the late Vice President S.I. Koroma..

➠ Another old girl who became very prominent in the field of politics is Paramount Chief Ella Koblo Gulama. She was born in Moyamba in 1921 and became a member of the Moyamba District Council. She was elected to the House of Representatives in 1957, being the first woman member of the Sierra Leone Parliament. This was formerly known as the Legislative Council, but a new constitution in 1957, under the Governorship of Sir Maurice Dorman, increased the number of members and changed its name to the House of Representatives. Madam Ella Koblo Gulama was re-elected to Parliament in 1962 and became the first woman Cabinet Minister.

➠ Lati Hyde was the first female College Graduate of Fourah Bay College in Freetown. She entered this College in 1934 and graduated four years later. She had previously attended Annie Walsh School, and after graduation she returned there as a teacher. She went to the United Kingdom on a course of further study, and then returned once more to the Annie Walsh Secondary School in Freetown to make history again as the first African female principal of a school in Sierra Leone. In 1961 she received the MBE (Member of the British Empire) and became a Justice of the Peace in 1973. A year later she was awarded the Order of the Rokel. She travelled widely and served on several Councils and Organisations. A hall at Fourah Bay College is named after Lati Hyde.

She married Samuel J Forster in 1947 and had three children. Lati Hyde died in September 2001 at the age of ninety, and Sierra Leone lost a great woman.

➠ Another prominent woman in Freetown was Constance Agatha Cummings-John, née Horton. She was a Foundation pupil of the Freetown Secondary School for Girls in 1926, and was the first woman to go into politics in Freetown, becoming an elected member of the Municipal Council in 1938 at the age of only twenty years. In 1939 Mrs Cummings-John was one of two Vice-Presidents of the Sierra Leone branch of the West African Youth League, which had started in 1938. Mr Elias Bamin was the other Vice-President. A copy of the West African Youth League calendar for 1939 was given to me by Toufic, son of Elias Bamin, who said to me, "Keep it well, this is history." The poster-size calendar lists many important dates in the history of Sierra Leone. The Bamin family is still very prominent in Freetown.

More than twenty years later, in January 1966, Mrs Cummings-John became the first female mayor of Freetown. A few years previously she established a school at Congo Cross, The Eleanor Roosevelt Preparatory School for Girls, which opened on 23 January 1952 with Mrs Cummings-John as its Principal. The school was still standing in 2002, although the name had been changed. Her autobiography, 'Memoirs of a Krio Leader', edited and with an Introduction by LaRay Denzer, was published by Ibadan University in Nigeria, in 1995. I was surprised and gratified to see that LaRay Denzer made several references to my own book, 'Sawpit Book', in footnotes on page 2 and other places.

Constance Agatha Cummings John died on 21$^{st}$ February 2000 at the age of 82. Her Obituary appeared in The Guardian newspaper in London, written by Christopher Fyfe, the noted authority on Sierra Leone history.

➤➤ When I was going to school I was taught that 'Money talks, but not always in the purest English'. Much later, I was talking to a gentleman from the Middle East who had fallen for someone's sweet talk about buying a second-hand car for a lot of money. His own comment was, "Money talks, bullshit works!" But Bob Dylan says, "Money doesn't talk, it swears!"

➤➤ A friend of mine called Osman Cole had a driver called Mohamed. My friend was very impressed by Mohamed's good work, because whenever he returned the car to the compound he would clean it thoroughly, inside and out. One day Mohamed had left with the car on an errand, and Osman Cole had to go out with another car. Along the way he came across his other car being used as a taxi by Mohamed to carry raw meat from the abattoir to the market, without telling the owner of the car. No wonder the driver cleaned the inside of the car so well!

This was not an isolated incident and I told Osman of my own experiences. Whenever I had cause to be away from Freetown during the school term, I would hire a driver to take my children to school and collect them in the afternoon. On more than one occasion the driver would be late returning the car to my house after the morning run. He would always have a good excuse, but on my return to Freetown some friends told me they saw my driver carrying passengers around the town in my car, and that was why he was late returning the car. Luckily for me my driver was only carrying passengers, not raw meat!

Sometimes I also employed a driver so that he could use the car to collect the children from school while I was working in my office. When the car was short of petrol I gave him money to buy at the petrol station on his way to the school, and he drove the children home and then came back to me at the office. I asked him for the change out of the money I gave him. He said, "Sir, there is no change, I put twelve gallons of petrol in the tank." I asked, "Just where did you put the petrol, the tank only holds eight gallons?"

Osman had another story regarding a friend of his. The friend had parked his car outside his house for the night, close to his bedroom window so that if anyone tried to tamper with the car in the night he would be woken up. Sure enough in the early hours of the morning he heard a noise and looked out of the window, to find that a thief had cut the rubber seal and had just removed the front windscreen of his car. He shouted at the thief to leave the windscreen alone. The thief looked up at him and said, "If you shout, I will throw the windscreen on the ground and break it!" The car owner knew that replacement windscreens for his make of car were very hard to come by and very costly, so he was forced to negotiate with the thief. The end result was that the owner had to pay the thief for him to put the windscreen down gently and go away. The owner then went out and took the windscreen inside the house for the rest of the night, and the next day had it refitted in his car at further expense.

➡ The last Saturday in every month in Freetown is generally known as 'Cleaning Saturday'. On that Saturday everybody is supposed to stay indoors and clean his or her compound up to 10.00 am. If you are found out on the streets before that time you are asked to explain why.

➡ One Saturday afternoon we were on our way to Aqua Club by way of Murray Town Road. Just before we reached the turn-off to the Club, we had to stop to allow a funeral procession to go by. The coffin was being carried on the shoulders of six men who were struggling up the hill towards the cemetery, with a crowd of mourners behind them. The coffin-bearers were staggering from one side of the road to the other, and one of them said loudly, "Mammy Sally, you noh wan go?" (Mummy Sally, Don't you want to go?), as if they believed that their difficulties in getting up the hill were due to the reluctance of the corpse to go to its final resting place in the cemetery. Did Mammy Sally really not want to go ....?

➡ A married businessman in the provinces, whose secret girlfriend had gone to Freetown to have his baby, arranged with her to send a telegram to him when the child was born. So that his wife would not understand the message, the girlfriend should say, "Bicycle arrived complete", if she had a boy. If a girl was born she should say, "Bicycle arrived, toolbox and pump missing"!

➡ When I was a boy we had all manner of games and rituals that we would carry out, and I was surprised to learn from my son John that he and his friends still did much the same things. One such thing was the method of committing ourselves to a bet. The person making the challenge would put out his little finger, saying for instance "I bet you sixpence that ..." The person being challenged would hook his little finger around that of his challenger. They would then call on a third person if one was present, to 'cut' them apart, by bringing the side of his hand down on the joined little fingers to separate them. This made the bet more serious than it otherwise would have been. If no one else was there, one of them would 'cut'. Sometimes the bet would be made a bit lighter by adding, "Payable when able" at the end.

John told me of making friends with some English boys when he was on holiday, and when a bet was made as to who would score the first goal in the football match they were watching, he stuck out his little finger to make the bet. This took the other boys by surprise, and they asked him why he was sticking his little finger out!

➼ One of the games we played at home was Warri. I learnt this game in the provinces and liked it so much that I got a set of my own to play with my family. The board is home-made and carved out of wood in the shape of a canoe. Twelve holes are made along the board in two rows of six, and dried beans are used as counters or 'men'. Each hole represents a town and four beans are placed in each hole. The two players sit one each side of the board and the game is played anti-clockwise, with each player taking all the beans from one of the holes in his own side of the board and sowing them one by one in consecutive holes until he has used them all, when the other player takes a turn. The full rules of the game are set out in Appendix C.

➼ The following story was told by my cousin Samir Courban, usually known as Sam, and I quote:

"I was tidying up the bedroom when there was a rap at the door. In ran Dean, who had been reading a book in the living room. He slammed the door shut and locked it with the key – 'De babu don cam!' he shrieked. Our neighbour had brought a chimpanzee down to town from his country village and it seemed to like our compound more than his. I didn't want to show Dean I was as frightened as he was! He pushed me out of the room and locked the door again behind me – I had no alternative but to try and sort it out. I skulked slowly down the corridor to the living room, mentally preparing myself to reverse and streak to the bathroom which had a key. I peeped around the corner and very slowly edged my way to the kitchen where I could hear some of the staff chattering. Halfway there I froze – there he was – the chimpanzee was standing at the living room door leading to the veranda, with the children's football under one arm. We looked at each other for a second or two, then I ran full speed to the kitchen.

'E don cam, E don Cam!' I exploded. The staff looked at me, amazed. 'Who dat don cam?' someone asked calmly. I was as excitable as my eight year old son – 'the babu – the babu' I stuttered, pointing to the veranda. It was all over in minutes as they ran to chase it over the wall and back home. It was relief all round when the neighbour decided the chimp might be better off back in its village up country."

➼ When I heard Sam's story it reminded me of an incident involving another cousin, Mike Blell. Mike lived at Hill Station near 'Runnymead', the residence of the British High Commissioner. Mike had a large 'babu' himself, which was usually kept in a large cage in his compound. However, chimpanzees are very clever, and this one found out how to open the door of his cage. He slipped out of the compound without being seen, and the next thing Mike knew of it was when he received a telephone call from a very angry High Commissioner complaining that the chimpanzee was in his study and was scattering his papers all over the room.  Mike rushed over to Runnymede and retrieved his pet, apologising profusely for the damage the chimp had done.  I believe that chimp too soon found itself returned up country, as Mike was worried about the chimp escaping when he was away at work and causing him more embarrassment.

➤ Talking about chimps, I have a wooden set of the Three Wise Monkeys that was carved in Freetown.  I have heard that recently a fourth monkey has been added to the first three, See No Evil, Speak No Evil, and Hear No Evil.  This new one has its hands covering its private parts to represent, 'Do No Evil'!

I would like to see a fifth one added with its hands on its head, to mean 'Think No Evil'.

➤ The following incident was told to us by Nancy, my cousin Sam's wife.  Sam and Nancy had a fairly formal dinner party, and after the meal the guests preferred Turkish coffee to finish.  Nancy went to the kitchen but neither she nor her cook could find any Turkish coffee.  She was obliged to make do with a jar of Nescafe, but made it so as to resemble Turkish coffee and served it in the special small cups used by the Lebanese.  The guests did not know the difference, and praised the aromatic coffee and all requested a second cup.  When we were told this story years later Nancy included a poem which went like this:

### "Secrets

Another cup, they all agree
Showing off their pedigree
The aroma, they sigh, is so divine
'Tis only on the best they dine
They relish every sip they take
How can I tell them of my mistake
No fast food for them you see
And only ever fresh coffee
No traces of my special brew
Could be found by the kitchen crew
My conscience pricked me all night long
Nescafe didn't go wrong."

➤ Quite recently in England our daughter Linda gave us a surprise gift.  It was a poem she had written during her secondary schooldays in Freetown, and printed out on her computer and framed for us.  We had not seen it before, and enjoyed it so much we thought we would share it with you.

## Beauty

There is Beauty everywhere, for everyone to use it.
Look for it now and then, try never to lose it.
With a heart full of happiness and a feeling of being free,
Even mundane details are thought of with certain quality.

There is Beauty in people of all different races,
In little children with happy, innocent faces.
A piece of red ribbon made into a bow.
A tiny black ant, walking across your toe.

There is Beauty in birds, flying wild and free,
Chirping away with music clear and sweet.
From fierce huge Eagles gliding in the sky,
To colourful little Kingfishers happily flying by.

There is Beauty in the sand, the sea and the sun,
A little ship disappearing on the horizon
A soft calm wind blowing away your worries,
And a gentle rustle of leaves on overhanging trees.

There is Beauty in Life itself on earth,
Even in hardships between Birth and Death.
And after this life, another will begin,
A life in Heaven, full of joy, love and Beauty.

➼ There was a man called 'Dr' Musa who did something I had never seen before. He was an entertainer and acrobat who could be seen at all the major hotels in Freetown in the Sixties and Seventies. He would turn several somersaults using only one hand while with the other hand he held a plate full of uncooked rice. He so managed to turn his hand while somersaulting so as not to lose a single grain of rice from the plate. Another of his tricks was to walk on his hands and to bring his feet down as if to comb his hair with his feet. He followed this by repeating the somersaults but this time whilst carrying a glass of water on a small tray, without spilling a single drop. He ended up by drinking the water while still upside down on his hands and gripping the glass between his teeth. I have never seen anyone else drink water upside down. Musa became a familiar and popular figure in Freetown and at the hotels and bars along the beach at Lumley, where he would perform his feats, and the onlookers would express their appreciation of his skills by making small donations.
➼ Sierra Leone is noted for its beautiful beaches. I was told that some years ago the makers of Bounty Bars came to Freetown to film an

advertisement for Bounty Bars, the creamy coconut sweet covered in chocolate. It showed a bikini-clad young woman reclining under a coconut tree on a tropical beach enjoying a Bounty Bar. This advertisement was shown on United Kingdom television.

➼ In 1991 we decided to come to England for a while. Joan wanted to get a job, but found her secretarial skills were scarcely adequate for modern Britain. Her most recent work experience had been typing agreements for me at home in Freetown when my secretary was away. This was usually by candlelight, because we had many power cuts in those days that would last for days or weeks, and was done on an old manual portable typewriter she had had since she was seventeen (she asked me not to say how long ago that was!).

She was lucky enough to get a place on a course for women who wanted to return to work after having their children. Joan found herself the oldest in the class, most of the others having children of school age, while she had waited until all of our children had grown up and left home. The course included work experience, which Joan did in a solicitor's office. Not finding work immediately after the end of the course, she did further work experience at the offices of the local town council. She worked in the environment department, which dealt largely with complaints of varying kinds. Many of them were about the collection of refuse. She came home one day and told me about a man who had been swearing at her on the telephone, and threatening to come up to the offices and empty his rubbish all over her desk if she didn't get someone to come and collect it immediately. The call ended with the man apologising to her, but all the same she tried hard to get his complaint dealt with quickly, just in case!

➼ Living in the UK we soon discovered that computers were becoming almost as popular in people's homes as televisions. Our son-in-law, Kevin, had a monitor for his computer that was not working very well, so he decided he would examine it to see if he could get it to go again. He spent some time working on it, then switched on to see if it would go. It did not respond, so again Kevin went all over it to see if he could find a fault, but he couldn't. After working for hours he decided that the monitor was probably beyond repair and reached down to pull out the plug. It was only then that he discovered that the plug was lying unconnected on the carpet!

➼ When Yazid Fadlu-Deen was a small boy of about eight years of age, he attended Ronsab Primary School in Spur Road, Freetown. There was a lime tree in the compound, and Yazid was trying to pick some by stoning them. He threw a stone which went very high and missed the tree altogether, and he called out a warning to his friends to take cover. Yazid stood waiting to see where the stone would fall when suddenly he found out. The stone hit him on the head!

➼ It is not unusual for children to be given an Advent Calendar in the early days of December. The calendar would have little doors with numbers on, and the child would open one door each day corresponding with the date in December, to see a picture or find a small piece of chocolate, the last door being Christmas Day. One child who had been given such a calendar was anxious for Christmas to come quickly, so she opened several doors each day, thinking that would make Christmas come quickly. She complained bitterly when she opened the last door, well before Christmas, only to find that Christmas still had not come.

➤➤ The Lebanese community living in Sierra Leone, wanting to put some of their profits back into society, decided the most fitting way to do that was by educating the young people. They offered 130 scholarships in the Bo area alone to suitable candidates for a period of five years, being from form one to form five when the students would sit their General Certificate of Education examinations. The scholarships were for both girls and boys and were spread among the secondary schools in the area. The Lebanese community also made donations of money, and goods such as water pumps and medicines to the local hospitals.

➤➤ Sierra Leone has many organisations that are known by their initials, but they then like to find alternative words to fit those initials, mostly to make fun of the organisation. For instance:

SLBS (Sierra Leone Broadcasting Service) is converted to So Long Between Shows.

NPA (National Power Authority) – No Power Available

WAIT – West African International Time

WAWA – West Africa Wins Again (invented and used mainly by Europeans)

PNP (Peoples National Party) – Pikin Nar Pikin

PMMC (Precious Mineral Mining Company) – Plenty Money More Corruption

NPRC (National Provisional Ruling Council led by the youngest Head of State at 28 years) - Nar Pikin day Rule de Country

➤➤ There are many terrible and tragic stories of the events in Sierra Leone during the rebel war which started around 1991 in the provinces and escalated over the whole country. This war has now come to an end and I hope there will be lasting peace. As this book is intended to show the lighter side of life, I am not going to print those tragedies here, but as always in Sierra Leone, there is humour to be found in any situation and Sierra Leone has a saying that "Sa Lone cry nar laugh", meaning that a person who is laughing may really be crying.

We were told the following story, overheard among the people who were crowded around the Mammy Yoko Hotel at Lumley Beach hoping to get on board a boat to escape from Sierra Leone. One man was telling another that his van had disappeared and although he had searched high and low he could not find it anywhere. As he was talking, he looked up and said, "Here comes the Anti-Looting Squad". A van was driving past with the words "Anti-Looting Squad" sprayed on the side. Suddenly he shouted, "Hey, that is my van!" He had recognised it and then confirmed his suspicions when he saw the number plate, and chased off along the beach road after it.

➡ In the latter part of the war that has taken place over more than ten years in Sierra Leone since 1991, the United Nations has had thousands of troops from different parts of the world serving in Sierra Leone. Britain has also sent troops which have served alongside the United Nations troops in various capacities, such as helping to retrain the Sierra Leone Army. In February 2002 the British Prime Minister Tony Blair paid a short visit to Sierra Leone as part of his five day tour of West Africa. He is the first British Prime Minister to visit Sierra Leone since it gained Independence in 1961.

Tony Blair's father, Leo Blair, was at one time a visiting lecturer in Law and an examiner at Fourah Bay College in Freetown, making regular visits to Freetown for periods of two weeks at a time over two years in the 1960's. Mr Blair senior enjoyed his visits to the beautiful, friendly country and passed on his interest and concern for the country's distress in recent years to his son.

The first television broadcast made by Tony Blair from Sierra Leone was a sad one, a message of sympathy to Queen Elizabeth and the Royal family on the sudden death of the Queen's sister, Princess Margaret, which had happened at 6.30 am on the day he arrived at Lungi Airport. British television later showed Mr Blair meeting some of the British troops at Lungi, and then visiting the nearby village of Mahera with President Kabbah and others to meet some Paramount Chiefs. They were entertained in the traditional manner by singing, stilt walkers, dancers jumping through hoops of fire and many other entertainers. The Prime Minister stayed for about two hours, then boarded his plane to move on to Senegal, his next port of call.

A year later a celebrity of a different kind visited Sierra Leone. American actor Michael Douglas, who has been named by the United Nations as 'a Messenger of Peace' arrived in Freetown on 31$^{st}$ January 2003 for a five day trip to narrate a film being made by the United Nations about the experiences of child soldiers. He spent some time in Kono District seeing how the children there are being reintegrated into the school system. Michael Douglas, who has acted in or produced many films, including 'Basic Instinct' and 'Fatal Attraction', is the son of one of my old favourites, Kirk Douglas. I well remember seeing him in such films as 'The Indian Fighter', 'The Big Sky', '20,000 Leagues Under the Sea' and 'The Gunfight of the OK Corral'. In fact I remember my wife and I being invited to the opening night of the Byblos Cinema in Freetown run by Adnan Abess to watch 'The Heroes of Telemark' starring Kirk Douglas and Richard Harris.

# Chapter 19

# On Our Travels

In 1968, just before the Russians went into Czechoslovakia, we had an overnight stop in Prague on the way to England for the birth of our youngest child. Prague in those days had a black market exchange rate. I asked the hotel porter where I could change some money as I very much wanted to buy some crystal before we left the next morning. He told me to meet him by the lift in half an hour. I was there on time, and he was waiting for me. He beckoned me into the lift, and we went up and down and up again, and down once more, several times, arguing over rates of exchange, in complete privacy! It ended eventually to the full satisfaction of both of us, my friend of the lift got some English currency, and I was able to purchase more of the lovely glassware than I would have otherwise. Amongst the cut-glass crystal things I bought were some green wine glasses decorated with gold leaves, six large patterned beer glasses, and a large vase in pink glass with gold leaves, this last being the only item we still have. We managed to carry our purchases safely to England, then all the way to Freetown at the end of our holiday, only to lose most of it some years later.

The following day at noon we were at the airport to continue our journey from Prague. At the check-in desk, we were told the plane was overbooked and we wouldn't be able to travel until later in the day. Our flight had been booked in Freetown some weeks ahead, so I was not very pleased at this. Our luggage had been left at the airport overnight, and I asked the airport official where my luggage was now. He looked a little uncomfortable, then told me that my luggage was already on the plane, and that I would find it waiting for me when I arrived in London on the later plane. I objected to this, and insisted that either I and my family travelled on the plane I was booked on, with my luggage, or he had my luggage removed from the plane so that it and I would stay together. He excused himself for a moment, and then came back to say that he could manage to get us all on the plane. I drew the short straw and travelled in Economy, where we were all booked, while my wife, who was pregnant, and our two youngest children, travelled in style in first class. The moral of this story is, don't travel without your luggage on the same plane!

Whilst staying in London I bought a second-hand car cheaply to use around town. I remember once going to the Inner Temple (the Inn I belong to as a lawyer), and by mistake I took a wrong turning into a one-way street, and found all the traffic was coming towards me. I was immediately stopped by a policeman, who asked me where I thought I was going. I told him I was going to the Inner Temple, but added jokingly, "I must be late as everyone else is coming back!" The policeman was not amused, but he stopped all the traffic, let me make a U-turn, and gave me directions how to get there without getting into any more trouble with the police. I had a "Visitor to Britain" sticker on my windscreen; probably that saved me from the courts!

On returning to Freetown following the birth of our daughter, Linda, in England, we didn't encounter any excitement until our arrival at the Lungi ferry terminal on the airport bus. The ferry to Freetown had loaded up with cars, lorries and passengers and was beginning to pull away slowly but had not yet drawn up the ramp. The bus driver decided he wanted to get on the ferry and drove quickly down the slipway, with all the passengers on board, and got the front wheels of the bus on to the ramp of the ferry, which was still reversing slowly away from the slipway. The bus was being slowly dragged into the water. All the passengers shouted to the driver to stop and back up the slipway, as the ferry was full. Luckily for us, the driver heeded our pleas, and he knew that the ferry was not able to stop in time. The driver backed the bus off of the ramp and back up the slipway, where we had to wait in the heat of the afternoon sun for the next ferry to arrive.

The large ferry that did the Freetown-Lungi-Freetown crossing took about thirty vehicles, besides foot passengers. The journey took about forty minutes, and was usually quite smooth. We were more than halfway across the river when suddenly we heard the ferry's hooter going and the ferry came to a stop. We looked out to see what was happening. We discovered that the ferry's propellers had become entangled in the net of a fishing boat. It took about half an hour of diving by one of the ferry's mechanics to clear the propellers of the net, and then we could continue on our way.

It was now beginning to get dark, and the green hills of Freetown made a spectacular and welcoming sight as the lights went on in the houses and streets. We had a panoramic view of the Kissy and Cline Town area, with Mount Aureol and Kortright in the background. The blazing beacon of the oil refinery, locally known as 'panlamp', could be seen from far out at sea. When we landed at the Kissy ferry terminal we had to wait for the unloading of all the foot passengers with their various loads, from dried fish to live chickens, from cassava leaf to bunches of bananas, and from 'mattar-odo and pencil' (a large mortar made from the trunk of a tree and wooden pestle) to fanners (large, round trays woven like a basket in which rice was winnowed). The bus took us to the Paramount Hotel as was usual, where we got a taxi to Lumley. We had come home.

234

➤ On the Barra side of the River Gambia there is a place called Berending that is noted for the presence of 'sacred' crocodiles. These creatures were protected and no-one was allowed to do them any harm. I went one day with my family on a visit to see the crocodiles. After standing by the riverside for a few minutes without spotting anything, suddenly with no warning a large crocodile rose up at the water's edge and set off up the bank towards us at high speed. We didn't stop to think, we just took flight back to the car as fast as we could, and were relieved when the crocodile gave up the chase before we got back to the road where I had parked the car. When we returned to my sister's house at Barra where we were staying, we complained that no-one had warned us that the crocodiles were dangerous. "But they are not," said my sister, "The crocodile was only looking for food." My brother, who was also at Barra doing business, said, "You should have taken some dried bonga (fish) to throw for the crocodiles as an offering, the one that chased you was only hungry, not angry." New and surprising things happened every day at Barra. The next morning when we went into the parlour, we saw a chicken on the settee. We shooed the hen back to the garden, only to find that it had laid an egg on the settee! It must have been a hen that liked home comforts!

➤ We would go on holiday every couple of years or so, and 1973 found us visiting friends in Gillingham, Kent, for the weekend. We spent some time in their garden, admiring the wide range of flowers and vegetables grown by the husband in his spare time. His wife explained to us that although the area was some miles from the sea, at one time it had been under water and that it was possible to find fossils of sea creatures among the pebbles on the ground. I said to her jokingly, "If I find something interesting, may I keep it?" She laughed and said that I could, although it was not likely as she was yet to find anything herself. I looked down at the pebbles on the gravel path where I stood, and stirred them around with my foot. I saw one about two inches across that looked almost heart-shaped, and picked it up. It turned out to be a fossilised sea urchin. I showed it to my host and hostess, and they were surprised at my success. They are people of their word and allowed me to keep my find, saying "Finders, keepers." Many years later when we came to live in England I took it to a shop in Gillingham that sells fossils and semi-precious stones. The shop owner looked it up and, to my surprise, confirmed it to be a sea urchin from the crustacean period, in the region of 140 million years old. Yes, I did write 140 million years! Fossils of sea creatures are commonly found in chalk, which is plentiful in Kent. I am glad that I kept this interesting find all these years.

➤ In 1975 we left Freetown to go on holiday and spent a few days in Banjul. We were about an hour into the flight out of Banjul when the 'Fasten your seat belts' sign came on and the pilot made an announcement. He said that we were approaching some bad weather and that we should all remain in our seats with our seat belts fastened. We sat there on tenterhooks waiting to see how bad it was going to get, but in fact we continued quite smoothly. After about fifteen minutes the pilot came back on the air with a further announcement: "We managed to avoid that patch of bad weather by sheer skill!" All the passengers clapped!

Our next stop was Las Palmas in the Canary Islands for one week. Paddy Warren travelled on the same plane with us, and we took apartments in the same hotel. In the evening we went for a walk and Paddy showed me where he worked in Las Palmas twenty five years before for a shipping line near the jetty. The next day we took a taxi together and went up into the hills to have lunch at a restaurant called 'Hao'. The tables and chairs were set outside and were all made out of rustic tree trunks

We then went to Rome for a week, where the people speak Italian, after spending a week where people speak Spanish. I was happy to meet Francis Karemo, who was with the Sierra Leone Embassy in Rome, and to talk Krio with him. He was very helpful and had booked rooms for us at the Hotel Calabria and sent his car and driver to meet us at the airport. 1975 was a Holy Year for the Roman Catholic Church. The next day Francis took us to the Vatican City. Pope Paul VI was addressing the pilgrims from various countries in St. Peter's Square, where he gave public audience once a week. We received the Papal blessing. Before leaving, the Pope drove slowly around the Square in an open Landrover, and passed quite near to where we were standing.

We visited the Trevi Fountain and we each threw in a coin. The belief is that if you throw a coin in the Trevi Fountain you will return again to Rome. That happened more than twenty five years ago, and so far none of us have returned. But who knows! There was a small boy near us who was trying to fish out some of the coins near the edge of the fountain. Perhaps he wanted to get out of Rome? That evening I went to a hotel to attend a Rotary dinner (as was expected of visiting Rotarians). I found very few Rotarians there as most Italians were away on holiday. The next day we went back to St. Peters. Our children, Mary and John, made their confessions to a priest as part of the Anno Santo pilgrimage. We all went through the Holy Door, which is opened during Holy Year and will then remain closed for the next twenty five years. On Sunday we attended Mass at the Church of St Vincent, and Mary and John received Holy Communion as the final part of their pilgrimage.

One of the places we visited was the Catacombs of St. Agnese. We went with a guide and were very careful not to be separated from the party we were with, as the underground tunnels led off in all directions and it would be very easy to get lost. We saw some skeletons of the early Catholics who hid in the catacombs 2000 years ago.

I changed some travellers cheques at Lira 1,418 to the pound sterling. The bank told me that I could not change more than £100, if I needed more

I would have to go to another bank. I went to another branch of the same bank, Banco Santo di Spirito, when I changed a further £100 at the better rate of Lira 1,433 to the pound. I found this disparity rather strange. I bought two suits from a shop next door to our hotel, at a very reasonable price. We next went to see the fruit and vegetable market, where we found everything of very good quality and reasonable prices. We bought some excellent peaches very cheaply. By chance we ran into Francis Karemo, who had been telephoning our hotel to invite us to dinner that night.

That evening Francis picked us up and took us to his home in the hills – he compared the area to Hill Station in Freetown, cooler and above the noise and bustle of the city. We met Francis' family, his wife and their three children. It was his wife's birthday, and some other friends from Sierra Leone joined us. We had foofoo and bitters, and also groundnut stew and rice. Later that night Francis drove us back to our hotel, after a very pleasant evening of eating, drinking and good company.

The following day we visited St. Pauls Outside the Walls, a Catholic Cathedral (as distinct from St. Pauls Within the Walls, which is Protestant). Linda fell on the steps and sustained what she called a 'Roman bruise'. Outside we found a stall selling souvenirs, and I bought Joan two things which she still has, a small gilt box with a picture of the Trevi Fountain, and a small copy of the 'Pieta' (meaning 'pity' in Italian), a statue by Michelangelo of the Virgin Mary cradling the crucified body of Jesus, which can be seen in St Peters.

Late on the night before we left Rome, I got a call from Francis to tell me he had just heard the news of the death of a close friend of mine, Roland Harding, who was a much-respected Judge in Freetown. I had known him for many years, from the time he was a practising lawyer, and we used to visit each other's homes and chambers. He was born on 31 July 1901, and was called to the Bar at Lincoln's Inn in England in February 1953. It seemed particularly sad to us that he should die at this time because it was only a month before that Roland had announced his retirement from the Bench. A special session of the High Court was held on 2$^{nd}$ July 1975, with a panel of about fourteen judges who were present in Freetown at the time, to say farewell on his retirement. Some other judges were sitting in the Provinces and so could not attend. Speeches were made by the Chief Justice, the Attorney General and the President of the Bar Association.

During our week in Rome we visited the Sistine Chapel, the Church of St. Mary Magiorre, St. Paul's Within the Walls and several other old churches, as all visitors to Rome do. Francis Karemo sent his Italian driver with the Embassy car to take us to the airport, and we left Rome by Air Italia to go to England.

About twenty four years later – in 1999 – Francis Karemo and his wife were killed by the rebels in the civil war in Sierra Leone.

In England we visited St. Paul's Cathedral in London and Canterbury Cathedral in Kent. On the Sunday morning the family all attended mass at the church near where we were staying in Kent, a recently built church of modern design. Walking home afterwards, Linda, aged six at the time, said with a sigh of relief, "When that church is old we won't have to come and look at it because we've already seen it!"

A week or two later we spent a day in the historic town of Rochester, a twenty minute bus ride away. After a visit to the beautiful old Cathedral, we all went to see Rochester Castle, which is partly in ruins and had scaffolding supporting some of the walls that were not safe. We explained to the children that the Castle was built by the Normans some few years after the Norman invasion of Britain in 1066. Young John eyed the scaffolding and remarked, in a tone of disgust, "And they haven't even finished building it yet!"

After a month we returned to Freetown.

➡ After attending the Rotary Convention in Las Vegas, U.S.A., we decided to visit some old friends who moved from Freetown to Pasadena. We travelled by bus through San Antonio, where we saw the Roy Rogers Museum, which reminded me of the films with Roy Rogers and his famous horse Trigger that I used to watch as a boy. At one stop on the route, while we were sitting on the bus, a man came up to us and asked us if we had any fruit, such as apples or oranges. The man did not look poor, or in need of something to eat, so I replied that we had none, although we did have a few apples that we had bought to eat on the journey. The man took our word for it and moved on to someone else. Unknown to us at the time, we were at the border to enter into California, and also unknown to us, the man was an inspector, checking to see if we were carrying any fruit from one state to the other, which was not permitted. It was only when we told the story to our friends in Pasadena that they explained to us that the man was not a beggar and it was not allowed to bring fruit from other states into California, for fear of introducing disease to the crops. We had inadvertently become apple smugglers, but we live to learn.

➡ We were travelling to England on holiday, and the pilot of the KLM flight from Freetown to Amsterdam came on the air to give his usual greetings to the passengers at the start of the flight. He told us, "There are three pilots on board today and a full bus. One of us is walking along the aisle." All eyes looked up, and all we could see was a small African boy of about six years walking along the aisle towards the toilets. There was general laughter, as I said to my wife, "That can't be the pilot, at least I hope not!"

We had an overnight stop in Amsterdam, and my wife decided to buy some cigarettes. We found a shop that had all different brands of cigarettes around the walls from floor to ceiling. She looked around for a while and couldn't find the brand she was looking for, so she asked the shopkeeper, "Do you have More?" The shopkeeper looked at her with some surprise, waved his hand at the well-stocked shelves and said, "Isn't this enough. You want more cigarettes?" My wife had to explain that the brand she smoked was called 'More', and described it to him. He then turned to his shelves and picked up a packet of cigarettes called 'Time', which were exactly the same as the ones Joan was looking for, so she bought them.

➤ We all enjoyed our trips abroad, and the children in particular enjoyed the novelty of in-flight meals on trays with lots of little compartments. On one trip they showed me a small packet of peanuts they had been given and asked me to explain why it was clearly labelled 'Peanuts', and then had written underneath, "This may contain nuts"! I thought this was the caution over food labelling gone mad!

➤ When on holiday in England in 1988, we were invited to spend a week in Belgium with a friend and her partner. The man was very wealthy and had a lovely home, a few cars and a private plane. He came to collect us at the ferry port at Ostend in a little bright red sports car. We had a lovely ride to his home just outside Antwerp, but my wife commented to me that she was surprised that with all his money, our host had only bought a two-door car and not a car with four doors. I had to point out to her that the car we had just been riding in could hardly be called cheap - it was a Ferrari!

At the end of our visit, our host offered to fly us back to England in his five-seater plane. I jumped at the offer, but Joan was not too happy with the thought of travelling in such a small plane. She agreed reluctantly, and we took off from Antwerp airport to fly to Biggin Hill in Kent. We had a lovely view of the landscape; flying lower than we were used to in commercial aircraft gave more opportunity to see the details of the countryside we were flying over. At Biggin Hill we landed safely and were called into the customs shed for the baggage check. Our host accompanied us but had no luggage, for he was taking off immediately for his return journey home. We had little luggage as we had only been away for a week, but in all our travels we have never had our bags checked as thoroughly as they were on that day. When he had finished, the customs officer explained that the smaller airports had become popular with drug smugglers so he had orders to be very thorough with all travellers.

➤ In 1995 on Christmas Day we attended Mass in a Catholic church not far from Cambridge, England, where our daughter Mary, her husband Steve and their children were living. Our son, John, was also at the service with his son Alexander, aged just over two then. The congregation stood up to sing a hymn. Alexander found he could not see what was going on, so he stood on the pew between his father and grandmother. He listened to the singing for a while but did not know the hymn. He wanted to join in so he quietly sang "Baa Baa Black Sheep", which he had recently learnt in nursery school. My son and his mother looked down at the boy and then at each other and smiled. They did not try to stop the boy singing, for they felt God would accept the musical offering of a small child.

Mary, Steve and their sons, Josh and Justin, sometimes came to spend the weekend with us in Gillingham. Justin was a very tidy child, and at the age of eighteen months he would wander around the house looking for things he could 'put away'. Our daughter Linda, who had driven round in her car to see us, had to walk home because her car keys were nowhere to be found. After searching for hours we found them late that night tucked away in a drawer where Justin had put them.

After Mary and her family went back home to Cambridgeshire, we had a shock at about 2.00 am when we suddenly heard music from downstairs. We crept stealthily downstairs, thinking it was a thief that had mistakenly turned on the music centre, only to discover the CD player had been put on Timer and had switched itself on. We decided the culprit was little Justin again, as he had been busy with the remote control of the music centre that afternoon. We switched off the music and went back to bed, happy in the thought that it was not a thief after all!

When Josh was very young he loved playing with the telephone. He would pick it up and pretend to be having a conversation with someone, sometimes pressing a few numbers first. On one occasion when he did this, a worried look came over his face. He held out the phone to my wife and said, "It 's for you, Granny." My wife was surprised as the telephone had not rung, but took it from Josh only to hear, "The number you have dialled has not been recognised"!

➤➤ John Farrah, the son of my cousin, told me this story of a friend of his, a young man who was travelling with his girlfriend in Thailand on a package holiday. They arrived at a hotel in Bangkok and went to the Reception to check in. A porter later came up to the young man, thinking he was alone, and asked him if he wanted to see some Tigers. The young man thought it sounded very interesting and suggested to his girlfriend when she returned from changing her dress that they took up the offer. The porter led both of them a short distance away from the hotel, and turned down a side street. He took them into what the young man quickly realised was a brothel, and the porter said, "Here are Thai girls!" The young man was very embarrassed at having to explain to his girlfriend that the porter had said Thai girls and he had thought the porter had said tigers.

➤➤ Our son John is very fond of travel and adventures and in 1997 he led an expedition down the Amazon against the flow of the river, starting at the Atlantic coast in Brazil and ending at the Pacific coast in Peru. In Brazil, on the day that the expedition really started, John had a dream that a huge male lion came into their camp late at night. In the dream, John was the only one awake but the lion did not appear aggressive. The lion walked around the camp then settled down just outside John's tent and rested its head on its paws, but remaining watchful. John relaxed and went back to sleep. During the journey John thought about this dream often, pondering over the strangeness of it, not least that he should dream of a lion where no lions lived.

On the same day of the dream, the support team for the expedition visited a school in Peru and told the children about the three British men who were coming up the Amazon. One of the children, an eleven year old boy, was a descendant of a tribe that lived in the jungle. It was the custom of his people to take a creature as their personal totem, and his own spirit guide was a lion, but as he lived in a town he felt he did not need it and that the travellers needed it more. The boy asked his father if he could send them his lion. His father agreed and took his son to visit a Shaman, or doctor-priest, who performed the necessary ceremonies to transfer the spirit lion from the boy to take care of the travellers.

The school children were asked to do paintings as a competition, the winners to be chosen by the British adventurers at the end of their journey. Several weeks after John had his dream, the journey was successfully completed and the travellers visited the school in Peru. John saw the paintings and chose as his favourite a picture showing a boat on the river passing through the jungle. Birds and beasts could be seen along the river bank, including a lion which stood watching the boat as it passed. He asked the boy who painted it why he put in a lion as there were no lions in Peru. The boy then explained about his guide being a lion and that he sent it to them to take care of them. John asked why did the lion come to him in particular. The boy smiled and said, "Because you wanted him." John framed the picture and it now hangs proudly on his bedroom wall.

➻ Joan and I went to Florida in 1998 to visit our son Michael and his family for two weeks. Michael and his wife Afaf made us very welcome, and we had a lovely time with them and our four grandchildren. Farid and Andy, Michael's two sons, were very helpful taking us around in Farid's car to do our shopping, but we usually all travelled in Michael's 7-seater when we went sightseeing. One memorable trip was going for an airboat ride in the Everglades, which included a stop on an island where we watched a man wrestling with an alligator, although it was done with care so that neither man nor alligator was injured. The airboats are flat bottomed and are propelled by a fan fixed above the water-level at the rear. An ordinary outboard engine with a propeller would not be efficient in the Everglades as the water is shallow in most places and full of water plants, fish and even alligators. There is plenty of bird life, too, including the Purple Gallinules, the Blue Heron with its snake-like neck, and the Anhina, a bird which resembles the hornbill.

Michael and his two sons took me on a fishing trip one day. We went out on a fairly large boat that took paying clients out on day trips and supplied all the fishing gear. We went a few miles out from shore, and after a while I had a bite and brought in a small barracuda. I was quite pleased with myself and imagined having it for supper, but I was to be disappointed. One of the crew came up to me and said that I should throw the barracuda back as it was not fit to eat. I complained that where I came from we ate barracuda whenever we could get it. He insisted the fish should go back into the sea, and explained that in those waters the barracuda carried a disease that made it unfit for human consumption. I continued fishing and had another catch, a fish unknown to me, and was again told that it had to go back overboard. I was used to fishing for food, as well as the enjoyment of catching the fish, and found it a bit pointless if I had to throw back every fish I caught. Luckily my grandsons caught some smaller fish that they were allowed to keep, so we had our fish supper after all.

I must tell you about one thing I found strange. One day we went to a restaurant for lunch. There were platefuls of peanuts in their shells on most of the tables, for eating whilst waiting for your order to arrive. The custom in this particular restaurant was to throw the discarded shells on the floor in the aisles between the tables. We complied with the custom! I suppose this 'deliberate casualness' was done to give the restaurant a 'theme', and make it different from all the others.

Some days we just stayed at home with the family and swam in the pool. They have a large house and a large garden, which is mainly lawn with a few trees at the back and flower beds in front. The gardens are just separated from the neighbours' land by shallow dips in the land to mark the border; there are no fences.

One afternoon Joan went for a walk with Nadia, Michael and Afaf's youngest daughter, along the back of the gardens to a house a little way along where there was a horse. The horse had a stable and a grassy area around it was fenced in. They were lucky that the horse came out and walked over to them and put his head over the fence to be stroked, which was a thrill for Nadia. Then she and Joan came back the way they had gone, only to find that the sprinklers in Michael's garden had just come on, as they were set to do twice a day. Nadia and Joan tried to dodge the sprinklers, but in vain as the sprinklers changed direction just as they were within reach and they both got soaked. I was sitting safely out of danger on the patio with Michael, Afaf and Michelle, their other daughter, having a barbecue, and we all laughed when they came in dripping wet.

After a few days we left the family in Florida and went on to our daughter Mary and her family in Nebraska. We flew from Miami airport in Florida to Dallas airport in Texas, to get an internal flight to Omaha. We had about three hours to wait, and having had some lunch and looked around the shops, Joan decided she would like to smoke a cigarette. No Smoking signs were everywhere, but Joan caught sight of a sign saying Smoking Area with an arrow pointing to it. We followed the signs and arrows and walked for a long way, until finally we came to a door with a Smoking Area sign on it. We opened the door and went through, expecting to find a small lounge and perhaps a coffee bar. What did we find? We stepped through and found ourselves in the Carpark! We went back and checked the sign on the door but it was correct. We went out again and then we noticed one of those large ashtrays with sand in it, and a few butts were lying around on the floor. We had found the smoking area! Joan decided she did not need a cigarette that badly and we walked all the way back to where we had to catch our plane to Omaha.

Omaha, unlike Florida, is not visited much by tourists, but we still found much to see. We went with Mary, Steve and their three sons to various places, including a lovely zoo where they had a tropical area that reminded us of Sierra Leone. There was a walk-through aquarium where you could look up and see a shark swimming above your head as well as all kinds of marine life on both sides of you. It was just like walking through a glass tunnel under the sea. We went to a disused railway station that had been turned into a museum, and as well as all kinds of train memorabilia, there was a beautiful collection of antique glassware. One day we all piled into their seven-seater and drove across a long, wide bridge over the Missouri River into Iowa, the next State, where we spent the day in Council Bluffs.

It was fun spending time with more of our grandchildren. We watched Josh, the oldest, at his soccer practice, and also when he marched with his boy scout troop in the parade through Omaha, which included the local fire brigade, politicians, horsemen and several marching bands. Josh is still a keen footballer, and is now qualified to referee matches played by the younger boys. Justin is also keen on games but has not yet decided which is his favourite sport. Jason, the youngest, was less than two years old when we were with them in Omaha, but when in 2003 the whole family visited us in England, Jason greeted us with open arms and a big hug, even though he could not really have remembered us, a special moment for us.

➡ In 2001 I visited the Lebanon for a holiday with my wife and daughter Mary, nearly thirty years after my first visit. Our flight arrived at Beirut airport at 2.30 am and we found my cousin Malik Yanni and my good friend Souham Haroun were there to meet us. We stayed with Malik and his wife Leila and daughter Roula in a suburb of Beirut. Souham and his wife, also named Joan, lived a few miles inland in a place called Bik Faya. We planned to visit the birthplace of my parents, and do and see all the usual things that visitors to Lebanon do. Incidentally, Lebanon is mentioned about seven times in the Bible.

On a visit to a supermarket in Beirut, I was most impressed to find that the long moving ramp, like an escalator without the steps, that connected one floor with the next, was magnetised. As you pushed your loaded trolley on to the ramp, the trolley was securely held in one place until you reached the end, when you pushed the trolley off. Even if the power should fail, as happened one day when we were half-way up and the ramp suddenly stopped, the trolley stays safely in place.

We were taken to see the Marie Baz Museum which has a collection of waxwork figures of prominent people, both Lebanese and international. One of the figures was of Nabih Berri, who at the time of our visit was the Speaker of Parliament. He was born in Bo, in the Provinces of Sierra Leone, but left when he was still quite young.

One of our trips was down to the south of Lebanon. We were taken by a friend, Salim Sabrah, and his wife Nahla, in their minibus. We passed Jieh, Jonah's Beach, the place where the whale is said to have spat out Jonah after three days in its belly. Our first stop was at Sidon, where we saw the ruins of an old Crusader sea castle built in the early 11$^{th}$ century on a broad stone pier out in the sea. At Tyre we saw extensive Roman ruins with magnificent marble columns still standing, but the architraves have fallen. There is a straight Roman road leading to the old port which is now under the sea. The water is so clear it is possible to see walls and columns lying on the seabed. There is a forum where the Roman gladiators fought, and the remains of the Roman baths, where fires would be lit beneath the stone floors to heat the bathrooms. The Roman floors are of mosaic work, but after the Romans came the Byzantine people, who laid marble floors on top of the mosaics, and there are places where the marble is broken or missing and the mosaic can be seen underneath. We saw the remains of a glass-firing furnace, but even more interesting were the large balls of greenish-blue glass waste from those early days.

A Phoenician king of Tyre, Agenor, had a daughter called Europa. According to Greek mythology she was abducted by the Greek god Zeus and taken to the island of Crete where Europa bore him three sons, one of them Minos who became king of Crete. It is said that the area around the Mediterranean that was known in those days was called Europe in honour of her.

From Tyre it was only a short distance to Qana, where we saw some rock carvings said to have been done by the early Christians and a cave where the early Christians used to hide from persecution. The carvings were said to depict the Last Supper, Lazarus's Tomb, the tablets for the Ten Commandments, the Virgin and Child and other significant Christian events. These carvings were so old and weather-worn that we would not have known what they were had they not been pointed out to us.

We were then taken to a site in the centre of the village which, it is claimed, was the place where Jesus turned water into wine at the wedding at Cana. We saw the ruins of a building and some stone basins which had been used for making wine. Some children from the village came running out to sell us pictures showing what the building would have looked like in the time of Jesus. One small boy of about six years old came up to us to try to sell us some pictures. He explained to us, in Arabic, his own version of the Bible story. He said that this was the place where Jesus came to his daughter's wedding. He, the boy, did not see Jesus, as he had gone to Beirut on a visit at the time!!!

From Qana it was only a short drive to a house belonging to Salim and Nahla Sabrah in a village in the south of Lebanon. After serving us a delicious lunch of kibbi, salad and beans akara that Nahla had brought with her, they showed us around the large, newly completed home of two storeys and a basement.

Some days later we went to Baalbeck in the Bekaa Valley. Originally it was a Phoenician city dedicated to the chief of their gods, Baal. (Their chief female deity was Astarte.) Baalbeck is called Gods' Paradise, and the most famous temple is dedicated to Jupiter, the building of which began in 60 BC. The Temple of Jupiter, built on huge blocks of stone one of which is said to weigh over one thousand tons, is the largest Roman temple in the world, and it was built on the ruins of a Phoenician temple. It is there that you can see the famous six pillars, the tallest columns in the world, which stand outlined against the sky. Every summer the International Festival is held on the steps of the temple, bringing visitors from all over the world. The Festival started in 1956 and world-class artists from the world of music and ballet have performed there. In 1975 the Festival did not take place due to the outbreak of civil war in Lebanon, but with the return of peace the unforgettable Festival was reinstated in 1997. We heard that in the summer of 2002 Feyrouz, one of the greatest female Lebanese singers, gave her farewell performance in these magnificent surroundings.

Near by and on a lower level is the Temple of Bacchus. Carved on the lintel over the gateway is a large eagle holding a key in its claws, and there are many carvings of gods such as the winged god Hermes. On the outside were carvings of Mark Anthony, Cleopatra with the asp, the goddess Diana and others. There is so much to see and enjoy in this wonderful place.

After leaving the temples we were taken to the quarry just a short distance away where the huge blocks of stone were cut and saw the enormous 'Stone of the Pregnant Woman'. It is said that after being cut and shaped, the stone was just too heavy to be moved and still remains in the quarry, partly submerged in the earth. Local legend has it that a young married woman can touch the stone to help her to become pregnant.

By now we were all hungry and went on to the town of Zahle, still in the Bekaa Valley, to eat in one of the open-air restaurants by the river. The food was wonderful with mezza consisting of all the usual dishes and some new to us, such as pickled grapes, followed by roast beef, chicken and kafta served on skewers, with fresh fruit to follow. Joan was fascinated to see the large, very thin Lebanese bread being cooked in the centre of the restaurant. The young chef took a small piece of soft dough about four inches across and worked it with his hands until it had stretched quite a lot, then he laid it over a large rounded cushion and stretched it further until it was at least fifteen inches across and very thin. He then put it over a large dome-shaped pan with heat underneath to cook for just a short time. The whole process took only a couple of minutes and the result was rather like a pancake, and was served warm and fresh at the table.

Less historical than Baalbeck but just as awesome was the Grotto at Jeita that we visited a day or two later. We went in a small cable car up to the higher level where we followed a marked path on foot. The caverns are huge and the strange and beautiful formations of stalactites and stalagmites left us speechless. Although there was a large area open to view, we were told that only a small proportion of the caverns are open to the public. We then walked down to the lower level where we were taken in small boats for a tour on the underground river. Here lighting of different colours was used, and the boatman entertained us by pointing out various formations and telling us the names they have for them, such as Romeo and Juliet (like two figures on a balcony), and the more prosaic cauliflower and boxing glove. There was a small zoo outside with birds and mainly domestic animals, and a very friendly donkey which took hold of the corner of my wife's handbag and didn't want to let go, and a gift shop selling very pretty items in blue glass.

The Phoenicians were the early inhabitants of South Lebanon, principally the towns of Tyre and Sidon on the coast. Dating back to around 3,000 B.C., they were the inventors of the alphabet, being the first to use letters instead of pictures as a form of writing in 1100B.C. The alphabet was adopted by the Greeks and later by the Romans and is what we use today. This book is written today in this form, thanks to the Phoenicians! It is interesting that the first letters of the Arabic alphabet are: alef, be, te (a, b, c). Inscriptions in Phoenician have been found as far away as North and South America.

The Phoenicians were skilled at working with silver and glass, making utensils and jewellery. Many items such as necklaces, pendants and decorated glass jars have been found during excavations and can be seen in museums in Lebanon. They were famous for their invention of dyes, in particular the Tyrian purple dye, and it is said that the 'coat of many colours' given to Joseph in the Bible by his father Jacob was almost certainly made in Phoenicia. The craftworkers there would dye the material and often sew it into colourful robes before selling it.

The Bible tells us that Hiram, King of Tyre in the Lebanon, was a close friend of King Solomon of Israel. (Solomon was well known for his wise judgements, as witnessed by one story of two women claiming the same baby: see Kings III Chap. 3) Around 900BC when Solomon, who was the son of King David and Bathsheba and who reigned for forty years, was building his famous Temple, Hiram sent him firs and cedars from Lebanon. "The Tutankamun Prophecies" by Maurice Cotterell tells us that Freemasonry began with Chiram Abiff, a stone mason and architect for King Hiram.

The Phoenicians were great sailors skilled in building ships, and Hiram lent Solomon "shipmen that had knowledge of the sea" (I Kings, 9.27) when together they sent out great fleets of merchant ships and they came back once every three years "bringing gold and silver, ivory, and apes, and peacocks." In the Old Testament the terms 'Canaan' and 'Canaanites' were used for Phoenicia and the Phoenician people. Solomon became the richest man and Jerusalem the richest city in the world.

The New Testament, St Mark Chapter 7, verses 24 to 30, tells us that Jesus "went into the borders of Tyre and Sidon and entered into an house ..." where He cured a young girl of an unclean spirit. This mention by St Mark of Jesus actually visiting Tyre and Sidon, makes it likely that Qana, near Tyre in the south of Lebanon, is the true site of the wedding where Jesus performed his first miracle when he turned water into wine.

In the book 'The Africans - A Triple Heritage' by Ali A. Mazrui published by the BBC in England in 1986, I read about the theory of Professor Kamal Salibi, Professor of History at the American University of Beirut in Lebanon. He put forward the theory that the Israelite Kingdom of David and Solomon was not in the area known today as Israel, but lay further south in Saudi Arabia in the provinces of Hejaz and Asir. He supported this by pinpointing about 80 per cent of the Old Testament biblical place-names that he has examined, showing that the events took place further south than was previously thought.

Going back to the Phoenicians, Book Fifteen of The Odyssey by Homer, on page 332 of a recent translation by Robert Fagles, says, "One day a band of Phoenicians landed there. The famous sea-dogs, sharp bargainers too, the holds of their black ship brimful with a hoard of flashy baubles." Homer wrote this work probably in the 8th Century BC.

It is believed that the Phoenicians sailed around Africa in about 600BC, 2,000 years before the Portuguese are known to have done the same thing. They were the first sailors to keep their bearings in open seas, navigating effectively by the stars. The Phoenicians were also skilled in working tin, and it is thought that they sailed as far as Cornwall and the Scilly Isles in Britain to work the tin mines there at that time. As well as sailing around the African coast, the Phoenicians travelled around the Mediterranean Sea and colonised some areas, including Marseilles and Toulouse in France, Cyprus and areas of the Turkish coast and southern Spain. The word 'bible' originated from the Greek word for book, which the Greeks took from the Phoenician town of Byblos in the Lebanon, which was well-known as a trading centre for papyrus, the earliest form of paper. We have a painting of an Egyptian pharoah and his queen in our sitting room (a gift from an Egyptian friend) which is painted on papyrus made in the original way used by the Ancient Egyptians from the papyrus reed.

In the fifth century BC the Phoenicians started to mint their own coins in Tyre and Sidon, with various motifs, but frequently of merchant ships on waves. The early coins were made of silver, but later on they also made coins of bronze. The Phoenicians were very wealthy. The centre of Phoenician civilisation was in the coastal cities of Lebanon such as Tyre and Sidon, and they were full of luxuries such as precious metals, spices, cloth, and timber from the cedars of Lebanon and other trees. Then, after centuries of success and expansion, these cities were taken over by Babylonian and Persian imperialists. The Phoenicians moved their focus of activities to Carthage, a colony near Tunis in North Africa founded by them in the 9$^{th}$ century BC, which became the main centre for their seagoing trade. Rome became worried by the success of the Carthaginians in many different fields ranging from agriculture to the arts, and decreed that Carthage must be destroyed. The destruction, which was complete, took place around 146 BC and extended even to the literature, such as the work of the early Phoenician writer Sanchoniaton, and to spreading salt on the soil to spoil the agriculture.

I could go on and on writing about my ancestors, the Phoenicians of Lebanon, but you will have to read some of the hundreds of books written about them if you want more information.

We made a visit of several days to the birthplace of my parents. We took a taxi from Beirut to the house of my cousin Georgette Abi Hanna in Beit Malet, stopping briefly at Tripoli on the way to buy some Lebanese sweets from the shop of the famous Hallab Brothers. The next day we did the short trip to Rahbe Akkar, the village where both my father and mother were born and where many of my relatives still live. Our first stop was to my cousin Linda, who inspite of our having already eaten lunch, insisted we ate with them. When I saw what they were having for lunch, cassava leaf and potato leaf cooked with palm oil and served with rice, I couldn't be sure whether I was in Lebanon or Sierra Leone, and I couldn't resist joining them. We had seen on our travels in the south of Lebanon, stalls by the roadside advertising cassava leaf and potato leaf for sale. Nearly every other house held a member of my family, so we were kept busy going from house to house to drink coffee and catch up with the news.

I have relatives that now live in Essex in England, some miles away from me in Kent, and although we spoke often on the telephone and promised we would soon arrange to meet, it hadn't happened. Walking into the house of my cousin Linda in Rahbe Akkar who should we meet but her sister - my cousin Farida and her husband Farid from Essex! We also met a lady called Najlah Abdallah Abrahim, who is my first cousin although we had never met. She had recently returned from Columbia in South America and spoke only Spanish and Arabic, but she was very helpful to us. She came with us and directed our taxi driver to the homes of various members of my family, until we arrived at the home of her sister, my cousin Mounira. After a rest and some refreshment of fruit juice and arabic coffee, Mounira's son Raad, an old friend of mine from Sefadu in Sierra Leone but now living in Rahbe, took over the role of director while Najlah stayed to spend time with her sister.

In the villages of Lebanon almost every house has its own grapevine, and the local drink is Arak, distilled from grapes and flavoured with aniseed. Raad took us to visit a Lebanese friend from Sierra Leone called Abdallah, a professional man, who has retired to his farm in Rahbe Akkar and grows grapes and other fruits. He served us some peaches, which were very small but very tasty, different to any peach we had seen before. We were lucky that at the time of our visit he was distilling Arak for his own consumption and was kind enough to explain the process to us. The grapes are crushed and left to ferment for two to three weeks. This is then strained and the juice is put in the lower part of the still, which is then heated. It is necessary to check the amount of heat, because alcohol comes off at 80 degrees while water vaporises at 100 degrees. Alcohol steam comes off and condenses in the upper container, which is fed constantly with cold water to make the steam vaporize. The resulting spirit runs down a tube into large glass jars. Anise is added for flavour and the arak is distilled several times more. I was given a generous quantity to take home, and I found it very good.

Abdallah introduced me to a man who was working with him who turned out to be Elieh Sheada, only child of my mother's sister Rada, making Elieh my first cousin. We had an emotional meeting although we could not converse very much as Elieh spoke no English and my Arabic is halting. I was amused to learn that this 'only child' had produced eight children of his own, two of them boys.

As we were leaving Abdallah gave us as a parting gift a cross-section of polished wood from an old olive tree that had grown on his estate at Rahbe. It was quite thick so Raad offered to have it divided into two. We gave one piece to our daughter Mary who was with us, and the other now hangs on the wall of our sitting room in England. As we were about to leave for Beirut the next day, Raad arrived with the olive wood, some tasty Lebanese sweets, and a big bag of the speciality of Rahbe - radishes, very large, crisp and hot.

Having returned to Beirut, our next excursion the following day was a much shorter one. We were driven along the coastal road to Jounieh, then took the winding road up the hill to Harissa to see the beautiful white statue of Our Lady of Lebanon which has stood there for over a hundred years. We walked up the spiral staircase around the base of the statue, from where we could see for miles along the coast to north and south. There are several churches nearby and there were several weddings taking place the Sunday we were there. We looked in a small chapel, decorated with swathes of white gauze and lovely white flowers, the church was full of their perfume.

Next to the statue of Our Lady stood the huge modern Maronite Basilica. The architecture was impressive, unusual and elegant. We went inside and found the sweeping shape of the roof made us think of the sails of a ship. Finishing touches were being put to the decorations for the wedding about to take place. The church was very large and the seating was arranged something like that of a theatre. The entrance where the bride and groom would come in brought them to a broad flight of steps which led down towards the altar. There were large stands with flower arrangements placed at short intervals down the staircase, and men were placing candles among the flowers ready to be lit at the last moment. On a table in front of the altar were placed two gold crowns ready to be placed on the heads of the bride and groom. The windows around the altar were of clear glass with deep red curtains hanging in front of them, except for one window through which you could see, surprisingly near, the statue of Our Lady.

As we left the Basilica we saw the bride and groom arriving together, walking hand in hand towards the church. This was different to the usual custom in Britain and elsewhere, where the groom arrives first at the church with his supporters and the bride arrives a little later with her father.

All in all our trip to Lebanon had been a great success. We received a warm welcome from family and old friends, and visited some places we will remember for a long time to come.

➡ In 2002 I was able to fulfil a long-standing ambition when I finally got to visit Stonehenge in Wiltshire, England. I had heard that the public were no longer able to approach the stones close up but could only circle the site behind a rope barrier. This was not going to be enough for me, I had waited a long time for this and wanted to touch the stones. Luckily for me, when we telephoned English Heritage to book our visit we discovered that it was possible to touch the stones but only by joining a private visit, outside the normal opening hours of the site. We booked and paid in advance, and had an appointment for 7.30 pm (the site was closing to the public at 7.00 pm during the month of our visit). We got there early so we could go into the gift shop. I bought a large book on the history of Stonehenge, while my wife bought a china thimble and a fridge magnet, her favourite souvenirs of the places we visit.

By 7.15 pm a small group of young women had arrived which was also booked for the private viewing so the guide allowed us through the gate. We walked along a tunnel leading under the road and came up the other side with a full view of the magnificent stones. As we approached the guide unhooked the rope barrier and ushered us inside, remaining outside himself. While some of the stones themselves are huge, bigger even than I expected, the whole structure is smaller than I imagined, being only thirty-five paces across. We wandered among the stones without hindrance, touching them, leaning on them, and when I got a bit tired I even sat down on one!

The group of ladies, about eight of them, had moved into the centre of the stones and sat down on the ground in a circle. They said what appeared to be prayers in a kind of chant, which went on for some time. Then they started singing while they wandered slowly in and out of the stones at random, touching them as they passed. The singing was not in English, there were no words I could recognise, but it added to the mystical sense of awe given off by the huge, ancient stones. When we left these ladies were all sitting or lying relaxed against the stones, facing the sunset.

There are many conjectures as to who built the stones circles and why, but so far no one really knows. Excavations around the site have revealed that burials took place there, but it is not known whether the burials were an act of sacrifice or whether the people died naturally and were buried in that place to honour them. We were told that the earthworks, a large raised mound surrounded by a ditch (which is what the word 'henge' means), were from a much earlier time than the stones. Also the stone circles were not all built at the same time. One of the legends as to how Stonehenge came about is that the wizard Merlin, of King Arthur's Court, brought them to Wiltshire from Ireland by magic. Apart from the use of magic, this theory has been disproved because the stones were in place long before King Arthur came into being. Another suggestion is that the stones were erected by the Phoenicians. (Stonehenge was being built in England at about the same time the Phoenicians were establishing colonies in the Mediterranean). Certain of the stones are aligned with the sunrise at the Summer Solstice, and many people are convinced that the stones are an astronomical computer.

Stone circles are in fact not rare, there are over five hundred of them in Britain alone. Although Stonehenge is by far the most famous, stone circles can be found in England, Scotland, Wales, France, Japan, parts of Africa and other places. From what my wife and I have read, no one can be sure of the origins of any of them.

# Chapter 20

# Freetown Revisited

In March 2002 our son John invited us to join him in Freetown for Easter. The flight from Gatwick was full, as flights between London and Freetown usually are. We had been warned that there may be some overbooking of seats so we should check in early. We were so anxious not to be left behind that we were there before the Sierra National Airlines check-in desk was opened, so we were first in the queue! This was my wife's first visit since we left in 1991, but I had been back to Sierra Leone twice since then.

It was a night flight and we arrived at Lungi airport about 4.30 am. We collected our luggage and crossed the sea dividing Lungi from Freetown by helicopter. We saw the dawn coming up as we waited for John to pick us up from the helipad behind the Mammy Yoko Hotel. We were soon driving along the almost empty roads on that early Good Friday morning, looking out for familiar places as we enjoyed the warmth and sights of Freetown. My wife said that by the end of the first day she felt as much at home as if we had not left the country more than ten years before.

We stayed with John at a house in Hill Station, and the only sign of past military activity was the Unamsil checkpost right outside the gate. (Unamsil means United Nations Mission in Sierra Leone, a peacekeeping force.) The roof was supported on poles and the walls were made of sandbags stacked waist-high. There were always between two and four soldiers, armed with machine guns, on duty inside. Looking up at the hillside gave us quite a shock. Where there used to be a mass of green trees growing so close together the soil wasn't visible, there was a brown, sandy hillside with scarcely a blade of grass. I was told that the trees had been cut down to provide firewood for cooking for all the thousands of extra people living in Freetown due to the Provinces being unsafe. This is understandable, and probably unavoidable, but a pity.

In the afternoon we went with John to Alex's Beach Bar at Lumley, and met my cousin Nadia Mileris, who runs it with the help of her children, who are now grown up and married. We sat at a table near the beach and ate Jollof rice and drank Star beer. In 2001 Sierra Leone Brewery celebrated forty years of Star beer being made in Sierra Leone. It is a very good lager and has won several international awards for quality and Joan and I both thoroughly enjoyed drinking it again. In fact, what with the heat and the enjoyable social life, we drank more beer (mostly Star) in our three weeks holiday than in the last ten years in England.

After our meal we went to sit at the bar and chat, meeting up with friends we had not seen for years as they came in to the bar. One man was a colleague of mine, although younger, and we had a chat about days gone by and the condition of the legal Bar today. I moved on to speak to another old friend, and my wife told me later that my lawyer friend had gone to say hello to her and told her, "Your husband is a household name in Sierra Leone!"

In the evening we went to Paddy's Beach Bar, just a short distance from Aberdeen Bridge. Paddy was not there when we arrived, but he came in just after us and his face was a picture when he saw us, not having any idea that we were in the country. He was so pleased to see us and we had a drink together before moving on to chat to other old friends, like Toufic and Florence Bamin and their family. The Beach Bar is quite large with many tables for dining, and on Saturday evening most of them were full. Our son told us the place is even more crowded on Sunday nights. Joan noticed that the ladies, although quite smart, were much more casually dressed than she remembered from ten years before. Just before we left to go home a strong wind blew up and then heavy rain fell for a few minutes, quite unusual for March which is usually dry and the hottest month of the year.

On Easter Monday morning we drove along the three miles of Lumley Beach and found it was crowded with people who came to enjoy the holiday. The road was lined with traders selling various kinds of foodstuff and cold drinks, and people were playing football or swimming. We saw several towers for lifeguards along the beach that were not there before. The area where we had lived in Lumley was much more crowded with many new traders, bars and shacks. We drove along the Peninsula Road as far as Lakka to Pierre's Beach Bar, formerly the Cotton Club which was operated by a Frenchman called Yves Candeau. We were sorry to see that the lovely two storey wooden building that had housed the restaurant was no longer there. We learned that a huge tree growing right beside the building had fallen on it during a bad storm, and it was so badly damaged it was pulled down. There is a large swimming pool with a bar at one end of it, so that you could sit on a bar stool in the pool with your drink watching football on TV.

We had travelled in a group to Lakka by Landrover, and the driver came to pick us up to take us home at about 8.15 pm. The road was quite clear until we got near to Lumley, but from there on there was congestion. Traffic along Lumley Beach had been made one way only for the day, travelling from Cape Sierra to Atlantic Club. As we had Nadia, her son Vlado and his fiancée Nuria (now married) with us we went over Aberdeen Bridge to reach Cape Club to drop them off. We could see the traffic along Lumley Beach and it was not moving at all, so our driver decided to take a chance and turn back towards Aberdeen Bridge. At one point we were driving behind a poda-poda which was packed to the seams and had two more people hanging on the back and at least ten perched on the roof. I really do not know how it managed to move, and was glad when our driver was eventually able to overtake it as I was afraid of someone falling off in front of our wheels.

One place we really had to visit was Sawpit, where I was born and lived to the age of sixteen, and where Joan and I had lived when I first brought her to Freetown. We were really surprised at the amount of traffic on the roads. Many of the vehicles belonged either to the United Nations or to one of the many NGO's (Non-Governmental Organisations) operating in Sierra Leone at the moment. Sawpit itself (the lower part of Malamah Thomas Street) was a shock. Walking along, the shops were on our left with living quarters above them, but on our right, where we were used to seeing just a railing protecting people from falling over the edge and down the steep slope to the sea, were a row of small shacks selling second-hand clothes. The front edge of the shacks was supported on the path and railings. The floors were made of strong cardboard cartoons opened out flat and supported from underneath by long wooden poles, looking very precarious to us.

We came to No. 8 where I was born, still owned by Mrs Mary Anthony (same surname but not related to me) who moved in after my family left in 1949 and she has lived and carried on business there ever since. Mrs Anthony welcomed us and we stayed and chatted for a while. Joan took some film with our video camera of the area, and of No. 4 where we had lived when I first returned to Freetown with Joan in 1964.

We saw many young women traders who carried their goods in large plastic or enamel bowls on their heads. Generally we saw a group of young women together selling similar things and they went from shop to shop offering their wares. When they put their bowls down on the ground for ease of selling, it was interesting to see the variety of patterns in their hairdos. The hair was 'planted' (plaited) close to the scalp, perhaps going around the head in a spiral, or coming out from a central point like the rays of the sun, or many other styles.

Some of the shops were locked up, their owners living somewhere else, but I was able to meet up with some old friends and relatives who had continued to run their lives and businesses in Sawpit in spite of all the troubles. We walked around the neighbouring streets and I bought some material to have two Safari suits made in Freetown. I wanted to see the place in Gloucester Street where I had my chambers for many years, and when I found it I was surprised to see it is now a fancy-goods store brightly painted in multi colours. Next door was a shop selling African carvings and curios which I remembered, so we wandered in and ended up buying a hammock made locally from country cloth which I now use in the summer in my garden in England.

254

We went to find the CMS Bookshop as I was looking for recent works by Sierra Leonean authors. We were shocked to find it reduced to one small room in the lower part of Gloucester Street, with only a few books on the shelves. The 'Butu Bookshops' are still in existence and seem to be thriving, with many of them around the outside of Victoria Park with small kiosks to hold the books so it is no longer necessary to 'butu'!

The Sacred Heart Pro Cathedral (Catholic) and St George's Cathedral (Protestant) both appeared to be undamaged, but the City Hall, opened in 1978, was just a burnt-out shell, as was the nearby CID building. However the statue of I.T.A. Wallace-Johnson still stands in the road opposite City Hall. The huge Treasury building is also completely destroyed, the only thing undamaged being the war memorial with the names of all the Sierra Leonean soldiers who died in World War II.

On another day we paid a visit to the market at Victoria Park to buy some gifts to take to England with us. Joan and I were walking around looking at the wooden carvings. I was wearing a gara hat with pockets on it that I had bought in the Gambia some years ago. A trader called out to me, "Are you from Texas?" I answered "No, I'm from Sawpit" and the bystanders all cheered! There were quite a few people in the market, but the day we were there most of those there were traders, not shoppers, so we were the focus of attention. All the traders were very friendly and helpful and if they did not have what we were looking for they would find it from one of the other stalls. Several of the traders recognised me. We tried to shop from several different stalls to give as many as possible the benefit of a bit of business from us. One trader who was selling beautiful gara tablecloths with matching serviettes (we bought several!) told us that he had another occupation. He could be heard on local radio as 'Taiwo' telling jokes in Krio. One item that was new to us was a map of Sierra Leone outlined on a piece of wood about ten inches square, with all the various districts demarcated and each filled in with real samples of what the area was noted for. There was beneseed for Pujehun, iron ore for Port Loko, and country rice for Kambia, etc, the whole board being varnished over to preserve and keep in place the glued-on seeds and so on. I bought several of these maps, and one of the nearby traders explained what all the various items were so that I could write it down. He was so helpful to us that I ended up buying a set of four small wooden hippos from him as I felt he too deserved some profit from our visit.

From the market we walked into Victoria Park itself and found it was busy with workmen putting up stands ready for an exhibition called "Tangains" which was to open the following day. We were pleased to see the pond is still there and freshly painted, although there was no water in it as yet. Victoria Park was established in 1897 and it is good to see that more than one hundred years later it is still popular and being put to good use.

255

Joan and I strolled hand in hand to Wilberforce Street to have lunch. As we passed the traders they commented to each other, "Look Mum and Dad!" and "Den de enjoy den old age!" We found Crown Bakery and Restaurant, run by a close friend of mine, Nizar Kesserwani and his wife Mai and had a tasty meal there.

We were very lucky in that the re-opening of the Law Courts after repairs and complete refurbishment took place while we were in Freetown, on Thursday, 4th April 2002, and my friend and colleague, Berthan Macaulay Jnr, collected us from Hill Station and drove us to the Law Courts for the ceremony. Another friend and colleague, Eke Halloway, now Attorney General and Minister of Justice but at the time President of the Bar Association, was Master of Ceremonies for the occasion. He made a very interesting speech; among other things he described the statues above the entrance of the Law Courts, an old man and a young man sitting facing in opposite directions, showing that the law is for the young and the old and is not partial or discriminatory. He also gave the meaning of the various objects they were holding. For instance, the sword represents firm decisions without fear or favour, the scroll represents the written law, and the rock on which the men are sitting stands for the solid foundation of the law. The Holy Bible placed at the feet of the old man signifies that only the truth is required in court. The eagle represents the height to which the law can go, and the owl stands for the wisdom of the law.

In my book Sawpit Boy I wrote that the building of the Law Courts started in 1910 during the governorship of Sir Leslie Probyn and was completed in 1916, at a cost of £850. The Foundation Stone was laid by Field Marshall H.R.H. Arthur W.P.A. Duke of Connaught and Streathearn on 15th December 1910. The well-known Cotton Tree standing beside the Law Courts was already a huge tree in those days.

President Tejan Kabbah was Guest of Honour at the re-opening, and sat at a table along with the Vice President, the Chief Justice, the British High Commissioner and other dignitaries. The audience was seated in chairs set out in the road, which was blocked off for the occasion, and the unmistakable Police Band was in attendance. In his speech, President Kabbah referred to attending a similar occasion nearby a few weeks previously when the new Ministry of Defence building was opened. This used to be the Paramount Hotel, formerly the social centre of Freetown, and which had been badly damaged during the rebel occupation of Freetown. It has been well restored and refurbished and its new use is suitable due to it being only a short distance from State House.

When the ceremony was completed and we had partaken of refreshments, we went across the road (Siaka Stevens Street) to the premises of Electrotech, owned by my friend John Hawa. We had arranged that he would take us up to the British Council, where the Freetown Rotary Club now meets for its regular Thursday lunchtime meeting. It was great to meet so many familiar faces among the members, my old friends were still there supporting the club as always. Some of them were amazed to see us as they had not heard we were coming to Freetown. In fact one particular friend, Dr Len Gordon-Harris, was so surprised that he stood up and shared his sentiments with the meeting. Just the evening before he and his wife Lorna had come across a photograph taken at our house, and they talked about us and wondered how we were getting on, and just the next day he was able to ask us in person! I could chat with old chums like Willie Conton (who sadly died in July 2003), S.H.O.T. Macaulay, Emile Carr, Dr Dave Wright and Adonis Aboud and others and catch up on Rotary activities in Freetown. I had brought a few items (small carvings in onyx, Rotary cufflinks and pins), with me from England that the club could use in their fund-raising raffles. The current President was unable to attend that day due to pressure of work, and as a Past-President and Senior Rotarian John Hawa was asked to preside over the meeting.

After the meeting John Hawa kindly lent us his car and driver to take us back to Hill Station. In the evening he came for us and took us to eat at Cape Club. He is an old friend and was particularly kind to us, taking us out to various places as he knew we did not have transport of our own, including to the restaurant at Lagoonda and inviting us to join him in eating Jollof Rice at his office.

The following day our son took us to Balmaya for lunch. The owner is Mrs Joy Samaké, an old friend, and it would seem that Balmaya has taken the place of the Paramount Hotel as a meeting place for Saturday lunchtime. Next to the restaurant Joy has a gallery where she displays and sells paintings by Sierra Leonean artists as well as wooden carvings, local musical instruments and fashions made from gara material. After a delicious meal, Joy kindly lent us her car and driver so that we could go to visit Mrs Talabi Lucan, a well-known author, mainly of books for schools.

Mrs Lucan lives at the end of Lucan Drive in Murray Town and was very pleasant and friendly. I asked her if she had any copies of her books to sell. She said she only had a copy of a small story book, 'Jeneba', but that she would not sell it to me, she would give it to me! She autographed the book for me, and then asked if I would autograph her copy of 'Sawpit Boy', which I gladly did. Mrs Lucan told me that she was writing another book, a biography of Paramount Chief Madam Ella Koblo Gulama, and after that planned a book on the late Mrs Lati Hyde Foster.

In the evening Dr Michel Aboud (another 'Sawpit Boy'!) and his wife Elaine came and collected us from Hill Station and took us to the Atlantic Club for dinner. We sat at a table near the sea, where we had sat so often on Saturday evenings in the past, and had a lovely meal and reminisced about the 'good old days'.

Someone I particularly wanted to see again was Hussein Jaward, Honorary Consul for Syria in Sierra Leone, so one evening I asked my son to take us to his restaurant complex on Lumley Beach called Family Kingdom. Hussein was happy to see us and took us for a tour of the premises. Around the main building were several large carvings done by Marco, a brilliant Sierra Leonean wood carver. There is a lifesize carving of a deer, which is one of the first things you see as you enter. Further in there is a dolphin, and near the back, placed over a small pit so as to appear as if in water, is a large and lifelike crocodile. There are also several smaller carvings of animals.

There is a special playground for children, and it is named for "H.E. P.C. KOMRABAI PETER PENFOLD". His Excellency Mr Peter Penfold was the British High Commissioner in Sierra Leone during the time of the civil war in Sierra Leone and helped the country a great deal and so was given the honour of being made a Paramount Chief. An unusual feature of the playground is a huge round wooden ball marked like a football, and in the sections are the names and dates of the countries that have won the World Cup for Football.

There is a small zoo with some monkeys, including a black and white Colobus, birds of prey, parrots, a heron, fish and a couple of turtles, one of them the jelly-back turtle. Around the outskirts of the compound are well-appointed chalets where tourists can stay.

Hussein kindly invited us to eat with him, and we had a delicious meal of couscous with chicken and salad.

The second Saturday of our holiday we spent with John visiting various places. We started the day going in to town with John in a Landrover to collect the car of a friend that had broken down in the centre of town. John towed it to a garage in Wilkinson Road, then we went on to Lumley to look for an old friend, Mahmoud Kudi, who used to drive for me years ago. We found him and arranged for him to visit us, and went on to see the piece of land I own in Adonkia. Our boundary is marked by a large piece of granite known as Beahbeah stone, and seeing it again brought back memories of the times we would go there when our children were small. We were lucky to find the elderly man who keeps an eye on the place for me right there on the spot and he brought me up to date on village gossip.

We continued along the Peninsula Road to Guma Valley Dam. The road was very bad and the ride was not very comfortable, but plans had been made to remake the road and I understand that this work is now well advanced. The dam was beautiful and peaceful as always, one of the loveliest spots in the Western Area. Joan was pleased to hear the tinker bird, whose call sounds like a small hammer striking on metal, and to see a heron standing on a rock near the water.

From there we went to Tokeh Beach. A friend of John's had rented a chalet for the weekend and was out in his boat fishing when we arrived, but some young men from Tokeh Village who are caretakers for the chalets took care of us. After bringing beach chairs out from the chalets and arranging them in the shade for us, they disappeared and came back with freshly picked coconuts which they opened for us to drink the milk. Another man came with a plate of sliced mangoes and a little later a third man arrived, dripping wet, with a bowl of oysters fresh from the sea, and we ate them with just a dash of juice from a fresh lime.

We went for a walk along the beach and saw many buildings that had been burnt and destroyed by the rebels, including private beach houses as well as nightclubs and restaurants. I looked for the building belonging to my friend Shakib Basma, but could not find it. There was a Unamsil checkpoint right on the beach where the soldiers could see a long way in both directions along the beach and also out to sea.

An hour or two later John's friend Roland came in on his boat and invited us to have dinner with him. He had caught a large barracuda near the Banana Islands, which was cut into chunks and cooked on skewers on charcoal. It was served with boiled potatoes, olives and warm tomato sauce and cold drinks.

We left Tokeh at about 8.00 pm and got home in about one hour. We had a wonderful day full of happy memories, wonderful scenery and exquisite food!

The next morning, Sunday, John took us to visit the Tacugama Chimpanzee Sanctuary near Regent Village. It is good that the forest there is still untouched and as we reached near the village we saw all the salad vegetables growing in neat beds as was usual for Regent. At the sanctuary the small chimps and new arrivals were kept in isolation in case of disease, but later were moved to shared cages and then to cages which are linked by wiremesh tunnels so that the chimpanzees can move around and visit each other. The final stage where the adult chimps are kept is in a large open area, or rather two areas, one of two acres with many chimpanzees ranging from young adults to quite old, and a one-acre site that has only a few chimps. These areas are almost untouched forest with a high wire fence surrounding them. The fence has a mild electric charge, not enough to do any harm but just to discourage the chimps from trying to climb out. There are heavy ropes slung between the trees for the chimps to move around and play. There is a platform with a thatched roof built on stilts with a wooden ladder leading up to it for visitors to stand to view, because when the chimps see a group of strangers they will throw rocks at them, as they did when we were there. The chimps were fed with mangoes and bananas and they soon lost interest in throwing stones, snatching the fruit and often climbing up into a tree to eat in peace. Among the chimps we saw the only albino chimpanzee known in the world. She had white fur and one blue eye and one brown, and they called her 'Pinky'. The other chimps appeared to be protective of her. A friend visited the Sanctuary in December 2002 and learned that sadly the albino chimp had died.

John is quite a frequent visitor to the Sanctuary and at the end of our visit my wife was chatting to the Chinese girl who worked with the chimps. John joined them and explained to the girl that Joan was his mother. The girl laughed and said to John, "Does your mother know she has a hairy grandchild?" John made things clear when he told us that he has 'adopted' one of the baby chimps and provides money for its food.

After leaving the Chimp Santuary we headed towards the Peninsula. On the road we passed a stall selling palm wine and could not resist buying some. At Lakka we came to a new hospital called the Emergency Surgical Centre for War Victims. The hospital was financed by a young Italian Pop Singer who saw the plight of the people as a result of the war in Sierra Leone when visiting the country with his then fiancée Antonella Bundu (we were told they have since married), a friend of our daughters and whose Italian mother Daniella was a friend of ours. We understand the young man raised the money by holding a concert and donating the income from the sale of CD's, probably in Italy. It was a praiseworthy undertaking by a caring young man.

We had been invited by Mike Rekab to join him at a privately owned beach house at Hamilton for lunch. Mike and I swam at a small secluded beach surrounded by rocks, the first time I had swum in the sea for years as I find the sea on the English coast far too cold! Mike had provided a varied and tasty buffet lunch which we ate in the open air watching the waves breaking on the rocks. Later Mike drove us home and we stopped at his house in Spur Road on the way for tea.

We went into town one morning to pay a visit to the Sierra Leone Museum. We were lucky that Mrs Dorothy Cummings, the retired curator, was also visiting that day, so we were able to have a chat about the changes in the museum since we were last there. One of the things still on show was the replica of the De Ruyter Stone, on which the Dutch Admiral De Ruyter carved his name when visiting Sierra Leone in 1664. This stone, engraved with 'M.A. Ruiter - Vice Admiral' is one of the oldest relics and monuments of Sierra Leone. There is an old wooden carving of Bai Bureh, another almost lifesize wooden statue of Sir Milton Margai, Gongoli and other masks, a collection of various African musical instruments, examples of African dress and of country cloth and other crafts, and many other things of interest.

That evening we were invited to eat at the Lighthouse Restaurant at Aberdeen. The restaurant itself looked much as we remembered it, but a hotel is being built on the seaward side of the carpark, with the outer edge of the building supported on concrete pillars going down to the beach.

We drove past the Mammy Yoko Hotel, which had been repaired. There was little to show the dangers and excitement people had experienced there in the recent past during the civil war, but at the moment it is the headquarters of Unamsil. Cape Sierra nearby is still operating as a Hotel, but mainly for business people because as yet there are very few tourists visiting the country. One night we paid a visit to the Lagoonda Casino and gambled a little on the roulette wheel. I lost, as I often did in the past, so that too made me feel at home!

During our visit Brookfields Hotel was occupied by the Kamajors, a civil defence force made up largely of local hunters. I understand the hotel has since been restored. The Bintumani Hotel at Aberdeen has also been renovated, by a Chinese construction company, and was reopened by President Kabbah on 1st February 2003.

I had been able to get in touch with my old friend and driver, Mahmoud Kudi, and found that he was now retired, but as he had his own car he was able to spend a day driving us around. We turned off of Wilkinson Road to go to Aqua Club. The place was deserted at that time of day, but the staff were around and we recognised Abu who had worked for the club from the time our children were quite young. He recognised us and was pleased to see us again. We walked around and found things much as before, although now there were some wooden sunloungers around the swimming pool. We saw the Programme of Events on the notice board and found there was some kind of function at least once a month, and that pleased us greatly. The two signboards with the list of Commodores from inception up to the present time were still in place above the bar.

We went through town and up to Fourah Bay College as I wanted to visit the bookshop. The students we asked for help looked confused when we asked for the bookshop and said, did we mean the library? Then we met a gentleman who looked like a lecturer and asked him the same thing. He told us we were too late, the bookshop had closed down a couple of years before, and he said it was a pity I had missed it as there had been a big closing down sale with many interesting books going at bargain prices. The lecturer turned out to be Dr Dudley Nylander, who remembered my sons Jamal and Michael very well, so I was happy to be able to put them back in touch with each other. Sadly, I have been told that Dr Nylander has since died.

On the way home we stopped to buy some jelly coconuts. The coconut vendor was walking along the side of the road pushing a wheelbarrow full of coconuts, and we stopped him and asked how much he was selling them for. He told us, "Le 400 each". We asked for six, and while he was busy lightly cutting the tops of the nuts, so that when we got home we could just lift the 'lid' to drink the water (milk), Joan asked if she could take a photograph of him with his wheelbarrow. The man smiled and nodded and Joan took the snap. When it came for us to pay him he asked for Le2,700. Joan queried him that this was Le 300 more than he had told us. The man said simply, "You take picture!" We paid him what he asked and admired him for his enterprise!

One Friday evening Mike Rekab gave a dinner party for us and invited some friends.  We were picked up by Ahmadu and Kitty Fadlu-Deen, they had to pass where we were staying to reach Mike's house.  We met there Joy Samaké, Tani Pratt, Saio Kanu and his wife Yebu, and an Englishman David and his wife Hannah, a Sierra Leonean.  The next day, Saturday, we were invited to lunch at her home by Edita Haroun.  We sat in the shade in her garden and enjoyed a lunch of barbecued chicken and beef with salad, potato salad and moutabal.  Edita had a tame mongoose, Ricki, in her garden.

The following Monday evening we were again invited out to dinner, this time by Dr Bernard Fraser and his wife Frances.  They took us to a restaurant which was new to us, called Mamba Point Restaurant and Hotel.  They had also invited Dr Michel Aboud and his wife Elaine and daughter Katherine, also a doctor.  The restaurant is at Wilberforce and we found it quite cool there, probably because it is quite high above sea level.  We sat outside in the garden and one thing that attracted us (beside the food and good company) were the unusual palms growing around the tables, one with large fan-like leaves.  We saw two or three motor bikes with carriers on them and signs reading 'Mamba Point Pizza Delivery', a very good idea and not common yet in Freetown.

The next day we spent in Freetown going around to say goodbye to our friends and relatives.  We walked to the surgery of our friend Dr Michel Aboud as he had invited us to have lunch with him at his home.  Michel drove us through some of the streets of Freetown, including Waterloo Street where the charcoal sellers still line the street with the dusty sacks of charcoal, and further up to where the Strand Cinema is still operating.  In Siaka Stevens Street we met up with a crowd of SLPP election campaigners, all in good humour and waving fronds of palm leaf, the symbol of the SLPP, and with a Gongoli devil walking in their midst.  We turned off to the right into Kroo Town Road, full of traders selling all kinds of local and imported produce, in front of Kroo Town Road Market established in 1898 and still as busy as ever.  At Brookfields we drove past the National Stadium, formerly known as Siaka Stevens Stadium.

All too soon it was time for us to leave and we crossed back to Lungi by helicopter.  This time it was daylight and we were able to see the extensive rebuilding work going on at the airport.  Security was much stricter than in the old days.  There seemed to be many checks on our passports, we were moved on from desk to desk where different people checked our papers.  The final check came when everyone had to hold his passport, open to show the photograph, up beside his face and was photographed like that.  I understand this is to prove that when we checked in we held valid passports and our documents were in order.  We had a good flight home to England, and our daughter Linda was waiting for us at Gatwick Airport.

We had a wonderful three weeks meeting up with old friends and visiting the various restaurants and beach bars, all of which were doing quite good business. The Sierra Leoneans all looked surprisingly well and cheerful, and it is only when you get into close conversation with them that you come to realise that they all have their stories of personal tragedy to tell. There is an atmosphere of people wanting to get on with their lives and get back to normal as quickly as possible.

# Appendix A

A group of philanthropists in England, who supported the movement for the abolition of slavery, formed a settlement in Sierra Leone, called the Province of Freedom. Settlers from among the Black Poor in England were carried to Sierra Leone in 1787. Later a company was formed by mostly the same group of men, who called it the Sierra Leone Company. One of these men, Thomas Clarkson, had a younger brother called Lieutenant John Clarkson, who had been in the Royal Navy. John Clarkson collected some 1131 further immigrants and sailed to Sierra Leone in sixteen ships in 1792. John Clarkson was Governor of the Sierra Leone Company from March to December 1792. When he was about to leave Sierra Leone he wrote the following prayer. The prayer was framed and prominently displayed in many homes in Sierra Leone, and enjoyed "a veneration second perhaps only to the Bible". (For more on John Clarkson see "Historical Dictionary of Sierra Leone" by Professor Cyril P Foray, one-time Principal of Fourah Bay College, published by The Scarecrow Press Inc, London, 1977).

GOVERNOR CLARKSON'S PRAYER
For Sierra Leone

O Lord, I beseech Thee favourably to hear the prayer of him whom wishes to be Thy servant, and pardon him for presuming to address Thee from this Sacred Place. O God, I know my own infirmity and unworthiness, and I know Thine abundant mercies to those who wish to be guided by Thy will. Support me, O God with Thy heavenly grace, and so enable me to conduct myself through this earthly life, that my actions may be consistent with the words I have uttered this day. Thou knowest that I am now about to depart from this place, and to leave the people whom it has pleased Thee to entrust to my care. Guide them, O merciful God, in the paths of truth, and let not a few wicked men among us draw down Thy vengeance upon this Colony. Ingraft into their hearts a proper sense of duty, and enable them through Thy grace to conduct themselves as Christians, that they may not come to Thy house without that pleasing emotion which every grateful man must feel when paying adoration to the Author of life. But I have great reason to fear, O Lord, that many who frequent Thy Church, do not approach Thy presence as becomes them, and they may partly be compared to the Scribes, Pharisees and hypocrites. Pardon, O God, their infirmities; and as Thou knowest their weakness, from the manner in which they have formerly been treated, and the little opportunity they have had of knowing Thy will and getting acquainted with the merits of Thy Son our Saviour Jesus Christ, look down upon them with an eye of mercy and suffer them not to incur Thy displeasure, after they have had an opportunity of being instructed in the ways of Thy Commandments.

Bless, O Lord, the inhabitants of this vast continent; and incline their hearts towards us, that they may more readily listen to our advice and doctrines, and that we may conduct ourselves towards them so as to convince them of the happiness we enjoy under Thy almighty protection. Banish from this colony, O Lord, all heathenish superstition, and let the inhabitants know that Thou art the only true God, in whom we live and move and have our being. If these people who profess Thy religion will not be assured of Thy superior power, convince them, O God, of Thine anger for their profession without their practice; for Thou knowest I have brought them here in hopes of making them and their families happy, both in this world and all to eternity.

But I fear they may not be governed by my advice, and that they may ruin themselves and their children for ever by their perverse and ignorant behaviour. I entreat Thee not to let their evil example affect the great cause in which we have embarked, for I would rather see this place in ashes and every wicked person destroyed than that the millions we have now an opportunity of bringing to the light and knowledge of Thy holy religion should, from the wickedness of a few individuals, still continue in their accustomed darkness and barbarism. Thou knowest that I have universally talked of their apparent virtue and goodness, and have praised Thy name, for having permitted me to be the servant employed in so great and glorious a cause. If I have been deceived, I am sorry for it, and may Thy will be done; but I implore Thee to accept the sincerity of my intentions and my best endeavours to improve the talent committed to my care. Only pardon the infirmity of my nature, and I will trust to Thy mercy.

Should any person have a wicked thought in his heart, or do anything knowingly to disturb the peace and comfort of this our colony, let him be rooted out, O God, from off the face of the earth; but have mercy upon him hereafter.

Were I to utter all that my heart now indicates, no time would be sufficient for my praise and thanksgiving for all the mercies Thou hast vouchsafed to show me; but as Thou art acquainted with every secret of my heart, accept my thoughts for thanks. I have no words left to express my gratitude and resignation to Thy will. I entreat Thee, O God, if nothing I can say will convince these people of Thy power and goodness, make use of me, in any way Thou pleasest, to make an atonement for their guilt. This is an awful, and I fear too presumptuous, a request; yet if it should be Thy will that I should lay down my life for the cause I have embarked in, assist me, O Lord, with Thy support, that I may resign it in such a manner as to convince these unbelieving people that Thou art God indeed.  May the hearts of this colony, O Lord, imbibe the spirit of meekness, gentleness and truth;  and may they henceforth live in unity and godly love, following as far as the weakness of their mortal natures will admit, that most excellent and faultless pattern, which Thou hast given us in Thy Son our Saviour, Jesus Christ, to whom with Thee and the Holy Spirit, be all honour and glory, now and forever.  Amen.

\* \* \* \* \* \* \* \* \* \* \* \* \* \* \*

The above prayer, whatever religion you profess to be, will apply equally to anyone who has a bad intention for Sierra Leone.

# Appendix B

Below are the words of the National Anthem of Sierra Leone, written by Mr C. Nelson-Fyle in 1961 when independence was granted. The music was composed by Mr John Akar.

"High we exalt thee, realm of the free,
Great is the love we have for thee;
Firmly united, ever we stand
Singing they praise, O native land
We raise up our hearts and our voices on high
The hills and the valleys re-echo our cry
Blessing and peace be ever thine own
Land of our birth, our Sierra Leone!

One with a faith that wisdom inspires
One with a zeal that never tires
Ever we seek to honour thy name
Ours is the labour, thine the fame
We pray that no harm on thy children may fall
That blessing and peace may descend on us all;
So may we serve thee ever alone
Land that we love, our Sierra Leone.

Knowledge and truth our forefathers spread
Mighty the nations whom they lead
Mighty they made thee, so too may we
Show forth the good that is ever in thee
We pledge our devotion, our strength and our might
Thy cause to defend and to stand for thy right
All that we have be ever thine own
Land of our birth, our Sierra Leone."

# Appendix C

The rules of the game of Warri are as follows:

1. Place the board lengthwise between the two players.
2. Each player owns the half of the board nearer to him and the store hole at his right.
3. The object of the game is to win the greater number of pieces.
4. Four pieces are placed in each cup, there is one lap to the move, and play is anticlockwise.
5. A lap includes the following procedures:
   (a) The player lifts all the pieces from a cup on his side of the board.
   (b) He sows these pieces anticlockwise, one in each of the consecutive cups. A lap ends when the last piece in the hand is sown.
6. A move can begin from any one of your own cups. During the course of the game a cup may become so loaded that it contains 12 or more pieces. In this case the original cup is omitted from the sowing sequence and remains empty.
7. The player must leave his opponent a cup from which to play, and if all the opponent's cups are empty, he must if possible make a move which gives him a piece to play with; and if he omits to do so, he forfeits all his pieces remaining in play to his opponent. This does not include the pieces in his store.
8. Captures are made when the last piece in hand falls into a cup in the opponent's row, making its contents two or three pieces.
9. If the cup from which the capture is made is immediately preceded by an unbroken sequence of cups in the same row also containing two or three pieces, the contents of these holes are also taken.
10. When no more captures are possible, each player adds the pieces left in his own cups to the store, and the player with the greater number of pieces is the winner.

This game became so popular that it was available in certain toy stores in England and I bought a set so that we could play when there.

The following passages are taken from an article in Sierra Leone Studies of April 1926, written by J. De Hart at Hill Station in1918:-

"It is not uncommon on passing through a native village in this Protectorate to see a couple of men in a secluded spot squatting on their haunches and manipulating beans on a canoe-shaped board. Whoever has patience to keep these people under observation will find that they often remain playing for hours on end. This is the game of Warri.

In some respects Warri resembles backgammon, but, while backgammon is based on the chances of the throw, in Warri the element of chance is replaced by one of pure calculation which raises the game more to the intellectual level of chess. Like the native, once one starts playing one loses all sense of time. .........

If a player succeeds in clearing his opponent's side of the board, he wins all the men, if any, remaining on his own side of the board. This is called "cutting off one's opponent's head." So the game ends. .........

It will be found that a superior player entices nearly all the men to his side of the board, by means of sacrifices, and then uses the control thus obtained over the game to swoop round and cut off his opponent's head. It is a sound principle to aim at compelling one's opponent to play across into one's own side.

The origin of the game is not known, but it is probably of great antiquity .........

Very little is at present known regarding the geographical distribution of the game and information on the subject would be of great interest. It is widely played by various tribes in Sierra Leone as well as in other parts of Africa and the East. A game which may be similar is ......... played by the Masai tribe in East Africa. ......... a similar game is ...... played in the Malay Peninsula ......... The boat-shaped board also occurs in Malaya.

The reason of the boat-shaped board is not known. It may possibly be due merely to the fact that this is the most convenient shape of board to contain two rows of holes. It is, however, possible that the game had an early home among a river or seafaring people. It may have been carried over the world either by the ancient traders or by the apostles and teachers of Mohammedanism. In the West Indies ......... it goes by the reminiscent name of "Ouaoui"."